Beyond *the* Border

A Korean's Journey Between the North and South

Tae-hyok Kim *and*
Nicole Kim Rogers

For privacy reasons, some names, locations, and dates may have been changed.

Book cover designed by Owen Gent
Maps designed by Nat Case
Interior formatting and design by KUHN Design Group
Photos provided by Tae-hyok Kim and Bill, Michelle, and Nicole Rogers

First edition 2023

ISBN (Paperback): 979-8-3998-0664-8
ISBN (Hardcover): 979-8-3999-4124-0

Dedicated to all Koreans, North and South.
My story is one of many.

TAE-HYOK KIM

Contents

PART FIVE:
A New Life, 1953 - 1970

ABBREVIATIONS

ROK: Republic of Korea (South Korea)

ROKA: Republic of Korea Army (South Korean Army)

DPRK: Democratic People's Republic of Korea (North Korea)

NKPA / KPA: (North) Korean People's Army (North Korean Army)

UN: United Nations

PRC: People's Republic of China

PLA: People's Liberation Army (Communist China's Army)

DMZ: Demilitarized Zone

KMAG: Korean Military Advisory Group

PFC: Private First Class

Sgt.: Sergeant

SFC: Sergeant First Class

MSgt.: Master Sergeant

Lt.: Lieutenant

Col.: Colonel

NCO: Non-commissioned officer

MP: Military Police

OP: Observation Post

Eomeoni: Mother (more respectful / formal way of saying mother)

Umma: Mom / mommy

Abeoji: Father (more respectful / formal way of saying father)

Appa: Dad / daddy

Hyung / Hyung-nim: Older brother / more respectful way of saying older brother (if speaker is male)

Nuna: Older sister (if speaker is male)

Ahjumeoni: Sister-in-law

Samchon: Uncle

Doryun-nim: Young brother-in-law

Harabeoji: Grandfather

Halmeoni: Grandmother

Bahkat-chae : Outer building

An-chae: Inner building / main living quarters

Sarangbang: Men's / guest quarters

Aigoo!: Ouch! or Oh my!

Tennōheika (in Japanese): The Emperor

Tennōheika ni saikayray! (in Japanese): Bow to the Emperor! → it means the utmost salute to the Japanese emperor

Tennōheika Banzai! (in Japanese): Long live the Emperor!

Kempei / Kempeitai (in Japanese): Military Police

Ilbon-nomdel: The Japanese (derogatory term)

Won: Korean currency

Go mahp sumnida / Gamsah-hamnida: Thank you

Sampal Sun: 38th Parallel

Yeobo: Honey

Hyeun-mull-se: Tax payment in goods or crop, not in cash

An-yung-ha-say-yo: Hello

Ondol: Traditional Korean floor with a heating system underneath

Jang: Traditional Korean flea market

Zinbangs: Small, steamed rolls stuffed with sweetened mashed red beans

Yapo: Field artillery

Hwarang Ga: Korean Army Anthem

-ri (if the name of a place ends in -ri): Town

Rijang: Village Chief

Soju: Korean alcoholic beverage

Siljang: Head of inmates

Arirang: Korean folk song

Mansei!: Long live!

Dae-han-min-guk Mansei!: Long live Korea!

Gukgun Mansei!: Hurray, Korean Army!

Chun-maneyo: You're welcome

Gukgun: South Korean Armed Forces

Dongmu: Comrade

In mingun: North Korean soldier

Corps: 2+ Divisions

Division: 3 Regiments /
6,000-15,000 Soldiers

Regiment: 3-5 Battalions /
2,000-5,000 Soldiers (in ROKA usually 2,500 Soldiers)

Battalion: 3-5 Companies /
100-1,000 Soldiers (in ROKA usually 400-600 Soldiers)

Company: 3-4 Platoons /
60-200 Soldiers

Platoon: 3-4 Squads /
18-50 Soldiers

Squad: 6-10 Soldiers

REPUBLIC OF KOREA ARMY MILITARY RANK

General

Lieutenant General

Major General

Brigadier General

Colonel

Lieutenant Colonel

Major

Captain

First Lieutenant

Second Lieutenant

Warrant Officer

Command Sergeant Major

Master Sergeant

Sergeant First Class

Staff Sergeant

Sergeant

Corporal

Private First Class

Private

A partial list of people in the army for your reference while reading. It is not comprehensive, to avoid spoiling the story.

N.B. Although surnames were used in conversation, for the ease of the reader, the given name is sometimes used in the story—especially when multiple people have the same last name—and appears here in parentheses.

Lee Jong-kook (Jong-kook): One of Tae-hyok's best friends. Met in basic training. Always on guard duty during the war. His family were farmers, but his parents died when he was seven years old. He later dropped out of grammar school to work on his relative's farm.

Oh Munchan: One of Tae-hyok's best friends. Met in basic training. He was from North Korea. His family was well-to-do. He had come to the South and volunteered to join the army.

Lee Yeong-sik (Yeong-sik): Met in basic training. Tall, solidly built man from North Korea.

Kim Maneong (Maneong or Man-E): A close friend. Met in basic training. Regiment Administrative Personnel. He was a restaurant cook before joining the army.

Jin Chin-mae (Jin or Chin-mae): Met in basic training. From North Korea. He was street smart.

Chun Byung-ho (Chun): Met in basic training. Regiment Administrative Personnel. A laid-back guy. He would often crack jokes and entertain those on the front line.

Bong Jong-tae (Bong): One of Tae-hyok's best friends. Met in basic training. From Tae-hyok's native province, but Bong's home was south of the 38th Parallel in South Korea.

---

* also known as Administrative Personnel or as a Company Clerk

Pak Sam-hyun (Pak): Met in basic training. Regiment Administrative Personnel. He was kind and had a warm personality. Dropped out of grammar school to work on his foster parents' farm.

Kim Jae-kook: Met in basic training. Regiment Administrative Personnel. He was from North Korea. He had had an arranged marriage and didn't talk about his wife much. He was a nice guy and had a great personality.

Kwon Seo-jin (Quartermaster Sergeant Kwon): Met in basic training. He was in the Quartermaster Corps.

Chang Hyokoen (Hyokoen): One of Tae-hyok's best friends. Met during two-year border guard duty. Regiment Administrative Personnel. He was from North Korea. He had a younger sister whom he often mentioned. He always had a positive attitude.

Choi Ga-ram (Choi): Regiment Administrative Personnel. Tall, arrogant guy. He and Tae-hyok were responsible for the personnel records of the same company, but they didn't talk to each other much.

Han Geun-bok (Sergeant First Class Han): Regiment Administrative Personnel. Became a squad leader under MSgt. Lee.

Choo Young-ho (Choo): Regiment Administrative Personnel. Easygoing guy and well respected by everyone.

Master Sergeant Lee: Leader of the Regiment Administrative Personnel department. Tae-hyok's main leader throughout the Korean War.

Sergeant Park: Senior NCO of the regiment headquarters company. Temporary leader at the outset of the war. Was later promoted and put in another regiment (so was only with Tae-hyok the first month of the war).

Corporal Chae: Regiment Administrative Personnel. Warmhearted guy with a solidly built physique. He voluntarily did various chores which other soldiers were reluctant to do. Well-liked by everyone in the group.

Sergeant Sim: Regiment Administrative Personnel. Considered a very knowledgeable man because not only had he received a secondary education, but also, he had read widely. He also understood a little bit of English.

SOME OTHERS IN THE ARMY

Lieutenant Colonel Choi Namkeon: Commanding Officer of the 8th Regiment (while in basic training).

Master Sergeant Gyeon: 5th Company Sergeant of the 8th Regiment (while in basic training and beginning of border guard duty).

Kim Hakdong (Drill Sergeant Hakdong, Sergeant Hakdong, or Platoon Sergeant Hakdong): Drill sergeant during basic training. Platoon leader during basic training and border guard duty. Outgoing personality and overall a nice guy (though strict in basic training). He was respected and a good politician.

Corporal Pae: Assistant drill sergeant during basic training. Was mean at first.

Choi Kyu: Met in basic training. Tried to escape the training center.

Captain Lee: Captain in the 8th Regiment. Tae-hyok was assigned to perform detail duties for him. Was the most senior officer among the four company-level commanders within the battalion. Was promoted to lead a Special Battalion in Yeongwol. He assigned Tae-hyok to the administrative personnel department.

Master Sergeant Chang Hee-chul (Master Sergeant Chang): 5th Company Sergeant of the 8th Regiment. He was good-natured, had a buoyant spirit, was always positive, and created an upbeat mood.

Lieutenant Roh: 5th Company Executive Officer of the 8th Regiment. Had received the order about the "special assignment" from Lieutenant Colonel Choi Namkeon.

Lee Chunwoo: 2nd Platoon Sergeant of the 5th Company.

Kim Suk-won: Division Commander Brigadier General. He was a fearless leader. He led a Japanese battalion to fight the Chinese Nationalist Army during the Sino-Japanese War in the late 1930s. He carried a samurai sword. He joined the South Korean Army in the late 1940s and was commissioned to one-star general, commanding the Capital Division.

Captain Chung: Battalion Headquarters Company Commander. He was not that nice of a guy. He did not like Tae-hyok.

Sergeant Jee: Friend and foot soldier in the same battalion, and an experienced soldier.

Sergeant First Class Goe: Soldier in the same battalion, but from a different company.

Major Cho: Commander of the 3rd Battalion. Not many soldiers under his command liked him. He did not possess the qualities of a good commander; he was known to be selfish and not too intelligent. He drove in the jeep.

Sergeant First Class Rim: Temporary leader during a portion of the long march.

Major Jeong: Battalion Deputy Commander. He was extremely well respected and looked out for the soldiers under his command.

Introduction

We reached the observatory. Tourists were all around me.

"Out there is North Korea," our tour guide said to our group while pointing to the land ahead of us.

"You can see their flag, Nicole," she said to me. She knew my name by now as I had asked so many questions.

We were visiting the Demilitarized Zone (DMZ). You couldn't do so without a guide.

And there I saw North Korea. I looked through the telescope and saw a red and blue flag waving in the crisp, clear autumn sky. Beyond that was the place where my grandfather had grown up—a place I couldn't visit. Over the years, I had heard stories of his adventures, his years as a schoolboy, his experiences crossing the 38th Parallel, his time in the war, his family, my grandmother, and his coming to America.

He told us these stories and wrote them down so that we would know and remember them.

What comes to most people's minds when they think of Korea is K-pop, K-dramas, and Korean barbeque. Korea is known for its pop culture, skincare, cosmetics, and delicious food with spicy and pungent kimchi in every dish.

But when reading my grandfather's stories and talking to him, I started to see Korea as it had been—a unified nation that was later divided, separating families forever.

I journeyed through "The Forgotten War." A time when the United States could have listened to South Korea's repeated warnings that North Korea was going to invade, and pleas for equipment to stop such a potential attack. A war in which, at the time, the Republic of Korea Army (ROKA) was undermanned, undertrained, and underequipped. A war which, due to America's boldness and the engagement of United Nations members, made South Korea a viable country.

I heard the cries of refugees who were forced to search for new lives.

I saw the hope of the Korean people who have endured so much since the beginning of the 20th century. And like my grandfather, they say they have "no choice," so they keep living each day with hope. Koreans have a sense of determination and fortitude, coupled with empathy.

So this story—whether you call it an adventure story, a war story, or an immigrant story—is to remember Korea and to never forget.

To never forget that before North and South Korea, there was one unified Korea.

To never forget that political figures in power have an impact on many.

To never forget the hundreds of thousands of military personnel who served in the Korean War, sacrificing their lives for Koreans' freedom. Their bravery should always be remembered.

And to never forget the Korean people in the whole peninsula. There are still some individuals alive who remember journeying from North to South Korea as refugees, leaving their families behind and thinking they would see them after the winter had passed. They never did. Many families and generations will live on, never knowing their ancestors in North Korea and vice versa.

This story is to help remember.

—Nicole

A NOTE FOR READERS

The following stories are based on my grandfather's memory. He had written them down about thirty-five to eighty years after they occurred, and I filled in gaps based on interviews I had conducted with him. As such, specific dates may not be exact. Also, we have changed names throughout the book. Because surnames like Kim, Lee, and Park are very common, and many characters have them, we kept some of them but changed others so as not to confuse characters. In addition, Koreans' last names (surnames) precede their first names (given names). We have spelled Korean names, words, and towns phonetically. Some towns and cities have been spelled differently on maps over time. For example, Pusan is now spelled as Busan.

PART ONE

Growing Up in North Korea

1931 - 1946

I remember it as though it were yesterday—the morning assembly at my small school in North Korea, where our Japanese principal triumphantly announced that Japan had attacked the United States at Pearl Harbor. He called it a 'brilliant victory.' Young men from our peaceful Korean village were drafted into the Japanese military in the following weeks. I also vividly remember crossing the 38th Parallel—an invisible line that tore my once unified country into two. I journeyed at night to cross the border, my heart pounding while trying to avoid getting caught by the border guards. And, of course, I will never forget the Korean War—our determined advance north and our heartbreaking retreats.

Before we delve into those times, I want to paint a picture of the Korea that existed when I was young. I'll first tell you about my hometown, village, and house, and then go into some stories from my childhood.

I hope that by sharing my experiences and memories throughout this memoir, you'll see what Korea has undergone and the immense trials and tribulations my people have faced.

CHAPTER 1

Home

MY HOMETOWN GEOGRAPHY

My hometown, a village called Cheong-duk-gol ("hamlet of virtue") is in the mountainous central region of North Korea, only about seventy-five miles north of the infamous demilitarized zone (DMZ). It is nestled in a small valley, approximately half a mile wide and two miles long.

The main peak of Obongsan Mountain (Five Peaks Mountain) gracefully rises in the east, attended by two lesser peaks on its north and south flanks. The Saribong Mountain Range starts at the southern shoulder of the Obongsan Mountain Range, ascends westward, and crests as high as the Five Peaks. Then it begins to descend and gently rests on a few hundred-foot-wide rolling hills, like a flying eagle's wing brushing a grass field. At the edge of these rolling hills, a thick pine forest slowly rises to the northwest. The forest is well known for delicious pine mushrooms.

At the upper rim of the pine forest, gigantic grayish rocks are stacked like standing knives, soaring as high as 2,300 feet into the sky. Our ancestors named it Kalsan Mountain (Sword Mountain). Deocksan Mountain, as rugged and rocky as Kalsan, branches out from the northern wing of Five Peaks and extends toward Kalsan. Deocksan Mountain sinks its ferocious claws into the east bank of Big River, challenging its mighty adversary Kalsan. The angry Kalsan faces Deocksan by sinking its gigantic sharp talons into the west bank of the river, which prevents the two mountains from crashing into each other. Over millions of years, Big River has scratched the foothills of the enormous mountains bit by bit, creating spectacular, red, yellow, and gray rocky cliffs on each side.

One legend says that the region's guardian god dug a magnificent cave deep into a western foothill of Saribong Mountain millions of years ago, and that since then, the cave has continued to spew a huge amount of spring water. A four-season river was born from this spring, and our great-great…great grandfathers dubbed it "Big River" because it was the only meaningful river around. All the others were creeks. Big River runs westward, then changes its course northeast, flowing along the cliffs of Kalsan Mountain.

Another tale says that thousands of years ago, months of heavy rain inundated the land, and people drowned. But one rich, foresighted man built a boat, put his family and valuables inside and sailed in search of dry land. Alas, the boat crashed on the peak of Kalsan and sank, leaving broken clay jars and chinaware. No one knows anyone who has ever scaled the top.

This rugged Kalsan Mountain Range extends northeast and drops a few hundred feet before it rises again, creating a saddle point. My school route, the Dong-kogae Trail, winds back and forth up a steep, rocky slope of the range through this saddle point and down to the valleys. This mountain range branches out and joins many others. As it continues north, its ruggedness transforms into a gentle, gray line against the distant whitish-blue sky before fading.

On the top of a lofty, rocky cliff of Kalsan Mountain, Seoissneun Bawi (Standing Rock) stands prominently, as if guarding the valley. Seoissneun Bawi is a tall, lone brown and orange rock resembling a determined mother carrying her baby on her back and a treasure chest on her head. According to more frequently told folklore, several thousand years ago, a wealthy miser and his warmhearted wife lived in the valley. When some hungry, poor folks came to her, she lovingly gave them food. If he saw her giving generously, he would yell at her and take the food away from the poor. One day, when a Buddhist monk came to the house for charity, she gave him sumptuous alms.

He thanked her, but prophesied, "Tonight a disaster will fall on your household. Unless you evacuate your house before sunset, your entire family will die. Whatever happens, don't look back." Then he disappeared.

Frightened, she called her husband back from the field and told him what the monk had warned. A greedy man, he snapped back, "You are insane. If you believe him, you go alone." She pleaded with him earnestly to go with her, but he didn't listen. So, just before sunset, she hurriedly left the house, carrying her baby on her back and her treasure box on her head. Night fell before she had gone a little over a mile. Suddenly the sky split in half, and a huge fireball fell, burning her house. Shocked, she looked back, disregarding the monk's warning. At that moment, a lightning bolt hit her, petrifying her into Seoissneun Bawi, which stands to the present day.

Below Seoissneun Bawi, is a narrow, rock-strewn path along the riverbank. Whenever I traveled on this road, I became apprehensive that Seoissneun Bawi might fall on me. I would run as fast as I could through this precarious stretch.

MY VILLAGE

A narrow valley starts in the foothills of Five Peaks Mountain and runs westward, flowing into the Big River. My progenitor settled in this remote mountainous region more than four hundred years ago. His offspring have grown into an isolated, tiny farm community living in a cluster of farmhouses nestled in the middle of the small valley. This is my hometown, Cheong-duk-gol. I was born in that valley and lived there for the first fifteen years of my life.

Another village of seven houses, Kosari-pyun, was settled near the foothills of Five Peaks Mountain, less than one mile east of my village. Over a red clay hill, Nam-san (South Mountain), about ten houses are scattered on the north hill of Saribong Mountain. This hamlet was called Ankol (Inner Valley). The daylight in this hamlet was much shorter than that in my village because it was on the northern slope of the mountain. Altogether, about thirty families of less than two hundred people inhabited the region. Everybody knew one another by name, and most of us shared the same ancestor. We were poor but cared for each other.

The surrounding mountains and rivers were integral parts of our lives. Thick forests of tall oaks, chestnuts, and other deciduous trees, including mulberries, covered Five Peaks and Saribong. These forests generously supplied firewood and timber to build houses and barns. They also provided Big River and small creeks with a continuous flow of water. Every year, in the spring and early fall, the nutritious mulberry leaves allowed my hometown folks to raise silkworms and produce homespun silk. Rich acorns drew large populations of wild hogs, deer, rabbits, and other wild animals to the area. In turn, they invited predatory animals such as wolves and magnificent Siberian tigers. In the fall, some of the town folks would collect fallen acorns and make acorn jelly to supplement their diet. It tastes somewhat bitter but gives our taste buds a kick.

Every May, before the rainy season began, all the able men from the three villages would get together, chop down pine trees from the nearest forest, bring them on oxen back to the Big River, and repair its three dams, creating reservoirs. These dams irrigated narrow belts of rice paddies along the riverbanks. During the summer, we swam and fished in those reservoirs.

MY CHILDHOOD HOUSE

My hometown was a village of sixteen farmhouses scattered along a small valley. Based on the astrological principle, all of the houses were built facing south except for one, which faced east. Astrology aside, a building facing south has a practical benefit, receiving more sunshine in the winter and more shade in the summer. Most houses had a similar design, varying only in size; wealthier families had larger homes. There was no electricity, tap water, or even a manual water pump. Two wells were dug to supply potable water for the entire village.

My childhood home was a humble farmhouse with about 270 square feet of living space, including an unheated kitchen. Built on a small plot, it consisted of three buildings: an L-shaped *bahkat-chae* (outer building), a rectangular *an-chae* (inner building) which was the family's main living quarters, and a shed. These three structures enclosed a courtyard. The two main buildings had about six-foot-high ceilings, mud walls and slate roofs. The slates were mined from a nearby hill, and the shingles varied in shape and size. The shed had a millet-straw roof which needed to be replaced every other year.

The main entrance, which featured double doors made of heavy oak, was in the middle of the outer building. The *sarangbang* (men's/guest quarters) were on the right of the main entrance, and a stable for a family cow was on the left. Traditionally, male guests or friends were entertained in the *sarangbang*, while female counterparts were received in the main living quarters.

A doghouse was built between the stable and the entrance. The men's quarters had two doors, one on the front wall and the other on the left wall, to the base of which an oven was attached. The oven was just inside the main entrance and had a large kettle. In the wintertime, we used the oven to cook cattle feed in this kettle and to heat the men's quarters. A grain storage room was attached to the north wall.

All of the doors were made of light pine and covered with white parchment, which was opaque but provided excellent insulation. My father used the men's quarters as his bedroom and study. There, he had six thick volumes of our ancestral genealogy along with a few Korean novels and Chinese literature books. He kept the treasured genealogies in an antique pine chest. He was a respected country gentleman and the town's resident genealogist. People came to him for advice. In this room, he entertained his friends and made straw shoes for the family and rice straw ropes for farming. This *sarangbang* was also used to raise silkworms from mid-spring through early fall. During that period, my father would sleep in his distant cousin's *sarangbang*. It was twice as large as my father's, and village men of all ages would gather there for fellowship.

The *an-chae*, the main living quarters, were built on a two-to-three-foot elevated foundation. To access the *an-chae*, we would walk through the main entrance, cross the courtyard, and climb up four stone steps. The kitchen was attached to the main room on the left, and a bedroom was located on the right.

The floors of the main room and the small bedroom were constructed from finely packed clay and covered with coarse reed mats that would give us splinters if we were not careful. Underneath the floors, four or five stone ducts were built to convey heat from the oven in the kitchen to the chimney, heating the main room and the small bedroom. The portion of the floor closer to the oven was warmer. The *sarangbang* floor was constructed the same way. In this main room, we ate our three meals and entertained our extended families and friends. My mother and sister-in-law sewed clothes there. My grandmother kept her spinning wheel in the southwest corner and spun cotton for fabric every day until her passing. She loved spinning. I played and studied there, too. My oldest brother, Tae-jun, and his wife used the smaller bedroom. The warmest spot on the living room floor was reserved for my grandma, who slept there. Next to her, my second older brother, Tae-wook and I slept, sharing a mattress and a quilt. Often, he snored so loudly that I couldn't sleep. Next to us, my mother slept with Yun-ok and Won-sik (my niece and nephew) on a large futon and a quilt. My mother was their de facto mother. At the far side of the room, my unmarried second older sister slept. For a couple of years, four generations, altogether seven of us including me, slept in this main room, until my sister married. Every evening, we would bring our futons and quilts down from the quilt racks and spread them on the floor for the night. In the early morning, we folded them and put them back on the racks for the day. Since our outhouse was located far from the living room, and there was no light, in the winter, my mother kept a chamber pot inside at night for my young niece and nephew. I took advantage of it. She cleaned the pot in the morning. Recalling the chamber pot, I feel sorry for her.

We had to go outside the living room to access the kitchen since there was no door joining these rooms. Since the kitchen did not have heat, it must have been an arduous task for my mother and sister-in-law to cook there and bring the food into the living room to serve, especially in the winter-time. Even worse, they had to draw water from a community well a couple hundred feet away. Men did not draw water for women. On top of the oven, there were three cast iron kettles—two smaller ones for cooking grain, such as millet mixed with adzuki beans or corn, and for making soup, mostly veg-etables in soy sauce stock, and a larger one to keep hot water from freezing or to cook cattle feed.

There also was a much smaller auxiliary oven with two small cast iron ket-tles. From late spring through early fall, my mother and sister-in-law used this small oven to cook because there was no need to heat the living quar-ters. They also boiled silk cocoons to extract thread for homespun silk fabric.

The *an-chae* had a small backyard, fenced with pine branches. There was a warehouse in the middle of the yard, and a tiny stone altar for household gods at the edge of the fence. A round baked clay jar filled with rice and adzuki beans and covered with a stone lid and rice-straw thatch stood on the altar. A white cotton ribbon was tied around the neck of the jar. Sometimes, at midnight, my mother or my sister-in-law placed an offering (mostly food) there and prayed for the family's health and fortune. I would tease my mom, saying, "*Umma* (mom), you covered the jar with a heavy stone in order to keep rats from stealing the grain in the jar. So, how can these stupid, weak gods make us healthy or give us fortune when they cannot even control the disgusting rodents?" She would slap my back and respond sharply, "Don't ever insult these gods. They may get angry and punish you." I never believed in those gods. Sometimes I even kicked the roof off the clay jar. But no angry gods punished me. However, once I prayed to them so that I would be able to whistle like all my friends. Although it did not work, many years later, I was able to whistle without those idiots' help.

There was a threshing ground in front of the *sarang-chae*. Across from it stood the outhouse and a cattle feed shed. Ash from cooking and burned millet shells were collected and used to cover fecal matter in the outhouse. In the spring, the mix, which was much better than chemical fertilizer and cost farmers nothing but labor, was dug out and used as fertilizer for farming millet, corn, or adzuki beans. During the harvest season, we threshed the soy and adzuki beans, separating the grains from the shells. The grains were stored in the backyard and the shells were collected in the feed shed. From late fall through early spring, when green grass was no longer available, we cooked shells with soybeans to feed the cow, who loved this hot, tender feed and grew stronger for the coming farming season.

My father and Tae-jun regularly replaced the straw in the pigpen and cowshed. They piled the dirty straw in an open shed to expedite its decomposition. The resulting material was an exceptionally rich organic fertilizer used mainly for cultivating tobacco and cotton.

RIVALRY BETWEEN MY NIECE AND ME

I was born to a large farming family consisting of four generations, including my grandmother, my parents, my oldest brother and his wife, their children, and my three other older siblings. My oldest sister, however, had moved to live with her husband before I was born. During my boyhood, Korean culture maintained that a large family was a rich and blessed one. But we were poor.

Also, the Korean tradition automatically made the eldest son the head of the family upon his father's death. He inherited the entire family property, including the house and the land, which he distributed to his brothers as he wished. His sisters inherited nothing because they would be married away and would become members of other clans. Men literally called them *oae-in* (外人), or outsiders.

The oldest son also took on the responsibility of caring for his elderly parents. When his father died, his mother and his younger siblings would come under his care, which included arranging marriages for his siblings and organizing his ancestors' annual memorial services. Then, these brothers and sisters would move out, marry, and establish their own independent families.

People usually married by their late teens. Those who remained unmarried beyond age twenty were stigmatized as being unfit for marriage. Consequently, Tae-jun married when he was only seventeen, the year I was born. He and his family lived with my parents. Within a few years, he and his wife had a daughter named Yun-ok and a son named Won-sik. They later had another daughter named Sook-ja. I was only two and half years older than Yun-ok and five years older than Won-sik. As my parents' eldest grandson, Won-sik was the most privileged member of the family after my father and Tae-jun. I was at the lowest rank, except for my sisters.

I received my mother's full attention and love until Yun-ok's birth. Then, my mother had to be both a mother and a grandmother. When my sister-in-law gave birth to her first son, his needs took precedence because he would be the family's heir. So, my mother took care of Yun-ok. In turn, my grandmother became my de facto mother, and gave me her time and attention. Without her, I might have felt like an orphan even though my parents were still alive.

Despite my grandmother's love, I was jealous of Yun-ok for stealing my mother's attention and fought with her often, causing her to tell my mother that I had hit her. As far as my mother was concerned, I was always guilty. She hit me, but never chastised her granddaughter. My mother murmured, "Why are you giving me trouble? I wish I hadn't had you!" and sobbed. I felt sorry for her, but did not apologize because I believed that I had been unfairly punished.

One fine spring day when I was in second grade, a peddler who was suffering from polio came to my village. His pushcart tire was low on air, so he asked if I could get a pump for him. Since I felt bad for him, I borrowed a pump from one of my distant relatives in town. He thanked me with two packs of candy—a big deal to me. After returning the pump, I came home and proudly showed the candy to my mother. Only she and Yun-ok were in the courtyard. I gave them one pack and kept the other. My mother gave her portion to Yun-ok. Despite having one whole pack, Yun-ok asked me for more, and I refused.

My mother said, "Tae-hyok, give her more!"

"No! I gave her some already. And she has yours."

My mother yanked the whole pack out of my hand and gave it to Yun-ok. I thought it was grossly unfair that I didn't have any candy, and was so mad that I punched my niece hard. She cried loudly. My mother yelled at me and hit me. I became angrier and punched my niece again. My mother lost her temper, picked up a stick and struck me on the head. This blow split my scalp. Blood poured down my face.

I covered my wound with my hands and screamed, *Aigoo, aigoo* (ouch)! My head is bleeding!" Not knowing I was bleeding, she hit me again.

At that moment, Yun-ok's mother came home from the fields and intervened. She took me from my mother and let me sit on the kitchen floor. She quickly made wheat flour paste and plastered my wound. Apparently, she had realized that her daughter was the cause of this incident and said, "This will stop the bleeding. I am sorry that you got hurt because of my daughter."

I didn't respond and went to the inner room, sobbing. I was physically and emotionally hurt, but so tired that I fell asleep.

Sometime later, my mother shook me and said, "Tae-hyok, wake up! Eat your supper!" while she lifted my head.

I wasn't in a mood to eat anything and responded moodily, "No, I don't want to! Leave me alone!"

While holding me tightly, she said lovingly, "Tae-hyok, I didn't mean to hurt you. You made me mad because you punched Yun-ok. Please eat your supper!" Her compassion melted my anger. I sat up and she fed me. Even though my wound still hurt, her love made me feel better.

I suppose no woman wants a baby late in her life when she already has many children, and her family is poor. My mother was in her forties and already had four children, including two handsome, precious sons, Tae-jun and Tae-wook (Koreans sometimes give their children names the same first syllable), when I came along. My parents didn't need another child. But I was born anyway, an accidental baby. Nevertheless, I knew that she loved me, because once in a while she hugged me warmly even though she never said, "I love you." I never heard anyone saying "I love you!" in town because the culture regarded this expression as silly.

As Yun-ok and I grew up, I treated her as a loving niece, not a rival, and she respected me as her uncle. She was very talented. When she was ten years old, she knitted a pair of cotton gloves for me. They kept my hands warm in winter while I walked to school on the mountainous trail. Yun-ok and I became very close friends over the years.

BRIEF HISTORY OF KOREA AND KOREA UNDER JAPANESE RULE

From the 4th to the 7th century, three states existed in Korea: Koguryŏ, Paekche, and Silla. During this time, they fought each other, so just one kingdom would rule them all. Silla eventually took control of Paekche and later Koguryŏ, which became known as the 'unification of Korea'.[1]

At the turn of the twentieth century, the rising imperialist Japan occupied Korea, after defeating China in the 1894–1895 Sino–Japanese War and Russia in the 1904–1905 Russo–Japanese War. By eliminating both China and Russia from Korea, Japan became the de facto ruler of Korea. Then, Japan annexed Korea in 1910. Korea, a sovereign nation with more than four thousand years of history and thirty million people, was now occupied by Japan until the Allied powers liberated her at the end of World War II in 1945.

THE THREE KINGDOMS

KOGURYO

SEA OF JAPAN
(EAST SEA)

SILLA

YELLOW SEA

PAEKCHE

KOREA STRAIT

JAPAN

CHAPTER 2

Grammar School

February 1939 – March 1945 (Age 7 - 13)

GRAMMAR SCHOOL ENTRANCE EXAM

After the annexation in 1910, Japan made every effort to eradicate Korean culture and language to Japanize the Koreans. They practiced racial discrimination in every aspect of life and treated Koreans as second-class citizens. They used a two-tier pay system, in which Japanese workers were paid much more than Koreans for the same job. A military governor, an army three star general (equivalent to a U.S. four star general), ruled Korea under de facto martial law. All police chiefs, including low-level section chiefs, were Japanese. All principals and vice principals of public schools were Japanese. Koreans were forced to speak Japanese. The Japanese Occupation Authorities humiliated Koreans by forcing them to change the surnames that they had had for thousands of years and hundreds of generations to Japanese names. For instance, my father had to change our family name from Kim (金) to Kaneko (金子).

After the Pearl Harbor attack, they forcibly drafted young Korean men into the Japanese Imperial Military services or hard-labor corps. Even worse, they conscripted young, single Korean women as sex slaves and sent them to the front lines, forcing them to "comfort" the Japanese soldiers. How barbaric those Japanese were! After Japan had surrendered, those unfortunate women returned home and lived in shame. Many never made it home. Some died of illness, while others took their own lives rather than enduring slavery. The Japanese stole rice, millet, soybeans, and cotton from Korean farmers to support their war effort. They called it *kongchul (共出)* (voluntary offering).

The farmers were poor to begin with, and as the products of their hard work were exploited for the benefit of the Japanese, some starved.

Under this unbelievably harsh, abnormal environment, I started my grammar school life at the age of seven in late February 1939. Like most Korean children, I never had the luxuries of preschool or kindergarten. One cold February day, my father took me to Sungdong Public Elementary School, about six miles northwest of my home, for an entrance exam. I was both excited and anxious. When we arrived, many children were already at the school playground, most accompanied by their fathers, and a few by their mothers. As we waited, more children arrived.

Sometime later, two gentlemen came out of the school office and climbed onto a parade stand. One of them spoke into a big cone-shaped loudspeaker in Japanese, while the other spoke in Korean. They announced the exam procedure, but I didn't quite understand it. After the announcement, my father said, "There are more than one hundred applicants for only eighty places. You must wait until your name is called for the test. Tae-hyok, do well in the exam! I think you will. The results will be announced next week."

My father's words made me shiver. He took me to the entrance of the school office to shield me from the breeze and put his long coat over me, which made me feel warm and safe.

One by one, children were called into the exam room. They exited through the other side of the room after the exam, giving me no chance to ask how they had done. When my turn finally came, I stepped into the room with much anxiety. Although it was somewhat dark and unlit, warm air engulfed my body. There were five big desks in a semicircle, with five examiners in dark suits behind them. The first man welcomed me in Korean, saying "Come over here!" with a gentle smile. I approached him slowly and bowed. He asked, "Can you tell me your father's name and your home address?"

His smile made me relax. I cleared my throat and answered, "Yes, sir. My father's name is Kim Jung-goo." I then told him my address. Judging from his last name, I knew that he was Korean.

He said, "Well done, well done!" Then he told me to go to the next examiner. Meanwhile, the two men exchanged a few words in Japanese. The second man did not smile; he looked rather stern. I bowed to him politely. He nodded and bowed in return. He had a number of translucent triangles on his desk. In a smattering of Korean, he said, "Watch carefully what I am doing!" and arranged them into a couple of different shapes, then broke them apart. I watched him attentively. "Now, duplicate what I did!" I reproduced them exactly as he had done. He smiled and told me to proceed to the third examiner.

I bowed to the third tester as I had to the others. He gave me a sheet of paper and a pencil, and said in fluent Korean, "These are a few addition and subtraction problems. Solve them and write down your answers." Thanks to my older brother, who had taught me simple arithmetic, I gave him my answers without hesitation. He nodded approvingly while checking my answers. He turned to the other examiners and said something in Japanese. Then he came back to me and said, "You do not need to go through the rest. You may go home." I bowed to him and left the office feeling confident. Later, I learned that he was Japanese and was the school's vice principal.

My father was waiting for me at the exit. As soon as I joined him, he asked, "Son, what did they ask you? How did you do? I hope you did well."

"*Abeoji* (Father), I think I did well. I answered the questions without any problems. There were five testers. The third one told me that I did not have to go through the last two, and then he let me go."

As the date for the announcement of the results approached, I became nervous. When that day arrived, my father, Tae-wook, and I set out for the school. The balmy March sun made our journey pleasant. The announcement day and flea market coincided, making the school town busy. When we got there, many children and their fathers already crowded the playground. Some parents greeted each other and talked. Some children were wearing western-style clothes, giggling and shouting excitedly. Perhaps they lived in town and were familiar with the school. Most of the country boys, like me, stuck with our parents and kept quiet. We wore traditional Korean clothes made from homespun cotton, dyed in black.

Close to midday, two school officials came out of the office. One carried a roll of white parchment, about a foot wide, and the other carried two step-chairs. Suddenly, the multitude grew quiet. All eyes followed the two men. The parchment contained the names of those who had made the cut.

The two men climbed onto the step-chairs. As the man with the parchment started to unroll it, the other used thumbtacks to fix it on the wall above the windows. The names slowly began to appear in large black Chinese characters (Koreans traditionally write their names in Chinese characters). Then I heard a man shouting, "You made it, you made it!" His son anxiously followed his father, "Where, where?" The father held him up, but the boy could not read his name because it was written in Chinese characters. I heard another boy crying. His disappointed father yelled, "You stupid! You failed!"

His crying made me extremely nervous because my name had not yet appeared. I questioned myself, "Did I fail?" Then, about one third of the way through, my father and my brother shouted, "Tae-hyok, there is your name." Tae-wook put me on his shoulder and asked, "Can you see it?" My father had taught me how to read my name in Chinese, so I said excitedly, "Yes, I do! I do!"

SCHOOL DAYS

I would become a seven-year-old first-grader, one of eighty. This notion made me proud. The school would start on April 1, only a few weeks away, but time passed ever so slowly. Meanwhile, my father bought me a pencil, an eraser, two notebooks, and an aluminum lunch box for school. My mother sewed me a book-wrapping cloth from her homespun cotton and dyed it black.

Most children used book-wrapping cloths. Only those from wealthy families could afford to buy fancy knapsacks. I practiced wrapping my precious school supplies and lunch box with my cloth. First, I spread the square cloth on the floor. Then I stacked my notebooks and lunch box at one of the four corners, rolled it over and over, diagonally, all the way to the opposite corner and secured it tightly with a safety pin, leaving the other two corners free like long flaps. I put it on my back with one flap over my right shoulder and the other under my left armpit and tied the ends firmly in front of my chest. This way, I kept my hands free and could walk or run. The only problem was that condensation from my lunch box dampened my books and notebooks.

My school's opening day finally arrived. I wrapped my lunch box, notebook, and pencils excitedly. I was ready even before my father had eaten his breakfast. He and my fifth-grade brother would take me to school because it was my first day. Tae-wook had just transferred to my school from another that only went through fourth grade. I was waiting for them at the door when my brother saw me carrying my notebooks and lunch box on my back.

He said, "Tae-hyok, you don't have to take them with you today because we will be excused after the new school year opening ceremony and some paperwork."

After a couple of hours walking along country roads and the Dong-kogae Mountain Trail, we arrived at the school and saw hundreds of children in the playground. Awestricken, I asked, "Oh my goodness! *Abeoji*, are they all students?"

Tae-wook, answered on his behalf, "Yes, they are. Do you see those tall ones? They must be in the fifth or sixth grade. I bet you they are sixteen or seventeen years of age. The small ones accompanied by their parents must be first graders just like you." I listened to him silently. He continued, "I have a few friends in the fifth and sixth grades who transferred from my previous school. The upper-class pupils play soccer or basketball."

I knew soccer, but I had never heard of basketball. I asked, "Tae-wook, what is basketball? Is it like soccer?"

"No, it is not. A basketball is bigger than a soccer ball. In a soccer game, you move the ball with your feet and kick it into the opposite team's goal posts to score. But in basketball, you advance the ball by dribbling and throwing it into a net which is fixed on a board, about eight feet high."

Shortly after our arrival, the school bell rang loudly. A group of teachers came out of their offices and stood in front of their classes. The class leaders shouted to their students to line up like soldiers. One of the teachers climbed onto the parade stand and directed all the first graders and their parents to the far left. A few upper-class pupils helped us form columns. Then a beautiful, smiling young lady—our first-grade teacher, Miss Park—came and stood in front of us. She was dressed in a western style suit, her lips were painted bright red, and she wore a pair of round eyeglasses. I had never seen a woman dressed like her before.

Then the teacher on the parade stand shouted something in Japanese. Our helpers interpreted the shouting into Korean: "Attention! Turn toward the East," and we did. The teacher yelled again, "*Tennōheika ni saikayray!*" The helpers interpreted it as "Bow to the Emperor!" and we bowed. "*Tennōheika ni saikayray!*" means the utmost salute to the Japanese emperor. At that time, the emperor resided in Tokyo, close to one thousand miles east of us. I did not even know what he looked like. While we were still bowed, the teacher shouted again. The helpers said, "Now, turn left toward the teacher," and we obeyed. After this, the teacher on the stand led the Japanese national anthem, and all but most first graders sang. We practiced this rite every morning for the next six years, until I graduated.

The teacher came down from the podium. Then, the principal climbed up on the stand, wearing a pair of white gloves and standing at attention. Another teacher, also wearing white gloves, came out of the office carrying a white scroll on a black tray slightly above eye level. He moved ceremoniously toward the principal and raised his tray with extreme care. In turn, the latter received the tray, and the former stepped back. The principal ordered us to bow our heads and untied the ribbon, spreading the scroll and reading it solemnly. The scroll contained the most consecrated decree of the emperor. When the reading was finished, the principal rolled up the scroll, tied it with the ribbon, and put it back on the tray. Then the teacher who had brought the scroll stepped forward to receive the tray and returned it to the office. The headmaster ordered us to raise our heads and stand at ease. He delivered a long speech, and when he finished, he raised his arms to the sky and shouted three times, "*Tennōheika Banzai!* (Long live the Emperor!)" We followed him, thus concluding the ceremony. This ritual was performed in every ceremonial assembly.

'TENNŌHEIKA'

Every grade had a principal's hour once or twice a year. A few months after school started, the principal, Mr. Komiyama, came to our class for this hour. He gave us a lecture in Japanese about the Japanese Royalty, and Miss Park interpreted it into Korean. He explained that *'Tennōheika'* (天皇陛下) was the emperor and the divine being in human form, and *saikayray* was the utmost salute that was reserved for the emperor. We were required to be at attention every time the word 'emperor' was mentioned. He also told us that the current emperor's name was *Shōwa* and that he was the 124th emperor; that

Japan was proud of an unbroken lineage of 124 royal generations for more than 2,500 years, and that no other empire had lasted that long. He required us to memorize all 124 emperors' names, which was not easy.

A WILD SIBERIAN TIGER

Siberian tigers are fearsome, powerful, magnificent animals. They are carnivorous, solitary creatures weighing five hundred to six hundred pounds. They must eat at least twenty pounds of food a day to survive. They usually attack their prey from behind, pounce on them with their mighty front legs, sink their claws into the prey's necks, and choke them to death. Their usual habitats are cold snowy forests of deciduous and coniferous vegetation in mountainous areas.

When I was a first grader, I met one of these Siberian tigers on a rugged mountain pass on the way home from school. At the time, I thought it was an oversized wild cat.

I lived in a mountainous region of north-central Korea that lay within the Siberian tiger's habitat. Occasionally, some village folks would claim that they had spotted a tiger nearby. Elderly villagers would say, "If you ever encounter a wild tiger, you should look right into its eyes, and never turn your back nor run away. The tiger is afraid of you as much as you are of it. If you have cigarettes and a match with you, light a cigarette because the tiger is afraid of fire, as are all hairy animals."

My parents told me that years earlier, one of my great uncles and his friends had gone to the mountains with a tamed hawk for pheasant hunting. While stirring pheasants out of the bush, they came across a Siberian tiger. My great uncle hit the tiger in the head with his long staff, killing it with one blow. He and his friends brought the tiger's body to the village and showed it to the villagers. My parents also saw that it had gray and light brown rings on its body. Despite having heard many tiger stories, I never expected that I would encounter one up close.

Since my village was remote, without a decent road or transportation to school, we seven boys from the village, including Tae-wook and me, would walk. It was about six miles in each direction, along rock-strewn narrow country roads over Dong-kogae Pass, a heavily wooded, rugged mountainous trail.

I was the only first grader amongst us. The school was in Jang-keo Ri (market town), northwest of my village.

The school excused the first graders after only four sessions. Because the trail was dangerous and sparsely traveled, I would wait for my older brother and the other boys from our village to finish their remaining three sessions and come home with them.

One fine spring day, I was waiting for Tae-wook. Feeling bored, I looked around for something to do. I saw that the hills nearby were covered with pink azalea blossoms, and the country roads were decorated with golden dandelions and colorful wildflowers. I left the playground and started walking down the country road, enjoying the beauty of nature, and forgetting to wait for my brother and friends. Before realizing it, I was already at the foothill of Dong-kogae Pass, far from the school. I felt somewhat apprehensive and wondered whether I should return to the school. But I said to myself, "It's okay, it's daylight. You can make it home alright."

The pass was heavily wooded with tall, old pines. A few thin rays of sunlight filtering through the trees made the north slope of the pass dim and eerie. After climbing farther up, I sang loudly, picking up rocks and throwing them into the bushes to frighten away any animals around me.

Finally, I reached the peak and the sun shone on me. The peak had a flat stretch, a few hundred feet long, before it started to descend. The left side was an upward slope with a narrow grass strip before a pine grove took over, while the right side dropped steeply in a heavily wooded slope. I continued walking briskly.

Then, unexpectedly, a fist-sized rock rolled down from the upper slope and landed in front of me. I felt my hair standing on end. I looked up the slope and saw a big grayish cat squatting at the upper edge of the grass strip. It had an unusually big head, with dark rings around its neck. I picked up the rock and threw it at the cat with all my strength, screaming, "You, son of a bitch cat, go away!" The rock landed right in front of it.

I threw another rock and gazed into its eyes. When the second rock landed beside the first one, the cat slowly rose, turned around, and walked into the thick pine grove. I threw many more toward the place where the cat had been sitting. I yelled for some time even after the cat had disappeared into the pine grove. I resumed my journey home at a faster pace, singing. By the time I came home, I had forgotten all about the big cat.

As usual during the farming season, we ate our late supper under a flickering kerosene lamp, chatting about the happenings of the day. Then my brother drew our attention, saying, "They spotted a tiger in broad daylight today."

Almost simultaneously everybody in the room said, "Where?"

"Around the top of Dong-kogae Pass."

My parents asked, "Who is *they*?"

He answered, "A few people from Jang-keo Ri. They went to the Dong-kogae Pass area to gather fresh wild edible vegetables. But they came home early without picking much because they spotted a tiger in the distance and got scared."

Upon hearing the conversation, I suddenly felt a cold shiver down my back and a tremendous fear gripping me. I began to shake as if the tiger was jumping on me. I felt my throat close and stopped eating. I moved quickly to my grandma, who held me tight in her arms. I said in a quivering low voice, "Grandma, I saw that tiger at the peak of Dong-kogae Pass on the way home from school! I thought it was a big cat, not a tiger."

She said, "Tae-hyok, don't worry, the tiger is not here, it's gone into the deep mountains," while holding me closer. "You are safe now. It must have been a good tiger. Perhaps it was a messenger of the guardian spirit of the great mountains. The spirit will protect you from harm from a tiger or anything else. Do you remember the harvest festival last fall? Our elderly cousins and your father went to the high place at the peak of Duit-dong San (rear mountain) and made an offering to the guardian spirit of the great mountains with a big pig head? I bet you the spirit was pleased with the offering, and protects you day and night."

But even my grandma's reassurance did not help. I crawled even closer to her for fear that the tiger would snatch me out of her arms. Without knowing, I fell into oblivion. After that incident, I did not dare come home alone.

FIRST SNOW AND MY BROTHER'S LOVE

My school route consisted of narrow, rock-strewn dirt roads and the wooded Dong-kogae Trail over the rugged Kalsan Mountain Range, 2,300 feet above sea level. The top fifth of the trail was very steep. If you took a shortcut along a sharp slope, it might have been less than two hundred feet. Since most of this steep rise was a granite ledge with sparse vegetation, there was little to hold onto if you lost your footing. I felt like for every two steps upward, I slipped one step back. We, energetic, adventurous school kids from my village did not have the patience to take the long detour. Instead, we took the precarious short path. It was difficult for me, the only first grader, to climb it. Almost every morning, Tae-wook helped me by pushing me from behind or pulling me up from the front. By the time he graduated, I had become strong enough to catch up with the other kids without help. Without his brotherly love, I might have quit school, because I did not want to be left alone on this unforgiving slope.

Before I realized it, three seasons had passed since my first day of school, and winter had arrived. Every morning, my mother got up at the rooster's second crow and prepared breakfast and lunch boxes for my brother and me. Like most Korean farmers, we could not afford alarm clocks, so we used our roosters to tell time. Korean roosters crowed three times a day at hour intervals—once about three hours before dawn, and finally just before sunrise. Usually, they slept on the cross braces of barns because they didn't like confined cages. Apparently, they had time-sensitive biorhythms; their crowing time was fairly accurate.

My mother prepared hot vegetable soup and millet mixed with adzuki beans for breakfast. For lunch, she filled the boxes with millet and a few slices of spicy kimchi. During the summer, she cooked barley with lima beans and salted vegetables instead. We hardly ever had eggs because we couldn't afford them. My parents sold the chickens they raised and their eggs for cash for our family.

One early December day, when my mother woke us, we rose reluctantly and ate our breakfast half-asleep. She said, "The first snow of the season fell last night. The road must be slippery, especially the Dong-kogae Trail. Tae-wook, watch your baby brother." Normally, I didn't like to be called 'baby brother,' but for some reason this morning it sounded so lovely.

After breakfast, I bundled my books and lunch box in a wrapping cloth, slung it across my back and tied it tightly in front of my chest. Then my mother wrapped my head and neck with homespun silk to keep me warm. She also bound my shoes and feet with rice straw twine to create traction. I wore bulky traditional Korean padded trousers and a jacket, which were not very efficient at keeping me warm since they were too loose to trap my body heat.

When we stepped out, the cold early morning air filled my lungs, and I shuddered. It was still somewhat dark. We joined our friends from the neighboring village. The seven of us trudged single file on the virgin snow, which made a crunching sound under our feet. The first snow was always an exciting event to the children in this remote village where little entertainment was available. I was in the middle, with my brother right behind me. We chatted about the snow and laughed. But the colder we became, the less we talked. The sun had not risen over Obongsan Mountain, yet it brushed the top of the snowy Kalsan Mountain Range in a pale orange, below which the grayish-white slope fell sharply into the valley. As we approached Kalsan Mountain, the orange turned to white, and the white rolled down to the foothills. Finally, the sun cast its rays on us and sparkled on the white snow. We shouted, "The sun rose!" and were re-energized.

The roads were not as slippery as my mother had warned even though we wore flimsy rubber shoes which did not have as good traction as sturdy leather ones. No one in the village could afford better. An hour or so later, we arrived at the foothills of the Dong-kogae Trail. It was so cold that we gathered dead wood and started a fire using matches. During the winter, almost every one of us carried a small box of matches for emergencies. Soon the fire was roaring, and sparks flew into the sky. We stood around the fire and tried to warm our freezing feet. Some impatient kids took off one of their shoes and lifted their feet closer to the fire, while balancing themselves by holding the shoulders of the kids next to them. But the fire scorched the cotton padded socks before the heat warmed their feet. Some sparks landed on our jackets and the loose woven cotton started to burn. We yelled, "Hey, you are on fire!" and whoever was nearest pinched the sparks out and extinguished the small burn, leaving a hole in the child's jacket. This ritual went on throughout the winter whenever it was very cold.

After we warmed up, we started to climb the trail. The higher I climbed, the more insecure I felt, but the older kids did not seem to have any trouble.

Soon, Tae-wook and I fell behind. When we reached the shortcut, my brother said, "Tae-hyok, get a firm footing!" and pushed me from behind. About thirty feet up this steep rise, I lost my balance, fell on my stomach, and started to slip. Tae-wook tried to hold me, but he did not have a firm enough grip. He shouted, "Tae-hyok!" and helplessly watched me slide.

I searched for something to grab, but with nothing but snow in my bare hands, I kept slipping. I was too frightened to call for help. I landed on my back with a thud, and snow fell on my numb face. I was extremely frightened but wasn't hurt because I had landed on a thick underbrush bed in a gully. I stood up feebly, but I was scared and cold. My knees were knocking, and my hands were freezing. I shouted, "*Hyung* (Brother), help me!"

"Hold on, Tae-hyok! Don't move! You will be alright. I am coming down," he answered. Tae-wook climbed hurriedly down the slope, jumped into the gully, held me in his arms, and asked, "Did you get hurt?" while examining my bare hands and face. Before I answered, he said, "You look alright. Now, let's get out of here!" He surveyed our surroundings and pointed at a big pine tree within his reach on the slope between the gully and the road. He lifted me up to the tree, and I held it tightly. Then he climbed out of the gully to the tree and put his foot on the base of the tree. He lifted me as high as he could and said, "Now, crawl up to the road! Don't worry, I will hold you until you reach the road." When I reached the road, he warned, "Tae-hyok, don't move! Stay there!" I feared that I might slip down to the gully again if I stood up. So, I squatted and carefully turned around to watch my brother climb up. He scaled the gully bank without too much struggle. Meanwhile, cold penetrated my bones.

After he joined me, he said, "Little brother, you are shivering. We must get down to the main road. Now, ride on my back, and hold tight!" and I did. He sat down on his butt, cautiously slid down to the bottom of the shortcut, about twenty feet, and lowered me. He said, "Stay here!" while he put my hands into my jacket sleeves to keep them warm. He collected dead wood, piled it up, struck his match and started a fire using handfuls of dried grass. When it began to produce heat, he held me, stretched my freezing hands toward the flame, and rubbed them vigorously.

As my hands warmed up, my fingertips tingled. Soon my frigid body warmed up, too, and became flexible. I looked up at him and said, "Thank you, *hyung*."

"You're welcome, my baby brother!" he answered, and squeezed me tightly. "I am glad that you weren't hurt. Your cheeks are red." We stayed by the fire for some time until I had calmed down. He asked, "Now, can you walk? We are not going to school today. I am taking you home. Let's put out the fire before we leave." He smothered the fire with a thick stick, and the burning wood hissed in the snow. We kicked snow over the fire, and after we had completely extinguished it, he took my hand, and we headed home. I thanked him and thought how fortunate I was to have Tae-wook with me.

SNAKE

One June day, my second-grade Japanese teacher, Mr. Nonoyama, assigned us homework. We were to memorize the multiplication tables by heart, but I procrastinated. The following day, I was randomly picked to recite them and failed miserably. As a punishment, he kept me behind for a few hours after the rest of the class had gone home. After I had read the tables by heart, he let me go home. By then the orange sun was only a few inches above the western mountain. I worried about going home alone in the dark.

I hastily bid him goodnight and ran as far as I could before darkness set in. There wasn't a single soul in the rolling fields beyond the school town. Soon the sun sank behind the mountains. I picked up my pace, but my flimsy rubber-soled shoes slowed me down. So, I took them off and ran barefoot, carrying my shoes in my trouser pockets. I stumbled over rocks, and my feet hurt, but I had no time for self-pity and kept running.

By the time I reached the foothills of the Dong-kogae Pass, darkness prevailed. All I could see were the dim road and silhouettes of trees and bushes. It was quiet, except for some nocturnal birds' intermittently singing and the metallic noise from my brass chopsticks beating inside my empty aluminum lunch box. The monotonous sound somewhat calmed me. Occasionally, the noise frightened small animals out of their sleep, and they scared the hell out of me. Ascending the steep trail, I slowed down, took my lunch box out of my backpack, and shook it vigorously to scare off any big animals that might be around. Since the trail was too rough for my bare feet, I put my shoes back on. When my arms got tired, I sang loudly or yelled at the top of my lungs. Approaching the top of the pass where I had met a Siberian tiger face to face as a first-grader, I felt apprehensive.

When I reached the crest, I did not see any glowing eyes. But in case a tiger was on the prowl, I continued rattling the lunch box, howled, and resumed my running. After several stumbles, I arrived at the bottom of the pass where two farmhouses were. I saw light from lanterns and heard people's voices. I slowed my pace for a few moments and took a deep breath. I had come two-thirds of the way, but still had two miles to go.

Not too far from that hamlet, the road ran between irrigated rice paddies that became a breeding ground for frogs from spring through early fall. The frogs drew waterborne snakes that we sometimes encountered and scared us. We usually waited until they disappeared into the grass along the rice paddy levees. Sometimes a snake lay coiled in the middle of the road and raised its head, sticking its despicable black tongue in and out, and ready to strike. Frightened, we children would throw rocks at it or whack it with a staff and kill it. We were wary because water moccasin bites were fatal. I shuddered at the thought of walking along that stretch in the darkness, but I had to continue.

After putting my lunch box away, I tightened the wrap on my back. I took off my shoes again and resumed running. The box and chopsticks began generating loud noises. I prayed the noises would scare any snakes away.* Soon I reached the stretch between the rice paddies, and my hair stood on end. I ran as fast as I could. Halfway along the stretch, my bare foot landed on something chilly, round, and wiggling. Instinctively, I jumped, and my spine went cold as I waited to feel the snake's fangs. But it did not bite.

I realized that I was standing alone in a dark, silent valley. I had to get going, and I started running faster than before. Sometime later, I heard someone calling, "Tae-hyok, Tae-hyok, where are you?" It was the sweetest voice I had ever heard—my older brother's.

---

* According to some scientists' research, snakes might be able to hear very low airborne vibrations below 70 hertz, but they are absolutely deaf to higher hertz.

"*Hyung*, I am here! I am coming!" I repeated, "*Hyung, Hyung*!" while accelerating my pace to meet him.

Tae-wook affectionately put his arm around my shoulder and asked, "Are you okay? You are not sick, are you? The whole family is worrying about you."

I couldn't answer, but instead trembled.

He embraced me tightly and said, "You must have been scared all by yourself. Now you are alright with me. You must be hungry." He took my backpack. "You sweated so much, even your books are drenched. Let's go home. *Umma* (mom) and *Appa* (dad) are waiting for you." He pulled me by the hand.

After I calmed down, I told him that my teacher had held me behind for several hours until I had recited the multiplication tables by heart. Also, I recounted that I had stepped on a snake a mile back.

He stopped abruptly and asked in a serious voice, "You weren't bitten, were you?" It was too dark to see his facial expression, but I knew he was very alarmed.

"No!" I said, while putting my shoes back on.

"I am glad that you weren't bitten, but how did you know it was a snake?"

"I am sure it was because it was round and cold. It wiggled under my bare foot."

He didn't ask any more questions. He held my hand firmly and said, "Let's run!" We ran until we saw my parents waiting for us by a small mosquito bonfire burning in the middle of the courtyard. My brother hollered from the front yard, "*Umma, Appa*, Tae-hyok is here."

My parents sprang up. I ran to them, calling, "*Umma, Appa*!" My mother held me to her bosom, and my father gently rubbed my head. Peace enveloped me.

They fussed over me, and my mother went to the kitchen and brought my supper. "Eat your supper! You must be hungry."

SNAKE PERSONALITY

A few weeks later, Yeo-soo, an amateur hunter, caught a water moccasin from the nearby fields and showed it to the townspeople. He said that the moccasin was the deadliest among all snakes in the region. He held it up by its tail. It bent itself into a U-shape, stuck out its black split tongue and tried to strike Yeo-soo's hand. It reached just short of his hand and fell back. I shuddered. A few seconds later it tried again. Each time its head got farther and farther from his hand. After many tries, it gave up and hung upside down.

When he put it down on the ground, it started to move. Then he stepped on it. The snake first attempted to extricate itself, then turned its head back to bite his thick rubber boot. It took a few moments before it tried to strike. He said that if you stepped on a moving snake and quickly removed your foot, the chance of getting bitten would be almost none.

Yeo-soo pinned the snake to the ground with his long-handled Y-fork. Then he picked it up by the neck, exposing its sharp fangs. The creature twisted around his arm. He untangled it from his arm and held it straight on the ground by its neck with his hand and its tail under his boot. He asked an elderly man to clean his tobacco pipe with a rice straw.

The old man inserted a straw into the mouthpiece of his long pipe and pulled it out from the other end, coating the straw with black nicotine tar.

Yeo-soo took the straw from the old man and forced the nicotine-stained straw into the snake's mouth, deep into its belly. A few moments later, he pulled the straw back out. The snake twisted a few times, stretched itself out like a twig, and died. He explained that snakes had no resistance to nicotine but warned us not to try this ourselves.

I trembled at his demonstration, but I now knew why I hadn't been bitten.

MY UNIQUE WHISTLING

I have a musical instrument which is free of cost and maintenance. I carry it with me wherever I go. It doesn't weigh anything. I play it to raise my spirits when I am sad. The instrument is my ability to whistle.

My whistling is unique. I have yet to meet anyone who whistles like I do. When they hear me whistling, people often say, "Your whistle is beautiful! It's like an Indian flute. It's serene and soothing. How do you do that? How long did it take you to learn to whistle like that? Who taught you?"

I answer, "Thank you. I taught myself." I actually could not whistle at all until I was eleven. How I envied all my friends' whistling! I often prayed to my ancestral spirits at my family altar for the ability to whistle, to no avail.

One day, my prayer was answered. It was a cold, brilliant day during my winter vacation. I was home alone; the rest of my family had gone out to visit their friends in the village. Taking advantage of this quiet time, I lay on the warm reed-mat floor and did my homework. My school assigned daily vacation homework—a couple of pages of reading and arithmetic. While doing my arithmetic, I accidentally whistled, generating a rudimentary shrieking noise for the first time in my life. I was so excited that I jumped up and whistled, walking around the room. I forgot all about my homework, continued to whistle, and tried to improve.

Then my father walked into the room and noticed me whistling. He said, "Son, don't whistle! If you whistle in wintertime, they say that the weather becomes colder." I don't know how they acquired such a theory.

Since my desire to whistle was so intense, I went out to the courtyard and resumed whistling. Within a few minutes, the biting wintry wind stiffened my lips, and I couldn't even generate an ugly squeaking noise. No matter how hard I tried, my lips would not whistle. In sheer desperation, I moved my tongue up and down, and then a hissing sound came out. I continued to whistle until the cold weather drove me inside. Fortunately, my father was not there.

In his absence, I resumed my practice. The more I practiced, the smoother I got. As I became more adept, I started to coordinate the whistling and the movement of my tongue. This practice gave birth to a peculiar sound, like a flute. It fascinated me so much that I repeated it. Over time, my skill improved and matured. Even my father began to appreciate the sound. He never repeated the proverb about whistling in winter.

PRINCIPAL KOMIYAMA

To achieve its expansionist goal, Japan immediately began to Japanize Korea by replacing the Korean bureaucratic systems with those of the Japanese. It brutally ruled Koreans, exploited them, and tried to erase Korean culture and language. The Japanese discriminated against Koreans in every aspect of

Korean life during these four horrible decades. They took over every important Korean institution, including schools.

Through this imperialist policy, Mr. Komiyama, a Japanese teacher and soldier, became the principal of my school for five years between my first and fifth grades. He came from Nagano Prefecture, Japan. He was a racist, a militarist, and an imperialist—a perfect reflection of his imperialist nation. Our school day started with a daily morning assembly in the playground, Monday through Saturday, except in bad weather. Every morning, he preached to us that the Japanese were superior to any race in the world, except Germans. The Chinese were uncivilized, dirty people, and Koreans were slightly better than the Chinese. American and British people were beastly, barbaric, and imperialistic.

Despite the Japanese colonist policy, my school continued to teach the Korean language to all grades for two hours every week until Mr. Komiyama's arrival. As soon as he assumed the principal's position, he stopped this language class altogether and ordered us to speak only in Japanese. He also commanded us to report anyone speaking Korean to him. Then he would severely punish him/her. He demanded that we teach our parents Japanese and report to him if they don't want to learn it. Of course, none of us obeyed his idiotic demand. Certainly, my parents did not want to learn the language under duress.

During the Monday morning assembly of December 8, 1941, Mr. Komiyama climbed onto the podium and shouted, "Attention!" We came to attention like stiff poles. Then, he solemnly spoke, "Yesterday, *Tennōheika* declared war against the savages of America and Britain. The Imperial Japanese Navy Task Force attacked Shinjuwan (Pearl Harbor)." He proudly announced, "Our most advanced *kansai-sento-ki* (carrier-based Zero fighter bombers) bombed American battleships, and our suicide *sensui-kans* (mini-submarines) rammed into enemy warships. From the air and from under the sea, our navy inflicted total destruction on the American Pacific Fleet. A brilliant victory! The cowardly enemy will soon surrender." He was excited, but we children shivered in the wintry morning. He continued, "Soon, *Dai-Doa-Ko-Ai-Ken* shall be realized under the leadership of *Tennōheika*. (My humble translation of *Dai-Doa-Ko-Ai-Ken* (大東亞共榮圈) may be read as *Greater Asia Co-prosperity*

Sphere which meant all Asian nations prosper together.) Then he raised his hands high in the air and shouted, "*Tennōheika Banzai!*" Students and teachers alike followed him. He repeated this twice, and so did we. Then, we were dismissed to march into our classrooms, singing a military victory song.

• • •

That same winter, when I was ten, my third-grade teacher, Mr. Kim, passed away. Mr. Komiyama filled in the late teacher's position for the rest of the year. He treated us like soldiers. He strongly discouraged us from smiling because it was girlish, and Japanese soldiers did not smile. He ordered us to come to attention whenever *Tennōheika* was mentioned. If anyone failed to do so, he or she would be severely punished. One day, he taught us Japanese history and mentioned *Tennōheika*. For some reason, a couple of my classmates, Park Kwang-sun and Lee Sang-hyun, giggled while we came to attention. He yelled at them, "Stand up!" He slapped the two boys hard across the face and dragged them by the ears to his office. Fear swept through the class, and no one dared to move or talk, even in his absence.

About half an hour later, the two boys returned alone, covering their heads with their hands, and quietly slipping into their seats. Their pale, terror-stricken faces convulsed. Their eyes were reddish and swollen. Dried tears smeared their cheeks. They were too terrified to talk. When they finally moved their hands, we saw horrible, fist-sized bulges atop their skulls. I shuddered and gasped. Everyone murmured. No one had the nerve to ask what the principal had done to them. Since I was sitting just behind them, I asked them what had happened. Kwang-sun answered in a barely audible, trembling voice, "He beat us, one blow after another, with a bamboo sword."* He dropped his head and started to sob. What a cruel monster this principal was to beat such young boys!

Mr. Komiyama entered the classroom like a triumphant general. He closed the door with a bang and climbed onto the teacher's platform. Then, he picked up his whip from the dust receptacle of the blackboard and pounded the top

---

* The bamboo sword was used for Japanese Samurai martial arts.

of his podium with it. The piercing sound was terrifying. We jumped up, held our breaths, and came to attention, expecting a horrible punishment to fall on us. My heart sank, and my knees knocked.

The monster shouted, "Turn around and look at those two. *Tennōheika* is the reincarnation of *Amaterasu Ōmikami* (the supreme god of Japanese *Shintoism*), thus he is a god. If you fail to come to attention at the word of *Tennōheika*, you will be punished like them," and he pointed his whip in the direction of the two shivering children. "*Wakaruka?* (Do you understand?)"

"*Hai Kocho Sensei!* (Yes, sir, Mr. Principal!)" we responded in scared, low voices.

"You talk like a *Sina-jin* (Chinese). Talk louder! *Baka-yaro* (You, stupid)."

"*Hai Kocho Sensei!*" we repeated louder.

After a long, threatening monologue, he finally let us out for recess. Then, our class representative shouted, "*Kiriz, Keirei!* (Stand up, bow your head!)" This ritual was performed at the beginning and end of every class. After that, we silently went out to the playground and took deep breaths. No one talked during the recess.

The new school year began in April of 1942, and most of us advanced to the fourth grade. Those who failed to advance eventually dropped out of school and never came back. No new teacher came to replace the late Mr. Kim, and Mr. Komiyama continued to teach us. Every day, at the beginning of the first class, he informed us of the brilliant victories by the Imperial Army and Navy, and proudly said, "Because Japan is the *Tennōheika's* sacred nation, the living god's, we are winning the war and will soon conquer the savages. Afterwards, we will rule the world."

One late April day, he came into the classroom with a grave face and passed around a newspaper clipping showing two blind-folded westerners led by a few *Kempeis* (Japanese MPs [Military Police]). He shouted, "Look at these barbaric American soldiers. These cowards sneaked their plane over the *Tennōheika's* sacred land and dropped bombs." We instantly came to attention at the word of *Tennōheika*. He continued, "The bombs did not even explode because the living god caused them to be duds. Our superior *koshapoes* (anti-aircraft guns) shot the airplane down and captured the Americans. The Imperial Army executed them because they had violated the *Tennōheika's* consecrated land." He banged the top of his podium angrily and yelled, "We will punish the enemy severely." In the following morning's assembly, he repeated this speech to the whole student body.

In the early days of the war, Mr. Komiyama had frequently predicted that the gutless Americans would soon surrender. Instead, after their brilliant victories in the first few months of the war, the Japanese military faced American counterattacks which grew stronger every day, and they began to lose battles across the line. Yet, the principal told us that the Imperial Japanese Navy had sunk many enemy warships or inflicted heavy damages on them around the Solomon Islands, while the Japanese Navy sustained light losses; and its brave Imperial *Riku-sentai* (marine corps) and Army units killed tens of thousands of *ki-chi-ku* (animal) American soldiers on the Guadalcanal and Bougainville islands.

He also caricatured President Franklin D. Roosevelt as the ugliest, meanest devil with glaring eyeballs, a dagger-like nose and forward-curved chin like a truncated crescent; General Douglas MacArthur, then the allied supreme commander of the Pacific theater, was depicted as the second meanest devil with an elongated face, a pointed chin, and a face half covered by grossly oversized dark eyeglasses (back then, I did not know of the existence of sunglasses). He also portrayed the British Prime Minister, Winston Churchill, as evil, lampooning him as a bruised potato with barely visible legs. Mr. Komiyama ordered us to make effigies of the three men and beat them until they were pulverized.

In addition, Mr. Komiyama began verbal anti-American propaganda, depicting Americans as carnivorous and ugly. He told many gruesome, atrocious stories to us innocent children at the morning assemblies. These stories made me shudder.

One day, when I came home, I asked my father if Americans were truly carnivorous and ugly. He responded, "Son, don't believe those Japanese lies. I know that the Americans are more civilized than the Japanese. They value human lives more than the Japanese do. As proof, the Americans built the first modern hospitals and colleges for Koreans in Seoul and Pyongyang, many years before the Japanese occupied our country. One of my friends told me that they are handsomer than the Orientals. Son, don't tell anybody, Japan will lose the war to the mighty Americans. Then Korea will restore our independence from Japan."

As the war dragged on, Mr. Komiyama mobilized the third graders and the older children for war efforts, forcing us to perform hard labor in the name of serving *Tennōheika*. We harvested wild hay from hills and riverbanks for the Imperial Army's horses; mined gravel from a nearby riverbed and carried it in large dustpan-shaped baskets to repair potholes in the only highway that ran through town.

During the one-month summer vacation, Mr. Komiyama ordered each of us to gather one cow-load of wild grape vines. My friends and I harvested vines from the surrounding mountains, bundled them in sheaves and carried them on our backs to the school playground two or three times a week throughout the vacation. Then, trucks transported them to a processing plant in a distant place. The principal explained that scientists would extract a chemical from the vines to use for weapons.

He also had each student collect one cow-load of pine because aged pine roots contained rich resin. To fulfill my allotment, my father and I went to my family's mountain, cut down a very old pine, chopped it into short lengths and transported them on my family cow's back to a local packed-clay furnace where the pine was cooked to extract resin. According to the principal, engineers would separate special oil from the resin, adding it to airplane fuel to keep it from freezing in the air. The plant produced a large amount of tar-like resin and stored it in a big pool. Ironically, it remained there unused even after the war was over. What a waste!

We also grew various vegetables and beans which teachers took home, not for the military. One hot summer day, Mr. Komiyama assigned the sixth graders to draw septic matter from the school septic tanks with wooden pails to fertilize the garden. It stank horribly. So, two boys covered their noses with their handkerchiefs to avoid the offensive smell. This upset Mr. Komiyama greatly. He ordered them to remove the handkerchiefs from their noses and roll up their shirt sleeves. Then, he commanded them to plunge their arms into the septic filth. Afterwards, he assembled the entire student body and teachers on the playground and brought the two children in front of the assembly. Then, he climbed onto the podium and delivered a speech in an angry voice. "Farming is a sacred profession. Even *Tennōheika* himself plants rice in the spring to show how sacred farming is. Look at these two boys! They desecrated this profession by covering their noses to avoid the smell of the fertilizer. No good Japanese should cover their noses, like these *baka-yaro* (sons of bitches)," he said, pointing his finger in the direction of the two pupils. He shouted again, "*Wakaruka?* (Do you understand?)"

We all responded, loudly and clearly, "*Hai!* (Yes, sir!)"

Then, he dismissed the assembly, but to punish the two boys further, he kept them standing in the scorching sun for a few hours. How cruel he was!

As the Pacific War continued, the Japanese military faced a serious shortage of supplies, including oil. One spring day, when I was in the fifth grade, Mr. Komiyama announced that half of the playground would be cultivated to raise castor plants. He said that castor beans would produce rich oil which would be used to lubricate the imperial war planes and vehicles to win the war. As ordered, we brought our own hoes or shovels from home, plowed the hard ground, crushed chunks of soil, and sowed castor seeds. It took all day. The playground was already crowded. Now, it shrank. There would be no more soccer games or fall sports festival either. This made us sad.

• • •

Despite his imperialistic discipline, I have a few good memories of the principal. He taught us basic plane geometry, such as calculating the areas of triangles, circles, rectangles, squares, or the circumference of a circle. He made it easy to understand. Perhaps, because of him, I came to like geometry. He could draw a perfect circle on a blackboard with just one quick move.

He was an absolute disciplinarian, but he loved literature and art, wrote haikus or short stories, and read them to us. He taught us how to write poetry and encouraged us to do so. When we wrote simple poems, he did not spare his praise for our writings. He even said that writing would make our lives rich, which I did not understand then. He had a good collection of fine art and showed it to us.

I liked history. When I was in the first grade, I used to listen to Taewook read about Japanese history or discuss various events with his friends.

I memorized as much as I could and participated in their discussions. Once in a while, at the morning assembly, Mr. Komiyama shared trivia about historical events such as the current *Tennōheika's* birthday, how many generations of emperors there were or how old Japanese history was. As a first or second grader, I raised my hand high without embarrassment. He pointed to me, and I gave my answer. Then, he would praise me sumptuously by saying, "*Kim Tai-kaku* (my name in Japanese pronunciation) is the only true Japanese. The rest of you are Chinese." Apparently, I had made a good impression on him. On the other hand, some kids made fun of me because I had answered those trivia questions. I believe that the upper-class children knew the answers, but were either defiant, too scared to raise their hands, or didn't want to be put on the spot.

In fourth grade, I got caught playing hooky with a few friends on Chinese New Year's Day. Mr. Komiyama punished us by whipping our backs. But my punishment was much lighter than the other boys'. I believed he treated me leniently because of my knowledge of history.

• • •

On March 27, 1945, I graduated from the sixth grade. After that, I became a farmer to help on my family's farm because my family couldn't afford to send me to middle school. Korean middle schools constituted the seventh through eleventh grades.

CHAPTER 3

Farming Days

May 1945 - October 1946

A 150-RI JOURNEY IN ONE DAY*

It was early May of 1945, about a week after my fourteenth birthday. Our mailman delivered a bundle of old daily issues of the *Mainichi Shimbun,* the Japanese Military Governor's propaganda newspaper. My father handed it to me to read while he and the mailman chatted under a mulberry tree in front of my house. They were such close friends that they called each other 'brother.' Since the post office was located within the county office complex in Suan-up city, the mailman had access to many county officials, including the county police chief. Consequently, he heard a lot of reliable information about the world which he shared with us.

My father asked the mailman how much longer the *Ilbon-nomdel* (the Japanese) could fight the formidable Americans.

"*Hyung-nim,* based on what I have heard, they can't last long because America is many times richer, bigger, and far more advanced in technology than the *Ilbon-nomdel*. Perhaps another year? According to rumors, upon learning that the American troops have landed on the Okinawa Islands, the brutal Japanese County Police Chief cried, 'We will lose the war unless we get a divine intervention, like the *Kamikaze* (divine wind) that had swept away Kublai Khan's invasion fleet.' Recently, the County Draft Affairs Office has been issuing draft notices like a mad dog. The Japs seem to be desperate."

---

* Note: 150 ris are equivalent to 37 miles. 10 ris are 2.5 miles.

"One year is too long," my father lamented. "Tae-hyok, don't tell anyone what we are saying. Do you understand, Son?"

"Yes, I do, *Abeoji*. When the *Ilbon-nomdel* surrenders, what will happen to us?" I asked innocently.

The two gentlemen answered in one excited voice, "Korea will be liberated from the brutal *Ilbon-nomdel* oppression and be independent. They will be kicked out of our land! We will be free!"

I didn't quite understand what liberation and independence meant, but I became excited, too. The paper headlined that the brave Japanese Imperial forces had crushed the evil American forces landing on Okinawa, resulting in negligible losses for the sacred Japanese defense forces. I told my father that the paper claimed that the Japanese defenders had crushed the Americans.

The mailman said, "The paper is lying. Son, don't believe what it says!" Then he and my father continued their conversation. The postman said that he enjoyed his job and meeting various people, but he hated hand-delivering draft notices to draftees. Upon receiving the notices, invariably the young men would sigh, either looking up at the sky or lowering their heads. Their families fell silent, and their wives and mothers would start to sob. Their fathers would say, "For whom does my son have to die? Damn *Ilbon-nomdel!*"

For a while, neither my father nor his friend spoke. I thought about Tae-wook, who was nineteen years old. I feared that he might receive a notice, too. I didn't want him to be killed for the *Ilbon-nomdel*. I also remembered that one year earlier, Tae-jun, who was too old to be a soldier, had been conscripted. He had had to leave his wife and three young children to work at a steel refinery for about half a year. It was a very difficult time for both his family and my parents. I saw his wife and my mother cry when he was taken away.

Finally, the mailman broke the silence and said, "I must deliver a heartbreaking notice to Kim Jae-soo today. I know that his older brother had been called up for a two-year term almost a year ago and put to work at a cement factory in Madong. He had to leave his wife, two young children and elderly parents behind. He will not come home for another year. Now, the evil *Ilbon-nomdel* are taking his younger brother for the army. I cannot wait to see the day when the Japs kneel in front of American soldiers, begging for their mercy!" he sighed. Then he rose and said to my father, "*Hyung-nim,* take care. Tae-hyok, obey your father's teaching," and moved his feet heavily to Jae-soo's residence across the river, less than half a mile from my house.

. . .

Later that afternoon, my father said, "Granduncle-by-the-creek told me that Jae-soo has only five days before leaving for the army." In Korean culture, calling an elderly man by his name was considered taboo and an insult. Town folks would give him a respectable nickname, usually associated with the place where he lived. Granduncle-by-the-creek was the nickname given to Jae-soo's father, the oldest man in our village. My father continued, "The uncle asked me if I would allow you to do an errand for him. He wants you to fetch his older son, Jae-hyun, home from Madong so that the two brothers can see each other before the younger Jae-soo leaves. It will be a 150-ri journey to Madong, a full day's travel on foot. Will you do it?"

Since a few weeks earlier I had traveled 120-ri in one day to visit my oldest sister, I said without hesitation, "Yes, I will." After dinner, I went to Jae-soo's father, who was in his mid-sixties, to convey my intention and receive directions.

After thanking me, the old man told me that there were two routes to Madong. "One is via train; the other is a short-cut on foot. If you take the train route, first you must walk sixty ris to Sinmak Train Station, then take a train to Madong. People say that these days passenger train schedules are unreliable because of the war, which means you might get stranded in a strange town." He paused a few moments, then continued, "I thought of your trip to see your sister, which is almost the same distance as the shortcut. It is better to take that route. Come to my house early tomorrow morning for breakfast before setting off." Then he gave me directions to Madong and advised me to memorize them. He was illiterate. I asked him if he had ever gone that way. He said, "Son, I have never traveled beyond Suan-up." His answer made me apprehensive, but my adventurous heart urged me to say, "I can do it." I thanked him.

Upon returning home, I jotted down the routes on a scrap of paper and went to bed earlier than usual. The next morning, my mom woke me up before dawn, and I prepared for the journey. As I headed out, she instructed me to ask people for directions along the way lest I should get lost. My dad reminded me to consult my directions frequently.

There was not a single star in the sky. The weather was unseasonably warm and humid for May, an omen of spring rain. *Please, no rain!* I hurried to Jae-soo's home across the river. He and his parents welcomed me into their living quarters, which were lit by a castor oil lamp. As soon as I settled down, Jae-soo's wife brought breakfast. We all sat at a round table to eat millet mixed with rice, adzuki beans, and marinated fresh vegetables. Midway through the breakfast, I noticed that only my bowl had rice; the rest just had millet and beans. In this steep valley, rice was a scarce commodity. Having it on the table was considered special treatment. Since I was on an important mission for them, they had prepared it specially for me. When I was ready to leave, Jae-soo's father put a couple of ten *won* bills in my hand, saying, "Tae-hyok, it is not much, but you could buy lunch on the way if you find a roadside vendor." I wondered how much food it could buy. I knew it was not much, but to this poor family, it was a large amount. I thanked the old man. Jae-soo's wife also gave me a bundle of five steamed wheat flour cakes wrapped in a cotton cloth for lunch. Then Jae-soo's mother brought an umbrella and said, "Take this with you. I am afraid it is going to rain." She saved me from the risky weather. I thanked her. It might have been the last surviving umbrella in town. Since the war had begun, umbrellas with steel ribs and metal handles had long disappeared from the market. My family had owned one, but it had worn out a long time ago. I sold its metal parts to a metal collector.

To support the war effort, the Japanese prohibited manufacturing consumer products which required metals, such as steel, brass, or aluminum. They even confiscated brass kitchenware which had been passed down through generations. Usually, a Japanese policeman accompanied by a couple of hired Korean laborers invaded Korean homes and took those valuable brass items without compensation. People hid their wares underground. My parents, too, dug a deep hole in the floor of our barn and buried our brass, leaving a few less valuable items on the kitchen shelves. The Japanese even sawed away the guard rails of bridges and Buddhist temple entrances. I thought it a miracle that this family had kept this umbrella in good condition for so long and now lent it to me for the journey.

When I set out, the whole family expressed their profound thanks and walked me across the river, saying, "Take care of yourself." I quickened my step, carrying the umbrella and my lunch wrap on my shoulder. I didn't see a soul out in the farm fields until Kombae Village, about three miles west of my hometown. Since the country road split into a Y-fork in the middle of the village, I asked a farmer the way to Yoochon and how far it was. He told me to take the wider road for about twenty ris. I thanked him and continued my journey. The wider road gradually narrowed, leading to a winding trail which wound through a dense pine forest. This brought back the memory of having met a Siberian tiger at the top of Dong-kogae Pass six years earlier. A chill ran down my back. Thankfully, the pine grove quickly ended, and the trail began to descend and joined a main road leading southwest. There were no signs, but based on my knowledge of geography, I was sure it was the highway connecting Suan and Sohung counties.

I consulted the directions to find the way from the main road to Hungsoowon, but the old man didn't mention the highway. I looked around for a local farmer to get help, finding none. There wasn't even a single farm field in that narrow valley. Feeling somewhat uneasy, I walked over a mile and met a man in his fifties smoking his pipe by the roadside. His cow grazed the spring grass. After greeting him, I politely asked the way to Hungsoowon.

Pointing his long pipe in the direction of a rock-strewn, swiftly flowing creek a short distance away, he said, "Young man, it's a long way, about fifty ris. Take the trail along the upstream for about fifteen ris, then turn left. Continue ten more ris on the rising trail to the peak of that mountain. From the top, you will see the Kyŏngŭi Railroad on the other side of the mountain range. The trail crosses the railroad, and soon it ends at a highway. Take the northbound highway for ten to fifteen more ris, and you will enter the town. The trail is rugged, but you will not lose it."

After thanking him, I continued my journey. As the farmer had told me, it was narrow and rocky. But the bubbling creek was crystal clean, enticing me to drink its cool water. After three- or four-hours' travel, I was sweating and tired. I unloaded my umbrella and lunch bundle onto a rock, lay on my stomach by the creek edge, submerged my face, and guzzled the water. After quenching my thirst and wiping my face with my sleeve, I sat on a big smooth rock to rest.

Because the sky was cloudy, and I had no watch, there was no way I could tell the time. But I assumed that it was around mid-morning and that so far, I had covered about a quarter of the journey. After putting my umbrella and lunch wrap back onto my shoulder, I resumed my travel on the rock-strewn trail. Shortly the trail left the creek and began to ascend along the rugged hills toward a gray, soaring mountain range in the distance. But I didn't have to climb those mountains. The trail gradually disappeared into dry, brown-yellowish tall grass under which new succulent spring shoots sprouted. Strangely, the rising hills were vegetated with tall grass, sparsely mottled with old pine trees here and there, almost like an African savanna. There wasn't even one small farm field in the hills; perhaps it was too rocky to farm. Nowhere did I see another farmer, domestic livestock, or even a firewood collector. The stillness and the leaden sky gave me a spooky feeling. Just as the farmer had told me, the trail turned left toward a saddle in the range, with high mountains on my right. It seemed as if no one had traveled on it for a long time. The path wound up between two abandoned graves under overgrown grass; they looked almost ancient. Korean graves were round mounds covered with grass turf, about four-to-five feet high and ten feet in diameter at their bases. Usually, beautiful granite gravestones and rectangular tables were set in front of the mounds. But those two graves had none.

I had heard stories about evil foxes that dug into young girls' graves, fed on their corpses, and turned into gorgeous young women. They seduced men, especially young ones, into their dens to prey on them. Those weird legends and the two ancient tombs made my hair stand on end. I took my umbrella from my shoulder and held it firmly, with the metal tip forward, as if ready to ward off an enemy. Dripping sweat drenched my shirt. I quickened my pace to pass by the tombs, but another one loomed a short distance ahead of me. My anxiety rose to its pinnacle. I couldn't stand the tension. I screamed, "You, fox-shifter, come out. I will kill you!" Then, suddenly a real fox sprang out of the tomb and ran across the trail right in front of me! As it disappeared into the tall grass, I jumped high, and then charged after the damned creature. But it had vanished. My knees were knocking.

Anxious to get out of the area, I walked as fast as I could toward the crest of the trail, hoping no more ancient tombs lay ahead. After a couple more miles of hiking, I reached the top of the trail and saw railroad tracks on the far side of a plain down the foothills, like a pair of thin black ribbons parallel to each other. Beyond the railroad, a highway ran parallel to them, and the sun peeked briefly through a breaking cloud.

My body wanted rest, but my heart urged me to continue my journey. I started the winding descent. After a few hairpin bends, the trail disappeared under a canopy of thick arrowroot vines. Arrowroots are deciduous, perennial plants with multiple vines and round leaves as large as a pumpkin. The thick, pliable vines stretch along the ground or climb trees, then tumble down, creating thick canopies. Farmers collect them during late summer to tie sheaves of corn or millet stalks, or firewood in the harvest season. The roots are sweet enough to dig up and chew for their juice. The leaves contain easily digestible, rich starch which herbivorous animals love to eat. During the summer, Tae-wook and I used to go to the nearby hills and collect young leaves to feed our family cow.

The sight of the dense vines brought my fear back because my granduncle had been attacked by a tiger while he and his two cousins were gathering arrowroot vines. Fortunately, the cousins saved him from the vicious animal by beating it away, but the beast left deep, lifelong scars on his chest. Before entering the vine burrow, I held my umbrella firmly, ready to charge, and shouted to frighten away any animals. I walked cautiously into the tunnel, keeping an eye on all sides, singing and shouting as loudly as I could, but my throat kept choking. Midway under the thick vine roof, a rock fell from the slope on my right. Instinctively, I halted and turned in the direction of it, searching intently for any movement but finding nothing. I surveyed the area for a few more moments before resuming. I finally crawled out of the dim tunnel to an open hillside. My intense curiosity made me look up in the direction of the fallen rock, where I saw a man and a woman thinning young millet shoots in a rock-strewn field. I realized they were the cause of the rock that had scared me.

Suddenly my feet lost their strength. I lay down on the newly grown grass by the trail, closing my eyes, wondering how far I had come and how much farther remained to the cement factory. The sun peered momentarily through clouds, indicating it was nearing noon. Assuming that there were eight hours until sunset, I got up and began to descend the steep trail. Farther down the hill, a gulley cut the trail. I climbed down to the bottom where a bubbling stream flowed from the high mountain. It was a welcome enticement for a traveler who had trekked so long. I scooped a few handfuls of the clean, cool water. How delicious it was! As I approached the bottom of the hill, the trail became less rocky. I finally crossed the railroad tracks, and shortly got on the northbound highway as the farmer had instructed. Unlike today's paved multilane highways, this one was a dirt road with no white line in the middle and hardly any traffic. Both the highway and tracks were built on raised dikes, a few feet above the ubiquitous rice paddies. The endless fields amazed me. The black, straight tracks faded into the horizon where the cloudy sky and the rice fields met.

A dozen farmers irrigated or plowed their paddies to plant new rice plants. These people made me feel safe. My fears of fox-shifters and tigers faded. I walked briskly to reach my destination before sunset. However, I couldn't help thinking that since the war had begun, the Japanese had stolen many crops which my family had worked hard to raise to support their war effort. The Japanese would exploit these farmers as they had done to my family. "Damn the Japs!" I mumbled.

After a few hours' journey, the highway led into Hungsoowon, a cluster of one hundred or more houses and a railroad station. I asked a man how far it was to Madong. He said it was about fifteen miles to the north. A few minutes into the town, I came upon a small crowd surrounding two men in their early forties shouting at each other. Since they were yelling in Chinese, I didn't understand what they were arguing about. Suddenly the smaller man swung his fist across the big guy's face, and he fended off the assault. But the little one charged again. This time, the big man caught the opponent by the neck and choked him. Suddenly, a woman sprang out of the crowd and lunged violently at the big man with a shriek. The man crumbled on the ground with a moan, beating the woman on the head with one hand while trying to free himself with the other. Then the crowd came to separate the warring parties. This scene shocked me because I had never seen grownups fighting in my small valley. I was curious about the cause of their fight, but I had to carry on.

The highway and the railroad ran parallel to each other. When I had covered some distance, a lugubrious whistle drew my attention. *That must be a train!* I had seen pictures of trains in my schoolbooks before. My heart pounded in anticipation of seeing a real train for the first time. As the whistling drew closer, I heard strange, powerful mechanical sounds like something beating a heavy metal object. Then a black monstrous iron horse appeared galloping north and trailing a long tail like a dragon; thick smoke spewed from it into the air. The train sped away with clanging noises and was seen no more, but the smoke contrail hung in the moisture-laden air for a long time. I sighed and continued my journey. An unwelcome shower began to fall, hastening my pace. Walking under an open umbrella was quite cumbersome.

When I proceeded five more miles and approached a railroad crossing, another train, southbound, roared fast toward the crossing with a long ear-splitting whistle. I quickly turned and ran a good distance from the track because I had heard that if you were close to a train, the swirling wind it generated would suck you underneath it. I turned back and watched the awesome train roaring through the crossing; the ground rumbled under my feet like an earthquake. Despite being scared, I counted the box cars, but it moved so fast that I could only count nine. What a magnificent black horse it was!

After the train was gone, I crossed the tracks and moved on. The highway veered off the railroad, slightly northeastward, to a somewhat higher elevation. The land rose and fell, creating an endless undulation of landscape. Several small farm villages clustered along the highway. Healthy, young corn and kaoliang shoots on the rich farm fields had already grown to almost a foot, promising a good harvest. They would grow as tall as seven to eight feet by summer. Back in my hometown, scrawny corn shoots in rock-strewn fields had barely reached one third of the height of those here. Despite the falling rain, some farmers worked on their land. I wished my parents lived here, so they would have good land and could afford to send me to a middle school.

The May shower continued. My rice straw shoes which my father had woven absorbed the rainwater and became stiffer, hurting my feet. I took them off and walked barefoot. The Japanese authorities mobilized citizens twice a year, in the spring and fall, and had them dig riverbed gravel which they transported and spread over the highway to make the surface hard. Since stepping on gravel hurt my feet badly, I trod on the roadside grass. The rain stopped, and the clouds started breaking from the west. Soon the sun began to shine, indicating mid-afternoon, and a sweet, westerly zephyr dried my shoes enough so that I could put them back on.

After many more hours' journey over the pastoral landscape and through two more towns like Hungsoowon, I finally reached an outskirt of Madong and saw a soaring concrete chimney in the distance. I wondered how they had built such a tall smokestack. Just before sunset, I arrived at the gate of the big factory complex and introduced myself to one of the two Korean guards. I said I had come to visit Mr. Kim Jae-hyun.

He looked at me quizzically from head to toe and said, "Boy, you look tired. Where did you come from?"

"Suan-gun, sir."

"Do you mean that mountainous county?"

"Yes, sir."

He consulted with his partner and said, "You wait here. I will get him." The other guard told me to sit on a bench against the guardhouse wall. Jae-hyun then reappeared with the guard. The latter said to Jae-hyun, "This is your young guest."

Upon seeing me, Jae-hyun stood speechless for a moment, then exclaimed, "Tae-hyok, what a surprise! Glad to see you, but what brought you here?" He squeezed my shoulders affectionately.

"Your father sent me, sir. Your brother received his draft notice yesterday and has only five days before leaving for the army. He wants to see you before his departure. I came here to fetch you."

Instantaneously, a heavy mood replaced his happy spirit. Without a word, he walked to the window and silently looked outside for a few minutes. Then he mumbled, "Damn, they are taking my little brother, too." He returned to me and said, "Sorry, Tae-hyok. Did you see my children and my wife before you left? How are they doing?"

"Yes, I did. They are all well. I had breakfast with them, your brother, and your parents at your parents' place this morning."

"Thank you for the information. How did you come, via train?"

"No, I walked. Your father gave me directions for a shortcut."

"What? You walked?"

"He told me that it would be about a 150-ri journey. I left your parents' house before sunrise."

The two guards also exclaimed, "Oh my God, 150 ris on foot in one day! Boy, you must be tired."

Jae-hyun asked why I hadn't taken the train. I told him that his father had said that because of the war, the train schedule was unreliable. So, I chose to walk. He chuckled, "That is foolish." He briefly conversed with the guards and took me to his barracks. About thirty of his barracks mates were there. He introduced me to them, "This is Kim Tae-hyok from my hometown. He walked 150 ris today to fetch me."

They, too, exclaimed, "150 ris!" just like the guard had done. They were in their thirties and had also been drafted for forced labor at the cement plant. They asked Jae-hyun if some urgent event had happened in his family. He told them about his brother, and they expressed their sincere empathy. Someone boldly spat out, "Damn Japs!"

The next morning, Jae-hyun woke me up and told me that the director of labor wanted to see me. He and his group leader took me to the big boss, a short, arrogant-looking Japanese man in a green shirt, who sat behind an expensive desk. We greeted him, "*Ohayo gozaimasu!*" ('Good morning, sir' in Japanese) bowing our heads, and stood at attention. He neither returned our greetings nor looked up at us. He asked if I had a letter of proof from my district police chief about Jae-hyun's brother's draft notice and requested the group leader to interpret for me.

Judging from his rude tone, I suspected that he was looking for an excuse to deny Jae-hyun's application for a pass. Instead of waiting for the group leader's translation, I blurted out in Japanese, "Sir, Jae-hyun's brother received his draft notice two days ago to fight for the Emperor, and he has only three days before leaving for the army." Upon hearing the word 'Emperor,' the director jumped from his chair and stood at attention just as we had done during the morning assemblies at my elementary school. My Japanese principal had taught us that the Emperor was the incarnation of their highest god *(Amaterasu Ōmikami)*. Therefore, we had to stand up when the word 'Emperor' was mentioned. I continued, "Once he goes to the frontline, he might never come home alive. That's why he wants to see his only sibling before his departure." I repeated emphatically, "He is leaving his wife and parents to fight for the Emperor!" I took a deep breath and resumed, "We are simple farmers, and we did not know that such a letter was required. If he hadn't received his notice, I certainly wouldn't have made a 150-ri journey in one day, sir."

When I finished, he said in a surprisingly gentle voice, "Young man, you are a good boy, a brave boy. 150 ris on foot in one day!" and sat down on his chair. He took a pen and wrote a pass on his official stationery. He blew on the paper to dry the ink, stamped it with his personal seal and said, "Jae-hyun, I'm giving you a five-day pass. Make sure you return on time. Take care of this young boy. Go!"

Jae-hyun received his pass and bowed to him, saying, "*Arigatou gozaimashita!*" ('Thank you, sir!') a few times. The group leader and I, too, bowed and expressed, "*Arigatou gozaimashita!*" and left his office. We all took deep breaths. The leader said, "You spoke well. Without the emperor thing, the director might have denied Jae-hyun's application. Where in the world did you get that idea?"

I explained to him that when the director had asked for a letter of proof, my Japanese grammar school principal's ritual had crossed my mind. He recited it at daily morning assembly, "To die for the Emperor is the most honorable thing we can do," until he was recalled to the army. We were required to stand at attention whenever the word *Tennōheika* was mentioned. Without thinking, I used his ritual. I didn't know where my boldness had come from.

When we returned to the barracks, Jae-hyun's roommates stopped eating lunch and asked him if he had been granted a pass. Upon hearing his yes, they congratulated him. Since his pass would start the next day, Jae-hyun and his friends returned to work, leaving me alone in the barracks. He told me that we would take a train to Sinmak that evening.

The anticipation of riding a train stirred excitement in my heart, and I wondered what it would look like. *Was it like a king's room? Were there chairs? If so, was I going to be allowed to sit on them, or should I stand or sit cross-legged on the floor? Were there wooden benches like those in my grammar school rooms?* All those silly thoughts made me nervous. So, I went out to take a walk around the plant. Despite almost twelve hours' sleep, I was still so tired that I returned to the barracks and napped until Jae-hyun woke me up for supper.

We ate our supper hurriedly on the floor along with the rest. When we finished, the group leader said, "Jae-hyun, each of us chipped in a few *won* to defray your travel expenses. It is not much but take it." He put a thick bundle of paper money in Jae-hyun's hand, and they urged him to prepare for the trip. I was impressed by their camaraderie.

Jae-hyun was overwhelmed by their sincere friendship, generosity, and thoughtfulness. He wiped tears from his eyes and said in a quivering voice, "My dear friends, thank you so much! I hope your younger brothers will not have to go through what my brother does."

Jae-hyun put a few things in his small backpack, and we left for Madong Railroad Station. Despite a couple of blisters on my feet, I walked quickly, expecting to ride a train soon. The station was dark except for six glowing bulbs dangling from the high ceiling. A few dozen passengers were buzzing like honeybees. Jae-hyun held me tightly by the hand and elbowed through the crowd to a big window. While he was talking with the man behind the window through an opening, I watched those incandescent glass balls and wondered how they emanated such a brilliant light without burning wicks. I had seen similar light bulbs at the barracks the previous evening, but the exhaustion from the long journey kept me from appreciating the mysterious light.

Jae-hyun showed me a couple of double-finger-sized cardboard strips on which Madong-to-Sinmak was printed and said, "These are two train tickets to Sinmak for our 10 p.m. train. We shall arrive there by midnight and stay overnight at an inn. Then we will walk the rest of the way home, about a twelve-mile journey, tomorrow." He noticed me watching those glass balls and asked, "Tae-hyok, is this the first time you've seen electric light bulbs?" while leading me to gigantic glass doors.

"Yes, sir," I said while looking through the doors. "By the way, where is our train?"

"Our train originates from Pyongyang and will be pulling in shortly. Soon a railroad clerk will open the gate, and we will go through it to the platform where we will board the train. Do you see those people forming a line? They are going to take the same train as us. Let's get in line," he said, and led me.

Shortly, a clerk in a black uniform manned the gate and let the passengers go through. As our turn approached, my heart started to pound in anticipation. Jae-hyun surrendered our tickets to the clerk who punched them without a word. Then we went through the gate to a long platform. A few light posts along the middle of the platform illuminated our surroundings. A couple of soldiers approached the platform. Someone cautiously said in Korean, "*Kempeis* are coming." As they pompously paraded through the crowd, talking presumptuously and laughing loudly, everyone became quiet. Each *kempei* had a saber dangled from his side and a white band around his arm on which 憲兵 (*Kempei*) was printed. They talked and laughed as if there was no one around. Their presence dampened my excitement. Jae-hyun whispered to me, "*Juh gae saeki dul joshim hara!* (Watch out for those SOBs!)" A man next to us murmured to himself, "Why don't they shut up?"

Kempeis were Japanese military police who wielded almost unlimited power over Koreans by arresting, torturing, imprisoning, or even murdering them. They were brutal, feared entities.

A train pulled in along the platform with loud whistles and hissing noises. I looked at it with excitement. A huge fireball on its head cast brilliant light straight into my eyes and on the tracks, so I couldn't see the train until it had halted completely. All I could see was a chain of black passenger cars, dimly lit, with many glass windows. The engine stayed in front of the long train, far away from me, hissing incessantly. It was too dark to get even a glimpse of the engine.

After the arriving passengers disembarked, Jae-hyun led me into the passenger car in front of us. A few clusters of light bulbs fixed on the curved brownish ceiling threw faint light on the aisle between two columns of seats with high backs. Most of the passengers were sleeping, oblivious to our footsteps. Jae-hyun and I occupied one of the empty seats. It was covered in blue satin-like fabric, which I had never seen before; its cushion was thick, and it was more comfortable than my own cotton futon at home. Once settled in, I surveyed the cabin. It was longer and wider than my house, with numerous windows and numerous chairs on each side. Its high ceiling was arched.

What a fancy, marvelous car it was. I looked through the window next to me and saw a man in a black uniform, waving a lantern in a circle. I thought he was strange. Then a sudden jolt and whistling frightened me so much that I jumped off my seat and searched for something to hold onto.

Jae-hyun held me by the arm and said with a smile, "Take it easy. The train has just started to move. Sit down!" I sat down slowly, fearing another jolt. The train gradually picked up speed and soon drove into the night. Noticing my nervousness, Jae-hyun put his arm over my shoulders and said, "You must be very tired. Go to sleep!" His brotherly gesture calmed me, and I fell asleep until he woke me up and said, "We have arrived in Sinmak. Let's get off the train."

I looked out and saw many passengers disembark and climb up a long ramp. The area was brightly lit. There were countless trains parked, numerous locomotives slowly moving forward or backward, hissing and whistling. This place was busy and lively even at night. Jae-hyun explained that the Sinmak station was one of the most important depots along the Kyŏngŭi line which connected Gyeongseong (today's Seoul) and Sinuiju, the last big city on the Korean Peninsula-Manchuria border. We settled in an inn nearby and quickly fell asleep.

The next morning, we set out for a twelve-mile journey on foot. Good rest allowed us to travel briskly, and we arrived at Jae-hyun's parents' place by mid-afternoon. The whole family welcomed him enthusiastically, holding him by the arms or shoulders. His wife buried her face in his chest and sobbed; his young daughter dangled on his trousers, calling, "*Appa, Appa!*" (Daddy, Daddy!); and his mother held his hand against her cheek and cried. His father squeezed Jae-hyun's shoulder and exclaimed, "Welcome home, son. We missed you so much," and wiped his tears. Jae-soo did the same, "*Hyung*, thank you for coming home!"

Overwhelmed by their happy but temporary reunion, I was unable to hold back my tears. After watching them for a while, I silently slipped away and returned home content with having brought Jae-hyun home.

END OF WORLD WAR II AND
THE CREATION OF THE 38TH PARALLEL

World War II took place from September 1, 1939 to September 2, 1945. Germany surrendered on May 8, 1945, which is now celebrated as Victory in Europe Day (V–E Day). But the war in the Pacific continued. The United States, Great Britain, and China asked Japan to surrender in the Potsdam Declaration on July 26, 1945. However, Japan refused. Their hope was that the Soviet Union could help with their peace terms, but the Soviets were planning to attack Japanese forces in Manchuria and Korea.

On August 6, the United States detonated an atomic bomb over Hiroshima, Japan. On August 8, the Soviet Union declared war on Japan. On August 9, the United States detonated a second atomic bomb over Nagasaki. Roughly 110,000 to 210,000 people were killed by those two atomic bombs.[2]

Japan surrendered on August 14, 1945 and publicly announced this to their people over the radio on August 15, effectively ending World War II. Victory over Japan Day (V–J Day) also known as Victory in the Pacific Day (V–P Day) is celebrated on the 15th of August. Japan signed the "Instrument of Surrender" on September 2 aboard the USS Missouri.

But the United States and the Soviet Union had to decide what to do with Korea, which was a Japanese colony. The U.S. wanted to act fast for fear that the USSR was going to take over a good portion of Korea. Colonel Dean Rusk (who later became a U.S. Secretary of State) and Colonel Charles Bonesteel, both from the U.S. Army, looked at a National Geographic map, and wanting Seoul and Inchon to be in the American sector, decided upon the 38th Parallel.*[3] The territory north of the line would be temporarily controlled by the Soviet Union, while the territory south of it would be under U.S. control. This line was chosen in about thirty minutes. No one from Korea was consulted about it.[4] Korea and its people were divided into two states by this 38th Parallel border line.

---

* It is important to note that the 38th Parallel is a different line from the Korean Demilitarized Zone (DMZ) that exists today. Some cities and towns that were in South Korea (Kaesŏng, for instance) after the creation of the 38th Parallel are now in North Korea after the creation of the DMZ and vice versa.

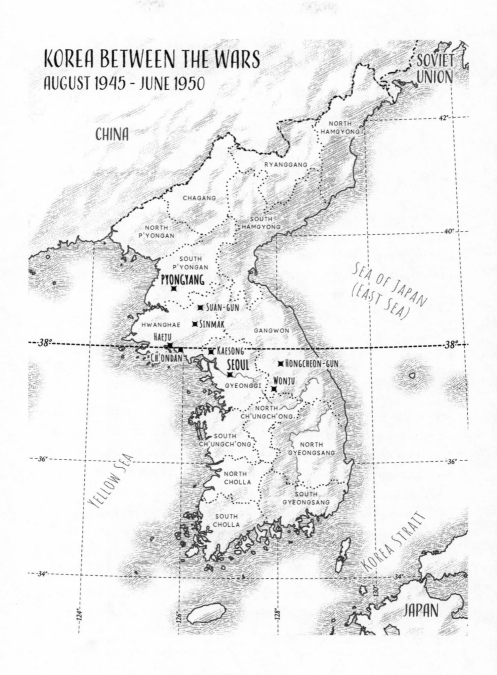

KOREA BETWEEN THE WARS
AUGUST 1945 - JUNE 1950

SOVIET
UNION

CHINA

NORTH
HAMGYONG

RYANGGANG

CHAGANG

SOUTH
HAMGYONG

NORTH
P'YONGAN

SEA OF JAPAN
(EAST SEA)

SOUTH
P'YONGAN

PYONGYANG

SUAN-GUN

HWANGHAE ■ **SINMAK**

HAEJU

GANGWON

--38°

38°--

CH'ONDAN ■ **KAESONG**

SEOUL

■ HONGCHEON-GUN

GYEONGGI

■ **WONJU**

NORTH
CH'UNGCH'ONG

SOUTH
CH'UNGCH'ONG

NORTH
GYEONGSANG

--36°

36°--

NORTH
CHOLLA

SOUTH
GYEONGSANG

YELLOW SEA

SOUTH
CHOLLA

--34°

34°--

KOREA STRAIT

JAPAN

124°   126°   128°   130°

JAPAN'S SURRENDER AND
THE END OF WORLD WAR II

Word started spreading around our village that Japan had surrendered to the United States and its Allies.

"It's true!" the mailman told my father one day. My father came back inside our home and said, "We're finally free from the tyranny of Japan!" My parents and family were so happy.

We said "Congratulations!" to each other on the streets. Soon the brutal Japanese authorities left, and we truly experienced freedom. Oh, it was so nice! Young men from the valley who had been forced to serve the Japanese army or go to a hard labor camp for two years returned one month later. Jae-hyun, coming back from Madong, and Jae-soo, returning home from the army in late September, were among them. Their wives and their families all welcomed them, and they embraced and hugged. Our whole village celebrated. We gathered at each other's homes to congratulate each other.

But freedom only lasted a couple of months before North Korea brought in communism.

A WOLF PROVIDED A FEAST

It was late April 1946, a couple of days before my fifteenth birthday. I was on my way home from a Korean language class. After World War II had ended the Japanese occupation of Korea, my neighboring communities founded a one-room school to teach their children how to read and write in Korean. The school was over a mile from my house.

The road ran between rock-strewn farm fields and skirted heavily wooded knolls. Green, succulent new grass covered the idyllic hills and fields, enticing animals to graze. But the low clouds and misty drizzle created an eerie atmosphere. When I reached a knoll that jutted out from Nam-san Mountain, I saw an animal eating something on the road ahead. As I came closer, the animal looked up at me and then quickly returned to its food. I became somewhat apprehensive. I approached slowly for a better view. It was a wolf!

Fear crept into my heart. I pondered whether to avoid the wolf by taking a detour or to challenge it. I didn't want to turn back and take a much longer route, especially in the rain. I thought I could handle that lone wolf. I picked up a few fist-sized rocks and put them in my pockets, keeping one in each hand. I came to within fifty feet of the wolf, hurled the rocks at it, and screamed. Incredibly, the first rock hit the animal's side.

Shocked, it jumped in the air with a sharp cry and ran some distance from its prey. Then, it turned around and snarled at me, showing its fearsome fangs. My hair stood on end, but I continued yelling and throwing rocks. Another landed hard on its head. Moaning loudly, the wolf ran toward the knoll. I chased it to the edge, throwing more rocks even after it had disappeared into the woods.

After making sure that it was gone, I returned to the spot where the wolf had been eating and found a fawn lying on the roadside grass. Its belly was open, but it blinked and twitched its legs weakly. It tried to lift its head, only to fall back, then convulsed a few times and closed its eyes. It did not move. I felt sad over the death of the young animal.

I palpated its neck. It was still warm. I wondered what to do with the dead deer. Then I thought about how we had been deprived of meat for so long because the Japanese authorities had prohibited Korean farmers from slaughtering their own livestock. If I took it home with me, my mom could prepare a feast for our family. Home was close to one mile away. I decided to try.

I lifted it up by its legs, but it was too heavy to carry. I tore apart the belly opening that the wolf had already made. It reeked of blood, and I winced. I plunged my hands into the animal's abdominal cavity to tear out the intestinal organs, but they were too slippery for my grasp. So, I crushed quartz and made a knife, using it to remove the guts and draining as much blood as I could to make it lighter. I discarded the intestines in the bushes nearby and wiped my slimy hands on the grass. Then I put the deer on my shoulder and set off for home, frequently looking back to see if the wolf was following. Thankfully, it didn't!

When I arrived home, I hollered to my father, who was doing chores in his barn. "*Abeoji*, I have a deer with me!"

He was surprised, and asked, "How did you get it?" while unloading it from my shoulder. "It's still warm!"

I proudly told him my adventure.

Shocked, he said, "You what? You attacked the wolves and took their prey? You shouldn't fool around with a pack of wolves."

"*Abeoji*, there was only one wolf there."

He looked relieved and said, "You are lucky. Usually, wolves hunt in a pack." He paused a few moments and then sternly advised me not to mess with wolves again. Then he called my mother, retelling the story that I had taken a deer from a wolf.

"*Eomeoni* (mother), we are going to have delicious venison stew!"

My mother reacted like my father and warned, "Don't approach a large wild animal, especially a female with her babies. It can be very aggressive." Then she brought warm water in a basin and washed my sticky hands and neck. She also asked me to change my bloody jacket for a clean one. "Your birthday is just two days away. We shall celebrate it today with deer stew."

My brother, his wife, and their children joined us. I retold the saga, and they were astounded. My brother said bluntly, "You were brave, but stupid to take a wolf's prey. It could have harmed you."

My father and Tae-jun hung the deer carcass by the neck on the cow-stake in the front yard, skinned it, and chopped it into small pieces. Won-sik, Yun-ok, Sook-ja, and I watched and talked with excitement.

My mother and my sister-in-law cooked a delicious meal. How generous of that wolf to provide such a marvelous feast for my fifteenth birthday! It happened to be my best birthday celebration with my parents.

RICE PADDY WEEDING AND
THE DECISION TO LEAVE HOME

Since graduating from my elementary school, I had been telling myself almost ritualistically, "I must study mathematics, science, history, and anything I can to help me grow. But how? There is nothing in this poverty-stricken little valley but a score of farmhouses."

One summer day in 1946, I was bent over, weeding my parents' rice paddies along with my father, Tae-jun and Tae-wook. My bare legs were submerged in muck. The sun scorched my back and neck. The stench of compost and hot steam rose from the slime and suffocated me. Underneath the slime, my legs started itching. The itching turned to pain. I lifted my leg, and there were several muddy, creepy leeches sucking on me. I screamed, "Leeches!" I slapped hard to get rid of them. No luck. I hurried out of the muck to the levee, and shouted, "*Abeoji,* help me take these damn leeches off my legs!" My brothers laughed at my hysterical scream.

"They are not going to kill you," my father reassured me. He slowly came out of the rice paddy and sat down next to me, filled his brass pipe with tobacco, and lit it. After puffing a few times, he said, "Let me see your legs." He burned the bloodsuckers with the head of his pipe. They dropped off my legs one after another, wiggled a couple of times, and died. He said, "Now, they are gone."

What a relief! "*Abeoji,* thank you."

After putting out his pipe, he returned to the muck. Apprehensive about the leeches, I followed him reluctantly and resumed weeding. As soon as I bent over, something stung my neck. I slapped it, and a big horsefly was stuck in my muddy palm. I cursed, "Damn fly!" and crushed it; blood stained my dirty palm. I rinsed my hand in the muck and carried on.

My back was in excruciating pain from being bent over for so long. I straightened my body to alleviate the ache. To my horror, I saw a snake stick its head up and swim across the slimy water toward me. I yelled, "Snake!" I instinctively whacked it with my hoe. The detestable creature flew high and splashed in the muddy water, a few yards away. It whipped its tail, but it could not move. My brother rushed toward it and battered it to death with his hoe. He scooped it up and discarded it in a nearby bush. I was still shaking.

I murmured, "There must be a better way to make a living. I should get out of this godforsaken valley and go to Seoul to get an education and build a better life. I have nothing here. Even this small leech-infested field is my oldest brother's inheritance, not mine. I am only fifteen. I don't want to waste my life here." At that moment, I made up my mind to leave this valley.

How could I make it to Seoul? It was a completely strange city, far away in South Korea. Besides, I had no money for travel expenses. Since my parents were subsistence farmers, they were not able to provide me with cash. There was no job in the valley for me to earn money; no one could afford a hired hand.

If I was to make it to Seoul and get a job, I had to save as much money as I could to pay for my education. In Korea, tuition was required for all levels of school. Since I knew I would not make much money from delivering newspapers or doing odd jobs, I would have to live frugally to save cash. I decided to train myself for an austere lifestyle to achieve my education when I went to Seoul.

REQUESTING PERMISSION TO GO TO SEOUL

My hard-working parents would produce about four *pils** of homespun silk every year—the main cash source for our family. I knew that silk was the only way to provide my travel expenses. So, one early autumn day of 1946, I sat down with my parents and said, "*Abeoji* and *Eomeoni*, I want to go to Seoul for more education and better opportunities. Here in this valley, there is no way I can grow."

My father kept silent for a few moments and then responded, "Son, you know that we are very poor farmers. We cannot afford to support you. Besides, Seoul is far away from home, and South Korea is becoming another country."

"*Abeoji*, I do not ask you to support me for my education. But if you provide me with the money to go to Seoul, I will somehow manage to support myself."

My mother, who was quietly listening to our conversation, interrupted, "Tae-hyok, you are only a fifteen-year-old farm boy. You do not know the way to Seoul or how to cross the border. How will you support yourself in that big city?"

"*Eomeoni*, I have heard that in Seoul, young boys like me deliver newspapers or do odd jobs to support themselves. I am sure I can do it. I think newspaper delivery is much easier than weeding rice paddies and millet fields."

I continued my talk. "*Abeoji*, if you give me one *pil* of the silk from *Eomeoni* and *Keun Ahjumeoni* (older sister-in-law)'s supply I will sell it at the next flea market for cash. I think that will be enough for my expenses. You know Mr. Kim Myung-sup of An-kol, the limping man? He has already made a few business trips to Seoul. He bought some merchandise there, brought it back

---

* One pil is about 40 feet long and 1.5 feet wide.

to North Korea, and sold it for a profit. He is planning to make another trip to Seoul in the middle of October. *Abeoji* and *Eomeoni*, would you please allow me just one *pil* of silk? He will depart for Seoul in just four weeks."

He responded, "Your mother and I will discuss this. We will let you know later."

LETTER TO FATHER AND MOTHER

I waited for their response for one long week but heard nothing. Finally, I could not wait any longer. One evening, I wrote a short letter to my parents in pen and ink on an old newspaper, under a flickering kerosene lamp.

> *Dear Abeoji and Eomeoni,*
>
> *I have been waiting for your decision about my request for one pil of silk. Since I have not heard from you, I am writing this letter because I do not have the courage to ask you directly about your decision. Forgive me.*
>
> *I visited Mr. Kim Myung-sup at his house the other day to find out when he would be leaving for Seoul and to ask if I could accompany him. He told me that he would be leaving on October 11. This trip would be his last one until next spring. He also agreed to take me with him. Abeoji, there are only three weeks left before his departure. Unless you give me the silk very soon, I may not have enough time to sell it at the next market, which means that I may not make a trip to Seoul.*
>
> *Abeoji and Eomeoni, would you please give me just one pil? I beg you to let me go to Seoul so that I may attend a middle school.*
>
> *Respectfully,*
> *Your son*

I folded the letter and put it in my front shirt pocket. Right after breakfast the next morning, just before he left for the fields, I handed it to my father, feeling nervous. Then, I hurriedly set off to the millet field with my older brother and his wife. I spent the day cutting millet tussles, but my mind was on the letter and my father. As the sun was retiring behind the western ridges, Tae-jun said, "It's time to quit for the day. Let's load the millet bags on the cow and go home." I was tired but apprehensive about going home and facing my parents.

PERMISSION GRANTED

I usually sat next to my father at the dinner table, but on this evening, I sat at a distance from him. I pretended to eat, but I could not because I did not know what my parents' decision might be. In the middle of dinner, my father casually said, "Tae-hyok, your mom and I agreed to allow you to sell one *pil* of silk. But you should get at least 1,600 *won* (perhaps, less than fifteen 1946 U.S. dollars) for it."

Upon hearing this, I felt my future opening wide. I was ecstatic and thankful. My mood instantly transformed from uncertainty and nervousness to excitement. "*Abeoji* and *Eomeoni*, thank you very much. I shall take it to the next flea market," I said without a breath.

As soon as I finished my profound thanks, Tae-jun said, "If you don't get 1,600 *won*, don't sell it. Bring it home." He spoiled my excitement. I did not respond. One *pil* was one quarter of our family's income. Since he was the first son of my parents, he had a big say in important family decisions. I thought he wanted to let me know that I was taking a big chunk of the year's income. But I was determined to sell the silk for even less than 1,600 *won* because it would be the only way to cover my travel expenses.

TAKING THE SILK TO THE FLEA MARKET

On the eve of the next flea market day, my mother took out one *pil* of silk from her chest and gave it to me with caring remarks. "Tae-hyok, I have saved two *pils* of silk for your future wedding. I will give you one *pil* and I will keep the other for your wedding, whenever it may come." I hugged her and said impulsively, "*Eomeoni, go mahp sumnida*" (Mother, thank you very much), and accepted it with both hands. In those days, Koreans would rarely hug. I gingerly put the precious silk in the corner of a four-foot by four-foot cotton wrapping cloth, rolled the latter all the way to the opposite corner, tied it in the middle with a string and put the wrap in a corner of the outer bed-room, which I shared with my father.

The next morning, I put my precious merchandise on my back diagonally, one end of the wrapping cloth over my right shoulder and the opposite end under my left armpit, and tied them tightly on my chest. I went to the flea market in Jang-keo Ri with a few men from the village; it was open every five days, and about seven miles over the northwest mountain range. As soon as I arrived at the flea market around mid-morning, I unwrapped the silk and displayed it on the wrapping cloth. It was a beautiful October day. The market was crowded and noisy with vendors, buyers, sellers, and bargain hunt-ers. Quite a few prospective buyers offered me ridiculously low prices for the silk. Apparently, they tried to take advantage of my being a farm boy with no sales experience. A few of them came back with slightly higher offers, which I did not accept.

As the afternoon waned, I became somewhat nervous that my parents might take the silk back if I did not sell it. Also, I had a long trip back home. I did not want to travel all alone over Dong-kogae Pass in the dark. Then one merchant came by and checked the quality of the silk. He asked, "Young man, how many *pils?*"

"One *pil*, sir."

"The quality of the silk is not that great, but alright. How much do you want?"

"1,600 *won*. It's good silk. My mother spun it herself."

"I will offer you 1,300 *won*."

The offer was the highest so far, but well below the price of 1,600 that my father had suggested.

"I want 1,600 *won*, sir."

"That is too much. I will give you 1,350 *won*."

"1,600 *won*, no less, sir."

"I will offer you 1,400 *won*, no more."

"No, I want 1,600 *won*, sir."

"That is too much," he said, and disappeared into the crowd.

When he was gone, I regretted that I had not accepted his final offer. I feared that I might not be able to sell the silk, which meant I might not go to

Seoul at all. While I was feeling sorry for myself, the merchant came back and made a new offer. "Young man, I will pay you 1,450 *won*, absolutely no more."

I said, "Okay, it's a deal, sir," with a deep sense of relief. I knew my parents would forgive me for selling the silk for less than what they suggested, but I was very apprehensive about Tae-jun's reaction. I had to devise something to satisfy him.

SELLING AN HEIRLOOM

As soon as I came home, I collected as much recyclable junk as possible, such as worn rubber shoes, broken brassware, empty kerosene tin cans, scrap iron, and used hemp papers, including a family heirloom. I took them to Mr. Lee, a peddler and scrap metal collector, and sold them for 100 *won* to make up the shortage of 150 *won*. He would transport the junk on a cow back to Jang-keo Ri flea market and sell it to a recycling vendor for a profit.

The family heirloom was a poem written in Chinese characters in brush pen and soot ink on a thick scroll of hemp parchment, two feet by four feet. One day, a few years earlier, I had found the old scroll in the attic. It had collected dust and the ink had been smeared by rainwater. I took it down and asked my father, "*Abeoji,* what is this scroll?"

He unrolled it and said, with somewhat mixed emotion, "More than a hundred years ago, your great-great-great-great grandfather wrote this poem for a *kwa-koe* test (an examination to qualify for the imperial civil service). He was a well-known scholar in Chinese literature in his province, Hwanghae-do Province. When he was in his mid-thirties, the family invested much of its resources to send him to Seoul on foot, more than one hundred miles, to take the test. After passing the test, he wrote a letter to his family, informing them that he had successfully passed the test and expected to be appointed county commissioner for one of the counties in Hwanghae-do Province. He would come home and wait for an official appointment notice."

He paused for a while, sighed, and said, "But alas, on the way home, he drowned while crossing a frozen river. His body was not recovered until the river thawed the next spring. When they recovered the body about four miles down the river, they found this scroll in his backpack. It was wrapped in a thick waterproof waxed paper. His father sold a large part of his land to educate his son, your great-great-…great grandfather. According to your grandfather, my father, the Kim family was relatively well to do. But after the unexpected death of your great-great-…great grandfather, this family became poor." Then he rolled the scroll and tossed it back into the attic almost carelessly. I felt somewhat guilty for selling the heirloom for just 50 *won*, but nobody in the family, including my father, seemed to treat it as a family treasure.

During dinnertime, my father asked me in a tender voice, "Tae-hyok, did you sell the silk?"

I said, "Yes, *Abeoji*." Then Tae-jun abruptly asked me, "How much did you get?"

I responded, "1,600 *won*, *Hyung-nim* (an honorary expression for older brothers)," with hesitation.

He said, "Show me what you got!" I reluctantly took out 1,550 *won* from my pocket and handed them over to him.

He counted them and said, "It's only 1,550 *won*. You did not get 1,600 *won*, did you?"

I said, "Yes, I did, but I spent 50 *won* for my lunch," avoiding his eyes.

He said, "Lunch should cost only 20 *won*, at most."

He did not ask any more questions and handed the money back. Obviously, he knew I had not told the truth. I handed the money to my mother to keep until I left for Seoul.

PART TWO

A Divided Korea

1946 - 1948

CHAPTER 4

Crossing the Border

October 1946

DEPARTURE TO SEOUL

October 11, 1946. The excitement of departing for Seoul woke me up early. I went out to the nearby community well, drew a bucket, and washed my face in the cold water. It was a chilly morning. I returned to my bedroom and put on a clean traditional Korean jacket and trousers.

My mother had made the clothes from her own homespun cotton fabric dyed in dull black and sewn unevenly. Some people might have said that they were poorly sewn, but to me, they were beautiful and precious because she had made them for me for this trip with her poor eyesight and calloused hands under a flickering kerosene lamp after a full day's field work. She had extremely poor eyesight due to cataracts. She had thoughtfully added secret pockets inside the trousers, one on each leg. I secured my money in the pockets lest it should get lost or stolen. I put an extra pair of cotton-padded winter clothes and a pair of insulated cotton socks in my backpack, all used clothes which my mother had washed and mended a few days earlier. My rustling noises woke my father, and I expressed my respect to him with a "Good morning, *Abeoji!*"

My mother called from the inner building, "Tae-hyok, breakfast is ready."

My father and I crossed the courtyard to the main room that was used as the dining room as well as the bedroom for my oldest brother's family of five. When I entered the room, the entire family was gathered for breakfast.

My mother and sisters-in-law (Tae-wook had since married) had prepared a simple breakfast of boiled millet mixed with red beans and Chinese cabbage soup in soy sauce. They set two brass bowls of the millet and two bowls of soup on two small rectangular burgundy tables with low legs. My father and I took one table facing each other, and my two brothers took the other. All the women and children sat in a circle with their bowls on the bare floor. We all sat cross-legged on the reed mats on the heated clay floor. When my father, as head of the household, started his breakfast, we all began ours, too, chatting with each other.

My mother said, "Help yourself! You have a long journey ahead," while giving me more millet from her bowl. "Make sure that you stay overnight at your sister's home, about fifty ris from here. It would be a good day's journey with Mr. Myung-sup. I am sure she will be happy to have you overnight."

"Yes, *Eomeoni*."

My father said, "I think it's going to take four to five days before you cross the *Sampal Sun*." The *Sampal Sun* was the 38th Parallel which divided the two Koreas. "Be careful to avoid the communist internal security soldiers. If you encounter any, and they ask you where you are heading, tell them you are visiting one of your cousins in Pyongsan who is an internal security officer."

"Yes, *Abeoji,* but what is his name?"

"His name is Kim Tae-sam."

Then Yun-ok, my twelve-year-old niece, said, "*Samchon* (an honorary expression for the youngest uncle), are you going to Seoul alone? Do you know the way?"

"No, not alone. I am going to accompany Mr. Myung-sup in An-kol. He knows the way to Seoul very well. He has been there a few times already."

She continued, "Are you going to cross the *Sampal Sun* by day or night? Aren't you scared?"

Even though I felt uneasy, I answered, "I think by night. I am not scared. Mr. Myung-sup knows several safe spots to cross the border."

Then Tae-jun said in a very kind voice, "Tae-hyok, Seoul is a big city. You have nobody to help or guide you except Mr. Tae-yun, one of our distant cousins. You met him once a long time ago while he was visiting his parents. You were then around six years old. I got his Seoul address from his younger brother, Tae-un, my best friend. Here is a letter from him to his brother in Seoul. When you arrive safely, the first thing you should do is visit Mr. Tae-yun, introduce yourself, and give him this letter. Then he will surely recognize you. My friend told me that his brother is an engineer and founded a construction company. So, he might give you some kind of work." He paused for a few moments. Then he continued, "If life is hard, just come home!"

A few days ago, I thought he was so mean, but today he was so kind.

This unexpected information from my brother made me very happy. I said with excitement, "*Hyung-nim*, thank you!" I took the letter and put it in the bottom of my backpack so it would not get lost.

After clearing the tables, my mother said, "Your brothers, sisters-in-law, and I are going out to a bean field on the top of Nam-san to harvest red beans before the sun rises too high. Drop by the field on your way to Mr. Myung-sup so that we can see you off."

"Yes, *Eomeoni*. I will."

They left before me. A few minutes later, my mother hurried back and said, "I forgot to give you the leftover steamed sweet potatoes for lunch on the road." She brought three sweet potatoes wrapped in newspapers and put them in my backpack.

"*Eomeoni*, thank you!" I held her rough hands tightly between mine and silently said, "I love you, *Eomeoni*."

GOODBYE

My mother, two brothers, and their wives had already left for the field. Won-sik, my nine-year-old nephew, had left for school with his friends. Yun-ok stayed home to babysit Sook-ja, her six-year-old sister, during the busy harvest season. My father was clearing the dirt courtyard for the sheaves of harvested bean plants that could be spread there to dry as soon as the family cow had transported them in from the fields. Then everyone except the children threshed the beans. This whole process was done in one day to minimize loss, because ripened dry bean shells easily cracked open by themselves, causing loss of grains.

I double-checked that I had everything in my backpack. I discovered that the algebra book that Mr. Jae-sik had given me a few months earlier was missing. I had treasured that book even though I understood only a small part of it. I fetched it from my father's room and put it in my backpack. Mr. Jae-sik had attended middle school in Tokyo at the beginning of the Pacific War, but later returned home because American warplanes bombed the city every day.

I slung my backpack over my shoulder, left the room, and met my father in the courtyard. I said, "*Abeoji*, I am leaving now. Take good care of yourself, sir," and I bowed to express my farewell and respect.

But instead of responding to my goodbye, my father took my backpack gently from my shoulder and held it so that I might secure it on my back by putting my arms through each strap. Then he said, "Take care of yourself, too. Make sure to avoid internal security officers. Don't forget your cousin's name, Kim Tae-sam. Write to us when you get to Seoul. I do not know whether the letter will be delivered. Write anyway. If life is hard in Seoul, come home."

I said, "Yes, *Abeoji*, I will. Goodbye, *Abeoji*." Then I turned to my niece, "Goodbye, Yun-ok. Take good care of your sister."

She said, "*Samchon*, goodbye."

As I walked away, I turned to see my house one more time, and saw my father and Yun-ok standing by the gate waving their hands. My eyes became warm with tears, and I waved back.

When I reached the bean fields on the north slope of Nam-san, I saw my mother, Tae-wook, and my sisters-in-law cutting soybean plants with short-handled sickles, leaving the cut plants on the ground. I also saw Tae-jun collecting the cut plants and tying them tightly into sheaves with arrowroot vines. As I approached them, Tae-wook saw me and shouted, "Tae-hyok is coming." Everybody stopped harvesting and began to walk toward me. We met in the middle of the field. I saw my mother tie her *jeogori* (traditional woman's jacket) with a piece of rough rice-straw twine because its ties had torn. My heart was heavy for her because I knew that after the backbreaking harvest, she would sit by a kerosene lamp with her poor vision to mend the ties. I used to thread the needle to help her. I wondered who would do it for her from now on. I said, "Goodbye, *Eomeoni*; goodbye, *Hyung-nim*; goodbye, *Ahjumeoni*. Everybody, take care of yourself!"

My mother held my hands and squeezed them as if she wouldn't let them go. She said, "Tae-hyok, take good care of yourself!" while reluctantly releasing my hands. Then she turned around and brusquely walked away. I believe she didn't want me to see her crying.

Tae-jun said, "Make sure you keep Mr. Tae-yun's address and the letter for him," affectionately adjusting my backpack. "Take care of yourself. Come home if it is hard for you in Seoul."

My two sisters-in-law waited for their turns and said, "*Doryun-nim* (young brother-in-law), have a good journey. Take care of yourself."

I bid my final farewell and started walking away. But Tae-wook put his hand on my shoulder and silently followed me to the edge of the field. He stopped and said, "Tae-hyok, I am glad that you are going to Seoul to study. I wish you success. On the other hand, I feel sad to see you, my little brother, off to a strange big city beyond the *Sampal Sun*. South and North Koreas appear to be becoming two different countries because of the damned Russians. I wish our family were rich enough to send you money so that you would not have to work to support yourself." Then he hugged me and said, "Goodbye, my little brother. Good luck." He walked away from me while wiping his eyes. I wiped my tears, too.

CATCHING UP WITH MR. MYUNG-SUP

I arrived at Mr. Myung-sup's place in An-kol in the early morning to join him for the journey. The house was a two-room building with rice straw thatching and an attached kitchen without a door. A pine branch fence surrounded the house. At the gate, I called loudly, "Mr. Myung-sup, good morning, sir. This is Tae-hyok."

Two girls, around twelve and ten years old, came out of the building. The older girl said, "My father left a short while ago. He asked me to tell you that he had to leave early to cover as much distance as possible. I think you can catch up with him easily." Both girls were poorly dressed, and their hair was unkempt.

I thanked her and set off to catch up with him. The pass was rugged and wooded, and followed a small, fast-running creek. I started calling loudly, "Mr. Myung-sup, Mr. Myung-sup, where are you? This is Tae-hyok." Instantly,

I heard his response, not too far ahead. "Tae-hyok, I am here. Come up here." I caught up with him a few hundred yards up the pass. He was sitting on a rock with his cane on his lap. What a great relief! I said, "Good morning, Mr. Myung-sup. How are you, sir?"

"I am fine. I am sorry that I did not wait for you. You know I walk slowly because of my bad leg. You might get bored today. Anyway, let's get going." He was struggling to get up, so I helped him. He thanked me, and we started to move.

Mr. Myung-sup had lost his wife many years ago, and polio had attacked him not long after her death, paralyzing his right hand and leg. He was well versed in Chinese literature and a well-known astrologer in the region. He used to operate a *hak-dang*, a private academy, and taught youngsters Chinese literature, but the Japanese had forced him to close the *hak-dang*. Despite these hardships, I could see his strong will to live and his desire to bring up his two daughters by any means. His determination made him travel to Seoul with his impaired leg. He would buy merchandise such as medicine, cosmetics, and fancy clothes there, bring them to North Korea, and sell them for a profit.

In the beginning, we talked while climbing the steep pass. But soon we fell silent because the effort left him breathless. He was sweating even though it was a chilly morning. As I watched him limping, I could not help admiring his courage.

FROM THE TOP OF MOUNT SARIBONG

Panting, Mr. Myung-sup said, "This is a very steep pass, isn't it? Tae-hyok, let's take a few minutes of rest," then sat on a boulder.

"Yes, it is. I have never taken this road before. This pass appears to be higher than the Dong-kogae Pass," sitting on a ledge opposite him so that I could have a better view of the magnificent southern slope of Saribong Mountain. Rich gold, ruby, and jade leaves shone under the brilliant autumn sun. The mountainside was gently sinking into the sea of white morning fog. What a splendid show of nature! I looked at the farthest end of the whitish southern sky and dreamed of the big, glittering city of Seoul.

After a few minutes of rest, we started to descend. I let Mr. Myung-sup walk in front of me because I was afraid that otherwise I might walk too fast for him. I noticed that he had more difficulty balancing himself in descending than ascending. At the bottom, we continued our slow and silent journey on a rock-strewn narrow country road that ran along the valley for about four miles.

I broke the silence and said, "Mr. Myung-sup, I would like to stay tonight with my sister. When she visited us a couple of months ago, she asked me to visit her before I left for Seoul. I promised her that I would. Of course, you are invited to stay with us tonight. My sister and her husband have a lot of land and a roomy house with a large *sarangbang*."

He gladly accepted my invitation and said that we were about nine miles from there, a good place to stop for the day. I then climbed down the steep bank of a creek and drank a few handfuls of water to quench my thirst. I picked up big oak leaves, made a cup by folding them, and filled it with water. I climbed up the bank holding the cup carefully and brought the water to Mr. Myung-sup.

"Thank you very much, Tae-hyok," he said, taking the flimsy cup from me. "It is very kind of you. I really need it." He emptied it without breathing and said, "The water tastes good and fresh. Once again, thanks. Now, let's get going."

A RIVER WITHOUT A BRIDGE

The road ended abruptly at a riverbank and continued from the other side of the river. There was no bridge, only steppingstones to cross. The river was about thirty to forty feet wide and knee-deep. The previous spring, when I had visited my sister, there had been a flimsy log bridge, but apparently a flood had washed it away during the summer. I thought Mr. Myung-sup couldn't manage the steppingstones. So, I suggested that I would piggyback him across the river. He accepted my suggestion gladly, as he had been wondering how he would cross the river.

I took off my shoes, socks, and backpack, rolled my trousers up to my thighs, and asked him to do the same to make himself lighter. I piggybacked him across the cold river. Fortunately, he was lighter than I had expected.

After dropping him off on the opposite riverbank, I came back for the backpacks and shoes. My feet were freezing. After wiping them off, I put on my socks and shoes, and slung the two backpacks over my shoulders. This time, I used the steppingstones, then joined him, helping him put his backpack on.

MY SISTER AND A BIG DINNER

We resumed our journey for a few more hours and arrived at my sister's place in the late afternoon. While opening the big, heavy wooden gate, I called excitedly, "*Nuna* (sister), this is Tae-hyok, your little brother."

My sister ran out of the inner court with her one-year-old son, and her husband followed them. "Welcome, Tae-hyok. Good to see you again," she said, and affectionately patted me on the head as if I were a small boy. "How are *Eomeoni* and *Abeoji* doing? Everybody is doing okay back home?"

Since the culture regarded the husband as superior to the wife, I bowed to my brother-in-law first and then to my sister even though she was in front of him, and said, "They are fine. How are you all doing?" Then I introduced Mr. Myung-sup to them and told them that he was taking me to Seoul with him and that he had been there a few times already. I also asked them if he could stay with us. They said he was welcome.

My brother-in-law and Mr. Myung-sup exchanged greetings. Then my brother-in-law led us to the guest room. As soon as I settled in, I joined my sister in her family room. I said, "*Nuna*, how is your baby doing? He is cute." I extended my arms to hold him, but he cried.

My sister said, "Seoul is a big city and far away, beyond the 38th Parallel. I admire your courage and intention to go to Seoul to study, but how are you going to support yourself? You are only a fifteen-year-old boy, my little brother. I always knew you were brave. But I never thought you were this brave to leave home for Seoul. I don't think any boy in this town even thinks of leaving home alone for a big city, not to mention Seoul. Did *Eomeoni* cry when seeing you off?"

"No, she did not, but she held my hands tightly for a long time as if she would not let me go. When she finally released me, she said, 'Tae-hyok, take care of yourself,' and turned her back." I paused, reflecting on saying my goodbyes. "Excuse me, *Nuna*. I had better join Mr. Myung-sup; it is not nice to leave him alone," and I left the family room.

I went into the guest room and found Mr. Myung-sup snoring. I was tired, too, so I lay down using my backpack as a pillow and fell asleep.

My sister knocked on the door and said, "Tae-hyok, dinner is ready." She brought a portable dinner table to the guest room for us. Dinner consisted of cooked rice and chicken soup with kimchi. Apparently, she had slaughtered a chicken and prepared this soup while we were taking our nap. The aroma tickled my nostrils, and my stomach gurgled.

"Wow, it looks great, a feast, *Nuna*. Thank you very much," I exclaimed, while receiving the dinner table.

"You are welcome, my little brother. Help yourself. Mr. Myung-sup, you, too."

We ate the dinner with gusto, emptying the bowls and licking the dishes in no time. Mr. Myung-sup asked me to convey his thanks to my sister for her hospitality. I returned the table with the empty dishes and bowls to my sister's kitchen and thanked her for the delicious dinner. I spent some time with her and her family. I cooed over my nephew and attempted to hold him, but he shied away. After a few more tries, we became friends, playing together. Then he fell sound asleep in my arms. I handed him over to my sister, bid them goodnight and returned to the guestroom for the night.

In the morning, I said to my sister, "*Nuna*, thank you for everything. I shall be leaving."

She said, "You are," scooping up her baby and walking me to the gate. My brother-in-law joined us. Mr. Myung-sup met us at the gate and expressed his sincere thanks to my sister and her husband for their hospitality, then set out ahead to allow us a private moment. After his departure, my brother-in-law advised me that it was very important to keep myself in good health, especially away from home. My sister agreed with him, and said, "You take good care of yourself."

"I will, *Nuna*. I had better get going." I bowed to my brother-in-law first and then my sister, bidding them goodbye. He saw me off outside the gate, but she continued to walk with me to the edge of the town. My baby nephew slept peacefully in her arms.

"If it is hard, don't hesitate to come home." Then she pulled my hand, put a roll of bills in it, and said, "Tae-hyok, it is not much; buy lunches when you are hungry. Take care of yourself," and held my hands tightly.

I bowed my head and said, "Thank you, *Nuna*. Goodbye," pulling my hands from hers. I kissed my baby nephew on the head and said, "Goodbye, Prince." Suddenly I felt lonely because from now on, I would be without any family. I turned around, saw her wiping her eyes and waved my hand to say my last goodbye.

MOUNTAIN RANGE

It was mid-morning on the sixth day since I had bid goodbye to my parents. Mr. Myung-sup said, "Tonight, we are crossing the 38th Parallel. Do you see that big mountain range in front of us? We will climb to the top." The mountains which ran north to south loomed very high and were bluish in the mid-morning sun. I wondered how in the world Mr. Myung-sup could climb those big mountains with his handicapped leg.

I asked, "Is that range the border?"

"No, the border lies beyond the mountains, in a southern valley. We shall travel about five miles southward along the ridge to a trapper's lodge on the southern slope. We shall buy our supper there, sleep until midnight, and then cross the border in darkness. I guess nobody except trappers or medicinal herb collectors have traveled those mountains until the Russians closed the 38th Parallel."

"Don't the Russian border guards know about the trapper's lodge? Don't they suspect that people use it as a waiting station to cross?"

"Maybe they don't because the lodge is in the middle of the mountain, over two miles from the nearest border guard post. There is no good road to access the house. Even if they know about it, those damned Russians wouldn't dare to come up the mountains in the middle of the night. Are you scared?"

Even though a sense of uneasiness was growing in my heart, I responded, "A little bit. But it's okay because you know the secret road to cross the border."

We arrived at the foothill of the mountain range and saw a few farmhouses with millet thatch roofs, scattered along a rapidly running creek. The mountain was heavily wooded with tall oak trees. Underneath the trees, there was a track of trodden grasses, like an animal track.

Mr. Myung-sup said, "Do you see that track? We will follow it up the mountain." Before we entered the woods, he surveyed the surrounding area to make sure no suspicious person was around. He said, "Once in a while, according to the local people, a Russian running dog passes by here." A Russian running dog was a derogatory expression for a Korean communist who did what Russians wanted him to do. We started climbing slowly. The track was steep and sometimes slippery from rotten leaves. Mr. Myung-sup managed quite well considering his impaired leg. He was doing better than me.

ULCER AND PRAYER

A small insect bit my left shin, causing itchiness and then pain every time I took a step. We reached the peak by noon, and found the ridge sparsely vegetated, providing us with a broad view in all directions under the spotless blue sky. Mr. Myung-sup said, "Let's take a short rest. It's a scenic view." He sat down on a boulder.

Without responding, I also sat down on a moss-covered rock at a distance from him. I rolled up the left leg of my bulky Korean trousers, inspected my shin, and found that the untreated insect bite was swollen and had ruptured, exposing a bloody lesion, bigger than a quarter. Apparently, the bulky trousers had rubbed off the dead skin. Then I understood why every step caused the nagging pain. Unless I did something about it, I might have serious trouble crossing the border. I had neither salve nor gauze with me.

Out of sheer desperation, I closed my eyes and silently offered a simple but earnest prayer to the great spirit of this mountain. "Mighty spirit of the great mountain, I have traveled a long distance from home to go to Seoul. Tonight, I must cross the 38th Parallel. Please cure this ulcer so that I may cross the border safely."

I kept my eyes closed and waited for some time to hear the voice of the mighty spirit but got no response. So, I repeated the prayer a couple more times. No voice came, only the rustling of the autumn leaves. I concluded that either there was no mighty spirit residing in this mountain or he did not want to cure my ulcer.

IMPROVISED DRESSING

I searched for anything that could be used to dress my ulcer. I found a vine with palm-sized green, pliable, waxen leaves under a nearby bush. I plucked a few leaves, carefully layered them to cover the ulcer, and tied them with my trouser leg ties. This improvised dressing proved soothing and kept the trouser leg from hurting the ulcer. I wondered whether the great spirit of the mountain might have led me to the leaves. Then I collected fresh arrowroot vines, cutting them to be about thirty inches long with a sharp rock, and tied my bulky trouser legs with them. Even though my shin still hurt, I felt confident that I could make the border crossing. I was glad that Mr. Myung-sup did not notice my ulcer, or he might have advised me to return home or stay behind at the trapper's lodge for a couple of days until it had improved.

I walked around to distract myself from the pain. The magnificent panorama displayed brilliant foliage under the dazzling October sun. It was so bright that it looked ready to jump out of the trees. My gaze drifted southward and found a black railroad bridge over a big, silvery river in the distance. The sun was reflecting on the water. For some reason, I hoped that the bridge was in the South.

RIDGE TREKKING

"Oh, my goodness, I had a good nap. Let's get moving, Tae-hyok," Mr. Myung-sup said, and we resumed our journey along the ridge. For the first few hundred steps, I frequently checked my dressing, which held firm. Even the pain seemed to be lessening. A couple of hours later, we met a group of travelers resting, some lying on their backs using their backpacks as pillows, and others leaning against them. As we approached them, they greeted us with "Hi, come sit with us."

We responded, "Hello there, nice to meet you," and sat down by a friendly looking man in his early forties. I presumed that these people were headed for Seoul. Among them was a lady in her mid-thirties and a teenage boy. The rest of them were men in their twenties to forties. I noticed that every one of them wore western style fatigues and leather boots. I thought those clothes and boots fit for rugged trekking. My partner and I were the only ones wearing traditional black Korean clothes and rubber shoes like country hicks. The rubber shoes resembled canoes with flattened tips. The sole was so thin that it was painful if I stepped on a rock.

The friendly man said that they were from Pyongyang, heading for Seoul. He asked us if we, too, came from Pyongyang. Mr. Myung-sup answered that we were from Suan, southeast of Pyongyang, and headed for Seoul.

The amiable gentleman asked, "Why didn't you take a Pyongyang-Reohyun train to Reohyun and cross the border from there, instead of using this mountain trail? It would be much easier as Reohyun is only a mile from the border. The internal security police wouldn't suspect you and your son. Thirteen or fourteen years old?" I presumed he asked this because of Mr. Myung-sup's crippled leg.

"Perhaps you are right, but better safe than sorry. Russians are tightening the border every day," Mr. Myung-sup responded.

"I guess you are right," said the man.

Mr. Myung-sup said, "By the way, this boy is a son of my neighbor, and he is going to study in Seoul. Are all of you traders?" Traders would buy merchandise in Seoul and bring it into North Korea for profit.

He apologized to Mr. Myung-sup for his mistake. Then, he continued, "Yes, most of us are, except for the lady and the young man. The lady is to join her husband in Seoul. He escaped Pyongyang and went to Seoul a few months earlier because the internal security bureau found out that he was organizing an anti-communist movement and issued an arrest warrant. He is an intellectual and well respected in the Pyongyang area. The young man is returning home to Seoul after visiting his grandparents in Pyongyang." He paused for a few moments. Then he said, "All, get up. Let's move."

We moved southward in a file along the ridge. I saw a black railroad track running north to south along the left foothills of this mountain range, like a pair of thin black ribbons. This railroad used to connect Pyongyang and Seoul before Russian troops closed the border a year ago. I felt sad that my country had been divided into two. My people shared the same progenitors, spoke the same language, and enjoyed the same culture for more than four thousand years.

TRAPPER'S LODGE, WAITING STATION

It was October 17, 1946. A dozen of us arrived at a humble shack, a lodge for border-crossing travelers. It was a low two-room building with an attached kitchen, built on a small, flat patch of land on a heavily wooded slope. I wondered how this flat patch had been formed on such a steep slope.

According to Mr. Myung-sup, before the peninsula was divided into North and South, the owner of the lodge had collected medicinal herbs during the spring, summer, and autumn and trapped animals for fur during the winter. Immediately after occupying North Korea, the Russian Occupation Authorities had closed the border. Many North Korean refugees and cross-border merchants flowed to the South using this mountain trail to avoid arrests by the North Korean border guards. The trapper started providing those travelers with room and board; eventually it grew into a year-round lodging business because it was profitable.

As we walked into the small courtyard, a middle-aged man in traditional white clothes welcomed us and conversed with some of our group while he led us into the room next to the kitchen. The innkeeper said that we had company from Pyongyang. After taking off our shoes outside the door, we entered the room (about seven by fourteen feet) and greeted the others. That night, all fifteen of us travelers would eat supper in this small room and sleep four hours until midnight. Then we would set off to cross the border. As soon as we settled in, the innkeeper collected 50 *won* from each of us for room and board. I thought it was too expensive!

Sitting cross-legged caused a flash of pain on my shin. I excused myself, went outside, and opened the improvised dressing, exposing pus. The ulcer had not spread, but the leaves had dried, so I needed fresh ones. I looked around the edge of the courtyard and found new leaves that were bigger, fresher, and fatter than the old ones. I plucked a handful and replaced the used ones. I collected some extras, rolled them to keep them from drying, and packed them into my backpack for future use.

After dinner, some of the travelers lay on the floor while others leaned against the walls, stretching their legs, and chatting under a flickering kerosene lamp, mostly about what kinds of merchandise would be profitable in North Korea. Soon, they succumbed to fatigue and fell asleep.

I, too, closed my eyes, but my thoughts kept me awake. *Am I going to make a safe border-crossing tonight? How am I going to find Mr. Tae-yun's home in the largest city in the country? I have never even been to a small city before. Will he have a job for me? If he doesn't, what shall I do? No job, no money to return home. Winter will be arriving soon. Can I solve these problems by worrying about them? No, I can't. Right now, I would be better off sleeping before tonight's travel.* To cheer myself up, I thought about a Korean proverb, "There is a way out of every situation, no matter how bad it may be," and assured myself that everything would be alright, inviting sleep.

Pain and pressure on my leg woke me. I discovered that we were lying crammed together. The man sleeping opposite me had his legs right over mine. He was snoring loudly. I pulled my legs from under his and put them on top. Even though I did not have blankets, I was warm from the body heat, and returned to sleep.

Mr. Myung-sup shook me and said, "Tae-hyok, Tae-hyok, get up. Prepare to leave. We are leaving soon." I put on my flimsy rubber shoes, securing them with the arrowroot vine I had collected so they would not slip off in the dark.

The friendly man who had talked with us earlier said, "Everyone, listen to me. I shall be leading you tonight because I know the way. I have traveled this route more than five times over the last few months. The border is along an east-west pass, a couple of miles from here. The pass itself is a part of the borderline. It will take about three hours to get there."

The leader lit a cigarette and inhaled deeply. Then he continued, "There are two border-guard outposts along the pass: one at the bottom of the eastern foothill, and the other at the western foothill. The two outposts alternately dispatch a team of one North Korean border guard and one Russian soldier. During the day, they patrol a couple of hours apart, but the nightly schedule is irregular, though less frequent. This unpredictable schedule makes it more difficult to cross. Once we have reached the pass, we shall wait a few minutes to make sure no guards are around. If all is clear, we will cross."

After extinguishing his cigarette, he continued, "If any of you come across the patrol first, don't panic. Signal to the person in front of you and behind you. Then hide under the bushes and keep silent until they have passed. But if they find you first, they will shout, 'Halt, stay there!' sometimes with a warning shot. Don't stop unless they are right in front of you. Instead, run into the bushes or straight to the border as fast as you can. They might fire a few more shots at you, but don't worry, just continue to run because it's too dark and wooded for them to see you anyway. Furthermore, they would not dare to fire across the border because it is an act of belligerence. Once you are across, you are safe. South Korean border guards will welcome you if they happen to be patrolling there."

While listening, my heart started to pound. Unconsciously, I clenched my fists so tightly that my palms became painful and sweaty. The stuffy air in the small room heightened my nervousness. Almost everyone smoked, which made the air heavy. Perhaps they were nervous, too.

The leader said, "Don't get lost. If you do, return to the lodge, and try again tomorrow. For the next few hours, no talking, no coughing, until we have crossed the border. Now, let's move!" He led us out into a dimly moonlit night. The cool air was refreshing. I inhaled a lungful to calm myself. My wet hands began to dry. The smokers dropped their cigarette butts on the ground and stepped on them, twisting their feet to put them out.

The leader descended along the slope; we all followed in a single file. Mr. Myung-sup trailed right behind the leader, perhaps because of his handicapped leg. I positioned myself as fourth in line because I wanted to be close to him, but not too close, to give myself enough time to run away from the border guards if they detected us first.

We elbowed through chin-high bushes. They made loud rustling noises in the midnight calm. I feared that the noise might alert the border guards down the valley. After descending some distance, we turned upward on a steep slope.

When we reached the top, several gunshots broke the midnight silence, and a pair of bright headlights flashed in our direction. Frightened, we spontaneously ducked and hid under the bushes. We waited. We could hear people shouting down the valley and a dog barking. A few minutes passed, but it seemed an eternity. Then the headlights turned around and were gone. Quiet prevailed again. Nobody seemed to be looking for us.

The man in front of me whispered, "Let's move." In turn, I relayed the message to the person behind me. We sighed and resumed our journey along the trail leading to the border. After about two hours of silent trekking, we finally reached the pass that ran along the border, east to west. The man in front of me gestured to halt, and I relayed it to the man behind me. One by one we tensely crawled thirty feet from the border and crouched, three to four feet apart.

We all held our breath and intently surveyed the path for some time to make sure no border guards were near. The moon was low in the western sky, and it started getting darker. The leader signaled for us to cross the border one by one. Within a short time, we had all crossed safely and continued quietly a few hundred yards farther into a thick pine grove. Abruptly, the leader stopped and said, "We made it! We are all safe now. Let's take a short rest."

We exclaimed "We made it!" and huddled around the leader to thank him. Leaning against our backpacks and stretching our tired legs, we finally started to talk freely and laugh.

I was excited to have made it safely across the border. I reflected on the past year: dreaming of a seemingly impossible journey to Seoul; begging my parents for one *pil* of homespun silk for my travel expenses; bidding good-bye to my family. Now, Seoul was within one day's journey.

When someone struck a match to light his cigarette, the leader shouted, "Don't smoke, please, lest the cigarette cause a wildfire. No smoking until we arrive at the lodge in the valley." The man who had struck the match apologized.

Relaxed, we resumed our journey, talking and laughing. Soon we fell silent, just walking, too tired to talk. Mr. Myung-sup stumbled on the rocky slope in front of me, but regained his balance and continued his journey.

We reached a gently rising ridge, then saw hundreds of blinking lights in the distance. The leader said, "That is Kaesŏng City.* Those lights are from a U.S. military camp. We are at the top of Mount Songak, and we shall descend to the lodge at the bottom. The downhill trail is steep and rugged, but short. The lodge is less than one hour away."

SOUTH KOREAN BORDER GUARDS

As we climbed down the mountain, roosters crowed in the distance, announcing that dawn was near. In less than an hour, we reached a lonely, dimly lit

---

* Kaesŏng City used to be in South Korea. But since the 1953 Ceasefire Agreement, it became part of North Korea, just north of the DMZ.

South Korean border guard post at the foothill of Mount Songak. Two border guard policemen came out and said, "Welcome to free South Korea!" I couldn't see their faces clearly, but those words sounded so sweet.

"Thank you, sirs." I couldn't help thinking that less than a couple of miles north of this post, the North Koreans and Russians had closed the border. Anyone attempting to cross it could be arrested or shot. Here, the South Korean guards were welcoming us. Two opposite worlds with the same people and same country!

The guards continued, "You must be hungry and tired. There is a lodge a couple hundred yards down the road. It is open all night for travelers. You can buy breakfast there and take a few hours' rest. Have a good trip."

We thanked them and arrived shortly. The lodge looked bigger than the one where we had stayed that evening in the North. Our leader knocked at the gate and called the innkeeper by saying, "*Jooin Young-gam* (Mr. Innkeeper), I am here." Apparently, *Jooin Young-gam* recognized him by his voice, came out with a lantern, and opened the gate for us with a welcome, leading us to a large room. As soon as I settled in a corner, perhaps because the danger was over, I felt so tired and sleepy that I fell sound asleep until Mr. Myung-sup woke me the next morning. Even after a few hours of good sleep, I was still tired, and my body ached.

CHAPTER 5

Journey to Seoul

October 1946

FIRST MORNING IN SOUTH KOREA

It dawned on me that it was the first morning of the first day in the land that I had longed to see. My desire to see it was so powerful that I got up and went outside. I stood by the gate and looked over the fields while breathing in the fresh air. The sun rose high in the eastern sky and shone over the rice fields, which stretched beyond the horizon to the east, south, and west. I had never seen such a vast and rich farmland. A cool, dry northerly autumn breeze came down over Mount Songak and softly shook the drooping rice ears, generating golden ripples across the never-ending fields. I imagined that all the farmers living in this fertile land were wealthy; they probably ate white rice every day. Back at home, my mother would treat us with rice only for special events, such as Chinese New Year's Day, *Chuseok* (Harvest Festival Day), and our birthdays. We subsisted on a poor man's diet of millet, crushed corn porridge, soybean soup, and barley. But the throbbing pain in the ulcer on my leg cut short my sweet reverie.

I sat on a boulder, untied the arrowroot vine to free my trouser legs, rolled them up, and removed the dressing to check the condition of the ulcer. I removed the dry, brittle leaves one by one. The innermost one was stuck to the ulcer. As I removed it, the ulcer hurt. Yellowish pus covered the lesion. The surrounding area was reddish and swollen. I unrolled my trousers to hide it from people, fetched the wild vine leaves that I had collected at the trapper's lodge, and returned outside. I carefully placed the leaves on the lesion and secured them with my trouser leg straps. The new dressing somewhat relieved the throbbing pain. I discarded the arrowroot vines that I had used to tie my trouser legs during the border-crossing trek because I feared they might make me look too much like a mountain boy.

KAESŎNG - GATE CITY OF SEOUL

We set out for Kaesŏng City, about two miles due south, which was the northern gate city of Seoul. Thousands of North Korean refugees and traders would come to Kaesŏng and take trains to Seoul or to other parts of South Korea. It had been the capital city of the ancient Koryŏ Dynasty, which lasted from the tenth through the fourteenth century. The citizens of Kaesŏng were known to be proud and independent. During the thirty-five years of Japanese colonization, no Japanese business established a successful foothold because Kaesŏngites boycotted Japanese stores and businesses.

As the journey progressed, Mr. Myung-sup lagged farther behind because of his leg. I stayed with him because he had been my travel partner from the beginning of this journey, and he was the only person whom I knew well among the group. I wondered how he managed the rugged border crossing in the darkness without any trouble when he had difficulty keeping pace with the rest of the group on a level road. By the time we had covered half the distance to Kaesŏng, we could no longer see the main group.

Approaching the city, I saw a big dome with a tall sharp spire that loomed against a spotless autumn sky. The dome was so imposing, and the spire rose so high that my heart pounded from excitement and uneasiness. I had never seen anything like this. I could not help but ask Mr. Myung-sup what it was. He told me that it was the roof of the Kaesŏng Railroad Station, and that we would take the 2 p.m. train to Seoul there.

Soon, we entered a wide, straight street lined with trees and perfectly paved with rectangular granite cobblestones. Slightly raised walkways, covered with diamond-shaped concrete slabs, rimmed the street on both sides. The street led to a majestic red brick building with many windows and grand doors, capped with a magnificent green dome—the Kaesŏng Railroad Station.

Many shops with glittering windows and doors and restaurants lined the street. The owners advertised their bountiful merchandise in these windows in big, colorful Korean letters or Chinese characters. I asked myself what the merchandise was for and who would buy so much of it. I knew that once in a while my father would take some of his farm products to the Jang-keo Ri flea market during the off-farming season, sell them for cash and buy basic necessities for the family, such as salt, kerosene, sewing needles and thread, laundry soap, rubber shoes, fertilizer or farm tools, and sometimes a few pounds of meat if some cash was left over. In my hometown, we lived with so little. Here in Kaesŏng, everything looked so plentiful. I felt like I was in a wonderland.

As soon as I entered the huge railroad station hall with Mr. Myung-sup, a deep, loud ding echoed through the hall. I was frightened and froze at the doorstep, momentarily searching for the origin of the sound. Before it faded away, many more sounds came from high above the wall, one after another. I looked up and saw a gigantic round clock with two long black hands on a snow-white face. The shorter hand pointed at 11, while the longer one advanced slowly, one notch at a time, ticking heavily. I stared at it in amazement. Mr. Myung-sup hollered, "Tae-hyok, what are you doing there? You need to buy a ticket."

I joined him in the ticket line. There were already twenty to thirty people in front of us. He asked me, "What were you looking at back there?" I answered, "That gigantic clock."

He said, "That is big, isn't it? We must buy tickets before they are sold out. I heard somebody saying that only a few hundred tickets for the 2 p.m. train are available today. One ticket will cost you almost 100 *won*."

I took out a 100 *won* bill from my pocket. Paying this much was painful. A quick calculation told me that I only had about 1,000 *won* left.

After purchasing the tickets, we went outside to the railroad station plaza. Mr. Myung-sup told me to wait there for him while he went to do some research on merchandise. Leaning against the cool brick wall of the station, I watched many people come and go. I did not find even a single man wearing black-dyed, hand-woven, floppy Korean clothes like mine. Suddenly, I felt embarrassed and became conscious of my farm-boy attire.

THE FIRST AMERICANS

While I was feeling inadequate in this modern city, two men slowly drove a green car into the middle of the plaza, honking a few times, and halted. The first American soldiers I had ever seen! The excitement of watching the white soldiers distracted me from my feeling of inadequacy.

I had heard different stories about Americans before, but I had never seen one in person. My village folks said that Americans were so tall that you had to lean your head back to see their faces. They also described Americans with big noses, *kumbal* (golden hair or blond hair), white skin, and hazel or blue eyes set so deep that you could hardly tell whether they really had eyes or not. Americans were as hairy as monkeys, and the richest people in the world.

During World War II, Japanese anti-American propaganda demonized Americans as barbarians. After the war, Russians and Russian-trained North Korean communists vilified Americans as heartless brutes and filthy rich exploiters of the poor. One anti-American cartoon depicted a poor, sick, elderly American woman, lying on the street, asking for someone to take her to a hospital and waving her bony hand with a few dollar bills in it weakly, but nobody cared.

North Korean communists also spread false propaganda that the Russians, not the Americans, had defeated the Japanese and liberated Korea. But only Korean communists believed those flagrant lies. We knew that the Americans had fought the Japanese for four long years and defeated them. The Russians had fought the Japanese for only a few days before Japan's unconditional surrender on August 15, 1945. We saw American B-29s flying over the Korean skies many times, but not a single Russian plane.

Now in Kaesŏng, I could see two real Americans with my own eyes. I wanted to get closer for a better look but watched them from a respectful distance instead. Certainly, their faces looked white even in the distance. I noticed that their matchbox-like car had neither a roof nor windows.

My boyish curiosity could not hold me back for long. I stealthily approached them until I was five to six feet away. Their noses were much higher than those of Koreans, but not as high as I expected. The color of their hair was totally different from Koreans' charcoal black. The driver's hair was somewhat yellowish, and the passenger's was reddish-brown. It dazzled under the autumn sun. Both wore dark glasses. I was disappointed because I could not tell how deep set their eyes were or what color they were. I also could not see how tall they were because they stayed in the car.

The two were dressed in different uniforms. The driver wore a loosely fitted dull green jacket with big pockets and trousers. His hat matched his jacket. But the passenger wore a well-fitted, pressed yellowish-green uniform and rested one of his legs on the dashboard. He wore shiny, brown leather boots, too. His exotic boat-shaped hat did not have a visor. I guessed that he was higher in rank than the driver because he wore a fancier uniform.

But the most amazing thing was that both were chewing without putting anything in their mouths. I watched them for a long time until my travel partner came back and asked what I was looking at.

"These American soldiers, sir. They are chewing without eating anything."

He laughed and said, "They are chewing *chung-kum* (chewing gum)."

"What is *chung-kum?*"

"It is a finger-sized, flat, sugary sweet that melts in your mouth when you chew."

Meanwhile, the two Americans slowly drove away.

DELICIOUS *UDON*

Mr. Myung-sup looked up at the sun and said, "Tae-hyok, I am hungry. We should eat lunch before we catch the train."

"That is a good idea, sir. I am hungry, too," I responded. I thought he had a knack for telling time; after all, he was a well-known astrologist in my hometown. He led me to the far side of the railroad square where four or five makeshift outdoor beaneries stood side by side against a brick wall. As we approached them, the aroma of cooking smelled so good. These were mom-and-pop eateries. The vendors used flattop wheeled carts as their kitchen and tables. They put large white cotton canvases over the carts as roofs. On the front of the carts, they advertised their menu in black soot ink. Each vendor had two or three portable, baked clay ovens (*hibachi*). Some had built makeshift brick ovens. In retrospect, these clay ovens were like upside-down hats with broader, thicker bases than the top of Uncle Sam's hat. Small, rectangular vents had been made in the bottom sides. Their kettles were made of shiny aluminum, and had wide rims, about two inches below the tops, deeper than traditional black cast-iron kettles. They placed the kettles lightly on the top of the ovens, so that they could easily move them around as needed. Charcoal was used as fuel. One oven, which consisted of a round metal barrel and a bigger kettle, stood out. The barrel had a large rectangular opening in the lower end through which firewood was fed instead of charcoal. I later learned that the metal oven was an American military gas drum, cut in half. All these kettles and the oven were new to me.

The vendors hollered to attract potential clients. They served traditional Korean food, such as rice in vegetable soup with kimchi. Mr. Myung-sup said, "I like one vendor who came from North Korea and opened an eatery here. They serve delicious *udon*. Last time I was here, I ate *udon* at their place," and he led me to their eatery. They had a long, crudely built bench for customers in front of the cart. He greeted the vendor and his wife, who appeared to be in their early forties. As we sat on the bench, she asked my partner, "Is he your son?"

"No, he is a son of my friend back in my hometown. He is going to Seoul to study," he responded.

She turned to me and said, "Do you have relatives in Seoul?"

"Yes, ma'am."

"What can I serve you, young man?" she asked with a gentle smile.

"*Udon*, ma'am." I ordered it partly because my partner influenced me, but mostly because having grown up on a poor man's diet, it looked like a rich man's food. Back home, my mother and sister-in-law would grind whole wheat by hand to make *udon* with grainy, brownish flour and served it in simple soy sauce soup. It was thick, rough, and tasted somewhat tart.

The lady scooped a few cups of fine, white flour from a jar, poured it on a kneading board and made a hollow mound. I had never seen such flour before. She poured some water in the hollow mound, mixed in water to make dough, and kneaded it repeatedly with a rolling pin till it became a thin sheet. She sprinkled flour on the sheet, folded it in half, sprinkled more flour and folded it again a few more times into multiple layers. Then she dexterously cut the dough, spread it into individual strands and put them in boiling water. Sometime later, she took out a couple of strands with a pair of chopsticks to check if they were properly cooked, scooped up the cooked *udon* with a strainer, put them in two china bowls and poured hot anchovy stock over them. I watched this whole process with fascination and anticipation while my stomach growled.

She gave us the *udon* bowls with a heap of sliced *danmuji* (pickled Japanese radish) and kimchi as side dishes. It was flaky, tender, and delicious. The *danmuji* was crunchy and somewhat sweet, complementing the hot *udon*. I had never had such mouthwatering *udon* before. It was so smooth that I swallowed it instead of chewing it.

After lunch, Mr. Myung-sup and I returned to the railroad station. Many travelers crowded the hall. The lack of sleep from the night before had caught up with me. I looked around for an empty seat, but none was available. I sat on the bare concrete floor using my backpack as a seat and leaned against the wall for a nap. Mr. Myung-sup sat next to me, and soon began to snore. I dreamed about all the new experiences I had had earlier in the day.

Seoul, the city I had longed to come to for so long, was within a few hours' train ride. Just seven days ago, I had been in a remote hamlet where no modern wonders existed. I thought I was lucky to have made a safe trip across the border and witnessed so many wonderful things in such a short time, and drifted off to sleep.

1:00 P.M. TRAIN TO SEOUL

Suddenly, a booming voice woke me up. I stood up and looked around for its source—a big, dark bugle up on the wall. It said, "The 1 p.m. Seoul-bound train will be delayed. Please wait for a further announcement. Thank you." I did not see a man blowing the bugle, so I thought that someone was hiding in or behind the wall, or inside the big horn. But I wondered how a man could possibly fit into it even though it was the biggest horn I had ever seen. Mr. Myung-sup slowly got up and grunted, "That train never arrives on time. Every time I've come to Kaesŏng, it's been delayed one to two hours."

"Mr. Myung-sup, that big bugle," I said and pointed to it. "I did not see anybody blowing it. Apparently, he must have fit inside it. I wonder how small he is to fit inside it?"

He said with a smile, "Tae-hyok, no one is inside. A man in that office speaks into a machine, and electricity carries his voice to the horn," and he pointed to the ticket office. "It amplifies his voice so that everyone in the hall can hear him. I shall be back soon." He disappeared into the crowd.

I felt quite embarrassed about my ignorance, but the electric horn continued to fascinate me. I waited for more announcements, but the horn remained silent. I watched the crowd milling about, talking loudly or laughing thunderously. Some were dressed in very fancy western attire; some in casual travelers' clothes; some in farmers' fatigues; but most wore traditional white Korean white costumes. I noticed that many travelers appeared to be from North Korea, like me, judging from their northwestern accent. They carried large backpacks. Some began to form a line at one of the departure gates. I wondered if it was for the Seoul-bound train. Fearing I would miss my train in the absence of my experienced travel partner, I walked over to the line and asked one of the passengers if it was for the Seoul-bound train. He said tersely, "No, it is for Toseong." I thanked him, returned to my place, and found that Mr. Myung-sup had returned.

He asked, "Where have you been? I was worried about you."

"I went to find out what that line was for. I am glad you have returned."

Shortly after that, people started forming new lines at the same departure gates. It seemed that almost all the men in the hall smoked cigarettes. Mr. Myung-sup sought out the lines for the Seoul-bound train, suggesting that we should join them. He said, "The closer we are to the gates, the better our chances of getting seats." The lines grew longer, snaking around the hall and out into the square. When the train did not arrive, people started to sit down on the floor, using their backpacks as cushions, and the hall grew quiet.

After a long wait, the bugle blared again, "The gates for the Seoul-bound train will open shortly." Upon hearing this, people began to talk, laugh, and put on their backpacks. I also stood up and helped my struggling partner put on his backpack. While we were waiting in line, a long, black train slowly pulled in between two platforms with short, intermittent whistles, and came to a complete halt. Then, many passengers poured out of the train, rushed toward the arrival gates, filed in lines, and tendered their tickets to the gate clerks before they went out to the hall. Some passengers carried very large, heavy rucksacks. I guessed that they were cross-border merchants, like Mr. Myung-sup.

When all the arriving passengers had cleared the train, the engine blew a loud whistle for a few seconds, shot steam into the air like an angry bull, detached itself from the long train with a metallic clink-clank and slowly wheeled away from the platform. Every time the engine hissed steam from its side, the big, black metal wheel rolled on the railroad track. How marvelous it was!

After the engine had moved out of the platform, several railroad employees in black uniforms punched passengers' tickets and let them through the gates. Some pushed each other and rushed forward. Women with children and older people lagged behind. It was a chaotic scene. I walked slowly along with Mr. Myung-sup. When we reached the train, we found every car packed except the last two, which were posted with big white letters in Korean and English side by side. I didn't understand the English. Only a few American soldiers occupied these two cars, in contrast with the packed cars for the public. My partner climbed up to the steps of the car next to the one for the U.S. military. We managed to climb up into the car and squeezed inside the door. Many more people climbed up behind us and stood precariously on the plates connecting our car and the U.S. soldiers'.

A foul odor reeked from the slender door that I leaned against. I wondered what was inside. Mr. Myung-sup said, "Shit. We are standing by the toilet." We tried to elbow ourselves further inside to get away from the smell, to no avail. People talked loudly. Some yelled. "Well, we have to put up with this damn smell all the way to Seoul," he grunted. All the windows were wide open, but the air in the car was stuffy even with the late October breeze. Somebody farther inside shouted, "Get rid of that %@#$ cigarette!" The smoker shouted back, "Watch your %@#$ mouth!" It seemed like no one was courteous. The raucous talk slowly died down. My legs hurt badly, especially the left shin from the infection. I shifted my weight from my ailing left leg to my right to alleviate the pain. Eventually, I fell asleep.

A sudden jolt almost knocked all of us passengers down. It frightened me out of my catnap. But the packed crowd supported each other. Noisy talk erupted; everyone became lively again. I said, "Mr. Myung-sup, what caused that jolt?"

He said, "The locomotive banged the train to connect to the engine. I think the train is going to leave soon. Did it scare you?"

"Yes, sir. It did." But the train did not leave for some time. The outhouse odor dulled my sense of smell. A long, lugubrious whistle sounded; a big jerk accompanied with loud clattering made me realize the train was moving. As the train rolled lazily, the engineer sounded the whistle frequently. Many curved tracks in the railroad yard converged and merged with the track on which my train was running. The train came out of the railroad yard and into streets where rows of stores and low houses stood neatly side by side. Pedestrians walked around, and stores had colorful signboards above the eaves or hung on them. A wide road separated the track from the streets. When the streets ended, the train picked up full speed. Countless black telephone poles raced backward, making a swishing sound. Many swallows gracefully perched on the phone lines. Perhaps they were resting before heading south for the winter. The fast-moving train mercilessly whipped and twisted young wild acacias along the track. It also caused gentle waves of humbly drooping golden rice heads in the fields. Rich rice fields stretched as far as I could see. What a beautiful, fertile land it was.

After hours on the train, we arrived at Susaeck Station, the last station before Seoul. The orange sun was just about to sink behind the western ridge. The conductor walked along the train and announced, using a portable speaker, "Next stop is Seoul Station."

I would be in Seoul shortly. My heart started pounding. My body temperature rose; my legs trembled. A sense of uncertainty followed the initial excitement. I asked myself, "What shall I do if Mr. Tae-yun does not have a job for me? Have I made a mistake by leaving home and coming to Seoul, a big, strange city?" To calm my nerves, I recited an old saying, "Even if the heavens fall on you, there will be a hole through which you can climb up to a safe place."

As we slowly approached the city, my anxiety heightened. For some reason, the train stopped in the darkness and showed no sign of moving. People started to grumble and curse. To temper my anxiety, I asked in a low voice, "Mr. Myung-sup, why is the train not moving?"

He said, "It is waiting for a green light. Without that, it cannot pull into the station. But it is unusual to wait this long. When we get off the train at Seoul Station, it might be quite dark."

SEOUL

After a long wait, the train sounded a loud whistle and started to move slowly with a series of metallic clinks-clanks between rows of big buildings. There were lights in all the rooms, on all the floors, even outside the building. People bustled along under the streetlights. Back in my hometown, once the sun retired behind the western hills and dim flickering oil lamps were put out after simple suppers, darkness blanketed the entire valley and stillness prevailed except for the intermittent barking of dogs. Within a span of just seven days, I experienced two different worlds—a simple bucolic farm hamlet and a glittering big city.

We finally pulled into the brightly lit Seoul Station and stopped between two platforms. Huge crowds of passengers disembarked and converged hurriedly toward the arrival gates. I saw trains beside ours, parked at various platforms to our left and right. Mr. Myung-sup said, "Tae-hyok, follow me. We must climb up the covered ramp to get to the arrival gates." He pointed at the ramp in front of us, which many passengers were already ascending. I wondered where all these people came from. It was a long walk from the train to the gates. At one of them, we gave our tickets and walked into the brightly lit station hall. I was awestruck by this humongous hall with its high dome. I thought the Kaesŏng station was big, but this Seoul station was many times bigger. I was completely oblivious to being in the city that I had longed to see, until Mr. Myung-sup hollered, "Tae-hyok, what are you doing? Let's go out to the square and eat supper."

We crossed the station plaza. Lights from tall poles dimly illuminated the area. The square, covered with concrete, was very crowded. When we reached a wide boulevard, cars with glaring lights honked and drove past us.

Suddenly, further up the street, lightning zigzagged through the air. This frightened me so much that I grabbed Mr. Myung-sup's arm and asked him, "What is that?" He said, "Oh, that is from a *jeonchah* (trolley car). We must watch for oncoming cars before we cross the street." We stopped by a raised platform. A big, long, packed *jeonchah* with bells sounding slowly appeared and halted. Passengers poured out and went on their way. A multitude of people fought their way to the car and packed into it. When the doors closed, the bell sounded again, and the car started to move. We crossed the street and went inside a tall, fire-gutted brick building where we ate supper. Then, Mr. Myung-sup and I returned to the railroad station hall.

A PICKPOCKET AND MR. MYUNG-SUP

Mr. Myung-sup said, "Tae-hyok, I am going to Namdaemun Market (the South Gate Market) for shopping. I shall return in a couple of hours. I am going to stay overnight here and take the first northbound train to Kaesŏng tomorrow morning. It is too late for you to go to your cousin, Mr. Tae-yun. Why don't you spend the night here with me and go to him tomorrow morning? If you want to go shopping, you can come with me, but if you are tired, you stay here and rest. It is safe." I chose the latter, and he left.

After that, I explored the spacious hall, admiring its splendid architecture, stately marble columns supporting the lofty ceiling, and hundreds of glittering electric lights. I measured the floor, which was more than two hundred paces, and was astounded by its magnitude. My elementary school back in my hometown was a one-story wooden building with five classrooms and an office. It was the largest building in the region, but it was nothing compared to this. I imagined that this hall could easily accommodate many buildings the size of my school. I watched people coming in and out, talking loudly, and laughing. Intermittent whistling from the railroad yard attracted my interest, and I walked over to the arrival gates and looked at the faintly lit yard. There were many trains parked along the various platforms, and some locomotives slowly moved in and out. An unpleasant odor of burning coal from the engines made me retreat inside. I found an empty bench, sat down, and leaned against the wall to rest.

Sometime later, I saw Mr. Myung-sup returning from his shopping, much sooner than expected. He limped excitedly, more than usual; he was panting and looked very upset. He called me from some distance, "Tae-hyok, Tae-hyok."

I sensed that something was wrong, and stood up and responded, "Yes, Mr. Myung-sup. Is something wrong?"

He said in an agitated voice, "A pickpocket stole all my money. What am I going to do?" He breathed heavily; his healthy hand was trembling badly. He sank onto the bench where I had rested, bowed his head, and started to sob. After a few minutes, he calmed himself down, sighed deeply, and said, "I do not even have money to buy a return ticket."

I was terribly sorry for him. I could not even find words to comfort him. I was also dumbfounded, because in my small farm village, no one stole anything. I had never heard of pickpocketing. All I could say was "I am very, very sorry, Mr. Myung-sup." I thought this pickpocket must have been heartless to steal from this handicapped man.

I said, "Mr. Myung-sup, tell me how I can help you."

He looked up at me and said weakly, "Tae-hyok, thank you. If you have money, would you mind loaning me 500 *won* so that I may pay for my return trip? When I go home, I will pay it back to your father."

I agreed without hesitation. I went to a corner where no one was around, took out six 100 *won* bills from my secret pocket inside my bulky Korean trousers, and folded them in my hand so that no one would see them. This was exactly 60 percent of my total cash, which I would need in this big, strange city. Also, I knew I would not see him again for a long time. I didn't even know if he would pay back this loan to my father when he returned home. But I had sympathy for him. I decided to give 100 *won* more than he had asked for, because he was in a dire situation. I returned, sat next to him, and put the money in his palm when no one was near us. I said, "This is 600 *won*, Mr. Myung-sup. I hope it will take you home."

He whispered, "Thank you, Tae-hyok. You saved me from trouble." He was still trembling. He put it away very carefully in an inner pocket of his jacket and held my hand appreciatively. Koreans rarely touched each other to express their thanks, but he did today. He looked physically and emotionally exhausted. Without saying a word, he gazed at the wall on the far side absentmindedly for a few moments, lay on his chest instead of on his back and rested his head on his backpack, perhaps to protect his money. He soon fell asleep and started to snore intermittently.

I sat at the end of the bench with a sense of apprehension and surveyed my surroundings to see if a suspicious person was lurking around. It seemed that no one was paying attention to us. Occasionally, Mr. Myung-sup groaned, perhaps from the pain of the theft, and twitched his legs. Since I was tired, too, I leaned my head against the wall and dozed. Mr. Myung-sup's screaming and groaning woke me up. I shook him and said, "Mr. Myung-sup, wake up."

He sat up, sighed, and said, "Thank you, Tae-hyok. I had a bad dream. I was somewhere on the border; a robber tried to take my backpack from me, and I screamed for help, but no one was around," and he took a deep breath. "I am going to take the first northbound train to return home. It leaves at 5 o'clock in the morning. When the sun rises, you should ask a policeman for directions to your cousin's home." He paused for a while and then continued, "I hope he gives you some work. I know him very well. He was the most intelligent man in the whole valley. You study hard and become a learned man like him. When I return home, I will tell your parents that you have arrived safely in Seoul. Let's get some sleep. I have a long way to go." He sighed and lay down. The big clock on the wall struck midnight. The crowd had thinned to only a few dozen people. Perhaps they intended to spend the night here, too.

I found a sign for the men's room on the far side of the hall. I cautiously entered the brightly lit, clean room and saw fancy, white urinals. I had never seen such a luxurious men's room before. Back home, we would use outhouses and chamber pots on winter nights. But this men's room was so posh that I thought it was reserved for dignitaries. I immediately came out and searched for one for ordinary people outside the hall. I found a bigger one that was dirty and used it without fear.

I returned to Mr. Myung-sup, who got up a few minutes later, wondering how his daughters were doing. I said, "I am sure they will be alright. The townspeople will take care of them. Don't you think so?" He said, "I think they are alright." But he was restless. He groaned and sighed. Apparently, the loss of his money caused him much anguish and deprived him of sleep.

I took the bench next to him and lay down to sleep, but thoughts about my future in this big, strange city kept me awake. There was no heat in the hall, and the midnight chill made me miserable. I catnapped through the night and waited for sunrise.

The big clock on the wall showed only a few minutes past 4 a.m. But people started to trickle in for early morning trains. As soon as the ticket windows opened, Mr. Myung-sup bought a return ticket and walked to the departure gate for the 5 a.m. northbound train to Kaesŏng, as if he could not stand another minute in this heartless city. I walked with him to the gate to see him off. The gate was not yet open. He was the only one in line. Neither of us spoke very much. We just looked out at the dimly lit platforms. I was cold and walked in place to warm myself. Soon, other passengers joined Mr. Myung-sup and formed a long line.

At last, a railroad clerk in a black uniform came to the gate and announced several times, "This is the 5 a.m. train to Kaesŏng."

I said, "Mr. Myung-sup, I am sorry that you have to return home this way but have a safe trip. When you return, please tell my parents that I have arrived safely in Seoul."

He responded, "Thank you, Tae-hyok. Thank you very much for the loan. Take care of yourself." The clerk punched his ticket and let him pass through the gate. He limped toward the ramp. Even though he was the first passenger to pass through the gate, many others who went through the gate behind him soon overtook him. He slowly disappeared into the multitude.

When I didn't see him anymore, I suddenly felt lonely. I lingered at the gate for a few more minutes, hoping to see him for the last time, but didn't. There were many empty benches in the hall, but I returned to the one where I had spent the night and rested. For some reason that gave me a warm and cozy feeling, perhaps because it had been my resting place the previous night. The hall was crowded, and it was warmer now. Even though it was noisy, I closed my eyes and took a nap.

RIDING THE TROLLEY CAR

The weak morning sun filtered through the windows when I awoke. I put my knapsack on my shoulder and went out to the plaza. The autumn morning chill engulfed me. I looked around for a policeman. I saw a small police sub-station next to the railroad station building. This sub-station oversaw law and order at the Seoul railroad station. I entered and saw two police officers

in black uniforms seated at their desks. Their uniforms looked more dignified than those of the railroad clerks. I bowed and said, "Good morning, sirs.
May I ask you for directions, please?"

They replied, "Good morning, young fellow. What can we do for you?"

I took Mr. Tae-yun's address from my pocket and showed it to one of the
officers. "How do I get to this address, sir?"

He took it from me and said, "Young man, you buy a ticket at the ticket
box by that power pole and take a trolley car to Wonjung at that platform,"
and pointed to a raised platform in the middle of the boulevard. I saw many
people standing on it. "Get off at the fourth stop, Wonjung 2-ka. Ask the
driver to let you off there. Once you get off, ask people there how to get to
No. 6 Youngjung." He returned the paper to me and said, "Good luck. By
the way, are you from the Pyongyang area?"

I said, "No, sir. I'm from Suan-gun, Hwanghae-do. Sir, how do I tell
which car is for Wonjung?"

"Every trolley car has a sign in its front window showing its destination. A
smaller car runs to Wonjung. Do you follow me, young man?"

I responded, "Yes, I do. Thank you very much for your help. Goodbye sir."

I walked over to the ticket booth. Inside it, a ticket salesman sat on a high
chair. I said, "Sir, may I have a ticket please?" and pushed in a 5 *won* bill
through the window. He tossed out a ticket and change without saying a word.
On the ticket was a trolley car illustrated in light green and over the illustra-
tion, 電車票 (trolley car ticket) was offset in bold black. I kept it in my hand.

I rushed to the platform and joined the crowd. Several secondary school
students were among them. They wore uniforms and carried beige packs.
I was surprised that some were girls because in my hometown, most parents,
including mine, kept their daughters out of school. They thought girls should
help with household chores and get married when they had grown up. Fewer
than ten girls were in my class of more than eighty kids.

These girls wore navy blue uniforms. Their jackets resembled a sailor's
jersey; the skirts were neatly pleated and sharply pressed. They wore white
handkerchief-like neckties. Their faces were beautiful, fair against their neat
blue jerseys. Their black hair shone. I wondered if they came from a different world. I had never seen such radiant girls before. Back in my hometown,

all the girls wore country tweeds or homespun black cotton clothes. Their faces were tan from working in the blazing sun.

The boys wore black school uniforms and hats. The hats had white ribbons stitched around them. Shiny brass insignia was just above the visors, such as Yong Choong (龍中) or Kyung Kong (京工), Chinese characters that were abbreviations for their schools. I envied them and said to myself, "I will make money and get an education like them."

Sudden cranking noises caught my attention. A couple of packed trolley cars approached one after another and halted by the platform. I carefully checked the signs in their oblong windows as the policeman had instructed. None read Wonjung-bound. As soon as the doors opened, people pushed each other to get on the trolley car even before the passengers had disembarked. After the trolley car took in as many as would fit, it started moving without closing the doors. A few hung on each door and tried to force themselves in. The trolley advanced for ten or twenty yards and halted. The driver at the front door and two conductors, one at the middle door and the other at the rear door, yelled at those hanging on the doors and pushed them off. Then they closed the doors and left. Many people were left behind. A truck slowly drove by us, honking loudly. A few impatient boys ran after the truck, tossed their bookbags into the cargo bay, and skillfully climbed up on the truck.

More trolley cars came and went, but none was Wonjung-bound. I asked a man next to me if this was the right platform to get a Wonjung-bound trolley car. He answered, "Yes, it is."

After a long wait, a smaller trolley approached and stopped. Its window said, 'Wonjung-bound.' When no more passengers came out, the people on the platform climbed into the car. I joined them. To reassure myself, I asked the driver if this car was heading for Wonjung. He said, "Yes." To my surprise, it was not as packed as the others. I positioned myself just behind the driver.

Large glass windows were installed all around the car. The ones in front were much larger than the others and offered a better view. Long wooden benches, fully occupied, were fixed along the walls, with a large standing space between them. Many passengers stood in this area. Two rows of leather straps dangled from the ceiling for standing passengers to grab. A bell sounded right above my head. The driver shut the sliding door. Then he pulled a string above his head a couple of times. That sounded the bell in the back. He swiftly turned the brown handle on a brass cylinder in front of him. I asked the driver, "Sir, I am going to Wonjung 2-ka. Would you please let me get off when we arrive there?" He said, "Sure, young man." As he accelerated, the car swung left and right.

Seoul was the largest, most modern, and most glamorous city in the Korean peninsula. Everything there was new and spectacular to me. But I could not afford to enjoy it because I was preoccupied with counting the number of stops. Although the driver loudly announced the name of each stop, I feared I might miss mine. After the third stop, I asked him, "Sir, is the next stop Wonjung-2ka?" even though I knew it should be.

He said without looking back, "Yes, it is. You must be a stranger in Seoul, are you?"

I answered, "Yes, sir." As the trolley increased its speed, it swung wildly.

He announced loudly, "Wonjung-2ka, Wonjung-2ka." He slowed the trolley and stopped. He said, "Boy, you get off here," and opened the door. I thanked him and got off. I was the only one.

CHAPTER 6

Mr. Kim Tae-yun

October 1946

It was early morning, and not many people were on the street. Only a few small shops were open. I approached a shopkeeper sweeping the sidewalk in front of his shop and asked for directions to No. 6 Youngjung Street.

He stopped sweeping and looked at me curiously. Then he said, "Sure, young man. It's on the other side of this small hill," and he pointed the way. "You take this back street for a few hundred yards along the foothill. Youngjung starts from there."

I thanked him and followed his directions. There were only a few small houses along that stretch. At the end of it was Youngjung Street. The houses on this quiet street looked neater and bigger than those along the previous road. I noticed 'No. 1 Youngjung' on the front door of a two-story house. A few men with briefcases hurried along. Even though I reasoned that No. 6 mustn't be too far, I asked one of the gentlemen.

He stopped and said, "Do you see that big house?" pointing in the direction of a huge, stucco house, and continued on his way before I could express my thanks.

Approaching it, I wondered whether Mr. Kim Tae-yun would recognize me, how he would accept me, and if he would give me a job. At last, I stood in front of an iron gate set in a six-foot-high stucco fence. Behind it stood not just a house but a mansion. Awestruck, I took a quick look through the bars of the gate. Finding no one around, I surveyed the compound. Manicured flower beds surrounded the mansion and walkway. White chrysanthemums blossomed in full. On the farther side of the mansion, a couple of princely cedars shot into the spotless blue October sky. Russet Japanese maples and bonsai-shaped pines mottled a large rock garden which extended from the flowerbeds to the cedars. A much smaller, dark-brown building stood near the gate. Autumn leaves had fallen here and there. I wondered how rich Mr. Kim was to own this large, magnificent residence. I was afraid to knock at the gate. Even if I did, nobody would be able to hear me. I lingered, hoping he would soon come out of the house.

Sometime later, I heard someone coughing inside the gate. I peeked inside and saw a man sweeping the fallen leaves. He was not my cousin. I took the address from my pocket and rechecked it. If I had come to the right place, why was a stranger sweeping the yard? Had my cousin moved? If he had, I would be in deep trouble in this big, strange city. I knocked on the gate anyway and said, "Good morning, sir!"

He stopped sweeping and greeted me. I told him that I was looking for my cousin Mr. Kim Tae-yun. "I came from his hometown in North Korea. Does he live here, sir?"

"Indeed, he does," the man said, opening the gate and inviting me in. Then he turned toward the house and hollered, "You have a guest out here from North Korea!"

A lady in her early thirties wearing a colorful western style dress rushed out. The man repeated what I had told him, and she approached me, wiping her hands with her white apron. She said, "I am Mr. Kim Tae-yun's wife. You came from my husband's hometown?"

"Yes, Ma'am," I bowed to her and then introduced myself. "Glad to meet you. I am one of his cousins."

She returned my bow awkwardly and said hesitantly, "You came from North Korea alone?"

"Yes, Ma'am."

"Please follow me. I am glad that you came early. My husband has not left for work yet." She hurried toward the entrance of the big house, excitedly calling, "*Yeobo* (honey), you have a guest from your hometown!"

I heard a man's voice say, "Who?" Then my cousin appeared on the porch. Upon seeing me, he stepped down from the porch barefoot, saying, "You are Tae-hyok, aren't you?" Despite having seen me more than five years earlier, he instantly recognized me and welcomed me, patting me affectionately on the back.

His recognition made my anxiety disappear. "How are you, *Hyung-nim* (honorary expression for cousin)?" I greeted him.

He said, "I am fine. When did you come to Seoul?"

I raised my head and answered, "Yesterday evening, sir."

He continued, "Did you come all by yourself?"

"I accompanied Mr. Myung-sup. He returned home early this morning."

"It's good to see you. Let's go inside." He led me to a beautifully carpeted office. I had never seen carpet before. "You are the first person from my hometown whom I have met since returning to Seoul from China a year ago." He had worked for North China Development Corporation (a Japanese company) in Beijing as a civil engineer until World War II ended. Now he was the executive vice president and cofounder of a construction company.

"How are my parents doing? Are they well?" he asked. His parents lived in my hometown.

I answered, "They are fine, sir." As soon as we settled down, I said, "Sir, I have a letter for you. Your brother gave it to me when I left North Korea." I took it from my knapsack and handed it to him.

He took it and said, "Thank you, Tae-hyok." He anxiously opened it and started to read. He appeared to be tense; his hands were shaking slightly. He quietly read all three pages of the letter. When he finished, he said, "I am glad that you brought me this letter. My brother writes that my parents and his family are all well. Also, he says that he had a bumper harvest this fall, but the communist government took away 30 percent of it as tax. Is it true, Tae-hyok?"

"Yes, it is true. They call it *hyeun-mull-se* (tax in crop, not in cash). The North Korean communists exploit the farmers as the Japanese did during World War II. It is reported that the Russian occupiers take soybeans and corn, and ship them to Russia without compensation."

He said angrily, "That's awful. Damn communists! I hope the Americans and their allies get the Russians out of the peninsula and unify the South and the North soon." He calmed down and said, "Tae-hyok, you want to stay in Seoul and study, do you?"

I said nervously, "Yes sir, if I can find a job. Would you give me a job, please? I will do anything."

"I think I can arrange some work for you. Let me discuss this with my partners. I shall introduce you to them. They are wonderful gentlemen."

As I was listening to him, I was so thankful and excited that I unconsciously stood up, bowed to him, and said, "Thank you, sir. Thank you." Suddenly the burden of uncertainty was lifted from my shoulders.

At that moment, Mrs. Kim Tae-yun came in and joined us. I stood up to show my respect. She said, "Sit down, please. How are my husband's parents doing? Are they well?"

"They are doing well, Ma'am."

Her husband said, "Tae-hyok brought a letter from my brother. He wrote that my parents are healthy."

She said, "Breakfast is ready. Where did you spend the night?"

"I spent the night at the Seoul Railroad Station, Ma'am."

"You mean all night there? Weren't you cold?"

"Yes, I was, but it was okay, Ma'am."

Mr. Kim Tae-yun said, "*Yeobo*, he wants to stay in Seoul and pursue an education."

She said spontaneously, "Really? Good for you. You may stay with us until you find a job."

I was overwhelmed by her generosity. I bowed to her and said, "Thank you very much. I cannot find proper words to express my sincere appreciation, Ma'am."

Mr. Kim Tae-yun said, "I am going to talk with Mr. Namgoong and Dr. Park about hiring him for my company. What do you think?"

"I think it's a good idea," she responded. Then she turned to me and said, "You must be hungry, after spending the night at the railroad station." She led us to a room with a large round table.

Two children ran in and hollered, "*Appa, Appa*." Upon seeing me they stopped abruptly and grew quiet.

Mr. Kim Tae-yun said, "Come in, children." They cautiously walked to him. The younger one sat on his lap and snuggled into his chest. The older one stood by him, holding his arm. He rubbed the boy's head. "This is my son, Jung-sik. He is six years old. And this is my daughter, Jung-jah. She is four years old. Our youngest, Kwang-jah, is still asleep. Children, this is Uncle Tae-hyok. He came from my hometown. He knows your grandparents. He brought their *'Hello!'* to you. He is going to stay with us. Would you please greet him?"

The boy bowed and said, "*An-yung-ha-say-yo* (Hello!)" I responded with a smile, "*An-yung* (Hello!), Jung-sik. Nice to meet you. You are a big boy." But the girl buried her head in her father's embrace and said, "No, no."

Her father said, "She is shy."

I said, "Hi Jung-jah." She took a quick look at me and hid her face in her father's chest again.

The boy asked, "*Appa*, have I ever met them before?"

His father answered, "Yes, you have, but you were a baby—too young to remember them."

"Are they old, *Appa*?"

"Yes, they are."

Mrs. Kim Tae-yun came into the room with food on a big tray. I promptly stood up and said, "Can I help you, Ma'am?"

She said, "Thank you, but sit down and feel at home." She put the food on the table. "Now, let's eat breakfast." The children sat next to their mother. It was a scrumptious breakfast, but I could not eat much. Perhaps I was too tired.

Mr. Kim Tae-yun said, "I still remember that ten or eleven years ago, when you were about five or six, you proudly showed me a nickel and said that with that nickel, you would buy a train ticket to Seoul. I was visiting my parents on the way to my job in Ywon City." He laughed and continued, "I thought you were cute. How old are you, Tae-hyok?"

I said, "Fifteen, sir."

He put his hand on my shoulder and said, "Fifteen! You are a brave boy to come to Seoul all by yourself. When I came to Seoul for the first time, I was scared. I was then twenty-one years old. There was no conflict. This peninsula was undivided. We had the freedom to travel wherever we pleased. Now the country is cut in half." He paused for a moment. "I am glad that you have come to Seoul."

Mrs. Kim Tae-yun said, "Have you ever been to a big city before?"

Before I answered, Mr. Kim Tae-yun said, "I don't think he has ever traveled outside his small valley, except to attend school in Jang-keo Ri. Am I right, Tae-hyok?"

I said, "Yes sir, except when I traveled to a cement manufacturing plant in the Sariwon area last May. I went on an errand."

"Really?" he said. "It must have been a long trip. Did you take a train?"

"No, sir. I walked. It was about thirty-seven miles."

Mrs. Kim Tae-yun asked, "How long did it take you to get there, a couple of days?"

"It took one day, Ma'am. I left home before sunrise and arrived there just before sunset."

She was astounded. "You walked thirty-seven miles in one day? I cannot believe it. You must have been only fourteen then. I wonder how you ventured to cross the border. I have a fifteen-year-old half-brother in North Korea. I don't think he would dare to come to Seoul all by himself. Even if he wanted to, my parents wouldn't let him."

I asked, "Where does he live?"

"He lives in South Hamgyong Province, about 250 miles northeast of Seoul. I also have my parents and a half-sister there. I miss them. A few days ago, I went to a refugee liaison office for South Hamgyong Province. I checked the refugee list and found the name and address of my best friend from that city. I went directly from the office to her house and met her and her family. They had recently arrived in Seoul, and they were temporarily living with one of her cousins. She told me that my family would escape North Korea as soon as my father could sell his business. I hope they come to Seoul soon."

The boy asked, "*Umma*, your *Umma* and *Appa*, what are they to me?"

She laughed and said, "They are your maternal grandparents." His father also laughed.

The boy said, "*Umma*, I have two sets of grandparents. But I know none of them."

She said, "Your maternal grandparents might come to Seoul sometime soon. Then you will meet them."

He said, "That's great. I hope it will be soon."

Oblivious to our conversation, the little girl concentrated on her breakfast.

She stubbornly used a pair of chopsticks to eat her food, and spilled more food than she ate. Her mom cleaned the table in front of her.

Mr. Kim Tae-yun said, "My wife's father passed away when she was three years old." He turned to her and asked, "Do you have any memory of him?"

"No, I don't," she said. "My mother remarried when I was five years old. My stepfather raised me. To me, he is my father. He is a good father."

In less than a few hours with them, I learned much about them. But it was sad that Mrs. Kim Tae-yun, like her husband, hadn't seen her parents and siblings in North Korea for many years.

After breakfast, Mr. Kim Tae-yun took me to his company's construction site downtown. They were renovating two huge brick buildings on a wooded hilltop for the U.S. Army. The inside walls had been taken out. A few workers were busily ripping grayish pipes and dusty wires out of the wall. I asked him what the pipes and wires were for, and why they were tearing them out.

He answered, "The pipes bring water inside the house. The wires were for electricity. Because they are old and dangerous, plumbers and electricians will replace them. When they have been installed, the carpenters will put in new walls and ceilings. After that's completed, the painters will paint everything. Then the building will be like new. We plan to complete this project by next February."

Until then, I had never known that plumbing pipes and electrical wires were installed inside walls. This modern technology fascinated me. Back home, we drew water from a deep outdoor well, and lit the house with either a kerosene lantern or a homemade oil lamp.

While we were touring the site, Mr. Kim Tae-yun's partners joined us. After exchanging greetings, he said, "I would like to introduce a relative of mine from my hometown in North Korea. Tae-hyok, this is Mr. Namgoong, the president of the company, and this is Dr. Park, the executive vice president in charge of engineering."

I bowed to them to show my respect, and said, "How do you do, sirs? Glad to meet you." Mr. Namgoong was a tall, athletic-looking man, and Dr. Park was a scholarly gentleman.

They returned my greetings. "Glad to meet you, too, Tae-hyok."

Dr. Park asked, "Are you from the same town as Mr. Kim Tae-yun's parents?"

"Yes, I am, sir."

He continued, "Did you bring good news from them for Mr. Kim Tae-yun?"

I said, "Yes, sir. They are well."

Mr. Namgoong asked, "Did you come with your family?"

Before I answered, Mr. Kim Tae-yun said, "No, he came alone. He is a brave young man."

Mr. Namgoong and Dr. Park said almost simultaneously, "Certainly, you are a brave young man."

"Did you have any problems crossing the border?" Dr. Park asked.

I said, "No, sir," even though the gunshots from the North Korean border guards had frightened me, and the infection on my left shin had caused significant pain.

After the ice-breaking conversations, Mr. Kim Tae-yun and the two gentlemen disappeared into their site office. Since I knew that he would surely discuss my employment with them, I earnestly prayed to the gods to influence the minds of my prospective employers. I sat on a rock, closed my eyes, and said, "Please let them hire me so that I may make money and go to school. You know how eager I am to get an education. Please!" I repeated this simple prayer many times.

A while later, Mr. Kim Tae-yun opened the door and hollered, "Tae-hyok, would you come into the office?"

I said, "Yes, sir," and entered. My heart was pounding loudly, and my face felt hot.

Mr. Namgoong said, "Tae-hyok, we have decided to hire you as an office boy. You will be paid 200 *won* a month. Mr. Kim Tae-yun has volunteered to provide you with a dwelling place. You will do chores for Mrs. Kim Tae-yun when you have time. Do you want to work for us, Tae-hyok?"

I was overjoyed with his offer. I wanted to shout, "I am the luckiest boy in the world!" but I hid my emotions. Instead, I said cordially, "Yes, sir. Thank you very much," and I bowed to them. I could not believe that I had a job less than twenty-four hours after coming to Seoul. My prayer had been answered.

Once I calmed down, I thought how generous Mr. Kim Tae-yun was. I thanked him profoundly for giving me a place to live so that I could continue my education. Obviously, he knew that I could not make it without help. He also knew how hard it would be for me to pay for my education in this divided country. He had come to Seoul all by himself in his early twenties to study civil engineering and had supported himself by delivering newspapers or doing odd jobs. It was peacetime then, and Seoul was burgeoning. Now the country was divided. Hundreds of thousands of refugees came to Seoul from North Korea, China, Japan, and other Asian countries. Most of them did not have work. I, a boy without skill or much education, already had a job. How fortunate I was.

After Mr. Namgoong announced my employment, Mr. Kim Tae-yun took me to a vendor where his company would buy some building materials. He introduced me to a couple of people and told them that I would come to pick up his orders. Then, he led me to a business district where banks, department stores, and the central post office were located. The streets were crowded and noisy. These people wore fancy, expensive clothes. Mr. Kim Tae-yun took me to a bank with which the company did business. He showed me how to deposit and withdraw money. Everything looked glorious and strange. I thought I was in a dreamland.

We returned to his residence by suppertime. Mrs. Kim Tae-yun asked her husband, "How was your day? Did Mr. Namgoong and Dr. Park accept your proposal to hire Tae-hyok?"

He said, "Yes, they did. We hired him as an office boy and to do some chores for us. He will be paid 200 *won* a month."

She said, "Good. Congratulations, Tae-hyok. You can eat with us and live with us so that you may save all of your paychecks for your education. We have an extra room for you even though it does not have a heating system. We are not charging you anything. All we want is for you to be a good boy and study hard."

I was overwhelmed by her generosity. I bowed to her and said, "Mrs. Kim, thank you very much."

THE PUBLIC BATHHOUSE

Despite the fatigue from my long journey, excitement about my first job kept me awake. So, I got up early in the morning and decided to clean the home company office. It was a big, carpeted room by the main entrance with five desks. I found a feather brush and began whisking off the desks.

Mr. Kim Tae-yun came in and said, "Good morning, Tae-hyok. You got up early. How are you?"

"Good morning, sir. I am fine."

He said that he was going to a public bathhouse and asked me if I would come along.

After my ten-day journey, I needed to wash. So, without hesitation, I agreed. I was excited about going to a public bathhouse for the first time in my life. Back in my hometown, we did not have one. We bathed in the river during the late spring through early autumn. When the river water became too cold to bathe in, we boiled a small amount of well water in a metal basin, dipped a washcloth in the hot water and washed ourselves, only four or five times during the long period from late fall through the next spring. Before leaving for the bathhouse, I fetched my new clothes that my mother had made.

When I returned, he gave me a towel and a bar of soap, and said, "Let's go." Outside, the street was still dark. We walked a couple of blocks to a building with 沐浴湯 (BATHHOUSE) painted in red on the big entrance door. Mr. Kim Tae-yun slid it open, and we entered.

"Good morning, Mr. Kim," the owner, who sat behind a tall reception counter, greeted us. "As usual, you are the first customer this morning. The water is hot and clean. Who is this young man with you?"

Mr. Kim Tae-yun answered that I was one of his relatives from his hometown and had just arrived from North Korea.

The counter had two big arrows, directing men to the right and women to the left. When Mr. Kim Tae-yun paid our fees, the attendant gave us locker keys. We entered the men's locker room. It was not heated. "You take off your clothes and deposit them in your locker," Mr. Tae-yun said. "Take the key with you."

As instructed, I undressed and deposited my clothes in my locker. I felt embarrassed and wrapped my towel around me. Mr. Kim Tae-yun undressed without showing the slightest sign of embarrassment. This made me feel less awkward.

As soon as we stepped inside the bath hall, hot, thick steam engulfed us.

The steam made me feel as if I were lost in a thick fog. Above my head the ceiling lights looked like distant stars, and under my bare feet a grooved concrete floor gently petered down toward canals surrounding the perimeter of the room. In the middle of the floor, there were two huge rectangular concrete bathtubs, from which steam billowed. One tub was much smaller, but both had rims to keep water from sloshing out. Many round gallon-sized wooden pails were neatly stacked nearby.

Mr. Kim Tae-yun said, "I don't think you have ever been to a public bathhouse before. First, use a pail to scoop water from the larger tub, dump it over your head, and wash yourself with soap. Always rinse with clean water before getting into a tub. This is a courtesy." He warned me that the water in the smaller tub was much hotter than that in the larger one.

I thanked him for his instructions.

After washing quickly, Mr. Kim Tae-yun climbed into the larger tub, submerged himself up to his neck, and said, "Oh, it is good!" He started counting in a melody, "One and two, two and three, ..., ninety-nine and one hundred!" He repeated this a few more times. Then he got out of the tub and scrubbed himself with his soapy washcloth again, repeating the entire routine with the hotter water in the smaller tub.

As Mr. Kim Tae-yun had done, I scooped a few pails of warm water from the larger tub, poured them over my head, and washed myself with soap. I thoroughly cleansed the insect bite on my left shin with soap, and the warm water soothed the pain. Then I cautiously moved into the larger tub and submerged myself up to my neck.

After bathing in the larger tub, I scooped a pail of hot water from the small tub and doused my head. The hot water shocked me, and I shouted "*Aigoo!*" I wondered how Mr. Kim Tae-yun could tolerate the whole pail of hot water so calmly. Fetching another pail of hot water, I soaked my towel in the hot water and used it to rinse myself. Then I tried the water with my toe to see if I could do as Mr. Kim Tae-yun had done. It was too hot. So, I pulled my foot out of the water and sat on the rim.

He said, "Tae-hyok, it is not that hot. Dip your feet first and slowly submerge yourself in it. Sit still against the tub wall, then sing as I do."

As advised, I cautiously stepped into the hot tub until the water reached my neck. I sat against the side, clenching my teeth, but I did not sing. Initially it was too hot. As my body adjusted to the water temperature, I became peaceful and relaxed. I climbed out of the tub and thoroughly scrubbed and washed myself with my washcloth. I felt so good that I got into the tub a few more times. The fatigue and tension from my arduous border crossing journey thawed like snow under the spring sun.

An hour of bathing refreshed us. I grew to like the hot bath and wished I could go often, but I couldn't afford to, so I settled for once a week.

CHAPTER 7

Escape

December 1946

MR. TAE-YUN'S REQUEST

"Tae-hyok, I'd like to talk with you about my parents in North Korea," Mr. Tae-yun said unexpectedly. "I am much obliged to you for bringing firsthand news about them. I want to send them some money, but there is no way to deliver it, except by courier. The Russians have sealed the border completely. Right now, I cannot afford to visit them. I must take care of my family and my new business," he sighed.

He continued, "It has been six years since I last visited them. I miss them very much. They are old, and I wonder if I will ever see them again." He dropped his head and wiped his eyes with a handkerchief. He was a strong gentleman, but he could not hold back his tears. Seeing him cry, I felt a surge of homesickness, and missed my parents.

He said, "I have a great favor to ask of you. Would you deliver a package of money to my parents? I have complete trust in you, and you know the way. It is a very risky trip. I will pay all the travel expenses. Think about it. You do not have to decide right now."

I knew this was a serious responsibility, but promptly said, "Sir, I will do it." I felt very proud of myself that he had total confidence in me, a fifteen-year-old boy, to deliver a large amount of money to his parents.

He said, "Thank you, Tae-hyok." He squeezed my shoulders. "When would you like to leave?"

"The sooner, the better, sir. I would like to take advantage of the moonlight to cross the border. If it is too dark, I might get lost. Fortunately, so far, no severe snow has fallen along the route. Deep snow will make the rugged mountain pass very treacherous to cross the border. I would like to set out within two or three days."

PREPARATION FOR THE TRIP

The next evening after dinner, he took paper money from his suit pocket and said, "Tae-hyok, this 6,000 *won* is for my parents. I cashed in 1,000 *won* bills which will be easier for you to carry, and here is 1,000 *won* in smaller bills for your travel expenses." I was overwhelmed. 6,000 *won* was equivalent to three years of my work. I had never seen such a huge amount before. Being entrusted with it made me apprehensive.

I asked Mrs. Tae-yun for a roll of wide gauze, a pair of scissors, a needle, and thread. With curiosity, she brought them to me. I cut two pieces of the wide gauze, about one and a half feet long each. I then placed three 1,000 *won* bills flat on each of the two pieces. I folded the gauze around the bills and sewed the gauze loosely to make a thin envelope. Then I took off my socks, rolled up my long johns, fastened the envelope around my legs just above the ankles, and tied it firmly to my legs. I unrolled my long johns and put my socks on. I stood up and walked around the room a couple of times. Mr. Tae-yun and his wife watched the whole process with amusement. I stopped in front of Mr. Tae-yun and asked him to search me as if he were a North Korean border guard and I were his prisoner. He patted my legs down thoroughly. He said with a broad smile, "Even though I saw you hiding the money, I couldn't tell if you had hidden anything under your long johns. It is very clever of you. I think you will outsmart the North Korean border guards."

CH'ONDAN

Two days later, I took the 5 a.m. northbound train from Yongsan Railroad Station in Seoul. By 2 p.m. the same day, I arrived at Ch'ondan, the westernmost border town, over sixty miles northwest of Seoul. This was the last railroad station before the 38ᵗʰ Parallel. It was a drizzling, bone-chilling afternoon in December of 1946. I planned on crossing the border from this town by night.

I was a total stranger here. I wondered, "Where and how am I going to find some cross-border travelers, especially merchants, whom I might follow to cross the border tonight?" Most cross-border merchants knew the best route for crossing. I went to a marketplace and bought a bowl of hot dumpling soup from a roadside vendor. While eating, I asked the vendor if she would direct me to a place where I could meet people who would be crossing the border. She said there was a small lodge at the north end of the highway, a mile from her shop. These travelers would buy their supper and sleep for a few hours before setting out for their journey by night.

The U.S. Military Government in South Korea practiced an open border policy, allowing Koreans to travel freely across the border. However, the Russian counterpart in North Korea had closed the border shortly after having occupied the northern half of the Korean peninsula in 1945. The Russians and North Korean communist border security forces arrested those who tried to cross the border from either side. Except for the communists, Koreans did not regard the 38ᵗʰ Parallel as a national border because we had been one people and one country until the peninsula was divided by the United States and Russia at the end of World War II.

I arrived at the humble lodge in the middle of the frozen rice fields just before dusk. The innkeeper welcomed me and asked if I planned to cross the border that night. I said, "Yes," and asked, "Are there any merchants at your place who will cross tonight?" He said, "Oh, yes, a group of six merchants in the guest room." He led me to them and said, "This boy is going to North Korea. Please take care of him."

They said almost in unison, "Come in, young man." An older gentleman in his mid-forties said, "Are you traveling to North Korea all by yourself? You are only a teenager." I answered that I would visit my parents in Suan-gun in the northeastern corner of Hwanghae-do Province. He said, "That is about ninety miles northeast of here." I was glad to meet someone who knew my county. He continued, "Why did you come to the South all by yourself, to visit a relative?" I told him that I had come to Seoul to pursue my education. He chuckled in disbelief.

After eating their supper, the merchants fell asleep one by one. I was keenly aware of the fact that I was a total stranger to them. They had no obligation to take me with them. I feared that they might even consider me burdensome and depart without bothering to wake me up if I slept too soundly. So, I asked the older gentleman to wake me up when he was ready to leave. He said, "Young man, don't worry. I will wake you up. Have a good sleep before setting out at midnight." I had concealed the money so well that Mr. Taeyun had not been able to detect it. But sleeping among total strangers made me nervous and kept me awake for some time.

CROSSING THE BORDER

Somebody shook me awake and said, "Young man, get up. We are leaving." It was the gentleman who had advised me to have a good sleep. "You stick with us. Don't fall behind. Nobody will wait for you." While putting his heavy backpack on, he continued, "There is a railroad bridge to cross just before the border. You must be very careful when crossing it; it may be quite slippery. Keep quiet until we have safely crossed the border." I thanked him for his kindness. He said, "let's move," and stepped out of the room. We filed after him.

It was a hauntingly beautiful but cold moonlit night. The whole world seemed to be in deep sleep except us. We walked at a brisk pace. Although we tried to be as quiet as we could, our footsteps sounded abnormally loud. After a journey of over a mile, we arrived at the southern end of the railroad bridge. Despite the bright moonlight, I could not see the northern end of the bridge. The railroad ties of the bridge were frosted white. The moon shone ominously on the river below the bridge. Thinking of crossing the frosted bridge made me distressed.

We started to cross it in a column. I carefully stepped on the ties. But the professional merchants stepped past me quickly as if they were walking on the ground. I started in the middle of the column but quickly fell behind. By the time I had clumsily arrived in the middle of the bridge, all my companions were out of sight. I became extremely troubled. When I stepped on a tie, I slipped and found myself straddled on it. I instinctively grabbed the tie with my two arms. I looked at the river below the bridge and saw the churning black water. I was petrified! It looked as if an evil dragon would rise from it and swallow me whole. Ice fell and was devoured by the water. That could soon be me! I froze with fear, knowing that I could not scream for help. Even if I did, there was no one to come to my aid in this no-man's land. Overcoming my fear, I pulled my feet up and crawled over the ties one by one, like a four-legged animal, and finally reached the other end of the bridge. In retrospect, if it had not been for the ties, I would have fallen to my death.

LOST

By the time I stood up at the northern end of the bridge, the moon was gone, and darkness engulfed the land. It was silent. I was cold and lost. I did not know which direction I should take. Even though I knew North Korean border guards were posted along the railroad somewhere further ahead, I decided to stay with the railroad. I walked for some distance and heard the faint barking of a dog. I judged there might be a farm village not too far from the tracks. Leaving the tracks, I hiked through the frozen rice fields toward the sound of the barking. But for some reason the dog stopped barking. Without the sound, I had no idea which direction to take. I turned around to return to the railroad, but I could no longer see it. I was lost. I wandered around in the cold for a few hours. I didn't even have an overcoat.

Just before dawn, I was startled by a sharp metal clicking and a shout. "Stop there and raise your hands!" I stopped and raised my hands. My heart pounded. Shivers ran down my spine. A dark figure came closer and stopped in front of me. He stuck his rifle in my chest, inspected me, and said, "Boy, where did you come from? Where are you heading?" The gun horrified me. Then I understood that the sharp sound of metal clicking was from him loading his gun.

I responded with a trembling voice, "I came from my house over the railroad tracks. I am going to visit my friends in the next town."

In disbelief, he said, "You are visiting your friend? This early in the morning? There is no town around here. You are lying! You came from the South, didn't you?" I kept silent. When he pulled his gun away from my chest, I was deeply relieved, but I kept trembling. "You look younger than my teenage brother. My parents wouldn't let him go out this early in the morning, especially in the winter. Tell me, where do you live?"

I realized no lie of mine would mislead him. I said, "Sir, I went to Seoul two months ago to search for an educational opportunity. Now I am returning to my parents who live in the northeastern region of this province."

He said, "I am taking you to my guard station. Walk in front of me." He put his rifle on his shoulder and followed a few steps behind me. We walked across the rice fields to a narrow dirt road.

As we arrived at the border guard station, the sun rose above the eastern horizon.

The guard pushed me inside. He did not search me. This made me feel somewhat relaxed. I joined a dozen travelers who had been captured while crossing the border. Some were heading to the South, some the other way. I did not see anyone from my original group. The station was a dilapidated building in the middle of nowhere. All the windows were broken, except those in the office.

The prisoners, including me, huddled and shivered. As the day advanced, more captured travelers were brought in. The prison population grew to about three dozen within a couple of hours. By mid-morning, the sky became ashen, and it was windy. Rain started falling steadily. A lone cold cast iron stove stood in the middle of the bare concrete floor. There was nothing to burn. But the office had a stove which was burning hot.

The guards did not feed us all day long. We were hungry and cold. A couple of prisoners who were familiar with this area told us that there was a beanery over the hill, half a mile or so away. They proposed that we chip in 30 *won* each and ask the officer in charge of the guard station to buy some food for us. They said, "Of course, we should give him a part of the pool." We agreed and chipped in.

The two went into the office and negotiated with the officer in charge. He accepted our proposal and dispatched one of his soldiers to buy food. An hour or so later, he came back with two men and a woman. The two men brought two big clay jars filled with hot tofu and bean sprout soup on their A-frames (farmer's backpacks) along with many brass bowls. The woman carried a pail of cooked rice on her head. We formed a line. She filled the brass bowls with rice and gave us each one bowl. Then the men poured the hot soup over the rice. It was delicious, and I wished for more. The quantity of this supper was only half of the one I had bought at the inn the previous night. I paid twice as much. Some complained about the small amount, but nobody made a big issue out of it.

THE MARCH TO PRISON

After supper, I stood by a window with my hands in my trouser pockets and watched the rainfall, wondering what would happen next. Then an athletic, handsome prisoner in his mid-twenties walked over. He wore a college uniform and a thick, black overcoat. He said, "Good evening, young man. It's lousy weather, isn't it?" I answered that it was. He continued, "Are you alone, or were you separated from your family while crossing?"

I said, "I am alone. I did not have my family with me."

He said, "Let me introduce myself. I study medicine at Severance Medical College in Seoul. I am returning home to visit my parents in Sinuiju City, North Pyongan Province. You bear a striking resemblance to my youngest brother. I have been watching you since I was brought here this morning. You are thinner than he is. Were you going to the South or coming to the North when you were captured?"

I said, "I was coming to the North from Seoul to visit my parents."

"You mean you went to Seoul all by yourself? Don't you think you are too young to venture out on your own? Do you have relatives in Seoul?"

I said, "Yes, I have a distant cousin. He gave me a job with his company. I plan to register in an evening school next spring." As our conversation progressed, I felt more at ease talking to him.

He asked, "Where is your home?"

I said, "About ninety miles northeast of here," and asked, "Are you returning home to open an office in your hometown?"

He said, "No, I have not graduated yet. I shall graduate next spring. My father is a medical doctor, too." He kept silent and watched the rain fall. It became dark.

I broke the silence and asked, "Why have the Russian Occupation

Authorities closed the border when the American counterparts allow us to come and go freely?"

He bent and whispered into my ear, "Don't ask such questions to those whom you do not know well. It's okay with me, though. I will tell you why. Stalin is a brutal communist dictator. He is making North Korea one of his satellite countries. They say that he has murdered more than fifteen million of his own people. He doesn't want the outside world to see his brutality. He is making Kim Il Sung a running dog for him. America is a democratic free nation. People elect their president every four years and their representatives every two years. The American government does not hide what it's doing from their people, unlike Stalin. That's why the American Occupation Authorities allow Koreans to come and go across the border." He cautioned me, "Don't repeat what I have told you to people whom you do not know."

I did not understand everything he said, but I liked that America was a free country and that its government did not hide things from its people. I didn't even know what an election was. I said, "Thank you very much for the information and for your trust in me. I will not repeat this to anyone."

He continued, "One of my classmates at medical school told me that he had been captured by the North Korean border guards while returning to Seoul after he had visited his parents in Pyongyang. He was imprisoned for about a month. They tortured him and confiscated some valuable possessions. Before they released him, they warned him sternly not to go to the South. But when he was freed, he crossed the border anyway and returned safely to the school. I am sure that we will be escorted to Haeju Prison as soon as the rain stops. Once we are imprisoned, we will be there for at least two to three weeks, if not months. Also, they will torture us and confiscate any valuables as they did to my friend." He paused for a moment. Then he said, "No way will I go to prison. I will escape as soon as night falls. Would you like to join me?"

The prospect of imprisonment horrified me. I wanted to join him but decided not to do so. I said, "I want to, but I can't because I do not have a heavy coat to keep me dry and warm. Thank you very much for your offer."

He said, "You are right. Watch for an opportunity to escape. Do not go to the prison. They say the prison does not even have a heating system." Then he left me abruptly without a word. A few minutes later, he came back with an armful of rice straw, spread it on the concrete floor as a mat, and sat down. He invited me to join him. I thanked him and sat down. He said, "I need some sleep," took off his overcoat, and covered both of us. He soon fell asleep and started to snore lightly. As I became warmer, I drifted off, too.

Sometime later, he shook me gently, and whispered, "Tae-hyok, I am leaving now. Do not go to the prison. Watch for a chance to escape." He squeezed my shoulder firmly and said, "Don't get up. Pretend to sleep. Once again, watch for an opportunity. Goodbye."

I whispered back, "I shall. I slept well because of your overcoat. Thank you very much. Good luck!"

He rose and slowly pulled away his overcoat. Cold air engulfed me. He put his coat on and mingled with other prisoners who were walking in place to keep warm. He observed every movement of the guard and stealthily moved toward a broken window in the farthest wall, as if he were looking for a place to fend off the cold wind. He sat against the wall and pulled his overcoat over his head, pretending to sleep.

The guard frequently went in and out of his office. He seemed somewhat lax, perhaps because he was tired or because he thought no prisoner would dare to escape on a wintry, rainy night. Again, he went into the office. At that moment, my friend swiftly jumped out through the broken window and disappeared into the dark. A few moments later, the guard returned, but he did not notice that the young man had escaped. I never saw him again. I followed his advice to watch for an opportunity to escape so that I could safely deliver the money to Mr. Tae-yun's parents.

The rain turned to snow. I got up because I was so cold without my friend's coat. I joined the other prisoners. We huddled together in clusters anywhere we could fend off the cold wind and keep ourselves warm. We struggled to fall asleep. It was too cold for it. Some walked around to generate body heat; some walked in place; some sat on their backpacks and buried their heads between their legs. At last, the long, sleepless night gave way to the brilliant morning sunlight.

The officer in charge of the guard station came out of his office. His cheeks were pink. The stove in his office kept him warm, while the unforgiving wintry weather made the prisoners' faces blue. He hollered in a pompous voice, "You reactionaries, go outside and form a line." We went out to the snow-blanketed ground and formed a single line. His soldiers, armed with rifles, were waiting for us. "You are going to Haeju Prison." He assigned soldiers to the front, middle, and rear of the line, and shouted again, "These three soldiers will escort you. If anyone tries to escape, they will punish you severely." I said to myself, "No matter what you say, I am not going to prison. I will ESCAPE. I must deliver the money to my cousin's parents." He continued, "Don't act foolishly. Now depart." The soldier at the head of the line saluted his commander with "Yes, comrade." Then the soldier yelled at us, "Move!"

The long line of more than three dozen cold, hungry prisoners moved slowly and silently along the narrow road across the snow-covered rice fields. As the journey progressed, my body heat made me warmer. I started limping as if my feet were hurting. I fell behind the rear guard by a few steps to test his watchfulness. Every time I did, he shouted, "Boy, hurry up!" I hobbled faster to catch up. Around noon, we entered the outskirts of East Haeju, a town of about a hundred houses clustered along a dirt road. As the street became busier, the guardsman became more alert, yelling more frequently. Every time he screamed, I responded, "Yes, sir," and pretended to do my best to catch up with him. I hobbled a few steps closer and then drifted back farther when he wasn't watching. I knew that the more people surrounded us, the better my chance of escaping.

A massive, grayish wall loomed in the distance ahead of us. I guessed it was the prison. It might be within less than one hour's walk. Suddenly, I realized that my chance to escape was slipping away rapidly. My anxiety heightened. Unless I acted very soon, there was no way I could avoid imprisonment. I feared that the prison authority would search me thoroughly and confiscate Mr. Tae-yun's money before putting me behind bars.

The rear guard shouted again, "Goddamn boy, hurry up!" He almost frantically waved his rifle and yelled at the top of his lungs. I had been behind him by at least twenty feet. I saw the long stretch of prisoners passing through a busy intersection. It was a small marketplace. Many shoppers and pedestrians crowded the intersection. The guard turned around and barked again, "Hurry up." I yelled back, "Yes, sir," and pretended to hobble harder to catch up. I noticed that he was so busy keeping his other prisoners away from the crowd that he was lax in his attention to me. *This is my only chance to escape. If I don't make it now, I never will.*

As soon as I reached the first store from the intersection, I quickly slipped in through the front door, pretending to be a shopper. I swiftly stepped out to a narrow lane using a side door and briskly walked away from the intersection for a few hundred yards. I looked back and no guard was coming after me. I whispered, "I made it! I escaped imprisonment!" I was sweating profusely and found myself in the middle of a snow-covered rice field.

HITCHHIKING

I cautiously returned to the intersection where I had escaped the guards. I saw neither the guards nor the prisoners, but I was still apprehensive. I went to a back alley and felt safer. I went into a shop and asked the owner where I could get transportation to Sinmak. He said, "Young man, there is no regular transportation to Sinmak from this town, except the occasional truck. You might be able to catch one at an intersection a short distance from here. Once you reach Sariwon City, hitch a ride to Sinmak." He continued, "Or you can take a train from Haeju City, about three miles west of here. I think there is no train to Sariwon City this afternoon." The prison was in Haeju City. I certainly did not want to go near the prison.

I caught a ride on a loaded truck at the intersection that the shop owner had pointed me to just before sunset. I joined two other passengers riding on top of the load. As we went farther inland, the snow became deeper, and the mercury plunged. I was so cold that I scrounged a few empty rice-straw bags and put them over myself to fend off the cold wind and escape hypothermia. After many hours, the truck halted in front of a noodle house, and the driver hollered, "Hey fellas, we are going to eat here." It was great news. My body had become so rigid from the frigid temperature that I struggled to climb down. I practically dragged myself into the restaurant. An old clock on the wall showed midnight—about eight hours' journey in the bitter cold wind. I ordered a bowl of buckwheat noodles in hot broth and slurped it in no time. I was stuffed with the noodles, and the heated *ondol** (concrete floor covered with waxed parchment) thawed my cold body. I fell asleep right there until the driver woke me up several hours later.

I left Sariwon for Sinmak, about thirty miles southeast, in the same truck. Sinmak was southwest of my hometown and the nearest railroad station to it. The two travelers with me had gone in different directions. I was the only hitchhiker. It was a sunny morning, but a very cold one. This part of the trip was much more bearable than the previous one. I arrived in Sinmak in the late afternoon and paid the driver for the ride. I stayed with one of my distant aunts overnight.

A SWEET HOMECOMING

The next day, I left for home after having thanked my aunt for her hospitality. I followed the directions that she had given me earlier. As I traveled on the wintry road, the city faded behind me. I walked all day on snowy mountain passes and valleys, encountering no one.

After more than fifteen miles, I arrived home as the sun was setting. Tae-jun was splitting firewood in the courtyard. I called, "*Hyung-nim!*" He looked up at me and darted into the house without responding to my greeting. He shouted excitedly, "Tae-hyok is home!" The whole family, including my little niece and nephew, ran out of the house, held me by the hands and arms and repeatedly said, "Tae-hyok, welcome home!" They practically carried me into the warm house. What a sweet homecoming!

My mother held my hands between hers, and said, "Your hands are cold," while she rubbed them gently. "How was your trip, crossing the border? It must have been very difficult."

Even though I had had a rough trip, I answered, "*Eomeoni*, it was not too bad." I did not want to give her unnecessary heartache.

My father asked me, "How are Tae-yun and his family doing? Did he give you a job?"

---

* *Ondol* is a traditional Korean floor with a heating system underneath. Made of packed, smooth clay, it contains four or five tunnels leading from the waist-high earthen oven/fireplace (*agungi*) in the kitchen to the chimney. The floor is usually covered with parchment lacquered with soybean oil. When burning wood in the fireplace, the heat travels through the burrows to heat the *ondol* floor.

"Yes, *Abeoji*. He hired me as an office boy for his company. He and two other partners founded it. It is a construction business. Right now, they are renovating two large buildings for the American military."

He said, "That was kind of him. When you return to Seoul, give him my thanks for his kindness."

"Certainly, I will. By the way, *Abeoji*, I have something for Mr. Tae-yun's parents. Would you please send someone to fetch them?"

My father asked, "Tae-wook, would you please inform Tae-yun's parents that Tae-hyok has come home from Seoul? Bring them with you. They must be anxious to hear news of their son's family firsthand." They were close friends of my parents.

"Seoul is a big city," my brother said. "How did you manage to get around?"

I said, "Mr. Tae-yun drew a trolley car route map for me. I carried it wherever I went. I did not experience any trouble. If I had to go to an unfamiliar area, I asked people for directions."

My niece and nephew sat beside me and held my arms. They asked, "*Samchon*, is Seoul many times larger than our town? How many people live there?"

I said, "Seoul is a thousand times larger, and tens of thousands of people live there. The streets are so crowded that people often bump into each other."

Won-sik asked, "*Samchon*, did you see Americans? Are they tall? The other day, a couple of people from the Communist Party came to my school and told us that Americans were ugly and mean. They also said that Americans robbed Koreans of everything, leaving the South Koreans starving. Is that true?"

Before I answered, Tae-jun said, "These communists lie to our children. Americans don't steal anything from Koreans. Tae-hyok, tell him what you have seen of Americans."

I said, "Won-sik, Americans don't steal anything from Koreans. They bring food from America and distribute it to Koreans for free. Without this food, many people might go to bed hungry. The food includes wheat and corn flour, crushed barley, and egg-yolk powder. I, too, receive food rations. Sometimes they supply candies and cookies for children. And yes, they are very tall."

Shortly after, my brother returned with Mr. Tae-yun's parents and his younger brother. We all stood up and welcomed them. Before I greeted them formally, Mr. Tae-yun's father said, "We are glad to see you home. You must have had a hard time crossing the border. How are my son, Tae-yun, and my grandchildren doing? Are they well?"

"They are healthy and doing well, sir," I said. "You have one grandson and two granddaughters. Their names are Jung-sik, Jung-jah and Kwang-jah."

Mr. Tae-yun's mother sighed deeply and said, "We haven't even seen the younger ones. We saw our grandson once when his parents brought him to us six years ago. He was a baby then," and she wiped her tears with her apron. "I wonder when this country is going to unify."

I took the money from under my long johns and said, "Sir, these 6,000 *won* are from your son," and handed it to him. "I am glad that I could deliver it to you safely."

He took it with trembling hands, and silently looked at it and me alternatively for a few moments. Then he said, "Thank you, Tae-hyok. This is a lot of money." His wife and his younger son Tae-un looked on, astonished. They said in unison, "He shouldn't have sent us such a large sum of money. He should have used it for his family." The old man took one 1,000 *won* bill and said, "This is to thank you," and gave it to me.

"Sir, this money is a gift from your son. I do not deserve it. I will not accept it. Your son gave me a job. Without him, I could not stay in Seoul. He also gave me 1,000 *won* to cover my expenses for this trip." I pushed his hand back. My parents and brothers agreed with me.

"I wish you would accept it," he murmured. He gave all the money to his wife to keep and said, "Thank you, Tae-hyok. Please thank my son for the gift when you return to Seoul. Tell him that we are all healthy and well. Also tell him that he should not send us money anymore."

"Certainly, I will, sir," I answered. I felt lighthearted and happy at having accomplished my task. I spent two precious weeks with my family before returning to Seoul.

CHAPTER 8

Homecoming for Winter

November 1947 - April 1948

For the next year, I lived in a small room at Mr. Tae-yun's house and worked hard, saving every bit of money I could for school. I almost had enough to register for evening courses in English and mathematics. Despite my difficulties, my hope for an education soared.

Then, a thunderbolt! One late November day in 1947, Mr. Tae-yun told me that his company was folding because there weren't enough projects to support it. Today was my last day. Devastated, I dropped my head, staring pointlessly at the floor. He said something that I didn't hear. I took deep breaths. *What would I do? Winter would arrive soon.*

He waited for me to calm down and said that since he, too, would be out of work, he hoped to set up a small civil engineering firm in the next few months. While handing over my last pay, he advised me to return home for the winter, then come back to Seoul the next spring to work for him. He gave my shoulder an affectionate squeeze, and I dragged myself out of his office.

I had crossed the 38th Parallel which divided North and South Korea three times. Each crossing had become harder as the North Korean border guards patrolled more frequently. Just thinking about crossing the border again made me shiver.

Wanting to stay in Seoul, I looked for work until the first snowfall, but had no success. My savings were almost gone except for a small amount to cover my travel expenses to return home. I set out in mid-December via train to Kaesŏng City Railroad Station, the last stop before the border. I asked the owner of a beanery to direct me to a lodge where cross-border travelers or merchant smugglers would rest before crossing into North Korea at midnight.

He kindly gave me detailed directions to a lodge just south of the border, about three miles north of the city. He also told me that rumor had it that lately, North Korea had increased the number of border guards. Fewer people were traveling across the border these days.

His somber words led me to a quandary. If I didn't find a northbound merchant, I would have to cross the border all by myself along a completely unfamiliar trail. I feared that I might get lost and freeze to death. I set out and followed his directions toward the lodge anyway. After a couple of hours of walking through the snow along narrow country roads, I arrived at the inn late in the afternoon.

The owner of the lodge welcomed me and said, "If you are crossing the 38th Parallel tonight, you will have a few companions," while leading me to a small room.

Entering it quietly, I found six people sleeping. I took my place in a corner and thanked heaven for these traveling companions. Lying on the heated floor warmed my body. I fell asleep until the innkeeper woke us up for supper around 10 p.m. I said hello to the travelers for the first time since my arrival.

I put an extra pair of socks on to keep my feet warm for the snow-covered trail. A few inches of snow had fallen while we slept, and a full moon illuminated the fields and mountains. I tied a large white cotton square of cloth around my neck and waist to blend in with the snowy environment and to keep me warm. I didn't have a winter coat.

When we were ready to set out, one of the travelers in his thirties who spoke in the same northwestern accent as I said, "Young man, it's a clever idea to wear white. How old are you?"

"Sixteen, sir."

He continued, "Stick with us so you don't get lost. If you fall behind, no one will wait for you."

I thanked him for his kindness. A group of four or five more travelers joined us. Everyone except me had a large backpack. I had only one algebra book and a few small cans of DDT (pesticide that my family used in our home to kill insects and lice) wrapped in a square cloth across my back.

After a couple of hours of trekking through deep snow, the man in front stopped abruptly at a ridge and whispered, "We are crossing the border. No talking until we reach an inn on the other side of the mountain!" The travelers wore leather boots and hiked quickly, while I fell behind because my cheap shoes with thin soles did not provide me with a firm footing.

When climbing down to the foothills of the mountain, abrupt shouting and a few rounds of earsplitting gunshots broke the silence. Instantly, we ran in all directions. But because I was far behind the group, I just lay flat on the snow. I shivered despite the body heat from the arduous trekking.

A guard yelled, "Stop there! Don't move!" Then, another shot followed. Someone frantically responded, "Okay, okay. Don't shoot!" More shouting went on. But I didn't understand what they were saying. It was too far to hear clearly. Apparently, some of the merchants must have been caught.

I prayed to the spirit of the mountain to keep me hidden. Lying flat on the snow caused my teeth to rattle and my body to shiver. However, I did not dare move. I waited for what seemed like an eternity for the guards to leave. Eventually, the silence returned. Still, I feared that the guards might be nearby, watching me silently. But, since I was so cold that I couldn't stay put any longer, I cautiously stood up and surveyed my surroundings. The moon was sinking behind the western mountain crest. An absolute stillness dominated the night.

Phew, the dreadful North Korean border guards were all gone. My fellow travelers were nowhere to be seen. I was alone and had no idea which direction to go in to reach the safe lodge on the other side of the mountain that the trailblazer had mentioned earlier. I didn't even know which mountain he had referred to because there were many around.

While I wondered which route to take, a sudden, distant howl from a wolf scared me. Despite the risk of running into the border guards down there, I immediately began walking along the uncharted valley as fast as I could because I would rather be arrested by the guards than torn apart by the wolves. Stumbling and sweating, I emerged from the wooded valley to narrow farm fields. The snow in the fields, not as deep as on the trail, helped me accelerate my walk. After a couple more miles of travel, at last, I reached a rarely used, primitive country road between rice paddies. Then the faint crow of a rooster in the distance sounded sweet to my ears. It not only indicated a farm village somewhere down the valley, but also heralded the arrival of dawn.

I continued along the narrow road until it joined a wider, flatter one. By then, dawn had broken over the eastern sky, and a few tendrils of smoke rose from distant farmhouses nestled in the rolling hills. My fear of the wolves vanished, but the specter of the guards somewhere along the road kept me alert. If I found anyone suspicious, I would slip into a frozen rice paddy and pretend to skate.

By sunrise, I reached a highway (a dirt road) where about a dozen farmers, some walking together, others individually, were heading for a local *jang*, a traditional Korean flea market held every five days. I joined the farmers, pretending to be a boy from a nearby village, greeting them, "Good morning, sirs." I had no idea where or how far from the border I was, but I didn't dare ask them for fear that some of them might be communists or communist sympathizers.

As I followed them, I listened intently to their conversations, hoping they would mention which *jang* they were heading to, which might suggest my general location. One man said that after having paid 30 percent of his crop as *hyeun-mull-se,* he did not have much left to sell in the *jang* for family necessities, and wondered how his family would manage through the next harvest. Others commiserated with him and said, "We are in the same situation, and we'll die together," and laughed.

They frequently mentioned *jang* in general terms, but without specifics, so I could not figure out where I was. When I arrived at a three-way intersection, road signs in both Russian and Korean provided unexpected help. The signs showed distances to each town—Sinmak to the northwest, Singye to the northeast, and Namchon to the south. Although I had never been there before, I knew enough geography to have an idea of where I was. Apparently, I had covered at least eight miles from the border inside North Korea. I had also drifted northwest, perhaps by more than six miles, from my planned homebound route through Singye, where my sister lived. I figured that taking the road to Singye would add more than six miles to my journey and might be through higher elevation than that to Sinmak, where my former neighbor, a friend of my mother's, lived. I decided to take the road to Sinmak.

I quietly followed the farmers. Even though they did not walk faster than when I had joined them, I found myself falling behind. By mid-morning, they were out of sight. I was so tired and hungry that I sat on a cold rock by the roadside, rested my head between my knees, and fell asleep.

Then, somebody shook me by the shoulder and said, "Wake up. You could freeze to death here." The kind man pulled me up by the hand. "You must have had a long journey. There is a restaurant near here where you can buy a big bowl of *onban* which will energize you. Let's go!"

Despite the warm mid-day sun, I was shivering. I followed him, dragging my feet. Soon, we reached an eatery. He led me into a crowded room and said to the server, "This young man is cold and hungry. He needs a big bowl of *onban*." He left before I could thank him. A dozen customers were busily eating their lunch at a long rectangular table with short legs.

While eating, I heard someone say that the North Korean government had tightened the border because it wanted to freeze the currency and issue new money. He lamented, "I don't know what the hell is going on."

A couple of other people responded, "So that's why more border guards were patrolling last night."

Since I gathered that those two people must have been cross-border merchants heading for Pyongyang through Sinmak, I boldly asked them whether they were heading for the town, and how far it was. They said they were, and it was about forty ris away.

I asked if I could accompany them, and they kindly allowed me to do so. We set out for Sinmak immediately. When we arrived at the town in the early evening, they went directly to the Sinmak Railroad Station, and I went to the home of my mother's friend (a distant aunt) for an overnight stay.

She and her son Tae-kook, who was in his mid-twenties, welcomed me. I appreciated her generosity. But soon I regretted that I had come because Tae-kook, a railroad engineer, started to lecture me by praising Kim Il Sung (the founder of Communist North Korea under the tutelage of Stalin) and Communism. He also gave me unwanted advice that I should not return to South Korea because Americans were evil capitalists exploiting our country. Recognizing that he had become a hardcore communist, I nodded silently. I was glad he went to bed early because he had to go to work before dawn.

Early the next morning, my aunt's son left for work. I felt relieved by his absence even though I didn't think he would have turned me in to a local internal security office because I was a relative. A year earlier, when I had visited the family on the way home after having escaped the North Korean border guards, he had thought about escaping to South Korea. I wondered what had converted him to communism in so short a time.

At daybreak, I expressed my sincere thanks for her kindness and continued my journey of more than twelve miles on mountain paths and narrow country roads. Since, from my previous travel, I knew there was no eatery along the way, I bought a couple of cheap rice candy bars for lunch from a mom-and-pop shop on the outskirts of Sinmak using my last coins. I silently exclaimed, "Now, I am penniless! But I shall be home by the end of the day!" and I walked faster.

Shortly the city street connected to a country dirt road which ran between snow-covered farm fields. Even though there were low straw-thatched farmhouses along the way, I did not see anyone on the road. Perhaps the farmers were enjoying their breakfast around warm fire pots. As my journey progressed, all the farmhouses disappeared. The road gradually narrowed and started to climb up the southern slope of a mountain like a snake, sometimes under thick oak trees and pines.

The warm sunshine melted the snow where travelers had stepped, defining the path clearly, which made my travel easier. Lacking decent infrastructure, many people used these rugged mountain roads for their inter-town travels. Animal tracks crisscrossed the virgin snow beside the main patch. The wolf tracks made my hair stand on end. At midday, when I reached the crest of the trail, I finally saw a repairman on a gigantic utility transmission tower not too far down the other side of the mountain. I didn't like the northern slope of the trail because the snow was deep, slippery, and cold. I began to sing and yell to scare any animals away.

By mid-afternoon, I arrived at the foot of the path where a few farmhouses lay scattered around. Children in homemade clothes were playing on the glistening ice in a rice paddy. Before I went to Seoul, every winter my friends and I used to flood a rice paddy near my hometown to make a big ice rink and play on it just like those kids.

Suddenly my heart pounded. I knew that my home was only about five miles away, and the roads ahead were relatively level. Picking up my pace, I arrived home just before dusk set in. As soon as I stepped inside the court-yard, I hollered, "*Umma, Appa,* I am home!"

At my unexpected return, my whole family, including my young nieces and nephew, burst out of the house and welcomed me like a son who had been lost. They repeated, "Oh, Tae-hyok! Welcome home!" According to the Korean custom, I bowed to pay respect to my parents. Instead of responding to my greetings, they grabbed my hands and pulled me inside, saying "You must be hungry and cold." Yun-ok and Won-sik grabbed me by the sleeves and called excitedly, "*Samchon!*" My parents let me sit by a *hwaro* (fire pot). My mother held my cold hands over it and rubbed them gently. She did this every time I returned from Seoul. "Your hands are chapped and bloody," she said, warm tears dropping on the backs of my hands. She brought castor oil in a small dish and massaged it softly into my hands.

My father was a very kind man, but one of few words. He said, "Judging from your chapped hands, you must have had a hard time. I'm glad you came home," and patted me affectionately on the back. I was happy to be with my family, sitting on a heated floor.

RETURNING TO SEOUL

As Kim Il Sung, the Russian-appointed North Korean dictator, sank his evil claws deeper into the conservative society of my small hometown, my life at home became very stressful. I had to avoid the regional cell leader of the Communist Party. He was an uneducated farm laborer who had become an important party member, the only communist in the surrounding communities. Almost every week, accompanied by a representative from the county headquarters, he called for a propaganda meeting. He praised Kim Il Sung as the greatest leader and a patriot. He forced people to recite Kim's twenty-point policy statement, and demonized American capitalists as exploiters of the poor. The twenty points outlined Kim's plan to change Korea into a social-ist state. I doubted that the cell leader understood what that policy meant.

Even worse, the party forced all levels of schools to indoctrinate children with the same propaganda. It organized a league of Communist youth consisting of children seventeen and under throughout the country and instructed them to report to the party anyone who spoke against the great leader or the party. My hometown couldn't escape this network. One day, the branch president of my village, Chang-whan Lee, who was once a good friend of mine, visited me and invited me to join the league. I realized his visit was a threat, not a friendly gesture.

Since I couldn't put up with this stifling life any longer, I decided to return to Seoul as soon as spring arrived. When I told my parents about my decision, they said that life under the communists was getting harder as their grip tightened. The communist regime had taken 30 percent of the previous year's harvest as tax. Furthermore, those communists might brand me as a reactionary because of my sojourn in Seoul. Based on those omens, my family supported my decision wholeheartedly, even though we did not know when we might see each other again.

My parents provided me with 2,000 *won* in the old currency which Kim Il Sung's regime had replaced with new currency a few months earlier. The old currency was still in circulation in South Korea. I returned to Seoul in late April of 1948 after sneaking across the border by night, hoping Mr. Tae-yun would hire me as he had done when I had first come to Seoul. Alas, my hopes were dashed. He had gotten a low-paying government job instead of forming his own business. Due to his low-paying job and food rationing, he could not feed me, but he and his wife kindly offered me a place to stay while I looked for work. To avoid awkwardness during mealtimes, I left the house before their breakfast and came back late in the evening after dinner.

One fine May day, I was walking aimlessly through the streets with a million different thoughts. I was unemployed and hungry. I had been searching for work since my arrival, surviving on one or two *zinbangs* (small, steamed rolls stuffed with sweetened mashed red beans) a day for the last three weeks. My money was almost gone. I wondered if I should return to my parents in North Korea for millet and a bowl of vegetable soup. But life in Stalinist North Korea was stifling, and returning home would mean the end of my hopes for an education. No, I would take any job to stay in South Korea. But how could I find one? According to the newspapers, more than one third of the people in Seoul were out of work. I only had an elementary school education.

Then out of the blue, I thought about a houseboy position with the U.S. Army. Early the next morning, I went to a U.S. Army camp near the Government Complex in central Seoul. The camp looked empty except for a lone Korean guard at the main entrance. I greeted him and said that I wanted to apply for a houseboy job.

He chuckled and said, "Young man. There is no work here. All the American soldiers at this camp returned to America a few weeks ago, and all the Korean employees have been let go. As you can see, this camp is empty. Only a few Korean guards are still employed." He took out an American lighter from his pocket and lit a cigarette. He inhaled the smoke and exhaled, making rings. He continued, "All but a few hundred American soldiers have withdrawn from Korea. Thousands of Korean employees have lost their jobs." He paused for a few moments and repeated, "There is no work!" He sighed deeply and murmured, "I will lose my own job within a couple of weeks when the Seoul City Government takes over the camp."

Disappointed, I bid him goodbye and continued my job search, knocking at the door of every shop along Chong-ro Street, a retail center, to no avail. Discouraged and hungry, I went to Pagoda Park nearby and sat on a bench to rest, watching a few pigeons pecking at the bare ground. Perhaps they were searching for something to eat as I did for a job. Hunger and fatigue made me doze off.

PART THREE

The South
Korean Army

1948 - 1950

CHAPTER 9

Joining the South Korean Army

May - September 1948

Suddenly a loud honk woke me. I saw three South Korean Army soldiers hop off an army truck and set up a table with a placard reading RECRUITING FOR THE ARMY COMMUNICATION SCHOOL. Curious, I approached and asked how much the tuition would be, and what they would teach.

They laughed and answered that the school would cost me nothing and would teach me mathematics, physics, English, and more. The government would pay for everything, including room and board, clothing, and a monthly salary. I thought this was a heavenly gift that came at the right time. I signed up immediately. The lead recruiter told me to return at noon the next day, and they would take me to the school in Susaek, a couple of miles northwest of Seoul, with other recruits.

That evening I visited Mr. Tae-yun and his wife and informed them that I had signed up for the Army Communication School and would be leaving the next morning. I thanked them for their generosity.

Mr. Tae-yun said, "Don't mention it. I wish I could do more for you. But I am glad that you have signed up for the school instead of going back to North Korea. I am sure you will do well."

Mrs. Tae-yun congratulated me and said, "Before you leave, I would like to tell you something. As you know, my family lived with us for about a year after they escaped North Korea. During that period, my half-brother frequently stole money from my handbag and my husband's wallet. But you have never done anything like that to us even when you were out of work. We admire your honesty and integrity." She paused, then continued, "I do not know much about the army school, but I am confident that you will do well."

Her unexpected comment not only surprised me but also warmed my heart. After saying goodnight, I returned to my room to pack. All I had was a futon, a quilt, and a couple of books. One was my precious seventh grade algebra book which I had brought from home. The other was an old chemistry book which I had purchased from a roadside vendor when I had had a job. I had been teaching myself algebra fairly well but didn't understand chemistry at all. I decided to take them with me anyway and to give away the futon and quilt because I wouldn't need them in the army.

The next morning, despite their tight financial situation, Mrs. Tae-yun prepared a special breakfast for me, consisting of rice and beef soup mixed with egg drops. In those days, beef was scarce. After surviving on a couple of *zinbangs* a day for so long, I relished the feast and thanked her for it. After breakfast, I asked her if she could give my futon and quilt to anyone who might need them. I told her that I had washed the covers a few days earlier.

She said that there were many North Korean refugees who had little. She would give my futon and quilt to a refugee family down the street.

When I bid farewell to Mr. and Mrs. Tae-yun, they escorted me to the gate and said, "Take care of yourself. Visit us when you have a vacation. Goodbye."

I bowed to them again and left for Pagoda Park with my two books. I arrived hours before noon, with as much excitement as if it were the first day of high school. Despite my being so early, the recruiters were already in place, but they were not the same people I had seen the previous day. Their placard simply read, "Army Recruiters." I wondered if the recruiters from the communication school had already left with the other applicants. Approaching the new recruiters, I said that I had applied for the army communication school on the previous day and asked if they were from the same group.

They said, "Yes. You wait there with the other recruits until further notice." Relieved, I joined a group of men under an old pine tree. They appeared to be in their twenties, thirties, or even forties. I was the only one in his teens. A man in his early forties asked me in a northeastern accent, "Boy, what are you doing here? You are too young to be a soldier." He might have been sympathetic. However, feeling insulted, I moved away without answering. I had a premonition that the recruiters might drop me because I was a scrawny, underweight boy even though I had just turned seventeen a month ago. While I was looking for a job, some unkind shopkeepers had commented, "You are too skinny!"

Noon came and went without any transportation coming for us. Finally, late in the afternoon, two rickety civilian trucks came by, and the recruiters herded us onto them. The trucks jolted forward, spewing foul-smelling smoke. I had no idea which direction we were heading in because we were packed in so closely. Although the truck was open, the odious emissions and body heat from others choked me so badly that I couldn't take it any longer and elbowed my way out to the rail of the cargo bay to inhale fresh air. Then I realized we were heading northeast, not northwest to Susaek. I asked the men next to me, if we had signed up for the Army Communication School in Susaek, why were the trucks driving northeast?

They answered that they had signed up for the 1st Infantry Regiment, and we were heading for its training center in Tae-neung. They proudly said that they were lucky to join the most elite unit in the South Korean Army. Another man behind me said that he, too, had signed up for the communication school the previous day. He conjectured that the recruiters might first drop those recruits off for the 1st Regiment. Then they would drive us to Susaek. But an uneasy feeling crept into my heart.

We arrived at an army camp parade ground late that afternoon. I saw four or five groups of soldiers, three columns in each, march forward, turn around, and march back at their drill sergeants' barks. Their movements were so precise that they looked like a machine.

The trucks stopped in front of a two-story red brick building with a long one-story wing on each side. Then the leading recruiter hollered, "You all get off the trucks." When we all disembarked, the leader shouted, "Now you are soldiers of the 1st Regiment." Then he announced a roll call and instructed us to form a column as each name was called, pointing at the ground a few feet from him. He yelled at us as if we were already his soldiers.

Confused and disappointed, I went to the leader and said, "Sir, I signed up for the Army Communication School, not for the 1st Regiment. Please take me to the school in Susaek, sir."

d into my eyes and asked in a sarcastic tone, "What did you say?" repeated what I had told him.

̣̣̣ ̣̣̣ ̣med at the top of his lungs, "I heard you, little son of a bitch! You belong to the 1ˢᵗ Regiment, not to the communication school. You are not going anywhere. If you mention the goddamn communication school one more time, I will give you a *kihap* (beating). Get back to the group."

I was shocked. Fear-stricken, I returned to the group. Suddenly I felt lonely and wondered, "What is next? Where is my communication school? Have I lost an opportunity to get an education?"

He began a roll call. As it progressed, the column grew longer. At the end, I was the only one not called. He shouted, "Hey, boy. Come forward!" When I did, he asked my name, date of birth, and address. After taking my personal information, he ordered me to join the column at the last position.

He barked, "Attention! Number off from the front!" He then split us into two groups, Platoon 1 with odd numbers and Platoon 2 with even numbers. Against my will, I became a member of the 1ˢᵗ Regiment.

BASIC TRAINING CAMP

A soldier with three bright red chevrons on each of his sleeves stood in front of us and yelled, "Atten…tion! I am your drill sergeant…" After delivering a short speech in a roaring voice, he led us to the camp quartermaster where each of us received personal supplies. They consisted of a pair of fatigues, a pair of socks, a pair of leather boots, a T-shirt, underpants, a blanket, a stiff fabric belt and a hat. They were all used American military gear.

Having made sure that everybody received his portion, the drill sergeant led us to a barrack and assigned each of us to one of the many mattresses spread on the bare wooden floor in four rows. Then he ordered us to replace our civilian clothes with the military clothes that we had just received. I did as ordered and wrapped my civilian belongings in my shirt. They didn't supply us with duffle bags.

Unfolding my army clothes, I wondered how well they would fit my scrawny body. I was five-feet-six inches tall and weighed only 86 pounds. Everything was grossly oversized! The supposed-to-be legless underpants reached my knees. To keep the briefs from slipping down, I made a few holes along the waistline, snaked my civilian fabric belt through the holes, and tied it around my waist. It served me well. The T-shirt fared no better; the hemline dropped below my knees and the neckline almost slid off my shoulders.

The fatigues were made of sturdy fabric with alternating stripes of avocado and light green. They were coated with some rubbery stuff which emitted an unpleasant smell. Later I learned that the American military had coated fatigues to repel mosquitoes in the Pacific Theater during World War II. Upon donning them, I found that they were too large, and they transformed me into an instant clown.

Similarly, my feet were swimming in the dirty, worn-out boots I received. They had leggings attached. Since there was no way I could wear them, I exchanged them for a better pair, but even that pair was big. I put them on over the rolled trouser legs and tightened the leggings to secure them.

Another soldier who had only one chevron joined the drill sergeant. The sergeant introduced him as his assistant and told us to obey him. Then he left. The assistant picked a few recruits and led them to the camp kitchen. They brought food in five-gallon-sized aluminum buckets and piles of discolored aluminum plates and bowls. After having the bowls filled with food, he ordered the rest of us to form a single line and each take one plate of the main dish and one bowl of soup.

Since the camp provided neither a mess hall nor tables, we sat cross-legged on our mattresses, placing our plates and bowls on them as well. The main dish was a small mound of boiled, bloated wheat grains, not even crushed, mottled with rice. The soup was chopped Chinese cabbage in soy sauce stock. I wondered how I would digest those wheat grains. Despite how undesirable the food looked, I devoured it. Afterwards, I was still hungry.

I noticed that there were a few extra plates with heaps of food and soup bowls left on the floor. I expected that it would be equally distributed among us. A stocky guy wearing only a T-shirt and better fitting pants took all but one plate and stashed them away on a shelf above his mattress. Having survived on a couple of *zinbangs* a day for the past few weeks, I thought his action was grossly unfair. I protested, "Hey, you are not the only one who is hungry. Everybody in this room is hungry. Split the food!"

He stared at me and said, "Do you know who I am?"

"Yeah, you are a greedy pig!" Being forced to join the 1st Regiment rather than going to the communications school made me emotional and talk back.

Sudden whacks across my face, right and left! I saw stars in my eyes, and pain pierced my cheeks. I stumbled on the floor and yelled, "You, son of a bitch, why did you hit me?"

"How dare you talk to me like that? I am a *kobyung*," he said and kicked me in the thighs. "Don't you know I am a *kobyung*? You had better know what a *kobyung* is!" and he went back to his place.

I sat speechless for a while, and then tried to get up. But the pain in my legs pulled me back down to the floor. While I was nursing my physical pain and wounded ego, one of the recruits in his early thirties sat beside me. He said in the same northwestern accent as mine that I shouldn't challenge that *kobyung* even though I was right; and for my own sake I would be better off apologizing. I asked what *kobyung* meant.

He explained that a *kobyung* literally meant an old soldier. However, in a basic training camp, a private who had just finished his basic training was also called a *kobyung* and could be as cruel as a slave driver to new recruits for no reason.

After a few minutes' pondering, for my own peace of mind, I bit the bullet, went over to that SOB *kobyung* and said, "Sir, I am sorry for what I said to you. Would you please forgive me?"

He responded authoritatively, "I will forgive you this time. You should learn how to behave toward *kobyungs*. Do you understand? Go!"

I thanked him and left. He was shipped out to his new assignment the following day. I never saw him again. Alas, reorganization sent the recruit who had advised me the previous day to another company before I had a chance to ask his name.

The assistant drill sergeant instructed us to go to bed at the ten o'clock evening bugle and get up at the six o'clock morning bugle. During bedtime neither light nor loitering was allowed.

But the room became pitch dark long before ten because the North Korean authorities cut off the power supply to South Korea, which relied on it. The reason was that when the United States and the Soviet Union had divided the Korean peninsula into North and South Koreas at the end of World War II, more than 95 percent of the output of the hydro-electric power plants in the peninsula went to North Korea, leaving only a couple of small plants in South Korea.

When I lay on my dirty mattress, my thighs ached where the *kobyung* had kicked me earlier. How long would I have to put up with this kind of injustice? Should I escape in the dark? Where would I go? Would I return home to North Korea? No way. I will stay at this training center. A good day will come soon. Missing my family, I sighed. I silently said, "Good night, Mom, Dad, Tae-wook and Tae-jun," and drifted into oblivion.

The morning bugle blasted across the camp, and our assistant drill sergeant roared, "Get up! Get the hell out of here to the parade ground. Hurry up!" After frantically jumping into my clownish fatigues and oversized boots, I dashed out of the barracks to the parade field.

My drill sergeant barked that we should form a single column as we arrived. When I reached the group, he shouted, "You, little one, go to the end of the column!" He ordered, "Number off from the front!" I was the last number. Pointing at a sparsely vegetated hill at the end of the field, he said, "Do you see a *yapo* (field artillery) at the top of that hill? That is Yapo Hill." The hill looked about one hundred feet high. He continued, "Now, you slow ones need more exercise. Everyone numbered thirty and up, run to the top of Yapo Hill and then return. Form a new column as you get back. Do you understand? Now go!"

A couple dozen of us slow ones ran toward the hill as if we were in a serious competition. It was a RACE. I did my best to get as close to the front as I could, but the heavy boots made me fall farther behind. Looking up the hill, I found it was much steeper than I thought. The track to the *yapo* was like a sandy, dry riverbed, straight up to the top. The track was not constructed, but over the years since the birth of the regiment, thousands of slow soldiers like me had toiled up and down the hill, breaking the shallow topsoil and exposing the granite bedrock here and there. Whatever vegetation might have been there along the track had been plucked away or worn out by soldiers trying to get to the top.

The track was so slippery that I had difficulty finding firm footholds. Often,

I climbed one step up and slid back two steps. My boots made it harder. By the time I made it to the *yapo* after much struggle and returned, panting heavily, I was again at the last position in a new column. Twice more he made the slowest half of my column repeat that run. Each time, I came in last. At the end, I was dead tired.

After ridiculing and tormenting us for our slowness, the drill sergeant gathered all the recruits in three columns, each with the tallest in the front and the shortest at the end. Though I was the youngest recruit, I was not the shortest, thus avoiding the last position in my column. Then he directed us to do calisthenics according to his instructions. I did all the motions easily except for kicking. When I kicked the air, I feared that my heavy, oversized boots might fly off my feet. After a series of exercises, he dismissed us for breakfast. I was greatly relieved, but wondered how I could endure the brutal training with my boots.

"You should probably get new boots," said a recruit who sat next to me while eating breakfast. He introduced himself as Lee Jong-kook. Little did I know at the time that he'd become one of my best friends.

We kept talking and I learned that he and his family were farmers, but that his parents had died when he was seven years old. He later dropped out of grammar school to work on his relative's farm. Like my family in North Korea, they sounded poor.

In the training camp environment, drill sergeants were regarded as dictators. Recruits feared to approach them. However, I couldn't go on with these lousy boots any longer, so I mustered all my courage and approached my drill sergeant. I saluted him and said with apprehension, "Sir, my boots are too big and heavy for me to move around. Besides, they hurt my feet badly. Could you arrange for me to get a better-fitting pair, sir?"

He looked down at my feet and said, "Follow me." He took me to the camp quartermaster sergeant and asked him to give me a smaller pair of boots. Surprisingly the latter exchanged not only my ugly boots for a smaller size but also my clownish fatigues with smaller ones. I thanked him and my drill sergeant for my new outfit. It made me so much lighter and more agile that I felt like flying.

That morning, the drill sergeant, accompanied by his assistant, brought our platoon list and announced our army serial numbers. Then he sternly instructed each of us to memorize our individual dog tag numbers because all personal information would be recorded under this unique number and referenced by it. Each number consisted of seven digits, the first three representing our regiment and the last four our individual ID.

To avoid the Yapo Hill run, I woke up early the next morning, put on my uniform quietly and returned to sleep. When the wake-up bugle blasted at six o'clock, I jumped up and ran out of the barracks to the parade ground to get as close to the front of the column as possible. To my surprise, I was not the only one who had put on his fatigues and shoes before everyone else. A few ran out ahead of me, taking front positions in the column. Apparently, some of them must have gone to bed without taking off their clothes. When all the recruits had lined up in a single column, the drill sergeant ordered the same rat race as the previous day for those with numbers thirty and up. Thanks to my new boots and my early morning preparation, I easily avoided the Yapo Hill run.

While the slow soldiers were doing the rat race, the assistant drill sergeant taught the rest of us the Army Anthem, *Hwarang Ga*, which I had never heard before. Despite being choppy and unromantic, the song was immeasurably more delightful than the run. When the Yapo Hill runners joined us, the assistant ordered the entire platoon to form a parade and report to the drill sergeant. In turn, the drill sergeant told us that the camp was experiencing a water shortage, so we would have to do our morning wash in a brook less than half a mile down the hill. Then he shouted, "Forward march! One two, one two ... Sing *Hwarang Ga*." We marched toward the brook while singing the anthem. As hundreds of heavy boots trampled the dirt road leading to the creek, clouds of dust rose, causing me to cough frequently. I marched alongside two friends I had made, Lee Jong-kook and Oh Munchan. Oh Munchan was from North Korea as well. His father owned a movie theater, and his family was wealthy, but he had come to the South and volunteered to join the army.

Upon reaching the stream, the sergeant hollered, "Wash in fifteen minutes. Now go!" We scattered swiftly along both banks of the creek. Alas, the shallow water was almost dormant. Brownish green algae covered the creek bed. Various water-borne insects crawled on the brook bed or swam in the water.

"Gross!" Oh Munchan said to me and Lee Jong-kook. There were many shallow brooks in my hometown valley, but I had never seen any brook as dirty as this one. Apparently, the long drought had almost dried up the brook. To make matters worse, some guys had dug into the bed with their bare hands to collect more water, muddying it. I reluctantly dipped my hands into the dirty water, scooped some carefully to avoid insects, and washed my face without soap. Since I felt as though insects were squirming on my face, I hurriedly wiped it with my fatigue sleeves. My face might have been cleaner before washing than after. I wondered how long we had to put up with these miserable, unhealthy conditions. The fifteen minutes expired quickly, and the sergeant shouted, "Time is up. Get back into line. Quick, quick."

When we returned to the camp, the sergeant barked, "Atten...tion! Now, breakfast time. You finish breakfast and return to the parade ground, right here, by eight o'clock sharp. Do you understand?"

We all shouted back, "Yes, sir."

"Dismissed!"

We ran to the barracks, hurriedly ate our breakfast, and rushed back to the parade ground after wiping food particles off our plates with newspapers, handkerchiefs, or whatever was handy because there was no water available for washing them.

For the next few days, under the scorching summer sun, the drill sergeant and his assistant trained us to shed our civilian mentality and converted us into machines so that we would act as if we were one body. He taught us how to salute, turn left, turn right, turn around 180 degrees, march forward, march backward, and other basics for the making of a soldier. He dictated every movement according to his script. When he yelled, "Salute," we stood straight, with our chests protruding, our heads looking straight ahead, and our left arms down beside our left legs. Then we had our right arm, with open hand and palm down, stretched out horizontally at the shoulder level. Then we bent our lower arm inward, in an acute triangle, and had the middle fingertip slightly touch the forehead midway between our right eye and right temple.

While the sergeant inspected each of us for proper posture, we had to keep ourselves in the prescribed position for ten to fifteen minutes. Holding my arm up motionlessly for that long made it ache. If he caught you in an improper posture, he yelled in your face, "You idiot," and forced your offending limbs into place.

He always shouted. When he gave us a fifteen-minute break once every two hours, we drank a ladle of water from the aluminum pails which daily detail duty recruits had brought from the kitchen. Even though the water became warm under the sun, it tasted delicious and quenched our thirst.

After three days of training from 8 a.m. to 5 p.m., we became one good robot. We were able to march forward and turn around 180 degrees or turn right or left like one machine at his barks. In addition to our physical training, every evening, by candlelight, the sergeant taught us the Army Regulations and the names and ranks of our commanders from the president all the way down to the drill sergeant. Despite our exhaustion, we had to put up with this tedious lesson for several hours.

One afternoon, the sergeant and his assistant led us out of the camp to country roads. The roads were so narrow and winding that he broke our parade form into one long column and let us walk freely along the roads like school children taking a field trip to the countryside. We didn't know where we were heading, but we enjoyed the trip very much after four days of a restrictive environment. After about an hour's walk, we arrived at the guard house of a camp fenced with barbed wire, a couple of miles from our training center. The drill sergeant talked with the guard, a South Korean Army MP. The guard let us enter the camp, which consisted of a few quonsets. The facility was a former U.S. Army garrison from which the American soldiers had withdrawn earlier, and the property had been transferred to the South Korean Army. The drill sergeant ordered us to form teams of two and led us into the buildings where we found three or four piles of military mattresses. Then he instructed each team to carry one mattress to our training camp.

My teammate was a tall, solidly built man named Lee Yeong-sik, who was a few years older than me. He lifted one end of a mattress easily from a pile, while I, a scrawny seventeen-year-old, struggled with the other end. The heavy mattress had no handles, making it awkward to carry. But Yeong-sik was patient with me the whole way despite my being weaker. He even encouraged me during the march back and chatted about his life growing up in North

Korea to distract me from our load. The line of more than thirty teams of mattress carriers along the narrow country roads looked like an army of ants transporting their food. Moving mattresses without handles frustrated everyone and drained our energy. The return trip took almost three times longer, and by the time we returned, it was almost 5 p.m.

• • •

About one week after my arrival at the training center, the drill sergeant announced that a reorganization of all recruits throughout the center would take place. There would be no training that day. He instructed us to take our personal belongings and gather in the parade ground by 8:30 a.m. He emphasized, "Eight-thirty sharp!"

I went out to the parade ground with my personal belongings: a toothbrush and my two books. I always wore my round wristwatch, which had a gold-colored rim and a brown leather strap. My brother had given it to me when I had left for Seoul. At first it didn't work, but in Seoul, I found a watchmaker (one of our townsfolk) who fixed it for me. The training center authorities had collected our civilian clothes to prevent disgruntled recruits from desertion. I never saw mine again. Since my clothes were old, I didn't care much.

When I arrived at the parade ground, I found many recruits lining up by company and platoon. I estimated that there were about six to seven hundred clad in oversized, used U.S. Army fatigues and boots. As 8:30 approached, drill sergeants performed headcounts of their platoons and reported the results to their respective company commanders, keeping us at attention. When the commander of the training camp appeared in front of us, each company commander reported to him.

He then delivered a terse speech that some of the recruits would be transferred to different regiments. He ordered the company commanders to take roll calls of those who would be transferred. In turn, the company commanders instructed their drill sergeants to execute the separation.

I became anxious because transferring farther away from Seoul could jeopardize my plan to attend an evening academy to learn math and English when my basic training was over. But I realized that worry would not help. When the selection was over, I was one of those who would be leaving. I hoped that there would be an evening academy wherever I went.

A captain shouted into a megaphone, "Attention! Listen carefully. Those who were selected, go to my right. The rest, go to my far left." About three hundred of us recruits moved to his right. Then he came to my group and announced that we would be transferred to the 8th Regiment in Wonju-up, Gangwon-do Province, and that he would be escorting us.

My heart sank because it was known to be the most backwoods province in South Korea. I gathered that such a place would not have an academy where I could advance my education. I had signed up for the army communication school. Then some unscrupulous recruiters had kidnapped me to the 1st Infantry Regiment, a so-called elite brigade. Now I was being exiled to the backwoods. I wondered if my educational opportunity was slipping away for good. Was *palja* (fate) playing a trick on me? I sighed.

Having had his assistants do headcounts and regroup us into six groups of about fifty each, the captain ordered us to march forward to Cheongnyangni Railroad Station, about four miles from the training center, singing the army anthem. We sang loudly. The unforgiving, humid summer weather slowed us, and the singing faded away. We arrived at the station long past noon and were herded into a waiting freight train without lunch, about forty soldiers to each car, like livestock being forced into cargo trains in the western movies. We were hungry. After a long wait, the train whistled lugubriously, and with a big jolt, it lumbered out of the station.

As the train sped farther southeast, the hills grew into high, rugged mountains, and patches of farmlands dotted the narrow valleys. Low, straw-thatched, tired-looking farmhouses were scattered at the edges of the farmlands. Tiny rice paddies cascaded farther down the valleys like curved staircases. A few farmers clad in loose white cotton looked fatigued bent over their rice paddies under the scorching sun. They reminded me of the backbreaking farm work that had made me leave home for Seoul twenty months earlier at the age of fifteen for an educational opportunity. Now I was in the army, not in school. Perhaps my parents might be weeding the same rice paddy now. Then I became homesick, missing them very much.

As the train entered a tunnel with mournful whistles and loud, monotonous sounds, foul-smelling smoke blew into our freight car through the open doors and woke me. Darkness prevailed. I shut my eyes and closed my mouth and nose with my hands to avoid the smell. A few soldiers cursed, but the smoke blew in mercilessly. Thankfully, the train came out of the tunnel within a few minutes, reaching a bridge over a swirling confluence of two big rivers. After that, the train chugged along the northern foothills of big mountains and stopped occasionally at small country stations to let oncoming trains pass by.

After many hours, the train pulled into Wonju-up Station in the late afternoon. The captain and his assistants shouted, "Wonju-up. Soldiers, disembark! Hurry up. Line up." When we did, he ordered us to march forward by group number and sing the army anthem. Again? Despite being hungry and exhausted, we sang and marched almost a mile to the 8th Infantry Regiment Training Center, our destination. The center consisted of three two-story wooden barracks and was located by the main street in the middle of the town. Its parade field was much smaller than that of the 1st Regiment Training Center.

As we marched into the parade field singing as loudly as we could, two high ranking officers watched us from the bridge connecting two barracks, with commanders' whips under their arms; they were the regiment commander and his deputy. A group of five more officers watched us from under the bridge. Having us line up in review format, our captain reported to the commander. The commander and his deputy reviewed us, then climbed back to the bridge and delivered a terse speech, "At ease! I am Lieutenant Colonel Choi Namkeon, Commanding Officer of the regiment. Major Han is my deputy commander. Welcome to this great regiment. We will train you to be good soldiers. Dismissed for supper!"

The captain turned around and shouted, "Attention!" Then he faced the commander, saluted, and repeated, "Company dismissed." Instead of dismissing us for supper, the captain and an officer from the regiment processed the transfer procedure by exchanging papers and headcounts while keeping us in attention mode. I hated their indifference to three hundred recruits' well-being. We hadn't eaten anything since our meager breakfast early that morning.

After the commander and his deputy had driven away, a dozen officers and senior sergeants from the 8th Regiment reorganized us new arrivals into two companies, transferred groups 1-3 to the 5ᵗʰ Company and the rest to the 6ᵗʰ. I was assigned to the 5ᵗʰ Company along with Lee Jong-kook, Oh Mun-chan, Lee Yeong-sik, and some other friends. Then a high-ranking sergeant with six red chevrons, three upward and the other three downward, took charge of the 5ᵗʰ Company. His posture was imposing, and almost untouchable! With authority, he introduced himself as Master Sergeant Gyeon, the 5ᵗʰ Company Sergeant. He performed a headcount on us, but my name was not called. After finishing, he asked if he had missed anyone.

I bravely raised my hand and gave him my name and serial number. He double-checked his list and confirmed that indeed my name was missing. He sent a corporal to the 6ᵗʰ Company to check if I was on its roster.

Meanwhile, I wondered how they had missed my name, and if I was a persona non grata? Those unscrupulous recruiters from the elite brigade had hijacked me and then exiled me to this remote province without my personal information. Was it a bad omen? What the hell was going on with me?

I looked over at Jong-kook and his mouth dropped in surprise at my not being on the list. My friend Kim Maneong snorted. I could tell he found it funny.

"Problem?" the 5ᵗʰ Company Sergeant asked him sternly.

"No sir!" he responded and straightened up. Kim Maneong would joke with us, and I thought of him as a close friend. He was two years older than me. We called him Man-E.

Shortly, the corporal returned and reported that the other company did not have my name either. Then the company sergeant said, "You stay with us. I'll put you in the 1ˢᵗ Platoon. The regiment headquarters will issue you a new serial number."

A few days later, I received a new number, and officially became one of the 8ᵗʰ Regiment's soldiers. The mix-up cost me ten days of seniority.

By the time the reorganization was finished, dusk had rolled in. A sergeant came to my platoon and hollered, "1ˢᵗ Platoon, follow me," and led us into barracks on the second floor. After ordering us in line, he said, "I am Staff Sergeant Kim Hakdong, your drill sergeant. This is Corporal Pae, my assistant." Sgt. Kim appeared to be pleasant, but his assistant was bulky and mean. The drill sergeant called platoon roll and assigned us beds. When the bedtime bugle blasted, he dismissed us for the night.

The training camp was an old silk mill which had been converted to army barracks, consisting of three two-story buildings and one large warehouse. The two-story buildings had floors constructed of heavy-duty wooden planks. A seven-foot-wide platform, a couple of feet high, ran the entire length of the room along the windowless walls. That platform served as our beds for the next three months. We spread futons side by side. Although our bedding was uncomfortable, I quickly fell asleep until the next morning's wakeup bugle.

After one more day of elementary training, Drill Sergeant Hakdong issued rifles and bayonets. Holding a real gun for the first time in my life gave me a strange, tingling sensation. It was a scary feeling! The weapons were long, heavy rifles with menacing bayonets.

Jong-kook had been excited for this day. He had been talking to our group of friends about it for a while. "When are we finally going to get our rifles?" he'd often ask.

Jin Chin-mae was eager to get a rifle too when the subject had come up a couple of days ago. Jin's home was also north of the 38th Parallel, and he was a few years older than me.

"Don't worry, guys, the day will come," Chun Byung-ho told them amidst our group. Chun was a laid-back guy in his mid-twenties. He would always crack jokes to break the tension if training ever got too difficult.

Having us sit in a circle around him, the sergeant began to lecture about the rifles. He said that they were World War II Japanese vintage Type 99 rifles, which were manual. He taught us the names of the parts: muzzle, loader, trigger, magazine, safety lock, butt plate, and bayonet. He emphasized the importance of using the safety locks to prevent accidental shootings. For the next few days, he taught us how to hold the rifles properly for marching, inspection, salutation, and attention.

Then he taught us how to load ammunition into the magazine, aim at targets, and pull the trigger while standing, sitting, or lying on our stomachs. Of the three positions, shooting in standing position was the most tiring, as it required us to turn about 45 degrees to our right, spread our legs, load our guns, and raise them to shoulder-level. He shouted, "You hold it horizontally with your right hand on the trigger house and place your left palm under the rear hand guard with its butt plate firmly against your right shoulder and aim at the target. Then he ordered, "Load your gun, aim, hold your breath, shoot!" Keeping us in that posture, he and his assistant checked our posture. If they found anyone in the wrong posture, they yelled at him and corrected it. It took about fifteen to twenty minutes for them to finish their inspection. Holding the heavy rifle that long pained my arms and shoulders. Often soldiers stealthily relaxed their arms to relieve the pain. Once the mean assistant caught me doing so, and yanked my rifle from me and jabbed it into my stomach. It hurt badly.

Next, the sergeant had us apply them in combat exercises, such as charging, hand-to-hand combat, crawling forward, and under barbed wire. He demonstrated hand-to-hand combat by showing how to deflect the enemy's bayoneted rifle, lunging your bayonet into your enemy's chest, and pulling it out, or hitting him in the jaw with your rifle butt with all your strength. He emphasized, "You do it before your enemy does it to you!" In our exercises, we mounted our bayonets with their sheaths on to avoid accidents. He split us into two facing groups, then barked, "Mount your bayonets. Charge, Step 1, Step 2 ..." We followed his choreography by thrusting our bayoneted rifles and left feet forward simultaneously with shouts, deflecting our mock enemies' rifles, and gesturing to sink our bayonets into the enemies' chests. Of course, we stopped our bayonets five to six inches away from the enemies. I was currently battling Bong Jong-tae, who was from my native province, but his home was south of the border in South Korea. He became one of my best friends. In this exercise, I always lost the game because I was the youngest, smallest, and lightest soldier. Despite my quick action, Bong managed to fend off my rifle and sink his bayonet into my chest because he was bigger and stronger. Bong would always joke that I needed to do extra push-ups to gain muscle.

In the evenings, the sergeant taught us how to maintain our weapons by disassembling, oiling, and reassembling them. We practiced this repeatedly until we became efficient enough to do it blindfolded. We hadn't yet learned to fire them. He also taught us army regulations and the chain of command and required us to memorize them. I didn't have much trouble with that, but others had real difficulty. The mean assistant drill sergeant punished them by beating their calves with his leather boots, causing severe internal bleeding,

and leaving them limping. My friend Pak Sam-hyun was one of them. Pak
had dropped out of grammar school to work on his foster parents' farm. He
was almost illiterate, which may explain why he had a hard time memoriz-
ing everything. But he was the nicest guy. He was taller than me and strong
from his farming life, but no one wanted a beating like that. We surrounded
him afterwards to see if he was okay.

A few days after my arrival in Wonju-up, Drill Sergeant Hakdong assigned
me detail duties for the drill sergeants' quarters. The four drill sergeants and
Corporal Pae, the ugly assistant drill sergeant, occupied the quarters. The
duties were to get food from the training center kitchen and set the table for
the sergeants, three meals a day, and clean the room. These assignments were
above and beyond the responsibilities I had to perform as a trainee. They kept
me busier than other trainees, so busy that I did not even have time to think
about an evening academy. However, one good thing came out of the extra
work. I never experienced hunger during my basic training because the kitchen
sergeant allocated more food for the drill sergeants than they could consume.
I ate with them, while other recruits were always hungry. Since there was always
leftover food, I gave it to my friends in my platoon. In turn, they helped me
clean my weapon, fold my uniforms, and arrange them neatly for inspections.

RECRUIT CHOI KYU

On the first day at the 1st Regiment Training Center, I met a recruit named
Choi Kyu. We met each other again after arriving in Wonju-up. Despite
being older than me, we became friends because he, too, came from North
Korea, where his parents had owned a business, large tracts of land, and a
big house. After the North Korean Communist Government confiscated his
parents' properties and forced his family to relocate to a remote farming village, they became poor farmers. He had come to Seoul hoping to continue
his college education.

One Sunday afternoon, we were under the shade of a tree in a corner of the
parade ground to alleviate the summer heat and were talking about our training. He said, "Tae-hyok, I can't take this slave-like training anymore. When
I signed up, I never expected this hardship. Even worse, they transferred me

to this damn place." He paused for a few moments and continued in a serious tone, "I have no future in the army."

I understood his difficulty, because he had been born to a well-to-do family and had lived comfortably until the evil government had robbed them of their wealth. The basic training was rigorous, but I did not think it was unbearable.

He said, "I am going to jump over the fence by night and leave the army for good. I shall find a job in Seoul or in Pusan. If you don't see me in the next few days, then you'll know I have gone. Why not join me?"

"Even though I don't like this infantry training, I will stay with the army because I have no place to go except for returning home to North Korea. I don't want to do that. You go alone! Unlike you, I only have a sixth-grade education. No one would give me work."

"I understand. Tae-hyok, these conversations are just between you and me."

I said, "Trust me, this conversation never happened." But I didn't really think that he would desert the training center.

A couple of days later, the 6th Company Sergeant ordered all the trainees out to the parade ground and asked us to form a circle around him instead of the usual parade format. When we did, two armed guards brought a trainee from the guardhouse to the sergeant. At first, I did not recognize him because he kept his head down. The sergeant pulled the soldier's head up by the hair and turned him around 360 degrees like a merchant showing his merchandise to prospective buyers. He shouted, "Watch this coward soldier." I was shocked; it was my friend Choi.

The sergeant shouted in an angry voice, "You know him very well. He is one of you. Last night he scaled the fence under the cover of darkness to desert the army. But alert guards and MPs apprehended him early this morning. He will be punished for his crime." Then he ordered my friend to assume a push-up position and started beating him on the hip with a baseball bat over and over, each blow landing in the same spot. At every thump, my body twitched as if I were being beaten, too. His unbearable screams pierced my ears. I saw the appalled faces of Jin, Pak, and Bong across the circle, each wearing a look of disbelief. Chun was by them, but his eyes were looking to the side as if trying not to watch. Jong-kook stood right beside me and was taking nervous, deep breaths.

As the sergeant continued whacking, Choi collapsed to the ground, lying flat on his stomach. He stopped screaming, resting his face in his hand. Every time the sergeant's bat landed, my friend's body jerked, but now he just lay silently as if he were dead.

After a long beating, the sergeant turned around to face us and warned us not to desert the army like that coward. All of us fear-stricken recruits kept silent as if we were in the middle of a midnight graveyard.

My friend was court-martialed for his failed desertion attempt and given a six-month imprisonment. Since he was serving his term in the regiment stockade, which had been built inside the training center guardhouse, I saw him occasionally in the distance when the prison guards took the prisoners outside for exercises. His head had been shaved like a Buddhist monk's, and he wore a prison uniform with two big white English letters on his back, the meaning of which I did not know then.

A few days after my friend's punishment, Corporal Pae, the malicious assistant drill sergeant, summoned me into his quarters and ordered me to kneel on the floor. He had a half-cut-suspension stick from an army folding cot in his hand. Fear swept through my mind, a chill ran down my spine, and my heart began to pound wildly. I slowly did as I was told, looking into the corporal's eyes.

He barked, "You and your friend Choi from the 6th Company planned desertion, didn't you?" and he whacked me on the shoulder even before I could answer. "Confess!" He continued to beat me on the shoulders and the back.

Pain and shock prevented me from answering or screaming. I just shook my head rigorously. Suddenly, I screamed, "No, I didn't." I pleaded with him to stop beating me. But he didn't stop. I moaned loudly in pain, curled up on the floor. Excruciating pain flashed through my hips repeatedly. I didn't know how long the beating lasted.

The corporal yelled, "Get up. Don't you dare desert us. Do you understand? Get out."

I dragged myself to my bed and buried my head in my pillow. I heard someone ask, "Are you okay?" It was Oh Munchan. He brought a cool, wet towel. I tried to put it on my back but couldn't, so he did it for me. "I saw you being called into Corporal Pae's quarters and heard his angry shouting.

I'm sorry you went through that. I hope you feel better." His unselfish friendship comforted me.

Despite Corporal Pae's barbaric torture, I had to perform my duties for the drill sergeants' supper. I hated and feared the corporal. When I served his meals, often I was tempted to spit in his food, but my conscience didn't allow me to do so. However, as days went by, he gradually became nicer to me, and a few times he brought me apples or candies when he returned from his weekend pass. I appreciated his gifts but did not know what to make of them. Then one day, he called me into his quarters and said, "Private Kim, I am sorry that I beat you severely. Drill Sergeant Kim Hakdong provided me with the information that you had planned to desert and ordered me to punish you. In retrospect, I did it too harshly. Will you forgive me?"

Despite his rank and position, he earnestly asked for my forgiveness. I was deeply moved and said, "Yes, Corporal. I forgive you, sir." Since then, we became friends. When he was promoted to sergeant and transferred to another unit, he bought a goodbye-gift package of candies and encouraged me to be a good soldier. I appreciated the gift and the encouragement. Later I learned from one of his friends that even though he was the most educated among all the enlisted men in the company, he had not been promoted to sergeant when all his peers had been promoted. Unfortunately, he may have poured out his frustration on me.

U.S. ARMY M1 GARAND RIFLES

Midway through our basic training, we trainees received American M1 Garand rifles with bayonets. They were semi-automatic and sleeker than the Japanese bolt-action rifles. The new weapons consisted of many more parts than the Japanese counterparts. An M1 Garand rifle with a bayonet weighed twelve pounds, 14 percent of my body weight. It was some task for me to carry an M1 rifle. But I loved my new American rifle because it was more advanced than the Japanese rifle, and the memory of the Japanese occupation of Korea was still fresh in my mind. It was less than three years since Korea had been liberated from Japan.

WAR GAME, EVE'S APPLES

One steamy, hot mid-August evening, Drill Sergeant Hakdong announced that we would have a war game the next day. He instructed us to fill our canteens before going to bed. The following morning, we woke up earlier than usual, had breakfast, and gathered in the parade ground with full equipment. Then he and his assistant led us to a foothill of a mountain that was about a few hundred feet high, about two to three miles from the camp. During the march under the August sun, most of us consumed some of our water.

Upon our arrival at a small river skirting the foothills, the sergeant halted us and ordered, "Check your canteens. Refill them with the river water." We were happy to cool ourselves in the river and refill the canteens before the war game began.

The sergeant said that an unknown number of hypothetical enemy soldiers had occupied the mountain last night and dug in at the top. We were ordered to take the mountain back, but unfortunately, we had little intelligence. Thus, it was essential to send a couple of reconnoiters to collect intelligence about the enemy before we would attack them. Using the army volunteer system, he picked me and another trainee, Park, and ordered us to scout the enemy. Then he said, "Give me a hand signal if you find the enemy. We will follow you. Go!"

Park was in his early twenties and had a high school education. I thought he was well-qualified for scouting duty. I was only a scrawny seventeen-year-old with a sixth-grade education—not a good choice. I did not understand why the sergeant had picked me. Nevertheless, I was glad to accompany Park, an intelligent soldier.

We set out. While climbing the mountain, he said, "Tae-hyok, I am glad that the drill sergeant picked you and me because I like your enthusiasm for learning. By the way, where did you get your middle school algebra book? No one in the company except you brought a book with them when we joined the army."

I sheepishly told him that one of my townspeople had given it to me, and I had brought it with me from North Korea. I treasured it.

The August sun burned my back and my bare neck. Numerous flies festered, sucking my blood. I felt warm under my oversized American helmet and wanted to remove it. We turned around to the platoon and intermittently signaled, "Clear!" Then they advanced a couple of hundred feet behind us. About one third of the way up the hill, we were sweating and thirsty. Park said, "Hey, let's have a gulp." I leaned on my rifle and drank a few gulps of water from my canteen. How sweet and refreshing it was!

"Don't stop! Get going." It was the drill sergeant.

"Oh, Sergeant!" Moaning, we reluctantly put our canteens back into their cases and continued to scout. Near the top of the mountain, we found a small orchard consisting of about a dozen ancient apple trees, obviously abandoned. They bore green, undernourished fruit—enticing to us, since we had been deprived of fruit since joining the army.

Park said, "I am hungry for apples. Let's pick some," so we picked a couple and ate them. Despite being unripe, they were juicy and delicious. Forgetting our scout assignments, we picked as many apples as our pockets could accommodate.

Suddenly, somebody shouted, "Hey, what are you doing?" It was Drill Sergeant Hakdong. We froze.

"What do you have in your pockets?"

We answered with trembling voices, "Apples, sir."

He ordered, "Take all the apples out of your pockets, count them, and pile them in a heap on the ground."

As ordered, we emptied our pockets and counted them. We were surprised that we had picked enough apples for the rest of the 3rd Platoon (anyone who enlisted at the same time in my platoon transferred from the 1st to the 3rd Platoon during basic training). Piling them up in one heap was not an easy job.

When we finished, he ordered us to step back. Then he whacked us on the butts a couple of times with his Carbine rifle and said, "Raise your rifles high up into the air and stand at attention until further notice! You are not eating these apples." Then he called the rest of the platoon to take one apple each.

Park and I sweated under the hot August sun with our arms up in the air, while our friends enjoyed the apples we had harvested. Man-E, Pak, and Chun smiled at us sarcastically and gestured as if to share their apples.

My arms ached. I cursed, "Damn those apples!"

When everyone finished munching, juice dripping down their chins, the sergeant shouted, "You two, lower your rifles. Never neglect your assignment. Success in a battle relies on good scouting. Do you understand?"

"Yes, sir!"

"Dismissed!"

Eve's apples tempted us and got us into trouble, but we learned a precious lesson. Never neglect an order, especially on the frontline!

After basic training, Park advanced to the Korean Military Academy, and I stayed with the 5th Company.

TARGET PRACTICE

One day, toward the end of basic training, Company Commander Captain Lee Yong-chan announced that all trainees would have target practice using live ammunition. His announcement stirred excitement among the trainees, most of whom had never fired a rifle. Two, who had been drafted by the Japanese Imperial Army during World War II and fought in the Sino-Japan Theater, boasted of their experiences, telling us some scary stories. They said, "When you fire a rifle, it recoils, and its butt plate hits your shoulder so hard that it can inflict bruises or even knock you down." They scared me so much that I considered avoiding the target practice. But I reminded myself that I was a soldier and had been training for this moment for the last three months.

"You'll be fine," Kim Jae-kook reassured me. Jae-kook was from North Korea. He had had an arranged marriage and didn't talk about his wife much.

The next morning, we marched to the regiment shooting range, singing a marching song. After a couple of miles, we arrived at the foothills of a small mountain. They gently sloped down, then rose ten feet before dropping sharply to the bank of a small creek, forming an undulating field a few hundred yards wide. A dozen targets were set up in a row along the far side of the field. Below the base of the targets, a long trench was dug, parallel to the entire length of the row. I thought this was ideal for a shooting range because the rise at the lower rim of the field provided an excellent vantage point across the field to the targets, and the backdrop of the rising hills would swallow any stray bullets. There was no fence around the range, nor were there any guards.

Land-hungry farmers had cultivated the land for a thousand years before the nascent 8th Regiment was born. Lush green corn and soybean plants were growing healthily under the hot summer sun, promising a bumper harvest. But that day, there were no farmers around. Perhaps they had been warned to keep off the field.

Drill Sergeant Hakdong distributed a clip with eight rounds of ammunition to each of us and demonstrated how to insert it into the rifle's chamber. First, he held his M1 rifle at a 45-degree angle across his chest, locked the safety, pulled the operating rod back to open the magazine, inserted the ammunition clip, moved his thumb to the right to avoid the forward motion of the bolt, and released the operating rod to close the magazine. Then he took the clip out of his rifle and instructed us to follow him step by step as he repeated the demonstration. After that he ordered us to take the ammunition out of our guns and sternly warned, "Do not reload the gun or unlock the safety until you are ready to fire."

For the first time in my life, I held live ammunition in my palm and looked at it. The brass shells and copper bullets were so smooth that the brilliant summer sun reflected off them, needling my eyes. My hand was shaking slightly, and apprehension rose in my heart. *Was my shoulder going to be hurt? Was I going to be knocked down?* And more seriously, *who was I going to shoot in the future?*

Sudden ear-splitting shots, like gigantic popcorn explosions, woke me from my anxious reverie. A dozen trainees of the 1st Platoon fired their rifles at their respective targets in standing position. As they fired, the rifle barrels tipped upward, and their shoulders flinched back, though not violently. Nobody was knocked down. After a few shots, the Drill Sergeant of the platoon yelled, "Hold fire! Sit. Three shots. Ready, fire!" After that, the sergeant ordered them to lie down. They finished their practice, shooting while lying prone.

Drill Sergeant Hakdong hollered, "Hey, soldiers. Watch those guys firing carefully. You can see the sun reflect off those fast-flying bullets."

I looked in the direction of the targets and saw objects flash and vanish in a split second, like flints. At first, I thought they were flying insects, but they were bullets. Amazing!

Every time a series of shootings was over, a group of soldiers climbed out of the trench, waving a white flag. They were target-detail duties, recording scores and replacing used targets with new ones. Then they hurriedly retreated into the trench, waving a red flag. The white flag was for 'DO NOT SHOOT,' and the red for 'RESUME SHOOTING.'

When our turn arrived, Sgt. Hakdong shouted, "Squadron 1. Forward! You shoot two rounds in a standing position, three in sitting, and the last three lying on your stomach." Twelve of us stepped forward and kept standing at attention. My heart started to pound again. I took several deep breaths to calm myself. Then the red flag waved from the trench, signaling 'READY.'

The Drill Sergeant ordered, "Lock the safety. Insert the clip."

I lifted my rifle across my chest at a 45-degree angle, pulled the operating rod, inserted the clip of eight rounds of live ammunition into the magazine, and released the rod.

"Unlock the safety. Ready, aim. Hold your breath!"

I put my left leg one half step forward, lifted the rifle to shoulder level, and held it horizontally by the trigger house with my right hand and by the barrel with my left hand. Then I fixed the butt plate firmly against my right shoulder and pushed my right index finger through the trigger guard. I aimed at my target, held my breath, and waited for "Fire." Holding the 9.5-pound rifle steady tortured my 86-pound body.

"Stea…dy. Fire!"

I pulled the trigger. "Bang," and my body moved back momentarily, but my shoulder did not hurt. I lost my target. I accidently fired two more shots instead of one without seeing my targets. Then I sat and aimed. I shot three more rounds with some confidence. By the time I was lying down for the remaining shots, my apprehension had disappeared completely, and I calmly finished my live ammunition shooting practice. According to my drill sergeant, my score was not great, but it was a passing grade. "See, you did alright!" Kim Jae-kook told me afterwards. A few days later we had another live ammunition target practice in the presence of the regiment commander, his deputy, the battalion commander, and my company commander. Despite the presence of those high-ranking officers, I performed well and scored much better than the first time.

BOOT CAMP GRADUATION

The next day we wore our clean khaki uniforms and polished our weapons. Company Commander Captain Lee Yong-chan led us to the regiment head-quarters' parade field for our boot camp graduation ceremony. We lined up for review. As Regiment Commander, Colonel Choi Namkeon and his dep-uty approached the review stand, and Captain Lee shouted, "Company, atten-tion!" When the colonel stepped on the stand, Captain Lee ordered, "Salute!" and reported that we were ready for review.

The colonel returned our salute and delivered a congratulatory speech. Then Captain Lee led our parade, and the regiment commander reviewed us, holding his commander's swagger stick under his left arm. Despite my being there involuntarily, a sense of pride and self-confidence surged in my heart—*Now I am a soldier*—thus culminating my three-month long basic training.

NEW ASSIGNMENT

A couple of days after graduation, the company sergeant announced that our 5th Company would be deployed in the Hyeon-ri - Sangnam Area to guard the 38th Parallel that divided the two Koreas. A reorganization within the com-pany took me out of the 3rd Platoon and gave me a different assignment. My new job was performing detail duties for the company commander: I would report directly to him and receive his orders. I wondered why they had cho-sen me—perhaps because I was the youngest soldier? But I didn't dare to question them.

For the next several days, the whole company was busy preparing for the new deployment. Despite all the activity, life at the camp was relatively peace-ful and smooth because basic training was over. Drill Sergeant Hakdong super-vised our packing and cleaning without shouting. He often joked with us.

One morning, a fleet of a dozen civilian trucks rumbled into the parade ground and parked in a row. Since the young Korean Army did not have adequate transportation, the regiment had hired these civilian vehicles for our relocation.

As the bugle blared across the camp, the entire company gathered in the field with our weapons, army backpacks, and personal belongings in cotton duffle bags and lined up for inspection. After Battalion Commander Major Kang and Company Commander Captain Lee inspected us, the Major delivered a short sendoff speech. He said that because the regiment headquarters considered the 5th Company as the best trained unit among the entire regiment, we were selected to guard the border in the Hyeon-ri - Sangnam region. Therefore, we should be proud of ourselves. He charged us to serve the country well. His speech sounded good, but I couldn't help thinking that we had had just two live ammunition practices of only sixteen shots.

Captain Lee thanked the battalion commander and ordered us aboard the designated trucks. He told me that I would ride on the company vehicle. Then he walked over to his wife who was holding their baby son against her chest and bid her farewell. He kissed his sleeping son on the cheek while holding her hand. When he started to move, she held him by the arm, not wanting to let him go. After a few more words, she reluctantly released him. Then he signaled the convoy to move forward and hopped on the company's three-quarter ton truck at the head, leading the convoy. She waved until we saw her no more. I rode in the cargo bay of the leading truck with two other soldiers who were the captain's liaisons.

As we passed by the guardhouse where the regiment prison was, suddenly I came to think about my friend Choi who was serving his six-month term for his desertion attempt. Since all the soldiers at the training camp were barred from contacting the prisoners, I had no chance to say goodbye or to ask him why he had mentioned to his interrogator that I had been his accomplice before I left for my new assignment. I never saw him again.

The Hyeon-ri - Sangnam region is about fifty miles north of Wonju-up in the mountainous region of Gangwon-do Province, right on the 38th Parallel which divided the two Koreas. As we moved farther north, the mountains grew higher and more rugged. Shortly after noon, the convoy snaked up a narrow, rock-strewn dirt path and reached the top. This path might have been sparsely used since the division in August 1945. Even in early September, the majestic oak trees on the high mountain ridges had already begun to show colors. The crisp, cool air and the dazzling sun in the cobalt blue sky might be hastening the foliage process. Those spectacular, unspoiled views reminded me of the mountain scenery around my hometown.

We continued to move at a snail's pace along the ridge for a couple more hours before descending through an ancient forest to a small valley between two soaring mountain ranges. A score of farmhouses, mostly poor, were scattered along a bubbling creek. That was Sangnam Village in the Hyeon-ri - Sangnam Region. The village resembled my hometown. Ironically, I had ended up in a similar environment to that of my native village. Any hope of attending an educational institution was now gone. I wondered how long we would be stationed in this isolated hamlet.

CHAPTER 10

Peaceful Days

September - November 1948

As we entered the town in late afternoon, a bunch of excited children gathered and walked alongside the crawling convoy, as if they were escorting us. Some shouted, some giggled, and some ran forward and came back, waving their hands. Perhaps these country children had never seen so many vehicles and soldiers in one place before.

As soon as we pulled into an empty field, Captain Lee disembarked from his vehicle. He handed his leather briefcase to me and said, "Follow me!" Then he ordered one of his liaisons to fetch Company Sergeant Gyeon. When the sergeant reported, the captain instructed him to direct preparations for supper and to set up camp before sunset, because the soldiers had not eaten since breakfast, and the night in this highland would be chilly.

The children continued to enjoy our presence as if they were in an amusement park. Soon, older folks, mostly men and a few grandmothers, came along and greeted us, "Hello, soldiers. Glad to have you here." A tall, handsome country gentleman in his early fifties came forward and warmly welcomed us on behalf of the villagers. He introduced himself to Captain Lee as the *rijang* (village chief) and offered his help to the captain.

The captain thanked him and asked if he could find someone who could provide him with room and board. The *rijang* said that he had anticipated such a need and had already found a good family. He then invited the captain and his deputy for dinner at his residence. Both accepted. He graciously asked, "Captain, would you also bring this young soldier with you for dinner?"

Without hesitation, he said, "Yes, I will." But the *rijang's* unexpected invitation puzzled me because I was merely a private and just the captain's detail duty boy. Dumbfounded, I looked at the *rijang* and the captain alternately. Did he think that I was one of the captain's relatives?

Captain said, "Can't you say, 'Thank you, sir?'"

Instead of speaking, I just put myself at attention and saluted until the captain ordered, "At ease, soldier!"

Company Sergeant Gyeon directed the soldiers to unload our weapons, provisions, big cast iron kettles, and army tents, leaving the rest of the equipment on the trucks until the next day. He ordered the quartermaster and his cooks to prepare supper, then split the rest into several groups and instructed them to pitch tents. The quartermaster team set up an impromptu kitchen near the creek so they could easily draw water for cooking. Within a couple of hours, a tent city sprang up in the middle of the field.

After making sure that all the soldiers had been fed and the tents had been pitched for the night, the captain and his deputy went to the *rijang's* residence for dinner. I was so hungry that I wished I could eat the humble supper with the other soldiers. When we arrived at his beautiful, traditional Korean house, the *rijang* warmly welcomed us and led us to his *sarangbang* where a short-legged round dinner table was set.

When I entered the room, the sweet aroma of chicken soup and pungent kimchi teased my nose, and the tendrils of steam from the bowls of warm rice and soup caused my mouth to water and my stomach to gurgle. The gentleman and the two officers talked to each other and laughed for some time before settling around the dinner table. I just kept quiet, standing behind them. It must have been only a few minutes, but it felt like an eternity to my complaining stomach.

The host served Captain Lee first with *soju* (a Korean alcohol) in a small china cup. After drinking the *soju* in one gulp, the captain exclaimed, "It's good," and turned the cup to his deputy officer. He received the cup with both hands and thanked him. When the captain poured the *soju* from the white jar, the deputy thanked him again and emptied the cup. Then the deputy turned the cup to the host and filled it in the same manner as the captain had done. After the host drank, he gave the cup to me and said, "Young soldier, your turn."

I said, "Thank you, sir. But I have never learned to drink *soju*. I am sorry, sir." My two officers laughed and said that I was too young to drink alcohol, although I might have tried it if my captain had not been present.

After dinner, I thanked the host and bid everyone goodnight. Upon returning to the company, I went into a tent and collapsed on an empty field cot, falling asleep instantly and hearing nothing until the next morning's bugle. Exertion from the rough travel had made my muscles and joints sore. Still fighting sleep, I did some calisthenics to loosen up my body and rinsed my face in chilly creek water.

I then reported to the captain. He instructed me to take his duffle bag and other belongings to his room and unpack them. I arranged his belongings neatly and shined his shoes and boots.

The boarding house was a traditional Korean residential home of a good size, albeit smaller than the *rijang's*. It consisted of two sections, one for the family and the other for guests, connected by a wooden-floored hall. Captain Lee rented the guest quarters. The landlord's family comprised a farmer and his wife, who were in their late thirties, and their two young children. The room and board were the wife's business.

"Private Kim, it is lunch time." The captain appeared in the doorway. I jumped up and saluted. I had kept so busy that before I knew it, it was noon. He inspected his room and said, "Good work." When I started to leave, he told me that I would be eating and quartering with him until further notice.

I was confounded. Was eating and quartering with the commanding officer a privilege or a hardship? I just stood at attention for a few moments, then said, "Thank you, sir." I might eat better and sleep in a more comfortable environment than my fellow soldiers, but I would lose the close fellowship with the friends with whom I had joined the army at the same time and gone through the arduous basic training together. From now on, in front of the captain, I would have to watch my language.

The landlady brought lunch and prepared it on a shiny, chestnut brown table. The captain thanked her and sat at the table. I felt so uncomfortable that I kept standing by the door. Then he said, "Soldier, sit down, and let's have lunch."

Thanking him, I sat awkwardly across the table and waited until he began to eat. Even though I was hungry, I was so nervous that I couldn't enjoy my food. I just pretended to eat.

Noticing my nervousness, the commander said, "Private Kim, be comfortable and enjoy your lunch." While eating, he casually asked what part of North Korea I had come from and about my family.

I told him that I had come from Suan-gun, Hwanghae-do Province, and that I had left my parents and two older brothers behind.

"You must be missing them."

"Yes, sir."

"I miss my parents, too. They live in Onsong, North Hamgyong Province. Have you ever heard of Onsong?"

"Yes, sir. It is in the northeasternmost part of the Korean Peninsula, bordering China, sir." I was not surprised that he, too, had come from North Korea because many young North Korean refugees had joined the South Korean Army.

"You know Onsong! Not very many people know where it is." My answer seemed to have surprised him, and he continued, "Where did you learn about that town?"

"When my older brother was in the fifth grade, and I in the first, I borrowed his atlas and read it over and over. I found that Onsong was the farthest, northernmost town from my village, sir." As our conversation progressed, I gradually calmed down and enjoyed my meal. Shortly, we finished lunch.

The captain was usually a quiet man, but that afternoon he talked more than usual. "You like geography, don't you?" Before I answered, he asked when and why I had come to South Korea.

When I answered, he became more interested in my story and asked, "I know you are the youngest soldier in the company, but how old are you?"

"Seventeen, sir."

"That means you came to Seoul all alone when you were only fifteen? Did your parents allow you to go?"

"Yes, sir. Because I pleaded with them for many months, they finally gave in, sir."

"Then why did you join the army instead of attending school?"

I told him that I had lost my job and had no money because the construction company I had worked for had folded, and that I didn't want to go back to North Korea, so I joined the army.

He quietly listened, then said, "I see!" He abruptly said, "Tae-hyok, will you find a laundry service in town and take my laundry there? Get the price list, too. That's all for the day." Then he left for his office. He called me Tae-hyok instead of Private Kim, which made me feel more at ease.

I asked the landlady if she knew of a laundry service for the captain. She said that she would do it at a reasonable price. She was a hard worker and a quick thinker. It would be very convenient for her to do laundry because a clean, bubbling creek ran right behind her backyard. After giving her the captain's laundry bag, I went to his office and reported that his laundry had been taken care of. Then I asked him if he had more tasks for me.

Handing me a list of supplies, he asked me to take it to the company quartermaster. As ordered, he fulfilled the captain's request and asked his assistants to transport two sets of bedding supplies to the captain's quarters. I directed the men to put one set in the captain's room and the other in the adjacent room for me. Then I made the beds for both rooms. When I finished the work, it was not even mid-afternoon.

Since I had a few more hours before dinner, I visited my friends in the 3rd Platoon. They were busy beautifying their camp by leveling the field, bringing stones and gravel from the nearby river, and transplanting ornamental shrubs from the surrounding hills. Sweating, some of them had taken off their upper shirts. I felt sorry for them because I had easy tasks while they toiled. I shouted, "Hey, you guys. How are you doing?"

"Hey guys, Tae-hyok is here," Bong hollered. Despite only a few days of separation, they stopped what they were doing, gathered around me, and greeted me like a long-lost friend. Man-E fondly said "Where the hell were you? I missed you, son of a bitch," and laughed. Others, including Jong-kook, concurred. They asked how my new job was.

I said, "I missed you guys, too. You know what? I have to watch my language in front of the commander." Then I briefly described my new duties and said I would be quartering with the commander until further notice. I was careful not to brag.

Chun said, "That's great. Good for you, our baby soldier." Pak said, "You are lucky, skinny boy. What did you do to land such a good job? Anyway, we're so happy for you." After a few minutes, the sergeant hollered, "Boys, get back to work!" I joined them, helping with their beautification work until the five o'clock bugle. It was good to intermingle with old friends.

After bidding them goodbye, I dropped by the captain's office for evening detail. He handed me his daily meal schedule for the landlady; breakfast at 7 a.m., lunch at 12:30 p.m., and dinner at 7 p.m. If any change occurred, he would let her know in advance. I promptly took it to her. She thanked me and asked me if I knew his favorite foods. I told her I knew nothing about his tastes because I had begun to work for him only two days earlier.

• • •

Within a few days, my daily work settled into a routine. I cleaned Captain Lee's bedroom, made his bed, shined his shoes, and did various odd errands. All those things took me only a couple of hours, and the rest of the day I was free to study algebra and solve practice problems. I did well at factorizations but toiled at others. Even after solving them, I was not sure whether my answers were correct because the book did not provide answers. Every so often after dinner, I asked the captain if he would mind reviewing my solutions when he was not busy. He kindly checked them under a flickering kerosene lamp, explaining my errors.

Every day, after algebra, I went to the company headquarters and read the *Kyunghyang Daily News* (경향신문) from cover to cover. Even though it was four or five days old and consisted of only six pages, it kept me abreast of the world beyond this backwoods village. I enjoyed it with gusto.

A few weeks after we had been deployed in this region, we heard from the regional school in Hyeon-ri, about three miles north of us. The school invited the commander to its athletic meeting (a homecoming day) as one of the VIP guests. He asked me to attend the event with him. Upon arriving at the school, the superintendent welcomed us and led us to the VIP section but sent our driver and guard to the regular spectators' section. On the way back to the camp, the captain asked me if I had enjoyed the event. I replied, "Yes, sir. I really did."

A few days later he had a business trip to the regiment headquarters in Wonju and again took me with him. After taking care of business, he accompanied me to his house and introduced me to his wife and baby son. They were wonderful people. He and his wife asked me to stay with them while his driver stayed at the regiment motor pool barracks. I truly appreciated them for treating me as if I were one of their family members. Spending a couple of days with them mitigated my homesickness.

After two days' hiatus we returned to the remote company camp, and my routine resumed. One afternoon, as I read the newspaper, Company Sergeant Gyeon abruptly said, "Hey, Private Kim, did you have sex with Captain Lee?"

Doubting what I had heard, I asked, "Pardon me, Sergeant?"

"Did you have *keogan* (sex) with the Captain?"

Shocked, I jumped off my chair and boldly said, "No, I have not Sergeant! Sergeant, I respect you and am thankful for assigning me to the Captain's detail duty, but it is disgusting for you to suggest such a horrible thing. The Captain is a gentleman and a kind officer, not a dirty man. Don't insult him anymore!"

Clearly surprised to hear such harsh words from a low man on the totem pole, he said, "You are out of line," instead of apologizing. "I assigned you to the Captain's detail duty to keep an eye on you because we suspected that you might desert and return to North Korea. Now, you have turned into a fresh-mouthed soldier, talking to your company sergeant so boldly. Get out. No more reading the newspapers in my office."

"Yes, sir," I left the office. Depressed, I went to a quiet place by the riverbank and tried to digest what the company sergeant had thoughtlessly spit out about the captain and my assignment as his detail duty. If they had chosen this as a means of keeping an eye on me, their plan was a total failure because the captain had given me more freedom to move around without supervision than anyone else in the company, including the company sergeant. Had I wanted, I could have slipped out of the town and crossed the border into North Korea.

Why did the captain allow me, a mere private, such a privilege? I remembered that at the lunch table he had inquired about my family and why I had come to the South at such a young age and joined the army instead of attending school. Then it dawned on me that my honest answers had made him believe that I had been wrongly suspected as a potential deserter, so he had allowed me freedom.

Shortly after the unpleasant incident with the foul-mouthed company sergeant, he was transferred elsewhere, and Master Sergeant Chang Hee-chul replaced him. He appeared to be more well-mannered than his predecessor. I introduced myself to him and got permission to read the newspapers once again. From the beginning, we had an amicable relationship.

Despite my comfortable life and unusual freedom, uncertainty about my future in the army began to creep into my mind. How long would my current job last? Captain Lee was the most senior officer among the four company-level commanders within the battalion. The others were lieutenants. Rumor had it that he might soon get promoted to major and be transferred to a higher position. Then my current job would cease to exist, and I would be reassigned to one of the four infantry platoons. After having enjoyed such freedom, I might have difficulties adjusting to a regulated lifestyle where I would not have time to study algebra or read newspapers anymore. Should I ask the captain to transfer me to a clerical job? However, it was only a handful of weeks since I had begun to work for him—too soon to ask for such a favor! Besides, I didn't have the guts. I would wait until I had gotten to know him better, and for the appropriate time.

Meanwhile, I studied algebra and read everything I could get my hands on. I wished they had a library in town so that I might have access to more reading materials. After my studies, I explored the town, meeting the local folk, enjoying the surrounding scenery, and taking advantage of the beautiful fall weather.

Then one mid-October day, Captain Lee called me into his office and told me that the regiment had promoted him to lead a Special Battalion, and he would be leaving the next day. He asked me to pack all his belongings and go with him to help his family relocate. Even though this abrupt news disappointed me, I composed myself and said, "Congratulations, sir! But so soon, sir?"

"Thank you." He cleaned his desk and bookcase. "Yes, so soon!" He handed me a bundle of files and a few books to be packed with his other belongings. "Tell the host lady that I will not come to dinner this evening."

It was already late afternoon. That meant that the captain had only a couple of official hours as the company commander. I thought it was my only chance to ask him to assign me to a clerical duty. If I didn't ask now, there wouldn't be another chance. Just as I took a deep breath and mustered my courage, a group of senior sergeants knocked at the door and asked, "Captain, may we come in, sir?"

"Yes, you may!"

One of them said, "Sir, we've just learned that you've been promoted to command the Special Battalion in Yeongwol. Congratulations, sir!" They came in with a bottle of *soju*. "Sir, if you please, may we toast your promotion? We know it's not five yet," they said while putting the bottle and a small china cup on the table. The company sergeant, MSgt. Chang also came into the captain's office and joined them.

The captain, usually a taciturn man, laughed and said, "Alright. Thank you." Starting with the company sergeant, each one shook hands with the captain. Then they surrounded the table, and the man who had brought the bottle opened it. After filling the cup with *soju*, he handed it over to the captain and said, "Good luck, sir."

The captain accepted the cup, drank the *soju*, and handed the empty cup to the company sergeant before filling it. The sergeant did the same, passing it to the next person, and so on, circulating the cup as was the tradition. They were all in a good mood.

Recognizing that the circumstances would not allow me to request a favor from the captain, I quietly slipped out of the office with his books, returned to his quarters and packed all his belongings into a couple of army duffle bags. I cleaned my room, too. I regretted not making my request sooner.

The next morning, after reviewing the company and giving his farewell speech, the captain climbed onto the passenger seat of the company's truck. I, too, climbed onto the cargo bay. As the vehicle slowly moved, the company saluted him goodbye.

A week later, I returned from the trip and reported to the company sergeant. He told me that I had been reassigned to the 3rd Platoon to which I had belonged during basic training. Shortly afterward I reported to Platoon Sergeant Hakdong. He and all my friends welcomed me. From now on I would work and act according to the platoon leader's orders as all my friends did. This ended my halcyon weeks; now there would be no more freedom, no more algebra or reading papers. Sgt. Hakdong also told me that the company had been ordered to move to another town within a few days, and that I should pack my belongings. The whole company was busy preparing for the move.

Late in October of 1948, we moved to Hongcheon-gun, Gangwon-do Province, over ten miles south of Sangnam-ri, farther away from the two Koreas' border. It was a much larger town. There were a few general stores, a couple of restaurants, and a public hot bath facility. Our camp occupied an empty school building with six classrooms, an office, and a large playground. I didn't know where the school had moved. The company headquarters took the school office, and each platoon took one of the classrooms as its quarters. Since we did not have beds, in the evening, we spread our futons in three rows on the bare wooden floor. In the morning, we folded them back neatly as soon as we got up. We ate our three meals sitting cross-legged on the futons.

Once we had settled in the new environment, every day we had field training in various battle formations. After the extraordinary freedom I had enjoyed, the training was almost as arduous as basic training. Even harder was nightly guard duty. My first guard assignment fell between midnight and 2 a.m. on November 8, 1948—the worst shift. It was lonely and cold.

CHAPTER 11

I Am Not a Spy

November 1948 - June 1950

I had just finished the two-hour guard duty and returned to my bed without taking off my fatigues and socks to keep warm. There was no heat in the room even though the outdoor temperature was nearly freezing, too cold to fall asleep.

Just as I finally drifted off, Sgt. Yun shook my bed and said, "Wake up, PFC Kim. Lieutenant Roh wants you to report immediately. You had better put on a sweater and a heavy jacket. It's freezing out there." An armed guard stood by him. I felt apprehensive. *Why does he want me in the middle of the night?*

I got up reluctantly and put on my army sweater, field jacket, and shoes. He and the guard escorted me to the office where Lt. Roh, the company executive officer, was waiting for me. Staff Sgt. Kim Hakdong (my platoon sergeant), Sgt. Lee Chunwoo (the 2nd Platoon Sergeant) and my friend PFC Jin Chin-mae were also in the office. I saluted Lt. Roh and said, "PFC Kim reporting, sir."

He returned my salute and addressed all four of us. "Listen! I have received an order from the regiment commander to escort the four of you to Chuncheon City for an urgent, special assignment. I do not know what it is, but you will find out when you arrive. We shall leave immediately."

Special assignment! Are we going to fight the rebels?

A month earlier, two regiments of the South Korean Army stationed in the southern region, led by communist commanders, had toppled the two-month-old democratic South Korean government. They had murdered anti-communist soldiers, local officials, policemen, and their families, including children. The newly elected president, Syngman Rhee, had declared martial law to quell the rebels. The whole country was hypersensitive to the communist movements.

Lt. Roh picked up his carbine rifle, and he and the guard led us to a truck. I was surprised that the lieutenant didn't ask us to get our rifles for a special assignment. He ordered us to climb onto the truck cargo bed escorted by the armed guard. Then he jumped into the passenger seat and barked, "Let's move." Chuncheon City was located about twenty miles due northwest.

I was very apprehensive about this special assignment because both the escorting lieutenant and the guard armed themselves with rifles, but we did not. I wondered, "How urgent is this special assignment? Is it so important that the regiment commander has chosen two of the brightest and highest-ranking sergeants in the company? But Chin-mae and I are only private first class, two of the more than one hundred lowest-ranking soldiers in the company."

The truck left the parade ground, and the guard at the gate stopped us. After exchanging a few words with the lieutenant, the guard let us go. As we drove into a short, unlit dirt street, a house dog barked wildly. Then many more joined him, yelping in chorus. As soon as the truck got on an unpaved, rock-strewn highway, the driver accelerated, raising dust into the cargo bed. It was too dark to see it, but I smelled it, and my lungs became heavy.

After a long silence, Sgt. Hakdong asked, "Does anyone know what this special assignment is? It is very strange; I don't like it."

Sgt. Chunwoo responded, "You're a senior sergeant in the company. If you don't know, certainly none of us do. It is very spooky."

My anxiety mounted, and the freezing weather made it more intense. It was so cold that every one of us, including the escorting guard, raised our jacket collars. The truck bounced wildly up and down on the rural roads, kicking up rocks which rattled the bottom of the vehicle. The bouncing upset my stomach.

After a couple of hours' rough ride through the mountainous area, we entered the outskirts of Chuncheon City. As we drove on an unlit, winding street, the driver slowed the vehicle and pulled in front of a two-story building lit by a single light above the entrance.

The lieutenant came to the back of the truck and shouted, "Okay, this is your destination. Climb down!" We did. I looked up at the signboard just above the entrance door. It read "Chuncheon Office of the 8th Regiment Military Police." *What the hell does this special assignment have to do with the dreadful military police?* The Korean Military Police operation was patterned after the Imperial Japanese *Kempeitai* (MP) and known to be brutal. My uneasiness grew into intense agitation. He led us inside the station. An MP staff sergeant and a corporal were sitting by a glowing stove.

As we entered, the two MPs jumped up and saluted Lt. Roh. The MP sergeant said, "Good morning, Lieutenant. You must be Lieutenant Roh, sir?"

"Good morning, sergeant. Yes, I am. At ease. I suppose you have received a message from the regiment headquarters about a special assignment."

"Yes, sir." Then he led the lieutenant to an adjacent office and closed the door behind them. The four of us stood silently around the stove and warmed ourselves. I began to suspect that the so-called special assignment was really something else. The more I thought about it, the drier my mouth became.

Finally, Sgt. Hakdong broke the silence and asked the MP corporal, "Corporal, do you happen to know what the special assignment is?" Everybody turned to the corporal, but he answered, "I don't know, sergeant," without even looking at him. Silence prevailed again.

The door opened, and Lt. Roh and the MP sergeant stepped out of the office. Instinctively, our eyes turned to them. They stared at us gravely, especially Lt. Roh. He walked over and said, "The MP sergeant will explain the details of the special assignment. I shall be returning to the company. Take care of yourselves." Then he, the driver, and the escorting guard went back to our truck and left.

An ominous feeling gripped me, and my heart started to beat rapidly. Even though my body had warmed up from the burning stove, I started shivering. The dark brown wall panels of the dimly lit, old office depressed my spirit. The only consolation in this uncertain situation was that three friends were with me.

Two more MPs joined the other two, all armed with carbine rifles. They talked loudly. The MP sergeant shuffled some papers, ignoring our presence. It must have been only a few minutes, but uncertainty made it seem like longer.

Finally, the MP sergeant called my platoon sergeant Hakdong, and asked for his personal information: name, rank, dog tag number, date of birth, place of birth, and unit name. The MP checked the information against his paper.

Undaunted, Sgt. Hakdong asked, "Sergeant, I thought we were brought here for some kind of special assignment. Why are you asking all these questions?"

The MP said flatly, "Yes, you were. I will tell you after finishing this paperwork. Please wait." Then he collected the same information from each of us. After finishing the paperwork, he said coldly, "By the order of the regiment commander, you are detained in this station until further notice."

I was stunned. A chill ran down my spine. My legs lost their strength. I asked myself what crime I might have committed to be detained in this infamous MP station.

Sergeants Hakdong and Chunwoo simultaneously asked, "For what charges?" PFC Jin and I were too frightened to talk, and simply watched the MP and our two sergeants.

"I am not able to tell you for what charges. Captain Joh, the station chief, will tell you in the morning. Follow me!" He led us out of the office through the back door to a short, covered walkway, followed by two armed MPs. A bare incandescent light bulb fixed on the ceiling gloomily lit our way. The wooden planks of the walkway squeaked loudly, intensifying my anguish. The MP sergeant ordered us to stop in front of a massive lumber wall with a heavy door (about two feet by two feet) at the floor level and an iron-barred small opening high up in the wall. A heavy latch locked the metal reinforced door. An MP soldier was posted to guard the wall.

The sergeant ordered the guard to open the door. As the guard pulled back the iron bar, the metallic screech pierced my heart. When the door opened, I saw people lying inside. It was a stockade!

The MP sergeant ordered us to get inside one by one. The entrance was so low and small that we had to crawl in. He directed PFC Jin to enter first, then me. As soon as I knelt and stuck my head inside, a stench stung my nostrils. As I unconsciously recoiled, the sergeant barked, "Hurry up!" and kicked me in the butt. Suddenly my eyes blurred with tears. I was crying not for the pain, but for the humiliation and loss of human dignity.

I crawled inside and stood by PFC Jin like a lost soul. Then somebody tapped me on the shin and said, "Move aside." I looked down while wiping away my tears. It was Sgt. Chunwoo. Sgt. Hakdong immediately followed him. As soon as he came inside, the guard slammed the door behind us and locked it by sliding the iron bar into its slot. The screeching metal made me shudder. Now I was locked in a damned stockade, cut off from the outside world. I had lost all freedom.

The stockade was a rectangular cell, about eight feet by ten feet. A bare light bulb dangled from the middle of the dirty ceiling, dimly lighting the cell. The dark brown walls made the cell gloomy. Sleeping on the bare wooden floor, about twenty inmates packed the cell. No one moved. Apparently, our noisy presence did not disturb their sleep. They did not have enough blankets. The cell did not allow enough room for them to lie down. They leaned their upper backs against the walls, stretching their legs toward the middle of the room. Their feet toppled over each other.

The foul smell that I had tried to avoid permeated the room. A five-gallon aluminum pail stood in the corner by the door. That was the toilet. It did not even have a lid. I realized that it was the source of the stench. We were being ordered to live in this jammed stockade under these inhumane conditions: to eat there, sleep there, excrete there, and inhale the stink. Even my parents' pig back home had better living conditions because it had room to move around in its pen. I screamed inwardly, "How long are you going to keep me here? I am innocent! I do not deserve this subhuman treatment." Obviously, no one heard my silent agonizing scream. Perhaps my friends were screaming inside, too.

Sergeants Hakdong and Chunwoo lightly kicked those inmates sleeping nearby and said, "Hey, you guys, move over. Make room." Grudgingly, they gave us room to sit down. They went back to sleep. We sat side by side on the bare wooden floor, holding our knees between our hands, leaning against the wall, confused and lost.

Sgt. Hakdong abruptly sniffed a couple of times and said, "What is this fucking stinking smell? It smells like shit!" He sniffed a few more times.

Sgt. Chunwoo laughed heartily and said, "Can't you see that shit pail?" pointing to the corner. "From now on, if you want to shit, you have to shit in that bucket. You know what? Shitting in that fucking pail must be our special assignment." I thought he laughed to hide how wretched he felt. "Seriously, I don't know why they have locked us in this damn stockade. I haven't done anything to earn this. How about you, Sergeant Hakdong?" Without waiting for his response, Sgt. Chunwoo turned to me and said, "Look, PFC Kim. You are the baby of the company. How old are you, sixteen, seventeen?"

"Seventeen, sergeant." Suddenly I missed my parents so much. I buried my head between my knees. My mind drifted to reflect on the last two years of my life. I had come to Seoul at the age of fifteen, hoping to get an education. I had worked odd jobs to earn money, but I did not make enough to pay for school. Six months earlier, I had eagerly signed up for the Army Communication School because the recruiters had promised that the school would teach mathematics, physics, English, and radio technology. Instead, they had taken me to an infantry training center where none of the promised subjects were taught.

During basic training, I had expressed to one of my trainee friends that I did not like that the army lied to me when recruiting me. One day my drill corporal called me to his room and beat me because of what I'd said, causing severe bruises and internal bleeding. *Was it a crime for me to express my displeasure with the army? Is that why I am jailed now?* If it was a crime, then I had already been severely punished for it. I was so exhausted that I fell into a deep sleep in a sitting position.

BREAKFAST IN JAIL

"Bang, bang!" Rough poundings on the jail door frightened me out of my sleep. The sharp metallic screech of the latch pained my ears. As a guard opened the door, the pale morning sun filtered through it. He shouted, "Breakfast, come on, Messboy."

One of the inmates got up from his sleep and nervously responded, "Here I am, Corporal," and crawled over the mound of human sardines toward the door.

The morning sun reflected on Messboy's face. His complexion appeared much fairer than that of most Koreans. Perhaps a long confinement and the lack of adequate sunlight had whitened his face. The guard escorted him out of the stockade. I thought that Messboy must have had a name and rank before being incarcerated, but now his name was "Messboy." He was a tall, handsome young man in his mid-twenties, not a boy!

Every one of my joints hurt, especially in my knees. Every inch of my muscles was stiff and throbbing. A few hours of sleep in a sitting position made my whole body ache. I wanted to lie on my back and stretch, but there was not enough room. Instead, I stood up and massaged my legs and back, loosening my stiff muscles.

After the massage, I sat against the wall with my legs crossed. Nature urged me to pass water, but I did not have the courage to use the toilet. Suppressing the urge to go caused pain in my abdomen, which grew worse by the minute. But I continued to hold it, burying my face between my knees. Then I heard a noise like water from a faucet. I raised my head and found the source. An inmate was releasing pressure as if there was nobody around him. He took a long time to finish. As soon as he did, I took care of myself, too. Nevertheless, the pain in my abdomen lasted for a few more hours.

The jail door swung open again. Cold morning air blew in, sweeping the smelly, stuffy room. Messboy announced, "Breakfast," as he pushed two aluminum pails into the stockade one after another, before crawling in. The guard slammed the door and locked it again. The pails were identical to the toilet bucket.

Messboy brought the two food pails to the center of the floor. One contained thin Chinese cabbage soup, the other cooked rice balls, each the size of a small apple. Everyone except the four of us gathered eagerly around the breakfast buckets. Messboy handed out a rice ball and a scoop of the soup in a frisbee-like aluminum bowl to each prisoner. Neither chopsticks nor spoons were provided. But the other prisoners skillfully ate their rice and drank soup from the bowls hungrily.

I had absolutely no appetite. I had never eaten a meal next to a toilet. I left it untouched. My friends started to eat, but soon quit. The other prisoners, already finished, looked at our food like hungry vultures. They asked, "You are not eating?"

I curtly said, "No." My three friends also said no, pushing the soup bowls toward the prisoners. They promptly grabbed the bowls without even a thank you, split them among themselves and devoured the food. Watching them eating, I wondered if I was going to be like them if the MPs continued to detain me. The thought made me sick to my stomach.

Messboy collected the dirty soup bowls and put them jangling into the aluminum pails. He banged the jail door and shouted to the guard, "Corporal, this is Messboy. Let me out to clean the soup bowls." The guard let him out with the dirty utensils.

After breakfast, the other inmates talked and laughed among themselves as if we were not present. Then a sergeant said with dignity, "I am Sergeant First Class Kim. I am the *siljang* (head of inmates). You may call me Siljang or Sergeant Kim. You guys came in last night, didn't you?"

Sgt. Hakdong answered on behalf of the four of us newcomers, "Yes, actually early this morning."

"Normally a new inmate is supposed to formally report to the *siljang*, but I will waive the formality this time. Why did they put you in this damn stockade? Where did you come from?"

"We don't know why. None of us committed any crime. Our company executive officer escorted us to this MP station last night, supposedly for some special assignment. Now we have ended up in this filthy jail. We are from the 5th Company of the 2nd Battalion stationed in Hongcheon. I am Staff Sergeant Hakdong; this is Sergeant Chunwoo. Both of us are platoon sergeants. These two kids (pointing to me and PFC Jin) are under my command. How about you, *siljang*? How long have you been jailed?"

The *siljang* matter-of-factly said that he was the First Sergeant of the 2nd Company of the 1st Battalion stationed here in Chuncheon City. He had been jailed for the last five weeks. The MPs had arrested him as a communist sympathizer, which he was not. He added, "My hunch is that you guys have most likely been accused of being communist sympathizers, just like me."

"You mean they have kept you here for five weeks without any evidence?"

"Yes. They have interrogated me a few times already and tortured me to confess that I was a communist sympathizer and have actively participated in communist activities. Of course, I did not give them any confession because there was nothing to confess." His remarks made me shiver.

Sgt. Hakdong asked, "Every one of you is accused of being a communist sympathizer?"

The *siljang* said, "No, not everyone. Only two of us, me and Corporal Han," and he pointed to someone sitting across from him. "The rest have been jailed for various crimes; some for desertion, some for petty theft, a couple for attempted rapes."

INTERROGATION

Mid-morning, the guard opened the door and called, "Kim Tae-hyok."

Fear gripped me; my heart pounded. I answered anxiously, "Here." He told me to come out of the jail. I crawled through the small jail door. An MP corporal escorted me to a staff sergeant in the office. Without looking at me, the sergeant ordered me to sit on a rough wooden bench in front of his desk. I cautiously sat, hearing my heart's loud pounding, hoping that he would find me innocent and free me, but deep in my mind, worry lurked. Something very bad might be waiting for me. He kept a chestnut brown police club on his desk.

In South Korea, if you were found guilty of being a spy for North Korea, a communist, or a communist sympathizer, you could be sentenced to a long-term or life imprisonment, or even to death. Knowing this, I swore to myself that if they accused me of being a communist, I would never give in to any torture, no matter how harsh it might be, and give no false confession.

He opened a file on the desk and asked, "What is your name?" looking at the file, not at me.

"PFC Kim Tae-hyok, sir."

"How old are you?"

"Seventeen."

"Where is your hometown?"

"Suan-gun, Hwanghae Province."

"That's in North Korea, isn't it?"

"Yes."

"So, you were a member of the League of Communist Youth, weren't you?"

I said loudly and clearly," No, sir," to emphasize my innocence. As he picked up his police club and slowly walked toward my back, tapping his club lightly on his palm, my hair stood on end, and my heart shrank.

"Tell me the truth. You are a communist, aren't you?"

"No, I am not!"

A sudden blow struck my shoulder, and pain flashed through me. I screamed and sprang up from the bench like a frightened rabbit.

He shouted, "Sit down," while pressing my shoulder with his club. "You are a North Korean spy." Whack, whack. "Confess that you are a spy for North Korea."

"I am not!" I responded in a pain-stricken voice.

"Why did you come to the South?"

"I came to Seoul to get an education."

He whacked me on my back and asked, "If so, why did you join the army?"

"Because I did not have money to go to school, and I didn't want to go back to North Korea," I answered loudly despite the excruciating pain in my shoulders and back.

"You are lying. Confess that you are a spy." More blows, one after another, and I groaned. I lost count of how many more. The continuous beating numbed my shoulders and back to the point where I felt no pain, just a hot flash with each whack. The torture exhausted me physically and mentally to the point that I could not scream anymore. I stretched my arms on the desk, as if surrendering, rested my head between them and mumbled, "I am not a spy, I am not a spy," wishing to disappear from this world forever.

A sudden blow on my back woke me up. "Get up!" the sergeant barked. "Corporal, take him back to the cell." Apparently, I had collapsed, but I could not tell for how long.

He mumbled, "Seventeen-year-old boy, a North Korean spy!"

I murmured, "Sergeant, I am not a spy. I am not a North Korean spy," staggering, while the corporal escorted me out of the office by the arm.

The guard opened the stockade door for me, and I crawled in slowly because of the pain in my shoulders and back. I sat silently and leaned against the wall, gently rubbing my shoulders. Everybody quietly looked at me. Then my three friends came over and asked, "Are you alright, Tae-hyok? What did they do to you?" in concerned voices. They looked very grave, perhaps thinking the same fate awaited them.

I said in a quivering voice, "A sergeant beat me brutally with a police club over and over to force me to confess that I was a North Korean spy. I denied it repeatedly."

Holding me by the arm, PFC Jin consoled me, "Tae-hyok, you will be alright. I am sure they will free us very soon because we are innocent."

I fell asleep. When I woke up, it was evening. I felt better, but my shoulders and back throbbed. My whole body was stiff and sore. I unbuttoned my jacket and squinted at my battered shoulders. They were blue, black, and swollen. I assumed my back must be the same. The slightest touch caused me to wince and groan. Suddenly, I became homesick and missed my parents. I thought that if my mother had seen me, she would have held me in her arms, applied some soothing salve with her tender hands to reduce my pain, and comforted me saying, "Tae-hyok, you are going to be alright," even though she might be crying and her heart breaking. Messboy brought supper, but I was too shattered to eat.

EXERCISE OR TORTURE?

The second morning, my shoulders and back were swollen and achy. Messboy brought in our meager breakfast, the same as the previous meals. Even though I had had no food for two days, I had no desire to eat. Pain and anxiety robbed me of my appetite. As before, other prisoners took my breakfast and ate voraciously.

Soon after breakfast, someone barked, "Everybody out, exercise time. Out, out!" He banged the iron bars with a stick, producing loud, metallic noises.

The old-time prisoners groaned, "Not again." We crawled out.

When we all went out to a small dirt courtyard, a low-ranking MP sergeant barked, "Line up in one column, one column! Do you hear me?"

Nervously, we hurried into a long column. Two MP PFCs armed with carbine rifles guarded us on the left and right. The sergeant stood on the walkway in front of us and commanded, "Count off from the front," while tapping his palm with his dark-brown police club. There was a baseball bat against the guardrail. He acted as if the whole world lay under his boots.

We loudly numbered ourselves, "One, two, three," and so on. Thirty-two was the last one. Thirty-two men! I was amazed that so many people were imprisoned in that small room.

"Now, numbers one to eight to row one. Nine to sixteen to row two, seventeen to twenty-four to row three. The rest to row four. Form rows. Hurry up!" the sergeant shouted, banging his stick against the guardrail. I was placed at the far right of the second row. "You follow me, one-two-three-four, one-two-three-four," he said, showing a few steps of calisthenics. Then he shouted, "Row two, three steps back. Row three, six steps back. Row four, nine steps back. Go! Go!" He fastened his police stick to his white MP belt and picked up the baseball bat from the guardrail.

He barked again, "Now, push-ups!" We put our hands on the frozen ground and stretched our legs backward, ready for push-ups. The push-up position caused my injured shoulders and back great pain. The MP repeatedly shouted, "One, two. One, two!" and we repeated ups and downs. He walked between the rows like a conqueror and yelled at us to show that he was our absolute master, hitting the baseball bat on the ground. He yelled again, "Raise the right leg high! Keep it high!" Keeping one leg in the air put my entire body weight on my outstretched arms. This added more pain to my battered shoulders. My fingers were freezing. My arms yielded to the intolerable pain, and I lost my balance. My body wobbled, and I fell flat on my stomach. The cruel MP shrieked, "Straighten your body!" I tried, but couldn't. He struck my hip with his baseball bat!

Pain flared on my rear end. I unconsciously screamed, "*Aigoo!*" which he sarcastically imitated before hitting me again. Fear made me try my best to push up, only to collapse again. He clobbered me many more times, until I became numb.

Then he unexpectedly walked to the row behind me. He yelled at the people in the back rows, "Keep your legs high," hitting his baseball bat on the ground. Whack, whack. Agonizing groans followed.

After such torture, the MP yelled, "Stand up! Get in line!" Everyone struggled to get up. The pain in my hip made me stagger. He shouted, "That's all for now. Dismissed!" The two guards herded us into the dismal cell. The fresh pain caused me to limp. It was almost impossible for me to sit. I had to lean sideways against the wall to minimize the hip pain. But leaning on my side hurt my shoulder. My hip throbbed. I wondered how my fragile body could have endured such brutal blows two days in a row, and how much more

I could bear. The MP was supposed to let us exercise for our physical well-being. Instead, he hurt us. Why? Was he just cruel? Perhaps he derived pleasure from his power. Torture under the name of exercise became an almost daily affair throughout my imprisonment. Different MPs used different methods of abuse.

No lawyer was assigned to defend me. No one in the cell had a lawyer. In the American judicial system, a prisoner is innocent until proven guilty. But these MPs regarded us as guilty until proven otherwise. Messboy was court-martialed for being AWOL, without a lawyer representing him. The military police presented his case to the military court based on his confession. In turn, the court handed down a six-month imprisonment.

We communist suspects were barred from contacting anyone from the outside world. I thought if those MPs murdered me and buried my body somewhere, nobody would ever find me. There was no way to defend myself except not giving in to their torture and not making a false confession. This dreadful thought made me determined to endure, no matter how harsh things might become.

By the fourth morning, I felt hungry for the first time. I had eaten nothing for almost four days and now felt famished. Apparently, my body had decided to replenish its badly depleted energy to sustain life. I eagerly waited for meals—cooked rice and Chinese cabbage in thin soy sauce broth. When it finally arrived, I licked my bowl clean. I was determined to improve my health to survive this extraordinary hardship.

POLITICAL PRISONERS AND DUNGEON

During the next few days, more prisoners were brought to the already over-crowded stockade. The prison population grew to almost forty. We could hardly move around without tripping over each other. To alleviate the serious overcrowding, the MP authorities separated the six political prisoners (communist suspects) from the rest and incarcerated us in a damp dungeon. The six consisted of the four of us from the 5th Company and the two from the 1st Battalion, including the *siljang*.

The dungeon was a concrete chamber with a large metal door and no windows. A bare light bulb fixed in the middle of the dark gray ceiling weakly lit the underground prison. The door had a small iron-barred opening at its top. A dirty ventilator occupied a small area at the top of the wall, opposite the door. The dungeon was twice as large as the original stockade and provided us with ample space to stretch our legs. Neither blankets nor mats were supplied, just piles of rice straw. Water seeped in through the cracks in the concrete walls, gathered in the small canals along the corners where the wall and floor met and flowed through a hole in the lowest corner. It was so damp and cold that we covered ourselves with rice straw.

This straw reminded me of my two pigs back home. I had put plenty of rice straw in their pen to keep them warm during the winters. They were well fed, inhaling fresh air and bathing in the warm sunlight. The pigs happily snorted and snuggled cozily under the thick straw blanket. Now, as my pigs had done, I tried to keep myself warm under a pile of straw. But in this dungeon, I was hungry, breathed damp smelly air, and crouched in darkness.

I remembered that back in November 1945 (three years ago), just three months after Korea had been liberated from the Japanese occupation, two North Korean communist cadres had visited our remote valley, collected as many men as they could from the surrounding hamlets, and given us a seminar about communism, Stalin, and General Kim Il Sung.

Those cadres had fed us fabricated information. According to them, everybody would become equally rich under communism; the poor would be freed from exploitation by the rich; Stalin was the greatest leader in the world who had defeated Germany and Japan; the Soviet Union under his leadership, not America's, had liberated Korea from Japan; and General Kim Il Sung was the greatest Korean patriot and genius military strategist who had singlehandedly killed hundreds of Imperial Japanese soldiers in battle. They also depicted America as the greatest evil expansionist and exploiter of the weak. America would do anything to colonize Korea, just as Japan had done.

During this seminar, none of our elders expressed an opinion on the cadres' preposterous presentation, perhaps because our culture dictated that a host should not offend his guest's feelings. It also discouraged children from contradicting their elders' opinions. I was then just fourteen years old. But I could not keep silent because those cadres were telling us lies. I asked, "Sirs, if everyone gets equally rich under communism, then why did a Russian soldier and a Korean communist cadre like you come to our village a week ago and steal soybeans and corn from us, just like the Japanese did? Our families worked hard to produce them. I don't believe communism will make everyone rich."

The senior cadre responded, "Young man, the Russian soldiers have not received sufficient supplies from their country, and they need food until they get more supplies. I am sure they will pay your parents for what they took." But this never happened.

"I have two more things to say about what you told us. First, you said that the Soviet Union under Stalin's great leadership defeated Japan and liberated Korea. I do not believe that because the Russians fought the Japanese only a few days before Japan's surrender on August 15, 1945. But America fought Japan for almost four years, and she dropped two new atomic bombs on Japan. I saw American B-29 bombers flying high up over our school town a few times this past winter and spring, but I never saw a single Soviet plane during World War II. So, I believe America liberated Korea, not the Soviet Union."

The cadre interrupted me and said loudly, "Young man, you are grossly misinformed. Yes, the Soviet Army fought the Imperial Japanese Army for only one week. That's all their brilliant Russian Army needed to liberate Korea."

I continued, "Second, you said that General Kim Il Sung was the greatest patriot and military leader. According to you, he is only thirty-six years old. He is too young to be the greatest leader in Korea's history."

The two cadres became really agitated and said, "Young man, what is your name? I think you should attend the Communist Party School in Haeju or Pyongyang. It is a six-month training, and the party pays all your expenses. They teach you the history of communism and General Kim's saga fighting the Japanese. Have you ever been to Pyongyang? It is a big, majestic city. You might get a good job at the party's headquarters in Pyongyang or Haeju upon graduation. Think about it and talk it over with your father." Neither my father nor I liked the two cadres' suggestion.

Then, they continued preaching that communism would guarantee equal rights to all. They said that we should call each other Comrade because we were all equal. The senior cadre suggested that we could even call our parents

"Comrade Father" or "Comrade Mother" instead of using honorary expressions of *Abeoji* (Father Sir) or *Eomeoni* (Mother)!

That doctrine shocked and upset our tradition-honoring people. Suddenly the docile audience erupted and protested, "How dare you teach us such ideas! We love our tradition and respect our grandparents and parents. You ask us to call them *comrade*. We don't want to listen to you anymore."

Stunned, the cadres apologized and left. They drove our people to disdain communism even though they were poor farmers. However, as time progressed, the North Korean Communist Party promulgated various decrees to control our daily lives. The communist North Korean government branded those who did not support it as reactionaries, confiscated their properties, and forced them to relocate to remote, unknown places. Some of them were sent to hard labor camps or coal mines. My uncle was one of them. The government also expelled students who opposed communism from schools.

I had escaped Communist North Korea to Democratic South Korea to seek freedom and better opportunities and joined the South Korean Army. Ironically, despite my strong anti-communist sentiment, now I was accused of being a North Korean spy and was locked in this miserable dungeon, wondering how long they would keep me in these horrible conditions. Deeply depressed, I stood and walked around to dispel this feeling. The rice straw was so thick that I had to lift my foot high for every step as if walking on deep snow. I reassured myself that I could endure torture, no matter how harsh it might be, and give no false confession. Eventually I would be freed. I started conversations with the other inmates to stave off depression.

Since our imprisonment, the MPs had not allowed us to bathe or change our clothes. None of us had extra clothes. Consequently, we had lice, and their bites drove us crazy. The dungeon was too dark to do nit-picking. Frustrated, we cursed them. Someone said, "Your foul language cannot get rid of the lice. We need a can of DDT," and laughed, as did we.

Just about the time when my injuries from the first torture began to heal, an MP soldier escorted me out of the dungeon to the same interrogation room where I had been tortured a week earlier. The brutal interrogator was not there.

Alone in the room, this thought agitated me: *I am the youngest and lowest ranking among the four of us from the 5th Company and have been branded as a political prisoner like the rest. I have already been interrogated, severely tortured, and brought back to this horrible chamber for the second time, but none of my friends have been grilled yet. Why?*

Then the brutal MP staff sergeant came in and sat, gesturing me to sit on the same bench where I had been ruthlessly beaten. The memory of his brutality came to my mind. Fear flashed throughout my body, and every strand of my hair stood on end. But I swore to myself that I would not give in and make a false confession.

He opened my file and said bluntly, "You still deny that you are a North Korean spy." Without giving me a chance to respond, he continued, "Why did you join the League of Communist Youth?" while he slowly rose, picked up his police club and walked around toward my back. I cringed.

Even though I was scared to death, I responded in a firm, loud voice, "Sergeant, I am not a North Korean spy. I have never joined the damned League of Communist Youth. I never liked communism."

He whacked me a few times on the shoulders and said, "You are lying."

Severe pain sliced through my shoulders. I screamed, "I am not a North Korean spy, sir." Another whack! He slowly walked back to his desk and sat on his chair.

Unexpectedly, he changed his tone and said warmly, "PFC Kim, if you tell me the names of those Communist Party members or sympathizers you know, we will let you go free. There is no reason for you to sacrifice yourself for those bad communists."

I responded firmly, "Sergeant, I am not a communist. I have no communist friends. If I were a communist, I would not have come to South Korea. Please believe me." Suddenly I was emotionally overwhelmed and started to cry loudly, shamelessly, and uncontrollably, burying my head between my hands. I didn't know how long I cried. I composed myself and sat wiping off my tears.

The sergeant said, "Corporal, take him back to the stockade!"

I did not believe what I had heard.

The corporal said, "Let's go!"

I stood up and followed him silently but was greatly relieved as he led me out of the torture chamber to the dungeon. As soon as he pushed me in and locked the door, my cellmates rushed to me with deep concern and asked how I was feeling. I said without emotion, "I'm fine. The sergeant only whacked me a few times and let me go." Since I had expected more excruciating torture, I could hardly believe that the sergeant had cut his interrogation short.

INTERROGATION OF THE SERGEANTS

That afternoon, an MP called out both Sergeants Hakdong and Chunwoo for interrogation. I told my friend Jin Chin-mae, the *siljang* and the other cellmate that I hoped they would not torture our sergeants as ruthlessly as they had done to me.

The *siljang* said, "I hope so, too. Those interrogators are brutes. Pray for a humane interrogator!" The corporal from the first battalion concurred with the *siljang*. But PFC Jin kept silent, just looking down at the floor. He seemed to be in deep distress expecting that he would be the next. A few moments later he murmured, "I hope they are okay."

Anxiety kept me from sitting idly in the cold, dark, damp chamber. I walked around aimlessly, kicking rice straw into the air like a restless wild animal in a cage.

In the mid-afternoon, Sgts. Hakdong and Chunwoo returned. They appeared to be in good spirits. We welcomed them and asked, "How are you, sergeants? What did they do to you? Did they torture you?"

Sgt. Hakdong answered with a smile, "No, they didn't. The MP master sergeant who interrogated us is a friend of mine. He and I joined the Army at the same time and went through basic training together in the same company. Right after that, he was sent to the MP school in Seoul because he was very smart. He asked each of us, informally, if we were communists or sympathizers. We adamantly denied the accusation. Then we talked about the good old days, asking each other about our friends. He told us that we should not worry too much. He also said that we would be released soon." This news lifted our spirits.

Even though I was glad that neither Sgt. Hakdong nor Sgt. Chunwoo was tortured, I thought it extremely unfair that the MP authorities had treated them so differently. I was sick for many days from being beaten and was still suffering. But the two sergeants' interrogator had been nice and lenient with them. I wondered why. We all were locked in this underground stockade, accused of the same crime. Was it because they were the interrogator's friends, or because they were polished city slickers talking smoothly while I was an unrefined boy from the backwoods in North Korea? Whatever the reason, it was exceedingly unjust. But I had no voice down here in the dungeon.

Sgt. Hakdong continued, "After a while, the MP sergeant changed the subject and said, 'As you might know, the 6th and 14th Regiments stationed in Yeosu and Suncheon in the southwest region, led by communist commanders and officers, have revolted against our government. They have murdered many anti-communist officers and soldiers and their families. They have also killed many civilians. Unless we get these communists and their sympathizers out of the army soon, our country might fall into deeper trouble. Do you know anyone in your company or battalion whom you suspect of being a communist or a sympathizer? If you do, please tell me. Your information is very important.' We told him that we had heard Master Sergeant Chang, our company sergeant, complain about the army. Unexpectedly, the MP shook hands with us, then let us return to our cell."

Then I realized why their interrogator had treated them leniently.

THE TRANSFER TRIP TO THE MP HEADQUARTERS

The day of freedom never came. Instead, one day, an MP master sergeant, accompanied by an MP corporal, unexpectedly visited us in the dungeon and announced that we would be transferred to the MP's main office in Wonju because we were serious political prisoners. They left the dungeon as quickly as they had come in. My heart sank, and my anguish heightened immeasurably. I asked myself, "What happened to our promised release?" Unlike me, the two sergeants appeared to be upbeat, which confused me. A few minutes later, Sgt. Hakdong explained.

He said in a jovial voice, "Once I get to Wonju, I shall contact my family and ask them to bring some delicious food, even a bottle of *soju*. Life will be much better there than in this goddamn dungeon." Sgt. Chunwoo concurred with a loud laugh and said that he would do the same. Their light-hearted mood somewhat mitigated my anguish. I even wished that they would share their delicious food with me.

A few days later, on a cold December morning, two MP corporals escorted the four of us out of the dungeon to the senior MP master sergeant in his office, leaving the *siljang* and the other prisoner behind. He ordered a sergeant who was with him to prepare for the transfer. In turn, the latter handcuffed us in pairs, Sgt. Hakdong with me, and Sgt. Chunwoo with PFC Jin. Then he connected the four of us by tying the handcuffs with a finger-thick, long, white police rope, allowing a four- to five-foot distance between the two pairs. This handcuffing was my first such experience. I felt so humiliated. When he finished, the senior MP master sergeant inspected each of us. Then he ordered the sergeant and the corporal, armed with carbines, to escort us to Wonju.

The two escorting MPs led us on foot through the streets to Chuncheon Railroad Station. My handcuffed hand was freezing. Sgt. Hakdong pulled my hand and put it into his jacket pocket along with his own to warm them up. There were many people on the streets. Shopkeepers were busily arranging their merchandise while others were out sweeping in front of their shops. They stopped working and looked at us with curiosity. Some hurriedly passed us with a quick glance. Humiliated, I kept my head down to avoid people's eyes. A grandma carrying her grandbaby on her back murmured, "What crime have they committed that they are handcuffed and being dragged to prison? Poor souls!" Her murmuring pained my already suffering heart. I wished I had not heard her. I did not know whether she was expressing sympathy or indignation.

After over a mile march through the cold streets, we were led inside the railroad station hall. It was not heated but was much warmer than outside. The station was deserted except for the ticket agents. The MP sergeant disappeared into the station office, leaving us alone with the corporal. When he returned, they herded us out to a freight train. The sergeant climbed up into a boxcar first, then ordered us to follow. It was impossible for us to climb up to the boxcar because four of us were roped together. Noticing our dilemma, the escorting sergeant ordered the other MP to untie the rope to separate us. Each pair climbed up with the help of the corporal. Then he jumped up last.

The sergeant did not retie us. I was very thankful to him for allowing us a little bit more freedom of movement.

Cold wind blew right into the car through one open door, raising dust from the floor. The sergeant closed one door with a big bang, and the corporal slammed the other. The floor of the boxcar was dirty; many empty rice-straw bags had been strewn here and there. We collected a few of them and used them as mats and quilts to keep us warm. The escorting MPs also collected a couple of the bags and sat on them in the opposite corner. They wore heavy army winter coats, and we did not. After a long, shivering wait, the train whistled and started to move with a sudden jerk. Riding a boxcar was a royal treat compared to being in the underground dungeon.

Even though Wonju was about fifty miles south of Chuncheon by bus, the MPs escorted us by a detour through Cheongnyangni freight depot, located in the eastern outskirts of Seoul, thus making the trip longer by more than sixty miles. This was an unexpected bonus. The intermittent, monotonous, metallic ticking of the freight wheels sounded sweet. I truly cherished the fresh air blowing in through the freight's air vent instead of the damp, stale air of the dungeon. The small patch of sunlight through the vent lifted my spirit. For the past two weeks, I had not seen even a single ray of sunlight down in the dungeon. Forgetting that I was handcuffed, my mind drifted to my sweet hometown, tucked in a little valley, where my friends and I walked and played, giggling and hollering, on the narrow dirt roads. I daydreamed that we climbed the top of the Five Peaks Mountain (五峰山), shouted, and sang at the top of our lungs. Our shouts and songs echoed beautifully, and then faded beyond the mountains. What splendid freedom! A sudden jolt interrupted my sweet dream and brought me back to reality. Alas, I was still in handcuffs! I asked Sgt. Hakdong if we could look outside through the vent. In turn he asked the MP sergeant for permission. The sergeant nodded.

Sgt. Hakdong and I stood up and walked across the floor to the vent. It was a little bit too high for us to peek through it. We stacked up a few folded rice-straw bags, climbed on the pile, and peered out. Most trees were bare; the once-busy farm fields were empty and dotted with snow clumps. The snow-covered distant mountains were somewhat bluish white under the weak wintry sunshine. Under ordinary circumstances, I would have said, "How bleak!"

But today I saw it as the most blessed, marvelous land with wild birds flying high in the sky and animals wandering freely. We watched this idyllic scene through the small opening for a long time before we started to shiver with cold.

It was noon when we arrived at the Cheongnyangni freight depot where we would take a southbound freight train to Wonju. Five months earlier, I had been shipped in a freight train along with hundreds of other recruits from this very depot to the same Wonju for my basic training. I had volunteered to go as a free man. Now ironically, I was to be loaded on a freight car from the same depot to the same city as a political prisoner. We traversed many tracks to a Wonju-bound freight train, which would not depart for a couple of hours. It was a beautiful balmy day. The MP sergeant generously allowed us to bask in the sun and to walk around the train, still in handcuffs. All four of us enjoyed this magnificent sunlight for the first time since we had been imprisoned for almost four weeks. I was glad that there was nobody else around in the railroad yard.

We were hungry. It was more than six hours since we had had our breakfast. Sgt. Hakdong asked the MP sergeant if he would buy some food for us if we gave him some money. He agreed to do so. We pooled every penny we had and gave it to the sergeant. He in turn handed it over to the corporal and ordered him to buy some food for us.

Later, the corporal returned, clumsily carrying a big package wrapped with newspapers in his arms and holding his carbine on his shoulder. He handed the package over to Sgt. Hakdong and said, "I bought *zinbangs*." Sgt. Hakdong accepted it with thanks, put it on the freight car door threshold, and tore it open, revealing a heap of steaming *zinbangs*. He invited all of us, including the MPs, distributing three *zinbangs* to each of us. After three weeks of subsisting each day on a couple of handfuls of cooked rice balls sprinkled with salt, these soft, sweet, steaming *zinbangs* were more extravagant and delicious than a king's feast. I gobbled up the first two in no time, but the last one I nibbled so that I might enjoy the overflowing sweetness for as long as it lasted.

The MP sergeant hollered, "The train will be leaving soon. All aboard." This robbed us of our brief freedom in the open world. We all regretfully climbed up into one of the empty freight cars. As in the morning, the MPs took seats in one corner and we prisoners in the opposite corner. Soon, the train whistled gloomily and started to move. As the train gained speed, so did the biting wind. It tore through the open doors of the freight car. The MPs closed the doors to fend off the cold wind. Pale afternoon light filtered through the air vents and faintly lit the inside of the car. As I thought about the past four weeks' imprisonment, I appreciated this bit of freedom more and more, even though Sgt. Hakdong and I had been handcuffed together the whole time. A few hours from now, we would again be put in a crowded, unheated stockade. Before too long, the two MPs, loosely holding their carbine rifles on their laps, fell asleep and snored. They must have been very tired from this boring trip of escorting prisoners. But we enjoyed this trip tremendously, being away from the dungeon. I suppose that we could easily have overpowered the sleeping MPs and escaped if we had wanted to, but none of us considered such an idea because we knew we were innocent. We believed that we would be freed sooner or later. We also knew that an escape would make the authorities confirm that we were truly communists. Even if we had escaped safely, we would have had difficulties as fugitives without proper identification. Also, the authorities would harass the families of the two sergeants and PFC Jin, who lived in the region.

When we arrived at the Wonju station, it was dark. The MPs led us through the streets to the MP headquarters, a mile from the railroad station. Sgt. Hakdong said to Sgt. Chunwoo in a subdued tone, "I am glad it is dark so nobody will recognize me. This is my hometown, and my house is behind this shop." He pointed out a shop by the street. Sgt. Chunwoo responded, "Me, too, I have many friends in this town. I don't want them to see me in handcuffs. They might think I am a serious criminal." The downcast spirits of the two sergeants were quite contrary to their upbeat talk in the dungeon a few days earlier when the senior MP master sergeant had announced our transfer to Wonju.

Upon arriving at headquarters, our escorting MPs handed us, along with our relevant papers, to an MP master sergeant on duty. He cross-checked each of us against the papers. Then he ordered a couple of his MPs to take us to the regiment stockade. The stockade was built inside the guardhouse at the 8th Regiment training center, where I had finished my basic training three months earlier. During my training days, I had often seen prisoners being escorted in and out of the prison and wondered what crimes they had committed. I had thought that a huge gulf separated my world from the prison world. Ironically, now I would be incarcerated in that same prison.

A regular soldier, instead of an MP, was posted to guard the stockade, which made me feel somewhat better. After a brief talk with the guard, the two escorting MPs opened the stockade door and ordered us to enter. Like the other ones, a bare light bulb dangling from the ceiling dimly lit the stockade. More than twenty prisoners packed the small, unheated room (about ten feet by fifteen feet) with a bare wooden floor. As in the other dungeons, a toilet pail stood in a corner. But at least it was not an underground dungeon. When we entered, some of the prisoners welcomed us with a hello, while others showed no emotion. They asked us about outside news, but we did not have any for them.

The floor was constructed with thick planks, crudely laid, leaving many cracks between them. Three or four army blankets were spread over the floor to prevent the draft from blowing in through the cracks, leaving only a few extra blankets for more than twenty prisoners to share. I learned by midnight that this stockade was also lice infested.

TRAIN-EXERCISE

The next morning, two MPs, a sergeant, and a corporal stomped on the wooden steps outside our cell door and shouted, "Everyone out, exercise time. Hurry out!" We silently filed out. We knew that exercise meant brutal torture. The sergeant carried a baseball bat, and the corporal was armed with a carbine rifle. Both had big hunting knives dangling on their white MP belts. The sergeant barked, "Line up, dress right dress," while the corporal guarded us, holding his carbine in his hands. He barked again, "Right face. You are going to have a train-exercise. Lie down on your belly." We did as we were told. My belly and hands were freezing on the ice-cold concrete floor. I wondered what this train-exercise was. "Now, bend your legs forward. Everybody but the first person in the line, crawl forward between the two legs of the person in front of you. Stretch your legs over the shoulders of the person behind you. Now, push up." We did push-ups. We were connected to each other by having the two legs of the first person over the shoulders of the second person, those of the second person over the shoulders of the third person … all the way to the last person. We looked like a multitude of flying frogs landing simultaneously. He shouted again, "This is a train-exercise. Do you understand?" Nobody had the strength to respond.

I was the youngest and skinniest prisoner. My legs had developed endurance, but for some reason my arms were not as strong. Thus, even a simple push-up exercise wore me out. Now, I was ordered to support another man's heavy legs on my shoulders while having my own legs placed on the shoulders of someone who was taller than me. This exerted a tremendous amount of weight on my shoulders and skinny arms, causing excruciating pain. I groaned, as did many others. My upper arms felt like they were being yanked from my shoulder sockets. My arms became extremely weak, wobbled to support the heavy weight, and finally collapsed to the concrete floor. The MP sergeant yelled, "Push-up, push-up," and whacked my rear end with his baseball bat. Burning pain flashed through my hip. I was utterly exhausted, and lay motionless, resting my head on my hands. A few more whacks followed. I screamed! The person behind me, who had carried my legs on his shoulders also crumpled on my feet. Whack, whack. Soon the entire train derailed. The sergeant frantically barked, "Push-up, push-up," like a mad dog, and whacked, but nobody even pretended to try. Finally, the mad dog gave up trying to salvage the wreck, and yelled, "Everybody, stand up. Form a line." We all stood slowly, filled with pain and distress. The tearing pain in my backside almost made me fall. He yelled again, "Get back to your cell." When I returned to the jail, I carefully sat against the wall. While gently massaging my aching hips, I questioned why they tortured us so cruelly. The only logical answer to my question was that these low-ranking MPs wanted to show that they had absolute power over the prisoners. Exercise-torture was a daily ritual. Of all the various types of exercise-tortures, the train-exercise was the most painful and barbarous.

SERGEANTS HAKDONG AND CHUNWOO ARE FREED

A week had passed since the four of us had been transferred to the Wonju jail. During this time, none of us were interrogated further. We were always kept behind bars except when the MPs took us out for daily exercise-torture. I noticed that all the prisoners, including my two sergeants, looked pale and swollen. I thought that lack of sunlight must have caused the paleness, but what caused the swelling? Since no one in the stockade had a mirror, I could not see myself, but I believed that I looked the same.

Late one afternoon, I heard excited hollering in the distinct southeastern regional accent, "Sergeants Hakdong and Chunwoo, where are you? You are free! You are coming with me. Where are you?" I immediately recognized our company commanding officer Lieutenant Lee's voice. My heart began to pound, as I expected that I too would finally be freed even though he did not call my name. Unconsciously, I stood up and waited impatiently, clenching my fists.

The jail door opened, and I saw Lieutenant Lee trying to peek into the jail over an MP's shoulder. Upon seeing him, I became more excited. The MP took out a piece of paper from his jacket pocket and read, "Staff Sergeant Hakdong and Sergeant Chunwoo." He ordered, "You two come out," while putting the paper back into his pocket. My name was not called. My heart sank. Fear and uncertainty gripped me so completely that I felt cold. My legs lost the strength to support my body. I sat down and watched the two sergeants crawl out through the small jail door and salute the lieutenant. After returning their salutes, he stuck his head in the door and said, "PFC Kim, PFC Jin, you will be alright. You will be coming back to the company soon." Hakdong and Chunwoo crouched down and nodded their heads in agreement. I was so downcast that I did not even bother to respond. Then they were gone.

I sat motionless and buried my head between my knees, thinking about the two freed sergeants for a long time; the four of us were from the same company, arrested at the same time and imprisoned in the same jail for the same reason, being suspected of being communist sympathizers. Now they were free, but Chin-mae and I were still behind bars. I asked myself, "Why?" But I did not find any answer except that the authorities must have classified me as a more serious suspect. This suggested that worse was waiting for me. I shuddered as my anxiety mounted. Those serving long jail terms seemed indifferent to my agony. They made offhand comments on the two sergeants' release, commenting, "Good for them, those two guys."

PFC Jin Chin-mae gently tapped my shoulder. He sat next to me and said, "Tae-hyok, I don't understand why the MPs continue to keep us in this son of a bitch jail while they freed Sergeants Hakdong and Chunwoo. We were arrested together. Why didn't they let us go with them?" He sighed deeply.

I said, "Chin-mae, I do not understand either. I wish I knew why." We sat against the wall and silently looked at the other wall for a long time. Other inmates chatted and laughed loudly as if we were not present. Finally, I broke our silence and said, "Chin-mae, so far, the MPs have not treated you badly. I hope it stays that way until you are freed. But I fear that they might torture me even worse than before." Chin-mae didn't respond.

In the late afternoon, a small amount of sunlight would filter into the jail cell between the bars. This sunlight had been my only privilege that the MPs could not take away. Back in the foul-smelling dungeon in Chuncheon, I had not had any sunlight. But that afternoon, I did not see this precious sunray. Apparently, I missed it during the last hours of agony. I felt even more dejected. I saw only the dull ray of the light bulb of the guard post swinging in the winter evening wind.

MASTER SERGEANT CHANG

A couple of days after Sergeants Hakdong and Chunwoo had been freed, the jail door swung open, and a new prisoner crawled in. It closed with a loud bang behind him. He stood up and greeted us in a rather affable mood, "Hi, I am Master Sergeant Chang Hee-chul. This is not a good place to meet people, but nice to meet you all anyway."

I instantly recognized him as my company sergeant. I knew that sooner or later he would be arrested due to the information that the other two sergeants had provided to their interrogator in the Chuncheon prison almost a month earlier, but I had never expected to see him in this jail. "Hello, Sergeant Chang. How are you? I am sorry that I must see you in this godforsaken place."

"Hi, PFC Kim. I did not know you had been jailed. I am very sorry to see you here, too." PFC Jin also greeted him.

In the jail, the best location was the farthest spot from the toilet pail, which was in a corner near the door. The cell was now packed with almost thirty prisoners. The *siljang* would occupy the best spot. The *siljang*, usually a prisoner with the longest residency, and preferably with a higher rank, was unofficially designated by MPs to maintain internal order in the cell. The *siljang* was king.

When a brand-new prisoner arrived, the *siljang* would assign him the worst place—next to the toilet pail. That was where he would spend all day, except when taken out for exercise-torture; he would eat and sleep there until another new prisoner would come. Then the newcomer would take over his place, and his status would advance by one notch, a foot farther away from the toilet. But today the *siljang* ordered those prisoners next to him to move over to make room and invited Sgt. Chang to occupy the place. Sgt. Chang thanked him and sat next to him. I do not know why the *siljang* did this special favor for him. Perhaps it was because of his amicable greeting or his high rank.

Since we were not allowed any newspapers, magazines, or letters, we were totally cut off from the outside world. Naturally we were hungry for news. The *siljang* asked Sgt. Chang what was going on in the outside world. He said, "You may have heard that the 6th and 14th Regiments revolted against the government a couple of months ago. Their commanding officers turned out to be communists. According to the newspapers, our army has crushed the rebels. Many of the insurgents either surrendered or were killed, but many of the rebels escaped into the Chirisan Mountains and opened guerrilla warfare. Ironically the 6th Regiment commanding officer was the former commander of my 8th Regiment."

Shocked at what he had said, I asked him, "You mean Lieutenant Colonel Choi Namkeon?"

"Yes. Do you know him?"

"He called us recruits a bunch of dummies when I had just been transferred to the 8th Regiment Training Center right in this compound. He was then the Commanding Officer of the regiment."

My jaw remained dropped, but we soon changed the topic to other news.

The more we talked with Sgt. Chang, the more I thought of him as a good-natured guy. Even the daily exercise-torture could not suppress his buoyant spirit. He said, "My friends, depression drives us to even worse depression. But laughter lifts our spirits. Let me tell you some stories that will make you laugh." He started with military jokes and went on to longer tales. I, too, laughed for the first time since my imprisonment a month before. He created an upbeat mood.

Then he said, "Singing enriches our soul. Let's sing." He led us to sing *Arirang,* one of the most cherished Korean folk songs, and we all joined in. After *Arirang,* he asked if anyone knew a European song called *Oh, Danny Boy,* but none of us did. He explained that it was an Irish folk song and one of the most loved songs worldwide. Then he began to sing it in Korean. It was the most peaceful, elegant song I had ever heard. His voice was rich and princely, a refined tenor.

As it progressed, the music gently shepherded me to the most bucolic land imaginable. When he sang the high notes, I imagined an eagle circling higher and higher into the blue sky where a few lazy white clouds were floating. When the song gently glided down to the low notes, I fancied that whoever was singing to Danny Boy was lying on soft green turf by a small meandering river and gazing at the vast azure sky, while a flock of white sheep peacefully grazed nearby. His song never ended; rather, it ever so slowly wafted over the gently rippling grass and faded beyond the horizon, where the rolling hills and gently waving grasses trundled into the bosom of the blue-white sky.

He sang the final note, leaving a hauntingly beautiful echo of peace and tranquility behind it. No one even noticed the song had ended. Perhaps everybody was immersed in a happy dream, or nobody wanted to break the silence. Sgt. Chang asked, "How did you like the song?" We enthusiastically applauded and called for an encore.

Bang, Bang! "Be quiet!" the guard barked.

Suddenly we fell from our Shangri-la into the abyss of reality. We had truly enjoyed the short-lived bliss. But Sgt. Chang responded to our call for an encore and sang the song again in a low voice. My heart again became light. For the next few days, he taught us *Oh, Danny Boy* and a few other songs. I thought that he was an intelligent and widely read man. He was a good singer and storyteller, too.

According to rumor, Sgt. Chang had been a first lieutenant and a company commander in another regiment until a few months ago. He was the only one in his military academy class who had not been promoted to the rank of captain at the beginning of the year. He wore a captain's insignia anyway. For this, he had been court-martialed and demoted to a master sergeant. The division headquarters had moved him to a totally strange environment, my company. It was a kind of exile. Apparently, he had held a grudge and bad-mouthed the army in front of the other senior sergeants of the company. I wondered what had made this intelligent man act that foolishly. Consequently, he had been brought down from the rank of first lieutenant to an enlisted man's status. Perhaps this might explain his imprisonment.

A few days later, two MPs called Sgt. Chang out and escorted him away, as I had known they would sooner or later. I was apprehensive because he would surely be interrogated with severe torture as I had been a month earlier. With our morale enhancer gone, the prison lost its liveliness.

Sgt. Chang returned to the jail six to seven hours later. He barely crawled through the door. He groaned and collapsed on the threshold, unable to move farther, just lying there in anguish. The *siljang* prepared a makeshift mattress by folding a couple of blankets for Sgt. Chang. When Chin-mae and I held him by the arms to move him onto the mattress, he screamed in pain. His lips were parched; his eyes were closed. He mumbled, "I am not a communist. Please don't beat me." He was almost unconscious. I knew from experience how painful it was to lie on a wounded back. So, we put him on his belly.

He said faintly, "Water, water." Since he was not able to drink lying on his belly, Chin-mae and I turned him over. While Chin-mae helped him lift his head, I brought some water in a dirty aluminum bowl to his mouth. He took a few painful swallows and then kept his lips submerged in the water for a while, trying to moisten them. When he finished, we carefully put him back on the improvised mattress. He lay in pain and continued groaning and unconsciously mumbling in a weak voice, "I am not a communist, I am not a communist. Please don't beat me, please, please!"

After laying him down, I gently lifted his shirt to check how bad his wounds were. Black, purple, and blue clots of blood covered his shoulders and back. I shuddered, and had flashbacks of the distress, pain, and wounds that my interrogator had inflicted on me. But mine were minor compared to those of Sgt. Chang. I shuddered again, and immeasurable fear gripped me. No doubt the MPs would make me the second Sgt. Chang because I had been imprisoned as a North Korean spy suspect. They had tortured me twice already. I didn't want to think about it, but the presence of the injured sergeant kept me in agony.

Because of the two freed sergeants' information, Sgt. Chang suffered unimaginable torture. Seeing his suffering made me reaffirm my resolution not to give my interrogators any false confession or to name anyone innocent to avoid pain.

No medical care was available, not even salve or ointment to apply to his wounds, so he was sick for a few days before he felt well enough to sit up. His severe injuries gradually healed, but his upbeat attitude was gone. He didn't talk or sing anymore. He was completely withdrawn. We tried to lift his spirit, but to no avail. He had brought an unexpected spring to us in jail. But it was taken away as quickly as he had brought it in. The winter of depression prevailed again.

INTERROGATION BY ELECTRIC SHOCK

A week after Sgt. Chang's brutal torture, two armed MPs escorted my friend PFC Jin Chin-mae and me, along with two deserter suspects to MP headquarters. The MPs took the two deserters into the building for interrogation, ordering Chin-mae and me to wait in the open courtyard until we were called in. Standing outside in the middle of December made us very cold. We jogged in place to keep ourselves warm.

Suddenly Chin-mae stopped and said nervously, "Tae-hyok, I am scared to death after seeing what you and Sergeant Chang have suffered. This is going to be my first interrogation. I do not know why they have put me in this fucking jail. I am neither a communist nor a sympathizer. They could find that out from my parents, friends, and neighbors." His lips were purple from cold and fear. His face had a pale bluish tint. He shivered like a frightened rabbit. Tears ran silently down his cheeks.

I said, "Chin-mae, remember, the authorities have not interrogated you yet. It's been five long weeks since our imprisonment. That might be a good omen. They might have checked your background and collected some good information about you during that time. Who knows, you may be freed after a brief, formal interrogation. So don't fret too much." Though I was just as anxious, outwardly I was more composed, perhaps because I had already survived two interrogations.

He wiped his tears and said, "Thank you, Tae-hyok. I hope you are right. Had I known the army would treat me like this, I would not have joined. Goddamnit." He sighed. Anxiety squeezed my heart, and the wind drove icy needles through my frozen skin and deep into my bones. We resumed our jogging.

A half-hour or so later, an MP corporal escorted the two deserters out to the courtyard where we were. Then he took Chin-mae into the office. Just as he entered the doorway, my friend glanced over his shoulder with a fearful expression. His anxious face reminded me of my two previous tortures at the Chuncheon Prison. Fear clutched my heart. Suddenly my mother's prayer came to mind. She had built a small altar in a corner of the backyard of our house and would pray to the gods for the prosperity of our family. Occasionally, I eavesdropped on her prayer and thought it was silly. But today, in desperation, I closed my eyes and imitated my mother's prayer, "The gods of heaven and earth, today I pray to you for me and my friends. Please save us from further tortures, please…"

"Hey, you!" A hard slap on my back frightened me from my prayer. The same MP who had taken Chin-mae said in a harsh voice, "You come with me." He led me to a basement. A bare white light bulb dangled from the ceiling, hardly illuminating a room of four dark gray concrete walls with no windows and just one door. An old wooden desk stood in the middle of the cold concrete slab, behind which was a chair. On the desk, a white police stick and some gadget like a double-sized army field telephone were laid side by side. The stick caused a sudden chill to run down my spine. A rice straw mat was spread on the floor in front of the desk. The corporal told me to sit on the mat and wait. He left the room. Though it was warmer than the open courtyard, I couldn't stop shivering.

A few minutes after the corporal had gone, an MP sergeant came in with a folder and sat down on the chair, ignoring my presence. He opened the folder, took a quick glance at it, and said, "Stand up, soldier, what is your name?" without even looking at me.

"PFC Kim Tae-hyok, Sergeant."

"Do you know why you are here?"

"I do not know exactly why, but they accused me of being a communist spy, which I am not," I said loudly and clearly.

He whacked my shoulder with the white club and said, "You are lying. You are a North Korean spy, aren't you?" Another whack. "Sit down. Why did you come to South Korea from North Korea?"

I groaned loudly and said, "I came to Seoul to seek an opportunity for education, sergeant."

"Then why did you join the army instead of attending school?"

"I lost my job, and I didn't have money for my education."

"You are lying. Do you know what this is?" He pulled the giant telephone toward him. It did not have a receiver, but it had two long black wires, maybe seven to eight feet long, connected to its terminal posts.

"It looks like a big telephone," I answered.

"No, this is not a telephone. I will show you what this is." He stood up, came to me, and picked up the wires. "Raise your hands, stretch your fingers!" Then he tied the bare ends of the wires tightly to my index fingers. He returned to his chair. He held the telephone firmly with one hand and the crank of the phone with the other. I became extremely apprehensive because I did not know what he was planning to do to me. My mouth went dry.

He turned the crank for one or two clicks. A sudden shock, the like of which I had never experienced before, ran through my entire body. It startled me. I screamed and involuntarily pulled my hands back. I lost my mind momentarily. I had not known a telephone could generate such a powerful electrical shock until that moment.

"Now, you know what this is. It is not a telephone," he said with an evil smile. "You are a North Korean spy. Confess that you are a spy. If you don't, I will give you more of this." Teasingly he cranked the phone -- click-halt-click-halt...

For every click, I unconsciously groaned, "No..., no...," simultaneously flinging my arms back and forth, back and forth. I repeated, "I am not a communist, I am not a spy." I pleaded with him, "Please don't do it, please."

Sudden shocks one after another! With one loud "No...," I fell flat on my back. Billions of tiny balls studded with small needles bombarded every cell of my body. Wave after wave rolled up and down, inside out, outside in.

My four limbs were outstretched and convulsed like a dying animal. I faintly heard my evil interrogator cranking the phone. My nervous system stopped functioning. Paralyzed! My wide-open mouth dripped saliva. My urine spilled uncontrollably. Inexplicable sensations simultaneously raced through my body, something like severe burning, pain, itching, tingling, and freezing. I couldn't move, speak, or do anything to escape this hell. My mind became blurred, and I passed out.

I heard a distant hollering, "Get up, get up!" Then I heard it again along with a thud on my butt, though I was too numb to feel pain from the whack. My mind was so foggy that I could not tell where I was or what was happening. It took a few minutes before I realized that I was in the middle of a nightmarish interrogation, an electric shock torture. I was extremely tired and felt profound numbness throughout my body. I slowly sat up and mumbled, "I am not a spy," over and over. My mouth was so dry that my tongue stuck to my palate. "Water please!" But there was no water.

"Now, are you ready to write a confession? Or do you need more of this?" he said, tapping the phone with his police stick.

I repeated, "I am not a spy, sergeant. I have nothing to confess," in a slow, slurring voice. The prolonged electric shocks had badly numbed my whole body. I sat in my own urine, but I hardly felt it.

"Crrrrrank!"

I screamed, "Ouuuuu....!" and fell down. BLANK! I do not know how long I was unconscious. When I regained consciousness, I did not see the evil sergeant. Instead, two MP PFCs were looking down at me. My eyes were blurry, my head ached severely, my body convulsed periodically, and I was totally exhausted mentally and physically. The two soldiers asked me if I could stand up. I managed to sit up and remained there immobile for some time, sobbing. When I tried to stand up, my legs wobbled. The two soldiers helped me stabilize myself and said, "Can you walk?"

I silently, slowly started to walk without answering their question. When I lost my balance, they assisted me by holding my arms. Once we got out of that dreadful basement to the upstairs hall, I asked in a feeble voice, "Excuse me, can I have a glass of water please? I am very thirsty."

One of them said, "Sure. Would you hold him?" to the other and went to fetch water. He returned with water in an aluminum soup bowl and gave it to me.

I gulped most of it and drained the rest in my cupped-hand and wet my face. It made me feel somewhat refreshed. "Thank you very much," I said to them. They were the only compassionate MPs I had met since being imprisoned.

They walked me carefully all the way to the jail, a quarter of a mile from the MP headquarters. It was a long journey. When we arrived at the jail, they helped me crawl. As soon as I was inside the cell, I fell asleep until the next morning. When I woke up, I had a severe headache, and my body was extremely stiff and achy. The atrocity had caused indescribable distress. My friend Chin-mae and a few other cellmates, including Sgt. Chang and the *siljang*, expressed sympathy. I thanked them for their concern. Chin-mae appeared in pretty good spirits; I assumed his interrogation had not been as severe as mine. I was so exhausted that I lay down without eating breakfast and quickly fell asleep again.

FANTASIZING ABOUT ESCAPING

A couple of days later, an MP came to the jail and handed my friend Chin-mae an order of release. He said, "PFC Jin Chin-mae, you are free. You may go back to your company." My friend stood motionless, silent for a few moments, like a mannequin, perhaps because he might have thought that the MP was joking or that it was too good to be true. Then suddenly he shouted, "Thank you, thank you." I did not know whom he thanked. I was sure it was not the MP. He came over, patted me on the shoulder, and said, "Tae-hyok, be strong. I am sure you, too, will be released soon. Take care of yourself." He bid goodbye to everybody in the prison and crawled out through the small jail door to FREEDOM.

I was happy to see him go free, but I could not respond because I was emotionally overwhelmed. The four of us, Sergeants Hakdong and Chunwoo, Chin-mae, and I, from the same company, were arrested at the same time and imprisoned in the same prison. The two sergeants had been freed a couple of weeks earlier. Now Chin-mae had been released. Suddenly, I became friendless, lonely, and lost.

Apparently, the MP authorities considered me the most serious suspect. Why else would they continue to detain me? I began to imagine facing worse interrogations than those I had already suffered, or a court-martial. If a court found me guilty, it would hand down a harsh verdict, an imprisonment of many years. The political environment in South Korea was paranoid about communist insurgents. Thus, even a death sentence could not be ruled out.

These nightmarish fantasies made me think about escaping. I thought about returning to my parents. But returning to North Korea would mean an even harsher life. I believed that the North Korean security bureau had information that I had joined the South Korean Army by intercepting my letters to my parents and brothers. I had written several letters to them, naively using my South Korean Army address, but I had never received a single answer. If I returned to North Korea, the security bureau would certainly brand me as reactionary to communism and send me to a coal mine, a no-return exile. The Communist North Korean government branded those who did not agree with its ideology as enemies of the people. It was well known that this government had brutally purged people by exiling them to hard labor camps. Returning home would be like walking into a lion's den. I discarded the idea.

Then I considered changing my identity, going to a big city such as Pusan or Taegu, far away from the Seoul area, and starting a new life. Since I had come from North Korea, nobody but the army in South Korea had my personal record. Even the army had no picture of me. It had only my name and birthplace. If the new life did not go as well as I planned, I would rejoin the army using a pseudonym, and nobody could possibly find my real identity. I fantasized about my new beginning, putting this miserable prison behind me.

This new life could not start unless I escaped. Right now, it was almost impossible. Even if I successfully escaped, how could I get away from this town? It was a long way to a southern city. I did not have money to pay for food or transportation. It was the middle of winter. I might starve or freeze to death. After thinking about escaping for many days, rationality returned, and I quit these impractical dreams. Instead, I reaffirmed my determination not to give a false confession, no matter how brutally I might be tortured. Sooner or later, the authorities would find me innocent and free me. A good day will come soon.

INTERROGATION BY AN INTELLIGENCE OFFICER

About a week after my electric shock torture, two MPs called me out along with two other prisoners. I did not know why the other two had been imprisoned and did not ask. The MPs escorted us to the intelligence section of the regiment headquarters instead of the MP headquarters. The headquarters building was a long, dirt-colored quonset hut. During my basic training from May through early September, every day I would jog along with my entire company to this parade ground for the solemn five o'clock flag-lowering ceremony. That was less than four months ago. Now I was here again to be interrogated as a communist spy.

One of the two MPs led me to an office in the building. A lanky sergeant first class sitting behind a desk said, "Come in, soldier." I saw a telephone on the desk that appeared to be smaller than the one used to torture me at the MP headquarters. Cold sweat ran down my spine. I asked myself, "Is he going to torture me with that telephone?" I walked in hesitantly and saluted him, my heart pounding rapidly. My mouth was dry. He said in an unexpectedly kind voice, "Sit on that chair," pointing to one in front of his desk. He was leafing through a file, apparently containing information about me.

He said, "You are a communist spy, aren't you?" while leaning back in his chair.

"Absolutely not, sir," I answered in a firm and loud voice.

"How long ago did you come to South Korea, and how old were you then?"

"Two years ago, and I was fifteen years old, Sergeant."

"Where are your parents now?"

"In my hometown in North Korea."

"Why did you come to the South all by yourself, leaving your parents in North Korea?"

"I had only an elementary school education. I wanted more. I wanted to attend a middle school. But my parents are poor farmers in a mountainous farm village. They could not afford to support my education. So, I came to Seoul to seek educational opportunities."

"Then why did you join the army instead of attending school?"

"I lost my job, and I did not have money for school. I did not want to go back to North Korea. So, I joined the army."

"Then why did you plan to desert during your basic training?"

I was appalled. "Sir, I had never planned to desert. That is an unfounded accusation."

"Didn't you discuss desertion with someone in your company during your basic training because you didn't like the army?" he asked, while reading a document.

"Sir, I never planned to desert at any time, anywhere, or with anybody."

"My information says that you planned to desert with a recruit named Choi Kyu."

I took a deep breath and calmly said, "I came from North Korea. Choi also came from North Korea after the communist government confiscated his parents' land and house and forced them to relocate to a remote farming village; they were wealthy landowners and owned a big house. Both of us missed our parents so much that we would encourage each other in our spare time. But I never discussed or planned to desert with him."

"Then why did he say that you and he planned to desert?"

"One night, during basic training, he was caught in a desertion attempt. His company sergeant punished him severely for his ill-fated try and pressed him to confess who else was involved. Apparently, the punishment was so unbearable that he gave my name to the sergeant. Without investigating whether his confession was true or not, my drill sergeant flogged me severely with a baseball bat. I was unfairly punished, which I did not deserve, sir." I noticed that the interrogator kept his eyes closed. Since I did not know whether he was listening to me or dozing, I paused for a few seconds.

He opened his eyes and said, "Continue, soldier." He closed his eyes again.

"Thank you, sir. After my punishment, I asked myself many times why he had falsely involved me, a totally innocent man. I never had a chance to ask him why, because he was court-martialed for his crime and given a six-month imprisonment. Shortly after my basic training, I was assigned to border guard duty along the 38th Parallel." The sergeant opened his eyes and jotted down something in the file.

I continued, "Originally, I applied for the army communication school because the recruiters had told me that it would teach English, mathematics, and physics. But they took me to the 1st Infantry Regiment Training Center near Seoul instead of the communication school. Eventually I ended up with the 8th Infantry Regiment here in Wonju. I was very disappointed about not going to the communication school. I once expressed my deep disappointment to him, but I had never planned to desert. Sir, if I had, I could have easily deserted when I was deployed along the 38th Parallel." At this moment, I choked.

"Don't choke. You are a soldier. Now, go back to the jail and wait until you are called back again," he said in a gentle voice. He asked one of his subordinate soldiers, not an MP, to escort me back to the jail.

He did not torture me. His manner of interrogation was humane; no truculent attitude could be felt. He patiently listened to my long story. I felt a surge of hope that something good might be coming soon. Since then, every day, like a drought-stricken plant waiting for a sweet rain, I eagerly expected that an MP would soon come by and announce, "PFC Kim Tae-hyok, you are FREE!" But that good news did not come, and my hope for release rapidly faded.

* * *

The morning of the last day of the year had arrived, with no news of my release. Then, around noon, an MP called my name. I answered loudly, "Here," and jumped up and went to the door. My heart started to pound in anticipation, but instead of releasing me, he escorted me to the chief of the regiment intelligence, Captain Seong. He was a lean, smart-looking man in his mid-thirties. Since the top intelligence man was going to interrogate me, I feared that deeper trouble might be waiting for me; perhaps I would be turned over to a court-martial.

Instead, he welcomed me with a smile, stretched out his hand, shook mine, and said, "Be seated," pointing to a chair by his desk. I did not know how to interpret his smile and mild talk, whether it was a good omen or a bad one, because none of my previous interrogators had ever treated me as compassionately as this captain.

Unexpectedly, he said, "Private Kim, we have found you innocent. I am sorry that you have had to go through all these difficulties. Now you are free. You may go back to your company." The words "YOU ARE FREE!"

overwhelmed me so much that I could not speak. Finally, I composed myself and said, "Thank you very much, sir."

He continued, "I know you have suffered an extraordinary experience and hardship, but don't be bitter. Use them to build your character and serve our country well," while writing something on a sheet of paper. His words sounded like fatherly advice. He signed the paper and handed it over to me. "This is the certificate of your release and a pass for you to return to your company."

I received it with trembling hands and bowed my head slightly to show my respect. That weightless sheet of paper unloaded the heaviest yoke that had ever burdened me. It declared the end of the nightmarish fifty-three days of imprisonment and numerous tortures and cleared me of being a North Korean spy. It opened the prison gate and led me to the freedom that I had yearned for, for so long. Tears of happiness welled in my eyes and blurred my vision. I wiped my eyes with my bare hand to read this most precious paper. I said, "Excuse me, sir," and turned around; allowing the tears to fall freely for a few moments before wiping my eyes and nose. Composed, I turned back to the captain and said, "I am sorry, sir." I folded the paper carefully and tucked it in my pocket.

"That's okay, Private Kim. You are now free. You may return to your company today or tomorrow, whichever you choose. I don't think there is an afternoon bus to Hongcheon where your company is stationed. Perhaps you might be able to hitchhike from the bus station in town, if you are lucky," he said. The bus station was about one mile from the headquarters.

"I'd like to return today, sir." I didn't want to spend another minute in that jail. And I did not have money to buy a bus ticket even if an afternoon bus had been available. I planned to hitchhike on a truck.

He said, "I understand," and led me to the door, shook my hand and said, "Soldier, good luck."

I saluted him and said, "Thank you. Goodbye, sir." I walked briskly out of the building and took a deep breath. For the first time in fifty-three days, I was able to look up at the blue sky, distant snow-covered mountains, and fields without MPs at my side. I shouted in my heart, "I am FREE! I am FREE!" Then I turned toward the north in the direction of my hometown, closed my eyes, and said, "Mom and Dad, I am FREE! I am FREE now. I am okay. Take care of yourselves till we meet again when the country is unified." It was a beautiful, balmy December afternoon. I walked to the guardhouse and proudly showed the guard my pass. He took a quick glance at it and let me go.

I took a graveled highway toward the Wonju bus station. As soon as I reached the highway, I stretched my arms out into the sky and shouted at the top of my lungs, "I AM FREE, I AM FREE!" Of course, there was nobody on the empty highway to cheer or welcome me. Later, I arrived at an intersection and turned right toward the bus station. The station was located at the third building beyond the MP headquarters where I had been tortured with electric shocks a couple of weeks earlier. I had to pass by the headquarters to reach the bus station. I felt so apprehensive of that damned MP building that I crossed the street to avoid it and walked as fast as I could. Once I passed that dreadful place, I re-crossed the street and walked right into the bus station.

The station was empty, except for a vendor in his mid-fifties tending a small shop in a corner. He was heavily dressed and had a small fire pot in front of him. He sat on an empty wooden box, rubbing his hands to warm them over the burning charcoals. I approached and greeted him, "How are you, sir? May I join you?"

"Of course, young soldier. Sit down," he said, making room for me.

"Thank you very much, sir." I sat next to him and told him that I had to return to my company in Hongcheon before the day was over. "Is there a bus to either Hongcheon or Chuncheon this afternoon?"

"Not until tomorrow morning. You might be able to catch a truck. It would take a couple of hours to get to Hongcheon. You must be one of the 5th Company boys. Aren't you?"

"Yes, sir, but how do you know the 5th Company?"

"Your company used to be stationed in this town until it relocated there in September. One of my nephews served in that company. He has been transferred to the army headquarters in Seoul." Then a fully loaded truck pulled over in front of the station and halted. "I know that driver. I am sure he is heading for Chuncheon. Hongcheon is located halfway between here and Chuncheon." He went out to the truck, and I followed him. He exchanged greetings with the driver and kindly asked him, "Would you mind giving this young soldier a ride to Hongcheon? He must return to his company before the day is over."

The driver said, "Young man, hop onto the truck. We shall be leaving shortly."

I said, "Thank you, sirs," to both the vendor and the driver, and climbed onto the top of the loaded cargo bay. The truck coughed loudly and began to move northward onto the dirt Wonju-Chuncheon highway that ran between snow-covered, empty farm fields. When the MP station disappeared from my sight, excitement erupted in my heart. I couldn't help shouting, "I AM FREE! MY PRECIOUS FREEDOM!" and pumping my arms into the powder-blue sky. Then, suddenly I felt lonely and became homesick, missing my parents. A wintry gust whipped me and restored my mood. I realized that despite my extraordinary experiences, I was still a seventeen-year-old boy.

The wind died down, and the balmy sun warmed me as if it welcomed my freedom. After thirty miles' journey, the driver dropped me off in Hongcheon, wishing me good luck in the army. I thanked him and walked a short distance to my company. When I entered my barracks, all my friends warmly welcomed me, saying, "Tae-hyok, you are back. Where have you been? We missed you…." Lee Jong-kook, Oh Munchan, Kim Hakdong, Kim Jae-kook, Bong Jong-tae, Chun Byung-ho, Jin Chin-mae (who still looked a bit malnourished from prison), Pak Sam-hyun, Kim Maneong (Man-E), and Lee Yeongsik, among others all gathered around me. I was so happy to join them and enjoyed their camaraderie. I believed that they knew where I had been and thoughtfully didn't question my long absence. Having been cleared as a North Korean spy, I began the second phase of my army career with a brighter heart.

* * *

BORDER GUARD DUTY

My company's two-year border guard duty lasted from September 1948 to June 1950. A couple of months after my imprisonment, I was transferred to the Regiment Headquarters to be a company clerk. The job was easy and for the most part was a desk job. I oversaw individual soldiers' personnel records: their name, home address, and any injuries or deaths. I met a communication specialist at the headquarters, and I learned that he had applied for the Army Communication School around the same time as I had signed up and had received his training there. The school taught him how to use various communications equipment along with some math and electronics, but no English. He went to the place he had signed up for, but as for me, they probably gave me the wrong pickup time (it could have been later in the day), and the Army Recruiters were trying to hit their new recruit numbers.

Some of my friends became a part of the administrative personnel group: Kim Jae-kook, Pak Sam-hyun, Kim Maneong, and Chun Byung-ho. We met new people as well. Chang Hyokoen became one of my best friends; he was reorganized and transferred to the personnel department. He was four years older than me and had a younger sister whom he often mentioned. He always had a positive attitude. His family lived in North Korea. There was also Choi Ga-ram who joined us in late 1949. He was a tall, arrogant guy. He got married and had one boy before joining the army. We didn't chat with each other much in our spare time but were both responsible for the personnel records of the same company, so we had to work together. Han Geun-bok joined the personnel department and was a good guy. He was ranked

With friends from the 8th Regiment before the Korean War. Tae-hyok is on the far left.

slightly higher than us. There was also Choo Young-ho, who was at a higher rank than us as well. He was someone I completely respected, and whom I could tell would make a great leader.

My best friend Lee Jong-kook was assigned to the regiment headquarters as well, but not in the administrative department. They assigned him odd jobs. He was always on guard duty. Oh Munchan, Jin Chin-mae, and Lee Yeong-sik served in the same company together. Bong Jong-tae was placed in a different company but we remained best friends. I met Kwon Seo-jin in basic training. He was a staff sergeant, assistant to the regiment quarter-master officer. The personnel and quartermaster departments shared a large office floor. Kwon would see me studying my middle school algebra book and encouraged me to continue to study. I completely respected him, too, and we became good friends. Hakdong was promoted, eventually to Master Sergeant. We were all in the same regiment.

During our border guard duty, we had around four battles fighting North Korea. Hundreds of men from both North and South Korea died during those battles. I was promoted from Private First Class to Corporal. In mid-June of 1950, those of us in personnel were assigned Master Sergeant Lee as our department leader. We had a good group, and I had fully adapted to army life.

PART FOUR

The Korean War

1950 - 1953

OUTBREAK OF THE KOREAN WAR

Shortly after the end of World War II and the creation of the 38th Parallel (a border determined by the U.S. and the Soviet Union), the Soviet Union brought in a total of 150,000 troops[5] north of the border and the United States brought in 77,600 to the south of the border as both these nations had temporary control of the individual states. This lasted until the Soviet Union and the United States started to withdraw their troops in 1948. The Soviet Union also provided upwards of 2,000 military advisors to North Korea.[6]

Syngman Rhee had become the leader in the Republic of Korea (ROK) south of the 38th Parallel, and Kim Il Sung was made leader in the Democratic People's Republic of Korea (DPRK) north of the border.

It is important to note the series of events that led to the outbreak of the war. While the idea of war and the individual leading it was Kim Il Sung, the Soviet Union and China were heavily involved, too.

The Soviet Union, whose goal was to spread communism, wanted to communize the entire Korean peninsula. They held a meeting in December 1948 with representatives from North Korea and Communist China. In that meeting, the three nations decided to strengthen the North Korean People's Army (NKPA) as well as invade South Korea by mid-1950.[7]

On March 5, 1949, Kim Il Sung met with Stalin to discuss the unification of the Korean peninsula and war preparations. They agreed that the Soviet Union would loan $40 million to North Korea for military equipment and train the North Korean People's Army.[8] In March 1949, South Korea started to ask the U.S. for more military assistance.[9] They had been given World War II equipment, some of which was deteriorated and needed repairs and new parts[10], whereas North Korea received new equipment from the Soviet Union. South Korea's howitzers had half the range of those provided to the NKPA, and their antitank rocket launchers could not destroy enemy tanks. In addition, the U.S. equipment was meant for 50,000 men, but by March 1950, the ROK forces had 104,000.[11]

According to "The Korean War: Volume 1" by the Korea Institute of Military History, "The low quality of the transferred U.S. equipment was but a reflection of Washington's basic position on military assistance to the Republic of Korea: The ROK Army was to be organized first and foremost as a police-type force to quell domestic unrest and maintain internal security, and later to be developed into a defense force capable of deterring North Korean aggression. It followed that the ROK forces, equipped with the U.S. armament, would not be able to redress the military imbalance with North Korea."[12]

On April 28, 1949, Kim Il Sung met with Mao Zedong to seek support from China. He also shared his discussions with Stalin and the accord he had signed with the Soviet Union on March 17. Mao committed to provide the NKPA with Korean veterans who were in the People's Liberation Army.[13] The total ended up being 50,000 veterans.[14]

By May 17, 1949, Kim Il Sung, Stalin, and Mao Zedong agreed on war against South Korea to unify the peninsula and to be a communist country. Meetings between North Korea, the Soviet Union, and Communist China continued from 1949 to 1950.[15]

On August 20, 1949, Syngman Rhee wrote a letter to President Truman outlining that South Korea only had enough ammunition for two days and listed the ammunition and equipment needed in case a war took place.[16] They also figured they needed 400,000 men in their forces.[17] The U.S. in return said they would give $10.2 million to ROK in 1950. The Korean Military Advisory Group (KMAG) which was a U.S. military unit said they needed $20 million and that North Korea was more armed with men and equipment.[18]

Meanwhile, the Chinese Communist Revolution lasted until October 1, 1949, and as a result, the People's Republic of China (PRC) was formed in mainland China, a communist victory with Mao Zedong as its leader. The Government of the Republic of China fled to Taiwan. In January 1950, Jacob Malik, the Soviet representative to the United Nations (UN), left the Security Council meeting because the UN rejected his proposal for a PRC representative to represent China and therefore would replace the Nationalist

Chinese (Taiwan) representative.[19] Malik started boycotting the UN Security Council after the proposal was rejected.

The ROK Army Headquarters prepared an intelligence report on December 27, 1949, outlining the NKPA's personnel and equipment numbers and warning that North Korea would go live with an invasion against South Korea in spring 1950.[20] The ROK government kept asking for military assistance from the U.S. And the warning of the invasion was shared with the UN Commission on Korea.[21] ROK also had press conferences with foreign journalists saying North Korea was preparing for an invasion and that they needed U.S. military assistance.[22]

Then a significant event took place on January 12, 1950 (Washington time). The U.S. Secretary of State, Dean Acheson, gave a speech at the National Press Club outlining the U.S. Defense Perimeter in Asia. He excluded the Republic of Korea (South Korea) and Republic of China (Taiwan) from the perimeter. This signaled to Kim Il Sung, the Soviet Union, and China that the United States would not back South Korea up if North Korea invaded.

Kim Il Sung continued to meet with Stalin and Mao. He shared his plan, which was to first build up the North Korean military, then to propose to South Korea the idea of unifying the two states. They knew that South Korea would reject this, so North Korea would then start the war.[23] There had been some border skirmishes from 1945 to 1950, causing 10,000 casualties of North and South Korean soldiers, but no major invasion.[24]

South Korea repeatedly warned the U.S. that North Korea was preparing for war. On March 10, 1950, General Douglas MacArthur wrote an intelligence report to Washington and said he had intelligence that North Korea would invade in June.[25]

South Korea came up with an intelligence estimate on May 12, 1950 of the personnel and equipment numbers. These were higher than their December 27 estimates and were fairly accurate to the NKPA's actual numbers. They shared this report with the UN. Below is a list of actual numbers prior to the invasion:[26]

PERSONNEL		
	South Korea	North Korea
Army, Navy, Marine Corps, Air Force, etc.	105,752	198,380
EQUIPMENT		
	South Korea	North Korea
Tanks	0	242 T–34 tanks (with 85–mm gun)
Armored Vehicles	27	54
Self–Propelled Guns	0	176 (SU–76)
Howitzers	91 (of 105–mm M3 which had a range of 6,525 meters)	552 howitzers which included 76–mm 122–mm which had a range of 11,710 meters
Mortars	960 total 384 of 81–mm which had a range of 3,600 meters 576 of 60–mm	1,728 mortars which included 61–mm 82–mm 120–mm which had a range of 5,700 meters
Antitank Guns	2,040 total 140 of 57–mm 1,900 of 2.36–inch (both of these did not have enough power to destroy T–34 tanks)	550 (of 45–mm)
Antiaircraft Artillery (AAA)	0	36 total 24 of 37–mm AAA 12 of 85–mm AAA
Aircrafts	22 total 8 of L–4 4 of L–5 10 of T–6	211 airplanes which included Training and Recon– naissance Planes IL–2 Fighter Planes IL–10 Fighter Planes YAK–9 Fighter Planes
Warships	71 total 28 patrol ships 43 support vessels	110 total 30 patrol ships 80 support vessels

The invasion plan was finished on May 29, 1950. The date was set for Sunday, June 25. The plan was in Russian, thus showcasing that it was put together by Soviet military advisors, and then it was translated into Korean. Their plan was to end the war in a month, with Kim Il Sung being the leader of the entire peninsula and a new government being formed by August 15, Liberation Day in Korea. They planned to move quickly, before the U.S. could intervene. China said that if Japan or the U.S. entered the war, they would send in troops to back up North Korea.[27]

Prior to the outbreak of the war, the ROK forces had a total of 105,752 people, whereas the North Korean People's Army had 198,380. In some areas, this ratio was 1:4 and 1:7.[28] The U.S. agreed to provide $10,970,000 in military assistance (earlier saying $10.2 million) in March 1950. However, less than $1,000 had been sent to South Korea by June 25.[29] As for equipment, ROK had zero tanks and 22 airplanes, no antitank weapons for armored attack, and no antiaircraft guns. The NKPA had 242 T-34 tanks and 211 airplanes. ROKA could not use 15% of its weapons and 35% of its vehicles due to them not being repaired.[30] There was absolutely no comparison between the Soviet-trained and Soviet-equipped North Korean People's Army and the undertrained and underequipped Republic of Korea Army.

The ROK forces strengthened their security and then went under emergency alert. This lasted for 45 days. This was lifted on June 24. One-third of the soldiers went on leave. Some went to help their families during the farming season.[31]

June 25, 1950 marks the date that North Korea invaded South Korea. The number varies according to different sources, but up to 100,000 North Korea soldiers attacked.[32] The South Koreans were caught by surprise. There was a "Domino Theory" that if the United States didn't take a stand, more Asian countries would fall under Soviet control. America decided to get involved to halt the spread of communism. President Harry Truman said, "If we let Korea down, the Soviet[s] will keep right on going and swallow up one piece of Asia after another."[33]

Meanwhile, on June 28, at about 2 a.m., the Army Chief of Staff Chae ordered the Han River bridges to be blown up. What had not been considered was the evacuation of people as well as troops. Some of these bridges failed to detonate. The Pedestrian Bridge, however, was blown up and 500–800 people died. 40–50 cars were affected by the blast not on the bridge, thus bringing injuries to citizens. Seoul fell in three days. ROK troops would have to figure out how to cross the Han River if they hadn't already, and citizens who hadn't crossed would now be under North Korean rule.[34]

The UN Security Council held an emergency session on the situation in Korea. The Council adopted Resolution 83 on June 27, 1950 New York time or June 28, 1950 at 1:45 p.m. Korean time, which "recommend[ed] that the Members of the United Nations furnish such assistance to the Republic of Korea [...] necessary to repel the armed attack and to restore international peace and security in the area."[35] The Soviet Union representative was still not there as they were boycotting the UN Security Council due to their disagreement with Taiwan representing China, so they could not veto this. Now imagine if they had attended that meeting? The Soviet Union would have vetoed the resolution. For western nations, it had become a war against communism.

Truman stated that same day, "The attack upon Korea makes it plain beyond all doubt that communism has passed beyond the use of subversion to conquer independent nations and will now use armed invasion and war. It has defied the orders of the Security Council of the United Nations issued to preserve international peace and security."[36]

The ROK forces were doing all that they could with the little that they had. They even performed "human bullet" attacks on tanks in which they would come close to (or on top of) the North Korean tanks and throw in grenades. Many soldiers did not survive this. ROKA put up a fight and maintained a strong resistance, and the NKPA were unable to envelop their forces.[37]

The U.S. committed to sending ground forces to Korea on June 30, and General Douglas MacArthur ordered the 24th Division of the Eighth U.S. Army to be sent in from Japan. Prior to this, they had already sent naval and air forces.[38] Task Force Smith arrived in Pusan on the morning of July 1.[39]

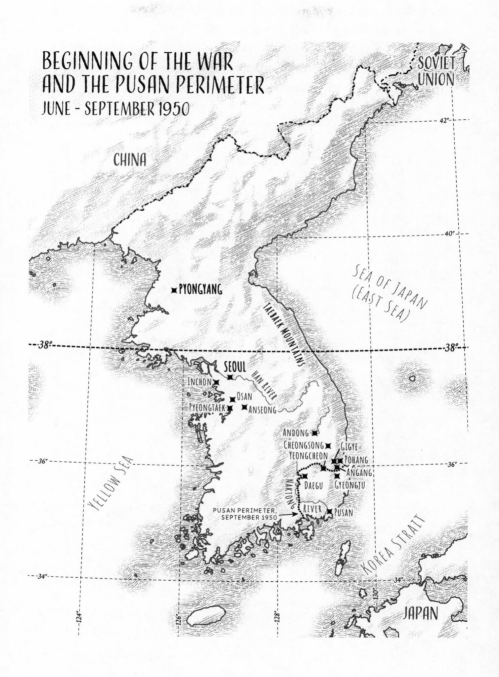

BEGINNING OF THE WAR
AND THE PUSAN PERIMETER
JUNE - SEPTEMBER 1950

SOVIET
UNION

CHINA

42°

40°

SEA OF JAPAN
(EAST SEA)

PYONGYANG

TAEBAEK MOUNTAINS

38°

SEOUL

INCHON

HAN RIVER

OSAN

PYEONGTAEK

ANSEONG

ANDONG

CHEONGSONG

YEONGCHEON

GIGYE

POHANG

36°

YELLOW SEA

NAKTONG

DAEGU

ANGANG

GYEONGJU

RIVER

PUSAN

PUSAN PERIMETER,
SEPTEMBER 1950

KOREA STRAIT

34°

124°

126°

128°

130°

JAPAN

The UN Security Council passed Resolution 84 (the Soviet Union representative still did not show up) on July 7, 1950 (New York time) which rec-
ommended that "all Members provid[e] military forces ... available to a
unified command under the United States of America."[40] That commander
became General Douglas MacArthur. On July 14, the command of the ROK
forces was officially transferred to MacArthur.[41] The ROK Army was now
under the command of the Eighth U.S. Army, the ROK Navy under the
command of the Seventh Fleet of the U.S. Naval Forces Far East, and the
ROK Air Forces under the command of the Fifth Air Force of the Far East
Air Forces.[42]

CHAPTER 12

The First Two Weeks of the War

June - July 1950

It was June 25, 1950, a beautiful Sunday with the sun shining. More than thirty guys in my barracks talked to each other excitedly and laughed loudly, generating an almost ear-splitting noise. It was the first weekend in Seoul since my 8th Regiment of the South Korean Army had been relieved from two years of border guard duty in the mountainous Central-East Region of Gangwon-do Province (江原道) and had been relocated to the Yongsan Camp in the southern part of Seoul. We had not yet fully settled in the new environment. Only a handful of soldiers were given a weekend pass. Fortunately, I was one of them. It was my first Sunday pass in Seoul since I had joined the army two years earlier. I was excited to visit my friends and Mr. and Mrs. Kim Tae-yun and research evening schools. I wanted to attend an evening school or an English and mathematics academy once I settled in this new camp. After breakfast, I put on a clean uniform and was ready to leave for the city.

Then, unexpectedly, a bugle blared across the camp to call an emergency mobilization. It continued to trumpet. I thought it was a drill and grunted, "Damn, why on this Sunday? I have my first pass to Seoul in two years." I grudgingly changed back to fatigues and prepared my equipment, including my rifle, for a combat drill. With a grave face, my company sergeant hurried into my barracks and hollered, "The North Koreans have opened a general assault across the 38th Parallel. It's a war! Prepare for combat readiness and assemble on the parade ground! Quick, quick!" He darted out of my barracks to the next.

We were stunned. No one spoke. The whole barrack became as quiet as a graveyard. But my heart started to pound fast. I could hear the beating. My thoughts flashed back to a border skirmish with the North Korean Army a year earlier. In that battle, I had been all alone, pinned down behind a rice paddy embankment by an enemy machine gun. The unceasing machine gun fire pulverized the embankment. Dust fell on my back and head. I thought I was going to die, but I survived. I wondered how this all-out war would differ from my earlier experience.

Chang Hyokoen murmured, "It's going to be a big war!" breaking the silence. A sergeant valiantly hollered, "We will win the war. We will destroy the goddamn North Korean People's Army! We will kill them all! We will reunite our country!" We all loudly chanted after the sergeant, "We will win, we will win! Kill them all!" Suddenly the silent barrack turned into a lively, energetic place. Everyone became excited and talked again. I, too, shouted with them. It dawned on me that soon I might be able to visit my parents, whom I hadn't seen since I had come to the South. This thought lifted my spirits.

Fully armed, we gathered at the parade ground in the mid-morning heat. The Regiment Commander, Colonel (Col.) Jong-chul Shu, stepped on the reviewing stand, and spoke into a loudspeaker, "At ease! Officers and men, listen carefully! At 5 a.m. today, without warning, the North Korean Armed Forces opened a general attack across the entire 38th Parallel. These invaders mobilized tanks, heavy guns, and even fighter-bombers. Right now, our front line soldiers are bravely fighting them. President Syngman Rhee has called a national mobilization and ordered our National Army to crush the communist devils. We shall prevail against the enemy. The Army General Headquarters has ordered our regiment to move forward. As soon as a fleet of trucks arrives, we shall move to the front line. Be ready!" Then he stepped down from the stand.

In the past, President Rhee and some of the high-ranking army generals had claimed that the South Korean Army could easily crush the North Korean People's Army, take Pyongyang, the capital city of North Korea, within a few days, and reunify the divided peninsula. The enemy's mobilization of tanks and airplanes made me apprehensive because the South Korean Armed Forces did not have any tanks or fighter planes. But I decided to believe what our leaders had said and that we would prevail.

We waited for our transportation, but it did not come. Meanwhile, the kitchen police (KPs) brought our lunch to the parade ground. We ate under the simmering June sun. At last, a fleet of civilian trucks and buses, not army trucks, arrived mid-afternoon. We packed them, and our convoy slowly moved out of the parade ground to Samgakji Circle (三角地). We sang army marching songs. Civilians—young and old, men and women—lined the streets to see us off. Some shouted, "Crush the enemy!" Some waved their flags and chanted, "*Mansei, Mansei* (Long live)!" Some silently watched, perhaps wondering what was ahead.

We responded with "We will win!" or "*Mansei!*" and waved back. When we got out of the city, reality sank in. We became quiet and tense. As we approached the front line, we heard distant artillery explosions. Pak said, "They must be the enemy's, not ours."

Choi Ga-ram tersely responded, "It doesn't matter. We are in a big war. Some of us may not come home alive." Nobody replied, and silence prevailed again.

We arrived at Gapyeong (加平), about thirty miles northeast of Seoul, late in the evening. MPs directed our convoy to a hill country a couple of miles farther north of Gapyeong. I heard the crackling of machine guns and rifle fire. Then I saw red tracer bullets flying from one hill to another. Machine gun tracer bullets are phosphorus bullets spaced at consistent intervals in the clip. They allow the shooter to see where their bullets are going. Intermittent artillery shells exploded on the hills, producing spectacular fireworks in the dark sky. When we disembarked, Col. Shu, the Regiment Commander, ordered my company commander to split our company into two groups, and deployed us to the hills along a narrow country road. As soon as we were deployed on the ridges of the hills, we dug foxholes, twenty to thirty feet apart. Col. Shu had only the regiment headquarters company under his command because his three combat battalions had not yet arrived. Our mission was to deter the enemy's advance. I wondered how we could possibly fight the enemy with just rifles. Furthermore, the North Koreans had already thrust three miles inside South Korea in less than a day.

As the night deepened, machine gun fire became sporadic. But we could not be less alert. Then early the next morning, we were abruptly ordered to go back to Seoul. We hadn't even fired one bullet. Why? Again, we packed into a convoy of civilian trucks and buses and left the battle zone. Our convoy quietly snaked southward along the same roads and streets we had taken northward less than a day earlier. Yesterday, we had proudly sung army victory songs with high morale, but today we were quiet. Today, the same spectators who had cheered us on looked nervous and bewildered. Some of them lined the streets and watched us forlornly, while others squatted in small groups with their heads drooped. We arrived unceremoniously at our Yongsan Camp late that afternoon. The sky was ashen and oppressive.

Our company commander informed us that we had to leave the Gapyeong area to defend the capital city. The enemy had taken Dongducheon (東豆川) and were approaching Uijeongbu (義政府), less than fifteen miles north of downtown Seoul. He directed us to return to our barracks and wait for a new order for deployment.

This shocked me. The crack division of the South Korean Army was responsible for defending the strategically significant Dongducheon-Uijeongbu Line (東豆川-義政府 線). I couldn't believe that this division had so easily lost this important city to the North Koreans. Now the enemy was about to attack Uijeongbu. My heart sank, and my morale plunged. For the first time, I doubted that we could stop the surging invaders. I believed all my friends had the same thoughts.

June 27, 1950 was a hot, humid morning. The sky was gray and low. We were uneasily waiting for the redeployment order, which never came. A few North Korean fighter bombers (USSR-made Yak) flew freely over Seoul without encountering any resistance, because the South Korean Air Force did not have a single fighter plane; all it had was a few L-19 reconnaissance planes. According to rumors, the North Korean planes bombed downtown Seoul.

Then, suddenly, a couple of fighter bombers with American stars on their wings appeared in the sky and intercepted the North Koreans. They chased the Yaks and shot at them. The Yaks tried to dodge the fighter bombers, but a fighter bomber hit one of them. The damaged Yak flew northward, leaving a smoke-trail behind it. The other Yaks escaped the American planes and disappeared into the northern sky. Seeing this spectacular dog fight lifted our morale. Rain started to fall, and we went inside.

As we were enjoying the morale-enhancing victory of the fighter bombers, the company sergeant brought more exciting news. He loudly, even proudly, announced, "The American President said the U.S. will help us!"

All of us spontaneously shouted, "*Mansei*! We will win!" We naively believed that America's involvement would bring an instant victory over the evil North Koreans and help us reunify our divided country. Even the heavy rain could not dampen our excitement. But as the day waned, and the evening rolled in, the booms from the enemy artillery bombardment became closer, louder, and more frequent. I wondered if the U.S. President had committed to sending in troops. Uncertainty prevailed again.

ANTI-TANK SQUADRON

It was raining cats and dogs on the evening of June 27, 1950, the third day of the Korean War. A series of distant booms were heard. A few seconds later, huge flashes, like lightning, came from the top of Namsan Hill in the southern part of Seoul and brightened the camp for a split second. Ear-splitting explosions followed. The windows of our barracks rattled violently. Enemy artillery bombardments! The heavy rain made these explosions more spectacular. This fantastic drama continued a couple of hours before slowing down. My camp was in Samgakji, at the western foothill of the hill. The Han River skirted the edge of the hill from the northeast to the southwest.

One soldier exclaimed, "The enemy tanks are already in Miari, just north of here. Oh, my God, my parents live there!"

Major Yang, the regiment deputy commander, appeared and gravely hollered, "Sergeant Park, organize a squadron and report to me immediately!" Sgt. Park was a senior non-commissioned officer of the regiment headquarters company. MSgt. Lee, my leader and our company sergeant, had been given another assignment that evening.

Sgt. Park responded, "Yes, sir," and loudly called names, "Corporal Pak Sam-hyun, Corporal Kim Maneong, ... Stand up and form a line!" He appointed me as his messenger. All nine of us were administrative personnel from the company. He reported to the major, "Sir, altogether nine."

The Major ordered, "At ease!" He paused for a moment, and then said, "You have volunteered to attack the North Korean tanks. According to the latest intelligence, the North Koreans are already in the northeastern outskirts of Seoul, only four miles north of us. We must stop them. Sergeant Park will be your commander."

We were stunned and scared. None of us had ever seen a real tank, and most of us had little fighting experience except for Sgt. Park and a couple of us who had fought a few border skirmishes.

Then Major Yang opened one of the army green boxes in front of him and picked up a sleek, round cylinder, about one foot long, and a clip of rifle ammunition. He said, "This is a grenade launcher, and this clip contains eight shells filled with gunpowder, but no bullets. You sit down and hold your rifle between your thighs at a 45-degree angle, then mount the launcher on the tip of your M1 rifle and load the magazine into the chamber. When an enemy tank approaches within one hundred feet, you aim at the track of the tank and pull the trigger. The grenade will fly and destroy the wheel, and the tank cannot move. Do you understand?"

Silence!

The major asked, "Have you ever seen a grenade launcher before?"

We responded in unison, "No sir." But I raised my hand and said, "Sir, I saw one in an American training film."

He winced. "Just remember what I told you. You will do all right. Get rest until I issue orders!" and left.

I wondered how, without decent training, we could possibly destroy the enemy's mighty tanks. How many of us would return alive? This mission was insane. No one talked. Perhaps the others had the same thoughts.

A few minutes later, the Major returned with a bottle of *soju* and a small china cup. He ordered us to form a line, handed the cup to Sgt. Park, and filled it. He drank it and passed the empty cup to the next soldier. The Major poured more *soju* for him. This ritual was repeated all the way to me. Even though I was not a drinker, I drank it because this might be the last night of my life. It tasted sour.

Then the Major gave each of us a *Hwarang* cigarette, known to be of low quality, and personally lit it. The scene was just like a Japanese Kamikaze pilot send-off ceremony. Despite being a non-smoker, I puffed my cigarette a couple of times. It was bitter, but I inhaled anyway. Suddenly I was choking and short of breath. I coughed violently and gasped for air. I tumbled on the floor and continued to cough, wheezing.

My frightened fellow soldiers came to help me and asked, "What's the matter, Tae-hyok?" The sergeant held my head and offered me water. I drank it slowly but coughed it out. Later I managed to drink a few drops, and it eased my throat. I drank more. A few minutes later, my cough subsided. I took a deep breath and sat upright against the wall. I said in a weak voice, "Thank you guys for taking care of me." That was my last cigarette.

Relieved, they said, "Glad you are alive."

Kim Jae-kook said, "We thought you were dying before the enemy could kill you," and laughed. Even the Major came and asked if I was okay.

Then he reminded us that our mission to defend the capital was extremely important, and said, "Destroy as many enemy tanks as you can!" He advised us to get some sleep and wait for our orders, before returning to his office.

We all lay on the bare floor using our army backpacks as pillows and tried to sleep. Then Man-E broke the silence and said, "Sergeant Park, have you ever used that grenade stick before?"

"Hell, no. I don't know what the f--- it is. Just shut up and get some sleep!"

Man-E murmured philosophically, "My sergeant doesn't know, I don't know, none of us knows. We will all die tomorrow."

The sergeant shouted, "I told you, *shut your mouth and get to sleep.*"

As night fell, my heart grew heavier thinking about my imminent suicide mission. I thought about my short life and my parents in North Korea, and silently said, "Goodbye, Mom and Dad." I tried to sleep but couldn't.

We all silently lay on the bare floor, wishing the fateful orders had never come. Gradually, fatigue overcame us, and we fell asleep one by one.

A series of fantastic lightings followed by earth-shattering BOOMS woke us. The windows rattled, and glass fell to the ground and broke. We jumped out of our sleep. Sgt. Park murmured ominously, "Those BOOMS are too big to be artillery bombardments. It's something else. I will ask the Major." He went to the Major's office and called, "Major Yang, Major Yang." No answer came. He returned and shouted, "No one is in the building except us. Let's go outside."

Chang Hyokoen asked, "Sergeant, what shall we do with these boxes of grenade launchers?"

"Forget about them. We are not taking them with us. No one knows how to use them anyway." He hollered urgently, "Let's get out to the parade field!" We did and huddled in the middle of the dimly lit parade ground. The whole camp was quiet except for the heavy rain and the intermittent enemy artillery bombardments. We looked at each other nervously and asked, "Where did they go?"

Sgt. Park cursed, "Goddamn, they are all gone. They evacuated without telling us. F---ing major. Let's get out of here before it's too late." He led us to the main gate where a lone sentry was posted. Sgt. Park asked him if he had seen Deputy Commander Major Yang.

He answered that the deputy commander and the headquarters' personnel had gone to Samgakji Circle.

Sgt. Park asked him again, "Did the Major say anything to you?"

"Nothing, Sergeant."

Sgt. Park cursed the Major again, "That son of a bitch!" He continued, "No one is around. Soldier, you had better come with us." Without saying anything, the soldier joined us.

Samgakji Circle was only a few hundred feet from the gate. Arriving at the circle, we saw hundreds of frightened refugees and vehicles crowding the circle and the main boulevard that led to the Han River Bridge.

Sgt. Park asked a refugee, "Sir, what's going on here?"

He answered nervously, "Sergeant, didn't you hear the big explosion? They say the Han River Bridge has been blown up. Anyway, I am going to the river to check if it has really been destroyed." He hurriedly led his wife and three young children toward the river.

We became apprehensive because the bridge was the only means to cross the river to the safety of the south bank. Sgt. Park led us there anyway. The rain continued. As we approached, more refugees crowded the road. Vehicles were in disarray and did not move. I realized they had been abandoned. I saw six army trucks with big guns in tow. The roads were completely clogged. Some people were turning back.

When we arrived at the riverbank, the rain had stopped, and the cloudy day dawned. Thousands of distressed people, including many soldiers and policemen, stood on the bank and helplessly looked at the destroyed bridge. We joined them and saw that the middle sections of the structure had disappeared. Later we learned that the engineering chief of the South Korean Army had prematurely ordered the blast. The river was high and swift, too wide and wild for anyone to swim across. Many trucks and buses had been abandoned on the remaining part of the bridge. We heard that it had been blown up without warning while many people and vehicles were crossing. Consequently, many people and automobiles shared the fate of the bridge.

At last Sgt. Park broke the silence by saying, "What shall we do? There is no way to cross the river, and the enemy will attack us soon. I do not see any ferry either."

Pak suggested that we try the Gwangnaru Bridge farther upstream.

The sergeant responded, "It is across the city, at least seven miles northeast of us. Don't you know that the enemy has already taken downtown? We'll all either be killed or made prisoners of war even before reaching the bridge. That is out of the question." Silence descended upon us again.

I was one of the few who came from North Korea. If we were captured, the North Koreans would surely recognize me as a North Korean native because of my accent and treat me worse than the others. I decided to cross the river by any means or to fight to my death. There was absolutely no way I would become their prisoner. I said, "Sergeant, we should return to the camp and set a defense position on the hilltop and fight. You don't want to become a prisoner, do you?"

Everyone responded almost in unison, "Are you crazy? Nine of us fight the mighty North Korean tanks with just these rifles?" while tapping their guns. "No way will we go back to the camp. Somehow, we must cross the river. And eventually regroup with our company wherever they are." They were right. I was too emotional and irrational. I neither wanted to die nor to become the North Koreans' prisoner. We had to cross the river. But no one knew how.

Since I had lived in this area before joining the army, I knew that there were three railroad bridges a few hundred yards down the river. I stared in their direction through the fog and saw the blurred image of the closest one. I yelled excitedly, "Hey, Sergeant, can you see those railroad bridges? If they have not been destroyed, let's use them to cross the river."

He responded hesitantly, "A railroad bridge? No way. It is too dangerous!" The others agreed.

I shouted, "Are you just going to wait for the enemy and surrender? No way will I become their prisoner! Goodbye!" I walked briskly toward the bridges. I reached the nearest one and looked all the way to the other end. Thank God, it was not destroyed. However, it did not have a walkway because pedestrian traffic was prohibited. The angry river almost reached the tracks. The dashing waters hit the piers and splashed on the ties, making them slippery. There was a space between every two ties that one could easily fall through if one lost one's balance while attempting to cross. No children or anyone carrying heavy loads could possibly make it across.

I cautiously stepped on one tie after another. I arrived at the first pier of the bridge and looked down. The muddy river splashed against the pier and wet my feet. Despite being scared, I continued to the second pier. Then, suddenly my feet froze. An incredible fear gripped me. There, two big bundles of dark brown, oversized hotdogs were tied to the tracks, one on each side. Dynamite! I raised my hand to warn the others, but I couldn't speak. I couldn't move. I heard footsteps and voices from behind. I noticed that the rest of my squad had followed me. My throat relaxed. Then I shouted, "Don't move! Dynamite!" For a few moments, no one stirred. No one talked.

Then Sgt. Park came by slowly. He did a quick inspection and murmured, "That is dynamite alright! I think there are more of these bundles ahead of us. Do you see the wires that connect the two bundles and lead over the bridge toward the other side?" I nodded. He continued, "We cannot keep standing here. We must move on." He hollered, "Hey, you guys, dynamite here! Move carefully! Don't step on it!"

We all moved with extreme caution to avoid the bundles and cables. Advancing, we saw more of them, every thirty to forty feet apart. Before seeing the explosives, the roaring river had scared me. Now, the dynamite frightened me so much that I became oblivious to the torrent. Suddenly, a horrible thought occurred: if someone detonated these explosives without warning, as had been done to the Han River Bridge a few hours earlier, then we would surely be blown up and fall in. Then, the angry flood would carry us into the Yellow Sea. No one would ever know what had happened to us. I shuddered. As I moved farther, my skill walking on the rail ties improved rapidly, and I picked up speed.

After a long, hair-raising crossing, we finally reached the end of the bridge. We shouted for joy, "We made it, we made it!" Even the sky had cleared, and the sun shone. We continued to move on, chatting loudly, for a few hundred feet, and found an ominous plunger detonator by the tracks. We all halted and looked at it. The cables from the bridge were connected to the plunger. Its handle was all the way up, ready to detonate the dynamite. No one was posted to guard it. Had someone been there and pushed the plunger, we could have been goners. We exclaimed, "We are alive!"

Sgt. Park said, "Let's get some rest." Keeping a respectful distance from the plunger, we sat down on the tracks. He asked, "Shall we blow up the bridge or not?" Some of us opined to blow it up immediately so that the enemy could not cross the river. Others said to keep it for some time so that our soldiers and refugees might use it as we had done.

While we were discussing what to do, three big American bombers flew over the bridges from the west, one after another, and dropped bombs. The bombs fell in two straight columns with a huge hissing noise, like a storm. Within a few seconds, they exploded with earth-shattering booms. We instantly threw ourselves flat onto the ground and plugged our ears with our fingers, burying our faces in the dirt. I raised my head a little and took a quick look at the spectacular explosions. Gigantic smoke billowed into the sky. The flying fortresses flew southeast. A few minutes later, three more came and repeated the fierce bombings.

When the stunning shows were over, and the mushroom clouds had dissipated, we rose and surveyed the bridges. They were extensively damaged. Many sections had fallen into the roaring river. The destruction kept us mute for some time. Then Sgt. Park broke the silence and said, "Well, the bombers took care of the bridges. We don't have to worry about the plunger. Let's move to Anyang-up, six miles south of here. We might meet some of our friends." We were hungry and tired but had nothing to eat. We dragged our feet toward Anyang-up, not knowing when we might return to Seoul. Some of us might never make it.

TWO UNFORGETTABLE GIS

July 4, 1950. The Korean War was just nine days old. A small group of us, administrative personnel from the 8th Infantry Regiment Headquarters Company of the South Korean Army, had headed to a small town, Osan (烏山), about thirty miles south of Seoul. Armed only with rifles, we had been fighting the heavily armed North Koreans in Gapyeong (加平) and Noryangjin (露梁津), losing each battle. It was especially bad in Noryangjin, where the enemy's heavy artillery from the front and their tanks from behind pounded, pinching us between them. Our regiment put up a fight and we were able to repel the threat for a few days, but alas, we lost. We sustained heavy casualties. The Battle of Han River was from June 28 to July 1. Our regimental commander was wounded, and a friend of mine was killed. Only one third of us in the regiment (nine hundred soldiers) managed to escape the hell.

At Osan, we met the first American soldiers. They belonged to a U.S. Army task force that had been hurriedly airlifted to South Korea from Japan a few days earlier and deployed around the northern edge of the town to deter the North Korean advance. Meeting them boosted our morale, for we believed that they would not only stop the North Koreans' advance but also turn them back to North Korea. We decided to stay close to the American troops so that together we might fight the invaders and return to Seoul. However, the American Military Police directed us to move on a couple of miles farther south to Pyeongtaek (平澤).

The heavy rain that had started the previous day continued to fall. A staggering exodus of tens of thousands of frightened, wet, cold refugees streamed southward, filling all the roads. Not knowing their destination, they were just trying to get away from the invaders. Mothers piggybacked their babies while gripping their older ones by the hand lest they should become separated. Only flimsy cotton clothes protected their babies from the pouring rain.

Two days earlier, the same children had cried under the sweltering sunshine. Now they wept under the cold rain. In addition to their babies, some of the mothers toted their belongings on their heads. Men shouldered heavy items and emergency provisions using farmers' back-racks or improvised backpacks; some with their youngsters on top. Some families were lucky enough to have two-wheeled push carts or ox-drawn carriages on which they heaped their belongings. Small children or elderly parents were perched on top of the heaps.

The rain persisted. To add to the refugees' misery, the roads flooded and became mired under the dragging feet. Despite the heavy rain and muddy conditions, the refugee flow continued throughout the day. The distant thundering of the enemy's artillery bombardments contributed to the refugees' anguish. The booming got closer and more intense by the hour. My country had never experienced such suffering before.

July 5, 1950. The rain showed no sign of ending. The flow of refugees trickled to only a few small groups, and then completely stopped by mid-morning. I wondered if most had already gone somewhere farther south. Had the heavy rain prevented them from leaving their homes; or had the North Koreans blocked the roads?

We anxiously but naively waited for the American soldiers to advance northward and push the enemy back to North Korea. Instead, the American artillery unit pulled their big guns out of deployment and docked them to the back of their trucks, ready to move southward instead of northward. We realized that they were preparing to retreat, and our morale plummeted. MSgt. Lee, our group leader, said gravely, "The Americans are retreating. We should prepare to move to Anseong (安城), about ten miles southeast. I have heard that our 8th Regiment is regrouping there." Lee had been ordered to lead another group the first few days of the war, so we had been temporarily under Park.

Just then a small group of wet and weary refugees approached from the north side of the town. They appeared to be a family of eight—two young mothers with two children each, an elderly man, and a boy in his early teens. Like other mothers, the women piggybacked their babies and led the older ones by the hand. The older children, bewildered and cold, were weeping. The old man and the teenager carried heavy loads on their backs. The weary old man came to MSgt. Lee and asked, "Sergeant, where are you heading?"

He replied, "Anseong (安城), sir."

The old man looked very disappointed and said, "Are the American soldiers retreating, too?"

"It seems like it." He asked, "Sir, where are you taking your family in this heavy rain without any cover?"

"They are my daughters-in-law, my grandchildren, and my youngest son. My two older sons are in the first division of the army; the oldest one is a captain and the middle one is a master sergeant, like you. They were stationed in the Kaesŏng area when the North Korean devils opened the war. I heard that the first division had fought gallantly, but they lost the battle after losing many lives. I worry about my two sons." He sighed deeply and continued, "Rumor has it that the North Koreans were rounding up the families of South Korean soldiers, policemen, and government officials. We feared that they would surely arrest us because of my soldier sons, so we left home yesterday morning and followed the refugees, but we lagged because of these little ones. We had to stop overnight at a barn off the highway a couple of miles north to give the children some rest. We left the barn early this morning despite this heavy rain." The old man paused and asked MSgt. Lee a very difficult question, "Now, sergeant, when do you think that you and the Americans will push back the enemy?"

MSgt. Lee looked down at the ground for a few seconds, cleared his throat, and mumbled, "I am sorry, I wish I knew, sir." The old man nodded as if he had already known the answer, and silently returned to his nervous family.

The merciless rain continued. A retreating American jeep pulled over. Two GIs hopped off the vehicle, came over to the wet and cold family and patted the crying children gently on the head. One of the GIs spoke to the old man, but he obviously did not understand English, and he turned his head toward us, seeking help. But none of us spoke English either.

The GIs took the crying children by the hand and led them to their jeep, gesturing to the rest to follow them. They put the children on the back seat, on top of the ammunition boxes. The children began to cry louder, kicking their legs in the air and calling "*Umma, umma!*" When the GIs helped their mothers climb up beside them, the children soon calmed down. Now the jeep was fully loaded with their weapons, ammunition boxes, and two mothers with their four children. This left no room for the old man and the teenager.

The soldiers spoke with each other, gesturing with their hands, apparently discussing how to solve this dilemma. Then they walked over to a nearby thatched barn, took out their bayonets and used them to cut away the straw-thatches and ropes to free a rafter from the barn roof. Then they put it across the jeep between the front and rear seats and secured it with ammunition boxes. The rafter was a sturdy round, smooth log, about eight feet long. It extended out over the jeep to the left and right, about one and one-half feet on each side. Then they helped the old man and the teenager climb up onto the rafter on each side, where they perched uncomfortably, clutching the front seats to keep from falling off.

With his entire family aboard the jeep, the old man bowed his head with a broad smile to the GIs many times to express his profound thanks. The GIs, with their own smiles, responded to the old man's thanks, hopped up onto the jeep and headed slowly southward on the muddy Pusan-Seoul highway.

While sloshing on foot along a narrow slimy road toward Anseong, I thought about those two American soldiers. When they found no room for the old man and his son, the GIs could have told them to walk, which would have split up the family. In the chaos of war, there would be little hope of reuniting again. Instead, their marvelous humanitarian deed and their ingenuity made me smile. It was like seeing a bright red rose in the middle of the desert. I thought this war was good versus evil, and the good was with us. Thus, we would eventually win.

WHERE IS MY GUN?

When the Korean War broke out on June 25, 1950, I was an infantry corporal in the Republic of Korea Army (ROKA). I was then a lanky nineteen-year-old boy, still at five-feet-six inches tall but now weighing 90 pounds.

My full equipment weighed approximately forty pounds, including one M1 rifle with a bayonet, two ammo belts, and an army backpack. This total load was equivalent to much of my body weight, and too heavy to carry to the front line. Since the M1 rifle with its accessories weighed about twenty pounds, I persuaded my ordnance sergeant to switch my gun with a Carbine rifle which weighed less than one half of an M1, reducing my load by at least ten pounds.

The invading North Korean Army consisted of 180,000 well-trained officers and soldiers armed with more than two hundred tanks, two hundred aircraft, and thousands of long-range field artillery guns and heavy mortars, all Russian-made. According to our intelligence, more than fifty thousand of them had fought the Japanese Army during the long Sino-Japanese War and World War II, either with the Chinese Communist Guerilla Army or with the Russian Army.

As opposed to this mighty enemy, the ROKA numbered ninety-five thousand officers and men, including all non-combatants; but all were not stationed at the border that day. We were not only undertrained but also poorly armed, some with antiquated World War II Japanese rifles.

From the onset of the war, the outnumbered, outgunned ROKA lost every battle it fought. The entire front line of the army crumbled within days. My 8th Regiment of over two thousand men was decimated to less than one third of its full force.

It had been raining almost daily since the beginning of the war. By early July a handful of us from the regiment headquarters company, headed by our Company Sgt. Lee, retreated to Cheonan-up, about fifty miles south of Seoul, where many American soldiers and trucks crowded the narrow dirt streets. A few American MPs directed us to a small farm village near Cheonan-up.

Upon arriving, we met scores of weary soldiers huddling like lost sheep. They said that after an intense artillery bombardment had pulverized their position and killed many of their friends, hundreds of the enemy infantry accompanied by tanks had attacked. The attack was so fierce that the company commander ordered them to retreat. Barely surviving the battle, they were separated from their commander during the chaos. Since the retreat, they had not seen him. I noticed a few of them had lost their guns.

Believing that the Americans would deter the North Korean advance and provide a safety cushion, MSgt. Lee gave us a badly needed rest while he tried to contact the regiment. Exhausted after many days of fighting, I took off my metal helmet, leaving the vinyl liner on to keep my head dry from the rain, and sat on the helmet. I held my rifle across my thighs and rested my head on it.

A prickling sensation irritated my cheek, and I slapped it automatically, which woke me. I found myself lying on my side in the wet grass, next to my helmet. Apparently, I had fallen asleep and unknowingly slid off my helmet to the ground. The rain had stopped, and the sun was heating my cheek.

Instinctively, I looked for my rifle, but it was missing. I began to search frantically for it, checking every Carbine holder in the area. Others complained, "What the hell is wrong with you?"

I snapped back, "Some asshole stole my gun. I am looking for it." Frustrated, I shouted, "Who the hell took it?" Nobody responded. They were too tired to care about my desperate situation. While searching, I stumbled on an abandoned Japanese rifle, Type 99, by the roadside and picked it up along with a couple of five-round magazines to use until I could get a new American rifle. Having received my basic training with a Type 99, I knew that it was a lousy gun for battle, because everything was manual. I tried to load it, but neither of the two clips fit into the chamber. Useless! Disappointed, I threw it into a nearby bush, cursing it.

Now, I am completely unarmed! What am I going to do without a gun on the front line? If I face an enemy, I will surely die. Fear gripped me from head to toe, and I shuddered. *I must avoid any direct contact with the enemy until I get another gun.* I cursed the bastard who had stolen my precious Carbine. However, my instinct directed me to devise a way to survive without a weapon.

Then I thought, *Get the Japanese gun back. It might become useful. If I encounter an enemy one-on-one, and happen to see him first, I could shout, 'Surrender!' as if I were ready to shoot. If he surrenders, then I'd have saved my life.*

I retrieved the Japanese gun from the roadside bush and found that it didn't even have a shoulder strap. I produced a few yards of twine and made an improvised shoulder strap for the gun. Strangely, carrying even a useless weapon over my shoulder made me feel somewhat better. However, I earnestly prayed to the spirits of my ancestors, "Please keep me from direct contact with the enemy until I get an American gun."

My intense nervousness caused me to have a few nightmares. One was of an enemy soldier who appeared out of nowhere in front of my foxhole and charged me with his bayonet. I shot at him, but my rifle did not go off. I screamed from pain and woke up. But it was only a dream!

Even though we didn't know where the regiment headquarters was, somehow my company sergeant received a new order through a carrier. We were ordered to move to a mountainous region, about ten miles to the east. According to the sergeant, an American Army task force which had just been flown in from Japan would deploy along the Seoul-Daejun highway, the enemy's main route.

I expected that the rugged terrain would slow the enemy's advance, reducing the chance of direct engagement, perhaps by a day. This new deployment lessened my anguish. The next morning, we were again ordered to retreat without a battle from the new deployment to avoid being trapped by the enemy who had broken through the American line on our left flank during the night.

Like a thirsty man in a desert, I waited for a resupply of weapons. I desperately wanted a usable gun. Meanwhile, my friends needed more ammunition to replenish their low stock. At last, a regiment ordnance sergeant arrived on a three-quarter ton truck with a new supply of much needed weapons and ammunition. I exchanged the useless Japanese gun for a brand new M2 Carbine rifle and two thirty-round magazines, including a couple of extra ammo belts. After four long days, I finally had a real gun. I kissed the rifle many times, held it high in the air, and shouted, "Now, I am alive!" My morale soared, and I feared engaging the enemy no more. Since then, I carried my beloved weapon wherever I went and tied its shoulder strap around my arm when I slept.

By that time, we had made it to Jincheon, and our division was placed under General Kim Suk-won. I was so thankful to have a new Carbine. I learned that General Kim had graduated from the Japanese Imperial Military Academy and led a Japanese battalion to fight the Chinese Nationalist Army during the Sino-Japanese War in the late 1930s. He had earned one of the highest Japanese military medals and been awarded the samurai saber. He had risen to the rank of full colonel by the end of World War II. After the Japanese defeat, he joined the South Korean Army in the late 1940s and was commissioned to one-star general, commanding the Capital Division. Apparently, he had carried with him Japanese army style tactics, and wielded his Japanese samurai sword. In the Battle of Jincheon, he directed battle right alongside us fighting soldiers where the enemies' bullets landed around him. Eventually, though, the front line collapsed. But then he went on a counterattack, and we took back our line. We had a fearless leader. We then went to

Cheongju, and later Boen. Six hundred members of our 8th Regiment were then reorganized into the 3rd Battalion of the 18th Regiment. We then fought in Yecheon and in Andong. In Andong, we cut off the enemy's advance and prevented them from heading to Yeongdeok.

'STAND OR DIE' SPEECH

By the end of July, the enemy had taken control of everything northwest of the Naktong River line, which was most of the Korean peninsula. The United Nations Command knew they could not risk losing any more land. The NKPA command were worried that more UN troops could be sent into a war which was supposed to have lasted only a month. On July 29, Lt. Gen. Walton Walker stated:

> *"We are fighting a battle against time. There will be no more retreating, withdrawal or readjustment of the lines or any other term you choose. There is no line behind us to which we can retreat. Every unit must counterattack to keep the enemy in a state of confusion and off balance. There will be no Dunkirk, there will be no Bataan. A retreat to Pusan would be one of the greatest butcheries in history. We must fight until the end … We will fight as a team. If some of us must die, we will die fighting together … I want everybody to understand we are going to hold this line. We are going to win."* [43]
> **—Lieutenant General Walker**

Lt. Gen. Walker achieved more than what he's acknowledged for in the battles up till September 1950 with the very little he had. While the UN and ROK forces kept getting pushed to the Naktong River Line, he refused to give up. He knew the importance of Daegu. He even would fly right above his men fighting and would scream at his troops, risking his own life while doing so.[44] Under his command, the UN and ROK forces put up strong resistance and significantly delayed the enemy. If it wasn't for Walker's command, one might wonder whether there would be no Pusan Perimeter and there would have been a Dunkirk.

CHAPTER 13

Reconnaissance

Early – Middle of August 1950

My battalion was redeployed on a mountain range north of a small farm village in Cheongsong County (Green Pine County), North Gyeongsang Province. The battalion commander ordered administrative personnel to camp under an old elm tree in the middle of the village, next to a creek. On the front line, heavy fighting went on all day and night, resulting in many casualties. We were relatively safe, out of the enemy rifles' firing range, even though sporadic enemy artillery shells exploded around us.

After a week of suffering from dysentery, which I had treated by drinking an entire mug of *soju*, I came down with malaria. Every two days I was stricken with a high fever and blinding headaches, which rendered me nearly immobile. Although I was weak, I was able to move around and perform my responsibilities between malaria eruptions. Because the medics did not consider malaria a serious illness compared to the heavy casualties in the battalion, I couldn't request to be sent to a clinic. I believed that the enemy's onslaught didn't allow time for the South Korean Army to set up clinics.

On the second afternoon in Cheongsong, I began to shiver. My teeth chattering, I curled into a fetal position. Despite it being a steamy August day, I felt as if I had been doused in ice water. I wrapped myself in my blanket, but the shivering got worse. Chang Hyokoen put his blanket over me and said, "I hope it will help you." I thanked him. The additional blanket didn't ease my shaking. This attack was more severe than the previous ones.

After four or five hours of convulsions, an excruciating headache followed, lasting for many hours, which deprived me of sleep while my fellow soldiers were snoring, except for our guard, my best friend Corporal Lee Jong-kook. I wondered how long this devilish malaria would torture me, and how long my health could sustain during the seemingly unending, arduous march, if I did not get well soon. Thankfully, my headache began to ease as the night deepened.

It was way past midnight, but I was unable to sleep. The hauntingly beautiful moonlight shone on the eerily silent valley, as if there was no war. The stillness and the silvery moon led my wandering mind back to my hometown in North Korea. On warm summer nights, my father often spread a big rice mat in our courtyard, and my parents and I lay on it with a mosquito fire burning. We chatted about the weather, farming, or our neighbors. Sometimes we gazed up at the moon or counted the stars until the mosquito fire ceased. *My parents might be watching this same moon as I am now. Maybe they are in their bed. Mom and Dad, over two long years have gone by since I last said, 'Goodbye. Take care of yourselves!'* I missed them so much, more so in my sickness. I wondered if we would meet again and hug each other. Tears filled my eyes and overflowed, wetting my cheeks. "Damn Kim Il Sung!"

The moon slanted westward and lost its brilliance somewhat, but still illuminated the quiet valley and the soybean field around the elm tree. I didn't like this quietness because it suggested that the enemy was planning a pre-dawn surprise attack. That's a tactic the North Koreans had frequently used from the onset of the war. I was not religious, but I prayed to the spirits of the valley or the mountains, whoever they might be, "Please do not let the enemy attack this morning. I am too weak to fight."

Even before I finished the prayer, a series of gunshots broke the silence. Jong-kook shouted, "Get up, get up." A red tracer bullet flew from a nearby hill across the valley. Everyone jumped out of his sleep, grabbed his rifle, and lay on the ground, ready for a counterattack. But the shooting stopped as abruptly as it had started. Captain Chung, the Battalion Headquarters Company Commander who led the supporting operations, asked which direction the shooting had come from. Jong-kook and I simultaneously pointed at the hill about half a mile northeast of us.

He said, "No one should be there. I don't like it." Then, unexpectedly a soldier approached us from the direction of the shooting. Jong-kook shouted, "Stop there. Password?" The soldier answered with the proper password and countered, "Yours?" After exchanging the correct passwords, the soldier joined us. Naturally, we asked him about the gunshots, but he didn't know who had fired them either.

After conferring with MSgt. Lee, Captain Chung led all the supporting functions to the other side of the creek. Then he ordered the sergeant to organize a reconnaissance team to survey the area where the gunshots had come from. The sergeant picked three non-commissioned officers (NCOs) under him, as well as me.

I thought how cruel he was to send a sick soldier to scout the enemy. I almost asked him to drop me from the mission because of my malaria, but I didn't because all of them in the group were my friends, and the battalion had lost more than one third of its force. I thought it would be cowardly to ask to be excused from the scouting mission.

After organizing the team, he gave us instructions to watch each other and to give a signal if we found anything suspicious or unusual ahead of us. He also warned us not to engage with the enemy unless it was unavoidable. Then he led us to the soybean field by the elm tree and ordered us to move in one line about twenty feet apart from each other. I was at the far-right flank. When we had cautiously advanced a couple of hundred feet, he signaled us to stop and survey the area. I crouched between soybean plants and inspected my surroundings. Nothing unusual! Then suddenly gunshots crackled behind me. I instinctively dropped flat on the ground and crawled back toward the elm tree, only to find that the shots were coming from behind the tree. *The enemy has already occupied the area! We are trapped. Don't be a target of theirs in the open field! Shoot back at them from the creek!* I army-crawled away and jumped into the creek. Then three or four men jumped into the creek right in front of me, giving me no chance to pull my trigger. *Oh my God, I am dead!* Then I heard a very familiar voice, a welcome voice. It was MSgt. Lee. *I was dead, now I am alive!*

I gestured to quiet them and whispered, "Sergeant, the enemy is here." "Where?"

"Right behind the elm tree. They fired at us from there."

"No, that was us. We didn't see anyone but gave warning shots anyway."

"You what?" Pure anger erupted in my heart, and I yelled at him, "You pulled back without telling me and fired from behind? You almost killed me, and I was about to shoot at you. What kind of leader are you?"

"I thought you were with us."

"Didn't you do a headcount?"

"Let's move, Corporal Kim!" he replied sternly.

"Sorry for my bad mouth, Sergeant." We got out of the creek and marched toward the place where the commander had sent us for the mission. Reaching it, we found a lone soldier waiting for us. He said that the headquarters had evacuated to the other side of the range up the valley, and conveyed the commander's order that we should follow them as quickly as possible.

By then the sun rays had begun to fan out above the tree line on the eastern mountains, illuminating the ridges of the northwestern mountains on our right. Someone exclaimed in an uneasy voice, "Look, something is moving on the ridge!" We all looked up and saw countless soldiers moving southward in a long column. We couldn't tell from so far away whether they were friends or enemies.

MSgt. Lee said, "I don't like it. Most likely, they are North Koreans. Let's get the hell out of here before they close the pass. It's the only way out of this damn valley." The trail wound to the top. He said that we could make it to the crest in less than half an hour. We slung our rifles on our shoulders and hurried. Despite being weakened by malaria, I managed to keep up with the rest until halfway up the trail. Slowly, I began to slip behind as the trail got steeper, but no one noticed because everybody was concentrating on climbing. Sweat drenched my fatigues and blurred my eyes. My legs wobbled. I was so tired that I just wanted to give up and lie by the roadside. However, my determination not to be captured by the enemy kept me going. I took out my canteen and gulped the water, which energized me somewhat. Corporal Man-E hollered, "Hurry up, Tae-hyok." I looked up and saw my friends shouting from the top, a few more bends from me. Shortly I joined them. Not knowing how weak I was, they said, "What the hell made you so slow?" I didn't even have the strength to respond. I lay on the grass and fell asleep quickly.

A shout woke me; it was MSgt. Lee. I don't know how long I slept, perhaps ten or twenty minutes, but I felt a little better. He deployed us on the ridge-line overlooking a few farm fields down in a small valley to the northeast and instructed us to keep an eye on the valley. On the other side of the hill, the trail descended sharply, ending at the bank of a large river which skirted the hill. A strip of willow trees like a green ribbon decorated the riverbank on the other side. Beyond that strip, rich farmland extended a couple of miles to the foothills of the rising hills in the west. A dirt highway connected a mountain range in the North and one in the South. A lone rice-straw thatched farm-house stood at the bottom of the trail with an outhouse at the edge of the courtyard. There were a few soldiers in the yard including the battalion adju-tant and MSgt. Choo.

I watched Sergeant Choo enter the outhouse, singing a folk song loudly. Corporal Chun exclaimed, "Oh boy, he is happy to release a big shit." Chun entertained us often on the front line. Nothing seemed to bother him much. Shortly, I heard mortar shells hiss, passing over our position. We were safe, but wondered where they would hit. A moment later they exploded near the outhouse, throwing dust and smoke high into the air. The frightened sergeant jumped out holding his trousers halfway up, exposing his rear end. Despite the tense moment, Corporal Chun said, "Poor sergeant, I think he didn't have enough time to wipe his ass!" and laughed. In a lull a few days later, Chun teased Sergeant Choo about it. Embarrassed, he shouted, "Shut your f@#$%&* mouth!" But a moment later he, too, laughed and said "Are you kidding? I didn't want to die in a shithouse!" We all cherished the brief, precious lull, forgetting the war for a few moments.

Shortly after seeing Sgt. Choo's drama, we returned to our positions from where we could watch a long column of enemy soldiers crossing the fields down in the valley. We fired at them. I aimed at one enemy soldier and pulled my trigger, firing at least six rounds, but he just continued marching. They were out of our rifle range. They didn't even bother to respond to our shoot-ing. Knowing that our guns couldn't reach them, they moved on with nary a bit of fear.

MSgt. Lee yelled, "Hold fire! Don't waste ammunition," and sent Cor-poral Lee Jong-kook to the battalion adjutant for further orders. But even before my friend departed, machine gun fire sprayed down on the five of us from the higher ridge on our left flank. Also, mortar shells exploded around us. No one was hit.

"Son of a bitch!" Corporal Chun yelled and turned to our enemy, aiming his rifle at them.

"Don't bother, Chun! They have the higher ground and are going to kill you with their machine guns before you take a shot! We'll fight back another time."

MSgt. Lee immediately ordered us to move to the hill. Separately we crawled into the wooded hill and then ran toward the river as fast as we could thinking we'd get out of their range. When we got there, I plunged in. The water was up to my stomach and flowed fast. I waded diagonally downstream to minimize the force of the flow, holding my rifle above my head. Midway, the flow almost knocked me down. Bullets splashed around me. Upon crossing the river, I ran into a willow grove and continued to run to get out of the enemy's rifle range.

After a good distance, believing that the enemy's machine guns couldn't reach me, I slowed down and looked for my friends. I hollered, "Sergeant Lee." No answer! "Sergeant Lee, Corporal Kim, where are you?" No one responded. Only our distant enemy's machine gun shots were heard. *I am lost!* Fear swept through my heart. I walked farther, expecting them; instead, I encountered two huge cast iron kettles under a big willow, full of hot cooked rice, but no one was around to tend them or eat. I halted there, hoping my friends would catch up with me soon.

The rice could easily feed one hundred soldiers. Obviously, some kitchen personnel cooked for their company, but the last enemy bombardment frightened them away. I wondered where and how they had brought these two gigantic kettles to the middle of the plain. Even though I had eaten nothing for the past twenty-four hours, I had little appetite. However, not knowing when the next food supply would be coming, I decided to eat some. I took out my Korean army mess kit from my backpack, filled it with rice and ate it using a pair of makeshift willow chopsticks. Without a side dish, it was hard to swallow. While I was eating, two friendly soldiers in wet army fatigues, whom I had never met before, came out of the willow grove, and exclaimed, "Rice! Can we have some?" I presumed that they, too, had escaped from the enemy, and their presence significantly reduced my fear of being lost.

"Help yourself. Someone cooked it and abandoned it."

They scooped rice into their canteen cups and devoured it like hungry pigs. One guy said, "We had better get going." They moved on while eating. I advised them to refill their mess kits for lunch and supper because food supplies might not come any time soon. They thanked me, and we all filled our mess kits with the rice. Since we were separated from our respective units, we decided to stay together until we reunited with our companies, introducing each other. Out of necessity, we became instant partners and departed together toward the highway, hoping to meet our friends.

The August sun poured heat on us mercilessly. Upon reaching the highway, we joined a small group of lost soldiers heading south, like us. Shortly we met the Division Commander Brigadier General Kim Suk-won standing in the middle of the highway and rattling his shiny Japanese samurai saber. He blocked the road and shouted repeatedly to the dispirited stragglers, "Climb up the hills and fight the enemies!" pointing his saber in the direction of the hills on his right. No one dared to pass by him. A few dozen demoralized soldiers were already following his orders and ascending the hills in a disorganized column. We, too, left the highway and joined the column. I looked for my friends, but I found none. Soon I lost my two partners. However, I didn't panic because I had many more soldiers with me now.

When I reached the hilltop, I found a larger throng of troops moving along the ridge. There must have been officers among the soldiers, but no one seemed to be in command. Even though I did not know where this column was heading, I followed it because I didn't have any other way to go. Despite my physical weakness inflicted by malaria, I managed to keep up with the troops. Perhaps the extreme circumstances had pumped adrenaline into my system.

Farther up the ridge, we met a company which had dug foxholes, ready to fight the enemy while protecting the moving soldiers and providing them with time to regroup. A lieutenant directed us to descend the mountains to a rendezvous down in a small farm village. I arrived there in the late afternoon, where many makeshift signs led the stragglers to their respective units. I followed my battalion sign and found my headquarters company's sergeant major and other friends. They welcomed me almost in unison, "Tae-hyok, you are alive! You made it. We thought you were dead," grabbing my hands and arms. I was moved by their genuine camaraderie. They told me that the previous night, the enemy had broken through a unit on our battalion's right flank and attacked us from behind. Since the division did not have a reserve combat unit to plug the hole and counterattack, the thinly deployed front line collapsed, forcing us to retreat in disarray.

• • •

Each unit conducted a headcount and regrouped. MSgt. Lee made a roll call and cross-checked everyone against the company roll. No one was missing. I did not know how well the rest of the battalion had fared.

We marched farther down the valley and were deployed on one of the surrounding mountains until the next morning. There was no engagement with the enemy throughout the night. The next day, our entire regiment was ordered to move southeast to the Gigye-Angang area.

It had been two days since my last malaria attack. I feared the devilish cyclic sickness might hit me at any moment. As I had feared, malaria erupted again in the afternoon during the march, making it extremely difficult to walk. Despite the sizzling August sun, I shivered wildly, and my teeth chattered. I wrapped myself in a blanket to fend off the chill, without much effect. My friends helped me. Some took my gun and backpack and carried them for me. I was profoundly grateful. We arrived at our destination by late afternoon. By then the chill had gone, but the severe headache lingered throughout the evening. Our three combat companies were deployed on the ridges of the mountain ranges in the north of the region. As usual, the battalion headquarters administration and ordnance personnel occupied two farmhouses at the foothills of the mountains. As soon as we settled in, I fell asleep until the next morning.

• • •

Early in the second morning in the Gigye-Angang area, the enemy began to shell the mountains where our combat units had been deployed. Our field artillery fired back at the enemy. This exchange lasted for a couple of hours, and then rifle and machine gun fire erupted. Fierce battles continued all day and night. In this battle we counterattacked the assaulters and captured a dozen North Koreans. It was a victory for us. Our morale soared. However, retaining the mountains produced high casualties.

After three days of fighting, we abandoned the mountains and went to the hills, a couple of miles farther south. A list of the dead and wounded from the battalion observation post (OP) showed more than two dozen dead and twice as many wounded. I noticed the name Bong Jong-tae, one of my best friends from my native province, among the dead. Suddenly my eyes clouded, and tears fell uncontrollably. When other soldiers had been killed, I had felt sad and scared. But this time, I cried over my friend's death. I inquired how he had been killed and where his body had been buried. According to his platoon sergeant, an enemy mortar shell exploded just behind his foxhole, pulverizing him. He was so badly torn apart that his combat friends buried him where he had been killed.

I remembered that he used to say, "If we get one week of vacation, you and I will visit my parents and spend a few days with them because your parents live in North Korea." (While we were from the same province, he lived below the 38th Parallel). But he was buried somewhere in the mountains, lost to his parents forever. I wished I could go up the hills and put a clear mark on his tomb, but I couldn't because they were under enemy control. If I died, I would end up like him, especially since my parents lived in North Korea. I was depressed.

To make matters worse, malaria reoccurred that afternoon. I wandered around trying to alleviate the grief of losing my friend until I found an empty farmhouse where I collapsed and fell asleep. Sometime later, a noise woke me. I had no clue where I was. I went out to see what was going on and saw a few soldiers cooking a large amount of rice in a cast iron kettle in the attached kitchen. I didn't know who they were or what unit they belonged to. I greeted them anyway, "Hello." They looked at me with an expression of 'Where the hell did you come from?' I told them that I belonged to the 3rd Battalion of the 18th Regiment and asked them what town I was in and if they happened to know where my regiment was.

A corporal in charge, in his late twenties, answered, "You, too, must be one of those poor soldiers who have lost their units. Damn war!" After telling me the name of the town, he gave me directions to my unit and the distance, a mile to the north. I thanked the corporal and immediately set out.

On the way, I ran into PFC Shin, a warm-hearted soldier whom I had met at basic training two years earlier. He had remained with the 5th Combat Company of the 8th Regiment along with his hometown friends while I had been assigned to the headquarters personnel section. However, after a reorganization of ROK Armed Forces, part of our regiment had been transferred to the 18th. Both of us were among those transferred. He said, "I do not belong to the 18th Regiment. I am going back to the 8th where all my hometown friends are. I can fight the enemy better with my friends. If I die, I want to die with them. Tae-hyok, take care of yourself. Goodbye."

"Take care of yourself, too." We shook hands and went our separate ways. His words made me homesick and lonely. He went to join his childhood friends, but I didn't even have a single hometown friend in the entire South Korean Army. All of them lived in North Korea. Some of them might have been drafted by the North Korean Army, and we might be fighting each other. Then a worse notion came to me. What if my older brother had been drafted? Brother against brother, friends against friends! This thought horrified me, and I cursed Kim Il Sung who had started this miserable war. I forced myself to shake off the painful thoughts, hastening back. I returned to my company around noon and reported to MSgt. Lee.

Before I offered my excuses, he shouted, "Where the hell have you been? You've been missing for an entire day."

"Sergeant, I am very sorry," I said, and explained what had happened. He listened to my story quietly. I continued, "Sergeant, do you remember when I asked you if I could be sent to an army clinic for treatment because I was so sick? But the company commander turned down my request because he didn't regard malaria as a serious disease."

"Yeah, you should have been hospitalized. But don't wander away again. You can be court-martialed for leaving your unit without proper permission. If malaria hits you again, you come to me so that I may show Captain Chung how sick you are and request that you be sent to a clinic. If he doesn't allow it, at least I can have someone watch over you so that you do not wander away again. Do you understand? Go!"

After the solid sleep at the farmhouse, mysteriously, my malaria never came back. My appetite improved, and my strength started to return. Also, our front line began to stabilize after a six-week series of defeats and retreats since the war had begun. The war had turned into a tug-of-war along the hills. One day we would take a hill from the enemy, and the next day the enemy would take it back, generating heavy casualties on both sides. But the North Koreans' loss was much worse than ours because we had finally been provided with heavy guns, and our fighter bombers pounded the enemy positions at will with napalm bombs and rockets. For instance, when one of our combat companies had taken a strategically important hill from the enemy, they reported more than 150 dead North Koreans strewn over the hill. They said that it was one of the most horrible scenes they had ever witnessed.

One hot August day, we administration personnel joined a short-handed combat unit to reclaim a hill which we had lost to the enemy a few days earlier. After a day-long battle, we recaptured the hill. When we reached the ridgeline in the dusk, the smell of rotting flesh was heavy in the still air. The enemy had abandoned their dead comrades when they ran for their lives. It was too dark to locate the bodies for burial. We had to put up with that incredible odor until the next morning. I was so thirsty that I climbed down to a gully in the foothills. I lay on my stomach at the edge of the creek, submerged my sweaty face in water and gulped it. Having satiated my thirst, I sat up for a few moments of rest. An undesirable smell, not too strong, tickled my nostrils. I thought it wafted down from the hill and tried to settle my queasy stomach. I filled my canteen and two others for my friends. As I walked up the hill, I hummed, having survived another day.

When I returned the canteens to my two lazy friends, they grabbed them, simultaneously thanking me and gulping the water. Then they spat the water out as fast as they had drunk it. Chun shouted, "What the f@#$%^&* water did you bring?" Pak exclaimed, "It tastes like rotten meat." They spat a few more times, trying to clean the foul taste from their mouths.

I was offended, and shouted back, "You ungrateful sons of bitches. I have done good for you. Instead of thanking me, you complain." I opened my canteen and sipped water to show nothing was wrong with it. It smelled rotten, but my stupid pride kept me from spitting it out. I pretended the water was good, quietly walked away from them, and then spat it out. The next morning, I returned to the creek to investigate what had caused the water to be so foul. *Oh, heaven forgive me! I saw a few bloated, dead North Koreans with their heads in the running creek.* My stomach churned, and I almost vomited. In those hot August days, rotten odors from human carcasses or dead horses were ubiquitous, but I had never even imagined drinking water polluted by dead bodies. War had stripped human dignity from each of us, enemies and friends alike. All day long, I had no desire to talk, just wanting to get off the cursed hill. Fortunately, we moved to another hill before the sunset.

CHAPTER 14

Why Me, Sir?

Mid-August 1950

When we captured North Korean soldiers, I would look at each of them to check if I recognized them. All my family, relatives, and friends lived in North Korea. I was the only one from my hometown who had come to the South before the war and joined the South Korean Army. On a hot, humid mid-August day, a North Korean POW on a makeshift stretcher was brought to the headquarters from the hills. With my heart pounding, I took a quick look at his face. He was a stranger, neither my brother nor a hometown friend. I took a deep breath, relieved.

For some reason, my curiosity caused me to look at this prisoner again. "Oh, my God!" A big, grotesque, maggot-infested cut in his belly revealed his wiggly, bloody intestines. They were bloody, bluish, and getting dry. Many other wounds covered his body. He was practically naked except that his private parts were hidden by his dirty, torn, dull green fatigues. Hundreds of flies swarmed all over the wounds. He kept his eyes closed, immobile. I felt so sick that I almost vomited. My eyes could take no more, and I turned away.

His faint groaning made me turn back. He opened his eyes, looking pitiful. He grimaced from pain and weakly cried out *"Aigoo!"* Upon seeing him in extreme anguish, a sense of sadness and sympathy swept through my heart. He could be my brother; he could be a friend of mine. I knelt by him, using my rifle as a cane, and said, "Don't be afraid. You are safe here. What can I do for you?"

Captain Chung, my company commander, ordered coldly, "Corporal Kim, take care of that POW!"

"Yes, sir." I interpreted his order to mean that I should evacuate the prisoner to an army field hospital. But his tone aroused an ominous feeling in me, so I moved the POW out of his sight. I asked the two civilian utility men who had brought the POW to carry him to a shady spot, about fifty feet away. After having him moved, I repeated, "You are safe here. What can I do for you?"

He opened his parched, trembling lips and whispered, "Water, please." I took out my canteen, opened the cap, and dribbled a small amount of water into his mouth while raising his head a little so that he could drink. After a few small gulps, he said, "Thank you." Smiling weakly, he closed his eyes.

I laid his head on the stretcher and asked him, "Where did you come from?"

He reopened his eyes and said slowly, "From Bukgando, Manchuria."

"That is in China, isn't it?"

"Yes, it is," he groaned.

"If you lived in China, how did you join the North Korean Army? Did you volunteer?"

"No, sir. On June 26, the district police chief, a Korean-Chinese, accompanied by a few armed internal security soldiers, came to my town, a Korean immigrant town, and rounded up all the able young men between eighteen and thirty. They forced us to climb up onto a truck and escorted us to a training camp in northeastern North Korea, across the Tumen River." He closed his eyes, as if speaking tired him. The river is the border between Eastern Manchuria and North Korea.

He opened his eyes again and said, "Sir, water please." I dribbled more water into his mouth. Groaning intermittently, he continued, "I was born in Dongchon, about four miles east of Daegu City, North Gyeongsang Province. When I was eleven, my mother passed away; a few months later, my father followed her. Afterwards, my older brother and his wife decided to immigrate to Manchuria to escape the Japanese oppression and to find a better life."

After pausing to rest, he continued, "The following year, after selling all our belongings, including the house and land, we moved to Bukgando, Manchuria, a completely strange, wide-open country. I missed my parents and hometown. When I was young, I often secretly cried." I saw his eyes wet, tears starting to fall, and he sobbed.

His sobbing overwhelmed me to the point that I turned and walked to the river. I, too, missed my family. I screamed in my heart repeatedly, "I hate you, Kim Il Sung. Why did you start this goddamn war? You son of a bitch, I will kill you." This screaming alleviated my emotions somewhat. I bent over the river, scooped up a handful of water, and wet my face. After wiping the excess water off with my dirty fatigue sleeves, I returned to the prisoner and found him sobbing no more. He seemed happy to see me.

A putrid odor reeked from his wounds; hundreds of disgusting flies were swarming around. I thought he needed immediate medical treatment, but nothing was available, not even a medic. I asked him if he wanted more water. He nodded weakly.

After letting him drink, I said, "Can you eat anything?" even though I expected that he could not. Surprisingly, he said, "I am hungry." That meant that his injuries were not as critical as they appeared. Apparently, his digestive system was still working. Again, he groaned.

I took a few pieces of *keun-bang* (Korean crackers) from my backpack, crushed them into crumbs in my palm and put a small amount into his mouth along with water. He chewed them slowly and swallowed. I fed him a few more times, but he was unable to eat any more.

He took a painful breath and continued, "My brother bought a piece of semi-cultivated land, including a small farmhouse from a Korean immigrant family that had moved to a big city. After many years of hard work, we made it into a large farm. My brother would proudly say it was five times larger than what we had had in Korea. We began to enjoy a comfortable life. I had to quit my elementary school to come to Manchuria. I was then in the fourth grade. I want to go back to school. But it is too late because I am now twenty-six years old." He seemed to be recollecting his life under this extraordinary circumstance, not knowing what was ahead of him.

I said, "You know what? You are in North Gyeongsang Province now. Your hometown may not be too far from here. What is the name of your hometown again?"

"Dongchon, near Daegu City, sir," he said, in a faint but brighter voice.

"Your hometown might be less than thirty miles due west. You can visit your hometown when this war is over."

Captain Chung hollered gruffly, "Corporal Kim, come over here!"

I rushed to him and with a salute I said, "Corporal Kim reporting, sir."

"How is the POW whom you are feeding?" he asked in a sarcastic tone.

"He is seriously injured, but not critically. If he is treated soon, I am sure that he will recover completely, sir."

"Shoot him and bury him!"

I was horrified, dumbfounded. I pleaded, "Sir, he is not critically wounded. He will be okay, sir."

"Goddamnit, I order you to shoot him!"

I unconsciously protested in a trembling voice, "Why me, sir? If you leave him untreated, he will die anyway."

He angrily shouted, "You son of a bitch, he is not going to get any treatment. He dies here. I will shoot you in the head if you disobey. Our field hospitals are overwhelmed with our own wounded soldiers. They don't have room for your pet POW. I am doing it for his benefit. Do as I have ordered. Get out of my sight."

In the face of his outrage, I lost the courage to plead further. I silently retreated, murmuring "Why me, why me?" He was my commander; I was low on his totem pole. I did not want to see the POW again; I wished he had died on his own. This would relieve me from this horrible anguish. On the way back, I approached the two stretcher carriers and asked them to dig a grave for the POW in the open field across the river so that he might not detect his imminent execution. I did not want to return to him but had to. I found thousands of detestable flies covering his wounds. I took off my fatigue jacket and swung it wildly to chase away those damned flies. Although it was a losing battle, I continued to swing the jacket until my arms were aching. One solace from this fighting was that I did not have to look at his face or talk to him.

Being so tired, I sat down on the grass a few feet away from the North Korean. This enabled me to avoid looking directly in his face. We spoke the same language and shared the same culture. Yes, he was an enemy soldier before he was wounded. Now he was a helpless, innocent human being, a fellow Korean. After listening to the heart-wrenching story of his unfortunate life, I felt he was a wonderful human being and a friend of many years. I did not even know his name.

It was so painful to look at this severely wounded, harmless man whom

I had been ordered to shoot. His only sin was that he was forced to fight the South Koreans, against his will, by the evil North Korean communists. He was left behind, severely injured, when his fellow comrades retreated from the hills. An irony of life drove us from the opposite directions and locked us in a tragic fate over which neither of us had control. I inwardly screamed, "Why me, why me?" I realized that this scream would not free us from this tragedy. I decided to minimize his anguish and give him peace of mind for the rest of his life, whatever time was left, ten minutes, twenty minutes or one hour until the two men would inform me that his grave had been dug.

I moved to his side and said with a smile, "Would you like more water?" He responded, "Yes, please." He drank and said, "Thank you very much," while I was lowering his head.

I asked him, "Do you believe in Buddha?"

"I do not know very much about Buddhism," he answered in a much weaker voice than before.

"I do not either, but they say if you have a harsh life in this world, you will be reincarnated as a happy, fortunate man in the next world." While holding his dirty hand, I continued, "Since you have had a very unfortunate life, Buddha might have compassion and reincarnate you as a very fortunate man in the next world. Why don't you ask him for his mercy?"

He opened his eyes and said, "Thank you, I will," with a weak smile and closed them again.

I continued, "My sister-in-law also lived in Bukgando, Manchuria for a few years when she was young. Just like you, she lost her parents when she was only nine. Her oldest brother took his whole family, including her, to Bukgando to escape Japanese persecution. He was a well-known scholar and a patriot."

Upon hearing Bukgando, he opened his eyes and asked, "Where in Bukgando?"

"I do not know. She just told me Bukgando. I came from North Korea to Seoul to study four years ago, when I was fifteen. I miss my parents and the rest of my family so much."

The two men who were digging the grave across the river came over and whispered into my ear that a grave had been dug. I wished I had not heard them. I felt as if my heart had suddenly stopped, and then cried out again silently, "Why me?" I knew I could not escape from this horrible distress because I was only an invisible soldier, an expendable existence without a voice in a vast military organization. I had neither the courage nor the heart to tell this hapless soul the truth: that I would be his executioner. Instead of telling him, I said, "My company commander has ordered me to escort you to an army field clinic, a mile south of us. I am sure they will give you good treatment."

He opened his failing eyes and weakly responded, "Thank you, sir," and closed them. My heart was aching so much that I wished to scream loudly but could not. I asked the men to carry him on the stretcher across the river and followed them. It was only three to four hundred feet away, but it seemed greater. I prayed for him to die before we arrived.

Finally, they lowered his stretcher beside the shallow grave. Apparently, the POW felt something very wrong and opened his eyes. He saw the grave, started to cry, and pleaded, "Please have mercy, Corporal. I lost my parents when I was young. I transformed a wilderness into good land. Let me live there, Corporal!"

I inwardly screamed and cursed, "You monster, Captain Chung. I wish you dead. Why me?" I bent over, held his hand, and said, "I am sure that Buddha will have mercy on you, and he will reincarnate you to be a fortunate man in the next world. I am terribly sorry. My commander has given me orders. And he said, 'You will not get treatment because the South Korean military clinics are overwhelmed with so many wounded South Korean soldiers. Eventually you will die after prolonged pain.' It would be better for you to die now than to suffer so much pain for such a long time and then die." I pleaded to Buddha, "Buddha, sir, have mercy on this poor soul!" I said in a trembling voice "Goodbye," and released his motionless hand. It appeared that a wound in his arm paralyzed it.

I stood up, raised my semi-automatic carbine rifle, and aimed at his head, but I just could not pull the trigger. I lowered my rifle, turned my face away, and wiped my tears. After a deep breath, I raised my rifle again and aimed at him, but once more I could not pull the trigger and lowered the rifle. I repeated this dreadful movement a few more times. I realized I was killing him, not once, but multiple times. Finally, I mustered all my courage and aimed at him again; my hands were wildly trembling. I turned my face away from him, pulled the trigger for one shot, and ran across the river without looking back. I sat down in the same place where I had befriended him for the last couple of hours, buried my head between my knees, and cried. Then I heard the two men calling, "Corporal, Corporal, he is not dead, he is not dead. You have to come and finish him off!"

I felt an unimaginable force hit me in the head. I did not respond to their call. They shouted louder, "Corporal, Corporal, come over," in fear-stricken voices. Apparently, my shot had missed because of my trembling hands.

I hollered back, "I don't care whether he is dead or alive. I did what I was ordered to do. Don't call me anymore!" Then somebody tapped me on the shoulder. I looked up. It was Sgt. Chang Hyokoen.

He said, "Corporal Kim, do you want me to finish him off?"

"Don't ask me. Do whatever you want. I shot him as Captain Chung ordered me." A few minutes later, I heard the volley of a carbine rifle. I could not dispel the crying plea of the POW from my mind. I said to myself, "Why me?" and kept my head down. Sgt. Chang tapped my shoulder and said, "Corporal Kim, it's done."

I did not respond, and tears welled up in my eyes again. I shot at men and saw them fall and die on the battlefield, but it felt different seeing them face to face and hearing their story. However, I was somewhat relieved; perhaps because someone else, not I, killed the POW, or because his incredible pain had ended. For the next few weeks, every time I fell asleep, this poor soul appeared in my dreams, with his grotesque bloody guts exposed, and pleaded, "Please have mercy!" I awoke sweating, sometimes screaming, "Why me, sir?" I pleaded with someone upstairs to lift this heavy burden from me but received no response.

CHAPTER 15

Battles in Yeongcheon and Angang

End of August – Middle of September 1950

By early August, the North Koreans had taken 90 percent of South Korea, and pushed the United Nations Forces (UNF) into the southeastern corner of the Korean Peninsula, called the Pusan Perimeter. The North Koreans escalated their offenses along the entire front, especially on the outskirts of Daegu and around Pohang, to finish the war by the end of August as the North Korean Leader Kim Il Sung had ordered. Daegu, by the Naktong River, was one of only two major cities left within the perimeter, about sixty miles northwest of the Pusan Port, and Pohang was a small fishing port at the northeastern end of the front line.

At the end of August, my battalion was fighting the enemy in the eastern part of the Palgongsan Mountain Range, north of Yeongcheon, between Daegu and Pohang. According to intelligence, our adversary was North Korean Army II Corps led by a battle-hardened Lieutenant General, Kim Mu Chong, who had fought the Japanese as a field commander of the Chinese Communist Army. Despite our air force's furious bombing, the enemy's intensive attacks inflicted severe casualties on us. After losing many lives, we were replaced by a reserve unit and moved behind the line to regroup.

During the move, our battalion took a few hours of respite at an elementary school playground. Despite the sizzling August heat, I fell asleep in a sitting position. Suddenly an ear-splitting machine gun startled me from my much-needed nap. Instinctively, I fell flat on the ground and buried my face in the dirt. After a series of about a dozen rounds, the firing stopped as abruptly as it had started. *Had the enemy broken through the combat line and advanced this far?* Despite being scared to death, I raised my head slightly and cautiously surveyed the area to find the enemy but saw everyone lying on the ground like me. Believing that the enemy was aiming at me, I quickly dropped my head back to the ground and stayed immobile. There was no good place to hide on this bare dirt playground.

Someone began shouting hysterically, "Medic---, medic---," followed by silence. Then he hollered again at the top of his lungs, "Don't die, don't die! Medic---, hurry up. Oh my God, you killed my boys, you killed my boys! Medic---," and began to cry loudly.

I jumped up and saw two or three medics dashing toward a spot just across the playground from me. Everybody was up and looking around in bewilderment. After ordering the men to stay calm, the commander, his deputy, and a few other officers and NCOs followed the medics, including my company sergeant, MSgt. Lee. Even though I was only a corporal and not asked to accompany him, I did so anyway. He didn't complain, perhaps because I was one of the few under him who had survived the war so far.

Arriving at the scene, I saw a sergeant holding a blood-drenched young soldier on his lap and a few other wounded ones on the ground. The sergeant wailed, "Don't die, don't die!" The soldier did not respond; his arms dangled onto the ground; his pale face showed no life; his chest continued bleeding, creating a puddle. One of the medics said something to the sergeant and gently pulled the lifeless body from him, but he didn't want to release it. Then the commanding officer whispered into the sergeant's ear, while gently tapping him on the shoulder. When he finally let the body go reluctantly, he mumbled, "Why did you have to die like this?" and cried. The other medics were busily applying first aid to the other wounded soldiers who lay on the ground groaning. Soon a couple of ambulances arrived and carried the injured and the dead away. Someone said, "He was killed by accident. That was sad."

After the ambulances had left, the commander ordered his intelligence officer to investigate how that terrible incident had happened and report the results to him quickly. I returned with a heavy heart. Since the war had begun, I had seen many dead, but the sergeant's anguish and the young lifeless soldier made me extremely sad. I did not know why. I wished I hadn't come to the scene. Later I heard that the dead soldier was a very close relative of the sergeant. An undertrained recruit had accidently pulled his automatic rifle trigger, resulting in that horrible incident. He was so frightened that he couldn't release the trigger until an older soldier yanked the rifle away from him. The poor recruit had reportedly received only four weeks of basic training before being sent to the front line.

Despite this tragedy, we were soon ordered to move on to Yeongcheon, a couple of miles farther southeast. As we marched on, rain started to fall. I hadn't even noticed that the sizzling sun had yielded to a thick cloudy sky. Someone behind me said to himself, "Even the sky is crying over the tragic death of the soldier." But no one responded. Sporadic enemy artillery shells exploded randomly here and there. No one panicked; we just moved on.

A BAD RUMOR

Since the beginning of the war, we had not had any encouraging news. The North Koreans had defeated us in battle after battle, inflicting heavy casualties and taking cities one after another. We had thought that the American soldiers would repel the invaders and unify the divided peninsula, but they were losing battles just as badly as we were. Even worse, the U.S. Army 24th Division Commander Major General William Dean went missing after the Daejeon Battle in late July.*

I was deeply saddened by this news, perhaps because I had expected that the U.S. Army under his leadership would defeat the North Koreans, or because I had read many of his policy decrees and public announcements, translated into Korean, and signed by him as the military governor of South Korea. He had held that position from 1947 until the new South Korean government was elected on August 15, 1948.

Then one day my company sergeant told me in a serious tone that he had heard that the Americans might soon withdraw from the Korean Peninsula to Japan along with three selected combat divisions of the South Korean

---

* After three years and two months of detention, Major General William Dean returned home in September 1953. The six-foot tall general lost 80 pounds from 210 to 130 during his bondage.

Army, about thirty thousand men. Then after regrouping and further training, they would return to retake South Korea from the North Korean occupation. Immediately, I wondered who would be chosen.

If the sergeant's remarks were true, then only combat soldiers would be
selected, leaving non-combat personnel behind. Surely the latter would become
POWs of the North Koreans and be classified as reactionaries of the communist
revolution, especially those of us who had come from North Korea. I knew that
the North Korean communist regime had sent many thousands of anti-communists, including students, to coal mines. I had also read a few publications
reporting that Stalin had sent over fifteen million of his own people to hard
labor camps in Siberia. They never came home. As a company clerk, would
I be classified as a combat soldier or as administrative personnel, even though
I had fought in numerous battles? *No matter what, I was determined not to be
a POW of the North Koreans; I would not spend my whole life in a coal mine.*

Then it came to my mind that at the onset of the war, the South Korean
Army numbered about ninety-five thousand men. Since the war had begun
two months earlier, my regiment had lost almost one half of its force. Based on
this, I estimated that the entire South Korean Army might have been reduced
to less than fifty thousand men. Thus, if a force of three divisions were to be
selected, we company-level clerks in infantry companies were more likely to
be chosen, because we had battle experience. I expressed my thoughts to the
sergeant, and he said that I made him feel better.

According to some historians, despite a proposal by a few high-level U.S.
military strategists and some politicians that all American soldiers should be
evacuated from the Korean Peninsula at this critical time, General MacArthur
met with Lieutenant General Walton Walker, and they declared, "There will
not be another Dunkirk." I recalled that declaration. I figured that this must
just be a bad rumor. The American and South Korean Armies continued to
fight the invaders along the Pusan Perimeter and defeated them.

THE STREET BATTLE OF YEONGCHEON

Yeongcheon was a small town in the northern part of the Pusan Perimeter.
It sat at a railroad junction of the Daegu-Pohang Line (East-West) and the

Central Line (North-South). Daegu City was less than twenty-five miles to the west, and Pusan Port about sixty miles to the south. All U.S. military personnel and supplies came through Pusan Port. The Central Line connected Seoul and Pusan through the mountainous central region of South Korea. Daegu and Pusan were the only two major cities left within the perimeter, the last foothold. Even though it was a small county administrative town, Yeoungcheon played a strategic role in the early days of the Korean War because of its geographic proximity.

According to intelligence, the most decorated 4th North Korean Army Division, which had occupied Seoul six weeks earlier, crossed the Naktong River and attacked the 24th U.S. Army Division that defended Daegu City in an attempt to take the city and advance to Pusan Port, thus finishing up the war. However, after almost three weeks of fierce fighting in August, the 24th Division and a U.S. Marine Corps brigade annihilated the enemy with the help of the U.S. Air Force.

The battalion intelligence officer told us that after the complete defeat by the U.S. Army in the northwestern Pusan Perimeter, the North Koreans recognized the strategic value of Yeongcheon that was defended by the 3rd South Korean Army Corps. Believing the South Korean Corps, unlike the American Army, was inadequately armed, poorly trained, and demoralized, the desperate North Koreans regrouped an army corps of thirty thousand men and began an all-out assault on the South Koreans in late August to capture this vital railroad junction. If they took this town, the North Koreans would let one half of its force march westward to cut off the supply line to the Eighth U.S. Army Headquarters and 24th Division in the Daegu area and attack them from behind. The second half would advance southward to occupy Pusan Port, thus winning the war.

After many days of fierce fighting in the hills north of Yeongcheon, one rainy afternoon, my battalion was replaced by a fresh unit and ordered to move into the town. We didn't know why because we were fighting well and had gained some ground, capturing a dozen North Korean soldiers. Nevertheless, we welcomed the much-needed lull, perhaps a few hours or even overnight.

By the time we began to move down the slippery hills, darkness had rolled over the landscape, and the rain fell steadily. As we marched towards the town, the enemy bombardments on the hills intensified. A series of spectacular explosions flashed the hilltops, and a chain of booms ensued. Apparently, the enemy had opened a nightly offense, taking advantage of the darkness and bad weather. Our airplanes did not operate at night or in bad weather.

After a few hours of marching on soggy fields and muddy roads, we arrived at the outskirts of Yeongcheon. The rain slowed, and the moon peeked through the clouds. Despite wearing a raincoat, my fatigues were drenched from the rain and sweat. Unlike American soldiers, who wore leather boots, we Korean soldiers wore quick and dirty Korean-made cotton shoes with thin rubber soles that absorbed so much water that every step produced squelching noises. Entering the dark town, a Korean Army MP directed us, with flashlights, to the two-story town hall building. A couple of army trucks were parked along the slushy street in front of the building, and a few dozen soldiers had gathered around the vehicles. The building was surrounded by a tall concrete fence with a large gate. Another MP shouted, "Into the building," pointing his flashlight in the direction of the entrance.

Once we entered the building, MSgt. Lee led us to the second floor. *Only one entrance for the entire building!* As we climbed up, the stairs squeaked loudly, as if to complain that we were too heavy. By then, the rain had stopped, and the radiating moon shone through the windows. The second floor was a large bullpen. I settled in a corner near the doorway to avoid being trampled by hundreds of feet and lay on the floor using my backpack as a pillow and holding my carbine rifle in my arms. *'Only one entrance for the entire building'* came back, warning me of something unexpected. *Grenades!* If only a few enemy rangers sneaked through the combat line, crawled into the courtyard, and hurled grenades into the building, we would all be torn apart. I shuddered, but extreme fatigue made me sink into oblivion.

Suddenly machine gun fire jolted me out of my deep sleep. "The enemy!" someone shouted. I jumped up and listened to determine where the noise came from, while securing my rifle and putting my backpack on, ready to run out into the open. My sergeant yelled, "Get the hell out of the building!" I recognized the sound of Russian-made burp guns firing rounds. I ran down the stairs ahead of the rest and checked the courtyard for enemies. The low moon and fog kept me from seeing clearly, but I found no enemies.

Then I rushed out of the building to the street and took stock of the situation, finding a multitude of soldiers shouting and running towards the outskirts. It was too dark to tell if they were enemies or friends by appearance, but their speech assured me that they were friends. The burp guns continued to fire farther down the streets. Our soldiers were going after the enemy.

An officer shouted to me and some others, "Run to the railroad bank, and attack from there!" He paused for a few moments, then continued, "Too dark to differentiate the enemy from our own soldiers! Make sure you kill the enemy, not our own!"

My friend Sgt. Jee and I ran towards the railroad bank, cursing the enemy. Then a soldier whom neither of us knew joined us and urged, "*Dongmu* (Comrades), rush, rush! The South Koreans detected us and attacked us." (We South Koreans do not call our fellow soldiers by *Dongmu*; only North Koreans use it.) Instantly, I looked and saw that he carried a long Russian-made rifle with a bayonet attached. My hair stood on end. As I brought my gun down from my shoulder, a blinding flash and an ear-splitting bang made me freeze. The stranger fell to the ground; he didn't even groan. Sgt. Jee had shot him, and said, "*Gaesashy* (Son of a bitch)!" Then he pulled my arm and said, "Hurry!"

We ran a couple of hundred feet, crouched behind a wooden fence, and evaluated our situation. Still panting, but somewhat less tense from the kill-or-be-killed moment, I said, "Sergeant, thanks for your quick action. That enemy soldier might have killed both of us."

He responded, "It was close. Are you alright?" while looking back down the street where he had killed the North Korean. The machine guns stopped firing and we couldn't find the enemy to go after them, so I asked him if we should return to the town hall. He said, "Not yet. Just wait a moment."

Then a group of soldiers ran toward us. Enemy or friends? We couldn't tell. We decided to wait as silently as possible and find out who they were. If they were the enemy, we would shoot them first. The few minutes before they reached the fence felt like an eternity. As they approached, I held my rifle firmly, ready to shoot if they were North Koreans. Sgt. Jee, an experienced soldier, whispered into my ear, "Don't shoot until I do." We listened intently to their sparse, barely audible speech. They sounded like friends.

When they came within twenty feet of us, Jee and I shouted from behind the fence, "Stop there! Password?"

They promptly stopped, holding their rifles ready to shoot, gave us the proper nightly password, and then shouted back, "Yours?" Immediately, we answered in unison the return password, confirming that we were allies. A slight mistake could have caused an unthinkable disaster. But we had narrowly avoided it. I breathed a deep sigh of relief.

The squadron leader and Sgt. Jee introduced themselves to each other. The leader was a sergeant first class (SFC), one notch higher than Sgt. Jee, and his surname was Goe. Even though they belonged to a different company, we joined them. SFC Goe asked Sgt. Jee's opinion about the next move. Jee told him that we had discussed returning to the town hall. Goe said that they were the last ones who had left the downtown, and that the situation was unsettled. Besides, it was still too dark to differentiate friends from enemies.

After a few moments, he continued, "I know this area well. Right now, the best we can do is to take up a position along the Yeongcheon River bank," and led us there. A narrow farm field separated the river and the edge of the town. He said, "We won't cross the river because the recent heavy rain has caused it to rise high and run swiftly. We will fight them back from here," he said, and deployed us along the bank. Sgt. Jee and I took our positions side by side along with the others, a few feet apart from each other. Then SFC Goe gave us a strict order to keep silent and watch the road from the town, the edge of the town, and the farm field for any movements. He emphasized, "If you see enemies or any suspicious movement, immediately report to me by contacting the one next to you. If they are very close, just shoot and shout 'Enemy!'" He sternly instructed us not to smoke because light and smoke might give us away. Then he strategically positioned himself at the midpoint of the long deployment.

I thought he was an intelligent and meticulous sergeant. Despite knowing him only a few minutes, I had full confidence in his leadership. As ordered, we lay silently, ready to shoot, on the wet grass and searched for enemy movements in the dark. Tension and the pre-dawn chill made me shiver. A wait-and-see game! Finally dawn broke, illuminating the road from the town and the soybean field in front of us. Except for sporadic distant artillery explosions, it was a brilliant, quiet morning, without even a breeze. Then, I noticed some soybean plants on the far side of the field shaking. My hair rose. I touched Sgt. Jee and the guy next to me with my rifle butt and whispered, "Something is moving," pointing my finger in the direction of the field. They gestured that they, too, had noticed the movements.

Then, unexpectedly, a half dozen North Koreans slowly appeared on the road. Suddenly someone began to shoot at them. We all sprayed a barrage of ammunition on them. A couple of them fell to the ground, and the rest were frightened and tried to run, but they, too, fell one by one. Almost at the same moment, a few heavily camouflaged North Koreans jumped up from the soybean field and fired at us. Sgt. Jee, the soldier next to me, and I showered our bullets on the enemy. I kept pulling the trigger of my semi-automatic rifle until my magazine ran out of ammunition. The strange-looking figures, too, fell to the ground, moving no more. Despite seeing no live enemies, I replaced the empty magazine with a new one and continued shooting into the soybean field. Then a couple of hands rose from among the soybean plants, less than one hundred feet from us, and waved, indicating surrender. We stopped shooting and shouted, "Raise your hands and stand up! Walk forward."

Three North Koreans slowly rose with their arms up and tried to steady their trembling bodies. Fear-stricken, they were unable to walk. Then suddenly someone shot at them, and all three fell to the ground. I was dumbfounded and screamed, "They are surrendering!" Sgt. Jee shouted, "Who the fuck shot them?" The squadron leader, SFC Goe, yelled, "Don't shoot!" But it was too late for those three who had wanted to live. They heard our shouting no more.

The killing of the three surrendering enemy soldiers disturbed me profoundly. Who had shot them and why? They might have hated the war as much as I did, and they must have wanted to live as much as I did. Some of them could have been my relatives or friends. Against their will, they might have been drafted by the North Korean authorities and forced to fight the South Koreans. For more than a thousand years, Korea had been one nation until America and Russia had divided the peninsula into North and South Koreas at the end of World War II, just five years earlier. *Now we are killing each other. Damn this war!*

Later SFC Goe shouted, "We are going back to the town." Then he split the squadron into two columns, assigning the first column to watch the left side of the road and the other to watch the right. We walked slowly, watching for enemies. We sidestepped the bodies of our enemies on the dirt road, whom we had killed only hours earlier. I didn't want to see them, but I couldn't help taking a quick glance at them either. Some lay on their back, some on their stomach. Thousands of flies swarmed over the corpses and blood puddles. The blood had already begun to dry. They had come to kill us, but we had killed them first. *Today, I am a victor, and they are losers. However, tomorrow, I might be a dead man.* Once upon a time, they must have been loving children. I wondered who would bury them. Even though they were my enemies, I couldn't help but pray for peace for them. If I were to be killed, I hoped I would die while we were winning so that my friends would bury me properly and mark my grave.

The war did not allow me to be too sentimental; the squadron moved on. Shortly we entered the town and walked past a dead enemy soldier, probably the one Sgt. Jee had shot earlier. Soon we met groups of South Korean soldiers who had hunted down the North Korean saboteurs and secured the town. After bidding them goodbye, without having a chance to exchange names with all members of the squad, Sgt. Jee and I rejoined our company, and SFC Goe and his men reunited with theirs. Returning to my friends made me feel secure and happy. We reported to our company sergeant how many enemy soldiers we had killed during the separation. He said, "Good job, but more importantly you came back in one piece." Then he performed a headcount and said, "We lost no one."

After receiving the headcount, the company commander informed us that according to a couple of the POWs we had caught, a few dozen saboteurs from the North Korean special forces had sneaked through an unguarded gap in our defense line to cut off our supply line. Fortunately, some of our reserve units had found and attacked the saboteurs before they could inflict any severe damage. He stressed that the platoon commanders should keep linking with their neighboring units. Then he deployed us on a mountain range to the east of Yeongcheon according to the battle plan.

The next night the enemy opened a massive offensive, with intensive artillery bombardments along the entire eastern Pusan Perimeter. They took the Pohang Port about ten miles east of us, putting incredible pressure on our divisional defense line. They were desperate to capture Yeongcheon, and we were determined to keep it. During the next few days, the town changed ownership a couple of times.

One day, during the seesaw battles, we were ordered to retake the town from the enemy. We dug in on one side of a street, the enemy on the other. That street became a no-man's land. We saw a couple of dead enemy soldiers left by their comrades in the intersection in front of us. Toward mid-afternoon, a group of piglets marched to the cadavers and began to eat them. It was the most grotesque, humiliating scene I had ever witnessed. None of us wanted to let the pigs violate fellow human beings, whether they were fallen enemies or not. Corporal Lee Jong-kook shouted, "Damn pigs," and began to shoot at them. We all followed. The pigs hurriedly retreated a few feet, only to come back, but they were small and quick.

Suddenly the enemy began firing at us instead of the pigs. Even though we couldn't see the enemy, we returned fire blindly in the direction of low, straw-thatched houses and foxholes. After a few minutes of exchanging fire, the battle ceased as abruptly as it had started. Perhaps both sides realized that shooting at unseen adversaries was wasting ammunition.

Despite holding our position firmly, one night, my battalion was ordered to move a couple of miles to the south and redeploy in the northern outskirts of Gyeongju, giving up valuable real estate to the enemy. Gyeongju was an ancient city, rich in history, and the capital of the Silla dynasty for almost nine hundred years starting from the 1st century BC. Going south caused anxiety among us soldiers. I wondered, "Has the enemy broken through our divisional defense line again, somewhere near our battalion? If so, how long can we withstand the massive enemy offensive?" But we kept our morale high, and we believed that eventually we would win the war because the mighty American army was fighting with us. As far as I knew, not a single fellow soldier from my company had defected to the enemy for the past couple of months, while more than a few scores of the North Koreans had surrendered to us.

After a few days of fierce fighting, we repelled the enemy and retook most of the land we had given up. Marching forward slowly, we found many dead soldiers along the roads and in the fields. A few South Korean soldiers were among them, but most of them were North Koreans. An enormous flock of crows gathered around the dead, noisily fighting each other. Their satanic caws gave me goosebumps. I shuddered. They were feasting on the eyeballs of the cadavers, rendering the dead even more grotesque. Someone shot at the crows, and a few of us joined in. The crows flew to nearby trees, cawing even louder. The platoon sergeant shouted, "Stop firing! Move on."

Someone murmured, "I don't want to die, but if I do, please let me die while we are winning. I don't want wild animals to eat my body." His remarks mirrored my thoughts. Another shouted, "Shut your fucking mouth! No one wants to die." Then he began to sing *Arirang*, the most cherished folk song, but soon it faded away. A heavy silence fell as we moved on toward an unknown fate.

Since the outbreak of the war, we administrative personnel had been augmenting combat units that needed extra hands. For the last several days, we had been helping a shorthanded platoon. While marching, my company sergeant pulled Sergeants Choi, Kim, and me (I had just become a sergeant), all company clerks, out of the column and ordered us to return to the company headquarters a couple of miles away. A few of the soldiers in the platoon were my friends. We had joined the army at the same time, received basic training together, and fought many battles side by side. Returning to the headquarters, a non-combat environment, was great, but I felt sad to leave them. *Some of them I might not see again.* I said, "Guys, take care. See you again."

They responded, "You, too. You were the skinniest and youngest among us when we joined the army two years ago. Now, you are a sergeant, but you are still bony. Put on some fat," and laughed. They hugged me firmly, patted me on the back, and said, "Goodbye, our baby soldier!" I felt a lump in my throat. Sadly, none of them ever made it home.

Despite capturing many North Korean POWs, my regiment was ordered to retreat, giving up the Yeongcheon area to the enemy again. Some murmured, "Are we losing the war?" Others said, "It must be a tactical retreat." No one knew why. Even our battalion's sergeant major did not have any idea. The combat units of the regiment took defensive positions along the treeless hills and the farm fields in the valleys a couple of miles north of Gyeongju.

We occupied several straw-thatched farmhouses by the narrow dirt Gyeongju-Yeongcheon highway, a mile behind the combat units' defense line. We set up a camp for the supporting groups, including ordnance, quartermasters, and administrative personnel. A dozen field artillery guns were deployed a quarter of a mile in front of us. The guns fired at the enemy positions all day long, shaking the farmhouses like an earthquake. I thought that without those big guns, our camp could easily be overrun by enemy tanks if they rolled southward.

After returning to my normal clerical duties from the front line, I became restless, so I visited one of my friends, Sgt. Jeon, at the quartermasters' camp, hoping it would lift my spirits. I saw a bull loosely tethered to a nearby poplar tree, lazily grazing on the roadside. Jeon said he had purchased it from a farmer to feed the battalion.

Since he hated slaughtering living animals, he recruited a volunteer to kill the bull for him. A sergeant from ordnance, whom I knew, loudly responded, "I will." He had an eccentric personality—sometimes happy, other times moody or distant. He bravely approached the bull, stopped a few feet from it and said, "You are going to die."

But the innocent bull seemed to welcome its executioner with gentle mooing and neighing. The butcher said, "This bull likes me, but goodbye." He raised his powerful M1 rifle and aimed at the unsuspecting animal's head. When I was just about to turn my back to avoid watching the killing of the good-natured bull, a sharp bang and an incredibly loud cry from the bull pierced my ears.

The bull raised its body, standing on its hind legs, its wide eyes pure white, showing no pupils. White foam spewed from its mouth; its front legs, bent slightly inward, were ready to pound its executioner to death. The beast looked like a magnificent, powerful warrior. It bellowed fiendishly and stood upright, defying death. The butcher was so shocked by the powerful beast that his face turned pale, his mouth wide open. His unblinking eyes fixed on the angry bull. The once showy, brave butcher sergeant now looked like a petrified mouse in front of a cat. The beast fell on the ground with a loud thud, landing on its side. Its legs twitched a couple of times, and then it was still for good.

After the bull had fallen, the butcher sergeant took off his helmet, wiped sweat off his forehead with his dirty army jacket sleeve, took a deep breath, and murmured, "That beast scared me to death!" He walked slowly to the steps of the thatched farmhouse and sat on them sullenly. Then someone hollered, "What's the matter with you? Cheer up!" But he didn't respond.

Crimson blood flowed from the bullet hole in the bull's head, creating a puddle on the ground. Even though it was animal blood, I couldn't stand watching it any longer; I had seen so much blood earlier. I regretted that I had lingered there too long. I returned to my group and took a nap until my company sergeant woke me.

That evening, I got a fist-sized ball of cooked rice and a small cube of beef boiled in salty soy sauce as a side dish along with all the other soldiers. I welcomed the supper hungrily, especially the meat, because beef was hard to come by on the front line. I took a bite of the cube and chewed it a few times, savoring its delicious flavor. Then suddenly the memory of slaughtering the gentle bull robbed me of my appetite, and I stopped chewing. But I forced myself to eat the beef to fill my protein-starved body.

BATTLE OF INCHON
AND RECAPTURING SEOUL

By September 1950, the North Korean Army had made a huge advance, driving the ROK Army and the Allies to the Pusan Perimeter in the southeast corner of South Korea, an area that encompassed about 5,000 square miles. The perimeter ran for 140 miles. To turn the tide, General MacArthur knew he needed to perform a miracle. He dreamed up a landing at Inchon—something so risky and daring that many doubted it would work. Its code name: Operation Chromite.

> *"I can almost hear the ticking of the second hand*
> *of destiny. We must act now or we will die ... We shall*
> *land at Inchon, and I shall crush them."*[45]
> **—General MacArthur**

He recruited Major General Oliver Prince Smith at the end of August to come up with the plans. Smith was commander of the First Marine Division, but Smith would be reporting to his complete opposite, Major General Edward Almond, also known as "Ned the Dread."[46] He was MacArthur's Chief of Staff and the X Corps commander.

The Inchon landing, which commenced on September 15, 1950, was an ultimate success and came as a complete surprise to the North Koreans. There were very few casualties for an operation that grand. Thirteen thousand troops came ashore.[47] And in the South, the North Koreans were retreating from the Pusan Perimeter. It was a turning point for the U.S. and UN forces and ROK Army.

> *"The amphibious landing of U.S. Marines on September*
> *15, 1950, at Inchon, on the west coast of Korea, was one*
> *of the most audacious and spectacularly successful*
> *amphibious landings in all naval history."*[48]
> **—Bernard Brodie, military strategist**

Next up: take back Seoul. The Marines encountered upwards of forty thousand men.[49] The enemy had set up barricades, mines, and snipers.[50] The Marines fought and ultimately won her back at the end of September.

With the success of the Inchon landing and recapture of Seoul, MacArthur suddenly had his eyes on marching north and liberating all of North Korea.

CHAPTER 16

Welcome, Gukgun

September - October 1950

THE INCHON LANDING

September 15, 1950. It was late afternoon and raining steadily. Despite our air and field artillery bombardments, we were unable to dislodge the enemy's machine gun nests from the rocky hills which dominated our position. Our infantry units had attempted to destroy them several times during the past two days, suffering heavy casualties each time. Another attempt had begun early that morning and was still going on after more than four hours. A truck-load of a dozen wounded and dead were brought to the battalion medics. The chilly fall rain continued, depressing our already heavy hearts even further. *Would we win this war? We would! But how soon?*

A supply truck rolled into the muddy front yard of the farmhouse where we had been camping for the last few days, halting with a loud squealing of brakes. The driver jumped out of the vehicle and excitedly shouted, "The UN forces landed at Inchon Beach this morning! They have landed at Inchon!" He ran around in the slush, pumping his fists into the air like a boxer who had just knocked down his opponent.

We all hurried out of our camp into the rain in response to the shouting. Inchon was about 180 miles northwest of this front line, and it had been in the enemy's hands since the outbreak of the war. Also, the city is only fifteen miles west of Seoul, the capital of South Korea. *How could anyone land that far inside enemy territory?* Everyone thought the driver's news was too good to be true. Our company sergeant barked, "Shut up, you crazy boy! Don't spread such a stupid rumor."

But the truck driver repeated, "The American and Korean Marine Corps have landed at Inchon Port! They have!" Then he chanted, "*Dae-han-min-guk Mansei* (Long live Korea!). I heard the radio announcement at the regiment headquarters communication center. It is true. We will win the war; we will win the war!"

Just then the battalion communication sergeant rushed from his post to our battalion Sgt. Major and exclaimed, "Sergeant Major, I received a message from the regiment headquarters that the U.S. and Korean Marine Corps successfully landed at Inchon Beach this morning." He stretched his arms into the air and shouted, "*Dae-han-min-guk Mansei! Mansei!*" just like the truck driver. We all spontaneously yelled with him, "*Mansei, Mansei* ----! (We will win the war!)," and danced wildly in the rain.

After an impromptu celebration, we asked each other, "How did they do it? It's so far inside the enemy line!"

The Sgt. Major said in a sage voice, "I think General MacArthur did it. I heard he is a genius."

Later we learned that the general had indeed planned the landing strategy and executed it successfully. Despite this great news, the fierce battle continued on the hills. Our big guns and the enemy artillery exchanged salvos, inflicting heavy casualties upon each other for two more days.

Finally, our combatants crushed the enemy machine gun nests. The enemy offense crumbled, and they began to retreat. We chased the retreating soldiers, capturing scores of POWs. As my company was approaching the southern outskirts of Yeongcheon, someone called in a familiar but agonized voice, "Tae-hyok, Tae-hyok."

I looked in the direction of the voice and saw a dozen seriously wounded soldiers on the wet roadside grass; everyone was wrapped with blood-stained bandages. I felt sick to my stomach. Only one medic was taking care of them. Again, the same voice called me, "Tae-hyok, I am Yeong-sik," but I could hardly recognize him. Bloody gauze covered his head and the sides of his face; a large chunk of his upper arm had been blown away, exposing the broken bone. His fatigue jacket was drenched in blood. The horrible wound hadn't been bandaged yet. Overwhelmed, I froze in front of him, tears blurring my eyes, a lump in my throat. Sgt. Lee Yeong-sik, in his early twenties, was a friend of mine. We had enlisted together two years earlier and received basic training in the same platoon. I knelt and said, "Yeong-sik, Yeong-sik. I am sorry!" holding his uninjured arm. "You will be alright." That was all I could say.

"Oo---, damn, the injuries are killing me. Good to see you in one piece." He closed his tired eyes for a few moments and asked, "Tae-hyok, do you have a cigarette?" Before I could answer, he continued, "I know you don't smoke, our baby soldier." I was the youngest soldier at the training camp.

"Yeong-sik, I am sorry, I do not have any with me." I wished I had kept a pack. Whenever I received my cigarette ration, I distributed them to the others in my group because I didn't smoke and disliked the smell. I hollered to the marching soldiers, "Hey guys, any of you have a cigarette for my friend?" They responded, "I am sorry, I don't," and kept moving. I felt so sorry that I had been unable to get a cigarette for my severely wounded friend. After this painful parting, despite my aversion to the smell of cigarettes, I carried two packs with me so that I could use them to comfort anyone in agony.

Oblivious to my talk, he weakly murmured, "They are going to cut off my arm. I am going to lose my arm!" Then he sighed deeply and lay on his side with his eyes closed. He had bled so much that his dirty face was pale. He had once been a tall, sturdily built, self-assured young man with a big heart, but now he was fighting anxiety and an uncertain future.

I managed to open my choked throat to try to comfort him, "Yeong-sik, they won't. You will be alright. Ambulances will take you to a hospital soon. By the way, the Inchon Landing has destroyed the enemy offensive completely, and the North Korean devils have begun a general retreat. We are chasing after them. The war will soon be over." But he was too tired and in too much pain to talk.

I couldn't see my group, and I had to catch up with them. I held my friend's hand and said, "Yeong-sik, I have to go. Doctors will take good care of you. See you again." I released his hand, but he kept his eyes closed. I asked the medic to take care of my friend, hoping an ambulance would take him to a field hospital before it was too late. I watched as the medic went over and knelt to help him. Tears fell from my eyes. I quickened my pace to join my squad, but my blurry vision hindered me.

The Inchon Landing made us advance toward North Korea, but I felt sad that my friend couldn't join this magnificent march. He, too, had escaped North Korea and joined the South Korean Army.

• • •

After landing at Inchon, the UN forces quickly established a beachhead and crushed the North Korean defenders, capturing the city in three days. Then they swiftly advanced toward Seoul, threatening to cut off the enemy's major supply line connecting Pyongyang through Seoul, to the North Korean Army which had been fighting the UN forces around the Pusan Perimeter for the past six weeks. Recognizing that they were about to be trapped, the enemy hurriedly started a general retreat. Our forces jumped out of the trenches we had dug along the perimeter and began an all-out attack on the retreating enemy. We had been waiting for this glorious moment for three long months.

On September 18, my company, too, joined the magnificent campaign, chasing the North Koreans. Many wrecked North Korean tanks and trucks were strewn along the roads, some intact. The enemy had abandoned them in their hurried retreat. Just before the outset of our march, my company received half a dozen soldiers fresh out of training camp. I was temporarily put in charge of them until they would be allocated to the various platoons in the company, which I didn't like at all, especially during rapid marches. For days, we continued to hit the enemy and marched on, without much rest or food.

WELCOME, GUKGUN*

The towns along the Pusan Perimeter, where we had fought for the past six weeks, were empty because the inhabitants had taken refuge somewhere safer. Thus, when we retook those towns from the enemy, no one came to welcome us.

As we advanced farther north, away from the perimeter, many war-weary

* Note: The South Korean Armed Forces is called *Gukgun* in Korean.

people, young and old, men and women, enthusiastically celebrated *Guk-gun's* return, shouting, "*Mansei, Gukgun.* We've been waiting for you for a long time." Some pumped their arms into the sky, some cried, and others held our hands. "We are free!"

We were equally overjoyed and shouted back, "Thank you! Happy to see you again!" excitedly waving to them. Every town we retook gave us the same profound gratitude. It was almost unbelievable for the people in this region to give us such a genuine, ardent welcome because this southern part of the peninsula had been one of the communist breeding grounds until a year ago. The people harbored the rebel renegades. I wondered what had made the people give us such an enthusiastic welcome. Obviously, they had learned, in a very short period, that communism was not as good as the North Korean communists had preached.

The farther we advanced northward, the more exuberant the welcomes. When we crossed the 38th Parallel, the predecessor of the infamous DMZ, the North Korean civilians treated us as heroic liberators. Despite the marvelous victories we had achieved, we faced many gruesome realities of the war. Before abandoning towns, the retreating North Korean forces had rounded up numerous political prisoners and anti-communist suspects, and had machine-gunned them down, town after town. This kind of carnage had been committed equally by North and South Koreans.

REMEMBERING THE REPUBLIC
OF KOREA FORCES AND KOREA'S CIVILIANS

Thousands of Koreans joined the fight for democracy and freedom, and thousands died—not only people from below the 38th Parallel, but also those who came from the North to fight alongside the Republic of Korea. Not only soldiers, but also townspeople and students. While we're thankful and always will be to those who came from the United States and the United Nations to fight for Korea (and can't imagine the outcome if they hadn't), we cannot forget the heroic efforts that the Korean people themselves demonstrated during those three years.

From the beginning, the Republic of Korea was outnumbered in troop strength, underequipped, and undertrained compared to the Soviet-trained North Korean People's Army. But they still put up a fight, and due to strong resistance, they delayed the enemy's advance. They also withdrew when appropriate and reorganized. If they hadn't, the enemy would have easily encircled them. Under the United States command, Korean soldiers were sent to fight in the mountains and hills, due to their knowing more about their indigenous terrain, operating in close combat against the North Koreans, and performing flanking maneuvers.[51] They went on to win battles as well as capture enemy soldiers and supplies.

Thousands of civilian volunteers joined in to serve their country. Their hope: the reunification of all of Korea. North Korea had expected the South Korean civilians to believe in their cause, but instead there were uprisings against them. Students volunteered for basic training and then would partake in combat missions. So many of them fought in the Battle of Pohang to hold the UN's position. Even female students enlisted. The Korean Student Volunteer Army was formed, the ROK Army Troop Information and Education Office created a Student Cadre's Unit sending 1,500 students to the front line, and regiments were reinforced by student volunteers. The army also opened training schools. The Korean Military Academy merged with the ROKA Infantry School to train students.[52]

Policemen also attached themselves to the army and sacrificed their lives.[53] Korean civilians volunteered to be service workers, carrying weapons and supplies up the hills to the battle ground, performing engineering duties like building airstrips and roads, and evacuating the wounded.[54] There were about 50–60 volunteers per ROKA battalion.[55]

> *"Too little has been said in praise of the South Korean Army, which has performed so magnificently in helping turn this war from the defensive to the offensive."*[56]
> **—Lieutenant General Walton H. Walker, September 25, 1950**

Sadly, civilians were forced to live under enemy rule. Many had to serve (or aid in some way) the NKPA or else they would be executed. About a third of the men in a division were forcibly conscripted. They lacked the will to fight and would surrender to the UN and ROK Armies when they could. Others, including students, were forced to carry loads of supplies and food for the NKPA, or build and repair items.[57] Many citizens were massacred. Civilians were taken out in groups with their hands tied behind their backs and shot in front of a trench which served as their grave. At the end of September 1950, 5,000–7,000 South Korean civilians were found dead in Taejon city, with just six surviving to tell the story.[58] And in October 1950, in Wonsan, North Korea, 600 Koreans had been killed by the NKPA. 12,000 civilians were killed in Hamhung by the NKPA that same month.[59] The NKPA was killing their own people. South Koreans did this to North Koreans as well, which is inexcusable. We are one people.

But for those who truly fought for the meaning of freedom and democracy for all of Korea and those who died during this fratricidal war, we cannot forget those individuals—be it military personnel, civilians, or students.

SEA FOR THE FIRST TIME

After three long months of retreats and defensive battles, General MacArthur's brilliant Inchon Landing on September 15, 1950 turned the table on the North Koreans' initial success in the Korean War. The entire North Korean offense collapsed. The United Nations and South Korea forces broke out of the 140-mile Pusan Perimeter and began to attack the enemy. It felt good to be winning the battles we fought. Our regiment would fight, win, and then march farther north.

In just two weeks, we advanced close to two hundred miles through the Taebaek Mountain Region and arrived late in the evening at a small fishing village by the East Sea, north of Gangneung City. After bivouacking for only a few hours there, we ate a predawn breakfast and set out marching northward along a highway parallel to the seashore. It was too dark to see, but the salty smell and rustling sounds of rhythmic waves told me that the East Sea was nearby. I had heard many stories about seas and had seen pictures, but this would be my first view of a real ocean. Even though the war was going on, I was excited to see the sea, wondering if it was as vast as I had read, if the sunrise would make it look like a conflagration, or if it really danced.

As we silently marched, the dawn broke over the dark waters, and soon the lip of the red sun rose over the simmering, crimson waves. Numerous *galmaegi* (seagulls) dove into the burning water and shot up. The expanse did not end but faded away into the dark bluish horizon. In a few moments, the full orange sun rose over the reddish, dancing waves. How magnificent the sunrise was! I screamed, "The sea is burning!"

Choi retorted, "You dummy. The sea is not burning. The morning sun is reflecting on it."

"I know, but it looks like it's burning," I responded. "Do you want me to say, 'The sea is dancing in fire instead?'"

Corporal Lee Jong-kook loudly added, "Hey, Tae-hyok is sentimental. He is writing a poem," and we laughed. The laughter in the battleground made me feel relaxed. I wanted to stop there and enjoy the gorgeous sunrise and the simmering sea longer, but I had to keep going, and sighed.

I often looked at the sea and watched it turning blue, as the orange sun became brighter. I wished everything stayed the way it had been. As we marched farther north, from my left the mighty Taebaek Mountain Range dropped steeply into the East Sea. On my right, the sea sparkled under the brilliant October sun. The big mountain and the vast aquamarine ocean met along a gently curving narrow band of white sand, which ran from north to south. Small waves washed over the sandy beach, and broke into millions of white bubbles, which then burst, producing sweet rustling sounds. The sea did not rest. *Oh, how beautiful the sea is! When the war is over, should I come and live here?*

We continued moving for a few hours. The dazzling sun in the spotless, azure October sky beat down on me, and I began to sweat. My army backpack and rifle hung heavily on my shoulders. No one seemed to be anxious to talk. We were too tired. But seeing the sea for the first time was extraordinary.

SAMPAL SUN (THE 38ᵀᴴ PARALLEL)

Unexpectedly, the Company's First Sergeant shouted in an excited voice, "*Sampal Sun!* We are crossing the *Sampal Sun!*" Unlike most high-ranking NCOs, he was usually soft-spoken and dignified.

I echoed at the top of my lungs, "*Sampal Sun,*" broke away from my column, and ran toward the sergeant. As I was running, half a dozen other soldiers sprang from their column and followed me, repeatedly asking, "Where?" Shortly, I saw the sergeant holding a signpost with one hand and raising his rifle triumphantly into the air with the other hand. Reaching the post, I held the post just below the sergeant's hand and shouted, "*Sampal Sun,* you have divided our fatherland for five long years. Today, no more!" I looked at the post again. It was nothing but an impromptu signpost with '三八線' (*Sampal Sun* in Chinese characters) written in black paint on a horizontal piece of pine board. There was no barbed wire or fortified wall to signify that it was the border that divided the peninsula. It was the invisible line that had separated the North and South, and brought about a tragic war.

This *Sampal Sun* signpost brought back memories of my border crossings: my group being shot at by a North Korean border guard the first time I crossed, getting lost and then captured by the North Korean border patrol but still managing to escape the second time, journeying with Tae-jun and his business partner as they wanted to come to Seoul to purchase photography equipment, and the two other dangerous crossings.

I put one foot on the north side of the post and declared, "Now, I am crossing this 三八線 in broad daylight." I asked my sergeant, "What time is it?"

"It is 10:30, October 2, 1950!"

I kneeled on one knee, bowed my head, and whispered, "Dad, Mom, I have just crossed this fateful *Sampal Sun*. I will visit you in a few months when the war is over. It has been a long time since I bid you goodbye. I was then sixteen. Now I am a nineteen-year-old sergeant." I was overwhelmed, and tears welled in my eyes.

Somebody tapped me on the shoulder and said, "Sergeant Kim, let's move." It was the Company First Sergeant.

I didn't bother to dry my tears and joined the others, shouting, "The country has been unified today!" I began to sing the Korean Army marching anthem *Hwarang Ga* at the top of my lungs; the company joined me. What a glorious unification!

THE FIRST TOWN ABOVE THE PARALLEL

After a few more miles of marching along the dusty, narrow highway precariously carved along the foothills of the mountain, my company arrived at a small farm village, the first North Korean town above the 38th Parallel. The townspeople, poorly dressed, welcomed us enthusiastically, waving makeshift Korean flags and shouting, "*Dae-han-min-guk Mansei!* (Long live Korea!)" or "*Gukgun Mansei* (Hurray, Korean Army!)" A few men yelled, "We have been waiting for this glorious day for five long years!" and danced, grabbing our arms. A couple of farmers brought large sacks of fresh, natural pine mushrooms, handing out the aromatic treats with broad smiles. Pine mushrooms are expensive delicacies among Koreans for their exquisite taste and fragrance. They grow only in a certain kind of soil and pine grove from late September through mid-October, mostly in northern Korea. The farmers could have sold them in the marketplace for cash, supplementing their meager farming income. But today, they gave them away to celebrate our arrival.

Overwhelmed by the farmers' exuberant welcome, we repeatedly shouted

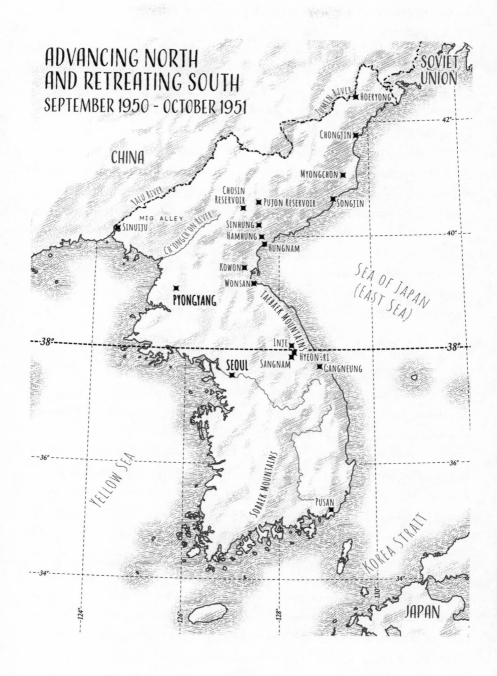

ADVANCING NORTH
AND RETREATING SOUTH
SEPTEMBER 1950 - OCTOBER 1951

SOVIET
UNION

CHINA

TUMEN RIVER

HOERYONG

CHONGJIN

MYONGCHON

YALU RIVER

MIG ALLEY

SINUIJU

CH'ONGCH'ON RIVER

CHOSIN
RESERVOIR

PUJON RESERVOIR

SONGJIN

SINHUNG

HAMHUNG

HUNGNAM

KOWON

WONSAN

PYONGYANG

TAEBAEK MOUNTAIN

SEA OF JAPAN
(EAST SEA)

42°

40°

38°

INJE

SEOUL

SANGNAM

HYEON-RI

GANGNEUNG

38°

36°

YELLOW SEA

SOBAEK MOUNTAINS

36°

PUSAN

34°

KOREA STRAIT

JAPAN

124°

126°

128°

130°

34°

back, "Thank you! Long live unified Korea!" These fervent farmers made me think about Kim Il Sung, the autocratic North Korean leader. He had preached that communism was a haven for exploited laborers and farmers. Also, he had promised that under his leadership they would prosper and would not suffer capitalists' exploitation any longer. After five long years of his regime, now these poor farmers passionately welcomed us, showing how much they disliked life under communism.

We wanted rest and time to chat with the townspeople to hear how their life had been under the dictator, but we had to move on. A new order directed us to advance westward to Inje-up over the rugged Taebaek Mountains, away from the spectacular coastline. After a few miles march, we reached a babbling creek, where we had a half-hour lunch break, a much-needed rest. I took my shoes and socks off for the first time since we had begun the long march more than two weeks earlier. My feet smelled like rotten meat. The skin of my soles was as soft as a baby's. As my feet dried, the skin pulled tight, causing throbbing pain which made me groan. I submerged my feet under the cold creek water for relief, but too soon came the order, "Battalion, move on!"

"Come on, I haven't even started my lunch yet," I moaned. Choi grumbled, "Don't disturb my nap." After filling my canteen with creek water, I hurriedly put my socks and shoes on and gathered my equipment. Confined in the shoes, my feet hurt. The weight of my equipment made the pain worse. I looked up the mountain we had to climb. "Oh, my God!"

The Taebaek Mountains soared into the cobalt blue autumn sky. Patches of high-flying white clouds appeared to circumvent the lofty peak. The pass snaked up along the steep slope in a stack of numerous switchbacks. Each switchback looked ready to bite the heel of the one above it. The road rose, disappearing into the woods. I sighed.

The battalion formed two columns and began to move. Each step hurt my feet so badly, but as I hobbled, they gradually lost sensation. A great relief! Some other soldiers limped, too. Since I had been nursing my feet during the break, I hadn't had a chance to eat lunch. While marching, I ate a fist-sized rice ball sprinkled with salt, which I had saved in my aluminum field mess kit.

As we climbed higher, the autumn foliage formed a spectacular display. While the supply trucks crawled on the narrow, rough pass, we foot soldiers took shortcuts, often beating the vehicles. The shortcuts were so steep that it felt as if for each step upward, gravity pulled me down two steps. Then, the company sergeant hollered, "Fifteen-minute rest!" What a sweet order.

After relaying the order to the soldiers behind me, I leaned against the road bank and settled my hip in the drainage ditch, resting my legs on higher ground to relieve the pain. As I was just about to close my eyes, the expanse of the East Sea came into view. Even though my body wanted to rest, my heart urged me to cherish the ocean one more time before going into the hinterland. In the distance, I saw three gray warships sailing northward, leaving white rooster tails behind them. One was much bigger than the other two. Having read a history book about the Pacific War, I assumed the ships belonged to the mighty American Navy, and that the big one was a battleship. Then I noticed that the sea level appeared to be higher than where I was, and that the horizon looked slightly curved. I thought we were at about one thousand feet above sea level, so why did the sea appear so high? Even stranger, the sea gradually rose from the beach until it met the whitish-blue sky on the horizon.

Kim Jae-kook kicked me lightly in the leg and said, "Tae-hyok, get up. We are moving out." Reluctantly, I rose and hobbled on my aching legs. The fifteen-minute rest had been so delicious, yet so short. As we approached the crest of the pass, the vegetation became smaller, and some trees had already shed their leaves. When we reached the top, the sun sank into the orange western sky, and the full moon rose in the east above the dark sea, illuminating the hauntingly silent, jagged Taebaek Mountain peaks. The company sergeant said that our orders from the regiment commander were to take Inje-up by daybreak, about thirteen miles from the pass. Despite being hungry and tired, we began to descend the rock-strewn pass without a break, to meet the battle plan. I bumped into a soldier in front of me, who had stopped abruptly without an apparent reason, and asked him, "What's the matter?"

"Oh, my God, I was sleeping! I am dead tired," he mumbled, and resumed marching. His mumbling made me even more tired.

Even though we were victoriously chasing the retreating enemy, suddenly an uneasy feeling crept into my mind: If the enemy ambushed us, how could we fight them, as weary as we were in this totally strange mountainous terrain?

Abruptly an incredible sensation pulled me back. I found myself standing precariously at the edge of a cliff. Fear struck like lightning, keeping me immobile for a few moments. The lifeless, pale moonlight skimmed over the ridges, making the valley a dark abyss that looked ready to swallow me. I cautiously stepped backward to the road. Apparently, I, too had fallen asleep while marching. One more step and I could have fallen into the deep gorge. I shivered! I rejoined the column and tried to stay alert, but sleep kept returning. Occasionally I took off my helmet and tapped my head with its rim or slapped my face to help me stay awake. Thankfully, I did not face another cliff, and arrived safely at the destination by morning.

INJE-UP

After marching all night, we arrived at the eastern edge of Inje-up in the early morning. The town was so quiet, not even a dog bark was heard. Tendrils of smoke rose from a few straw-thatched houses. This eerie quiet made me stay alert. The company commander issued a combat ready order. We checked our rifles and mounted our bayonets. As the sun rose over the roofs, we entered the town, following the reconnaissance squadron ahead of us.

As we advanced farther into the streets, a few weary old men in traditional white Korean clothes slowly came out of their homes and eyed us cautiously. Then their expressions relaxed, and they shouted at the top of their lungs, "*Gukgun* have arrived. *Gukgun* are here. *Gukgun Mansei.*" Upon hearing these declarations, hundreds of men and women, young and old, swarmed from their homes or hiding places, dancing and chanting, "*Gukgun Mansei.*"

The residents welcomed us as enthusiastically as those of the previous town. According to the residents, hundreds of North Korean soldiers had passed through in the past few days, and the local internal security agents and Communist Party members had left the previous night. Before leaving, the security agents had rounded up a score of men from their hiding places, whom they considered reactionaries, and taken them. The residents feared for the fate of those men. The remaining men hurriedly organized a self-defense militia to maintain law and order. Some of them armed themselves with abandoned North Korean Army rifles.

After the company sergeant posted guards, we had three meals, including the supper and breakfast we had missed on our march, and lunch. After that, we slept for a few hours on the grass or anywhere we found comfortable until mid-afternoon, when the sergeant hollered, "Company, move on!"

We continued to march day and night with intermittent rests of fifteen minutes, a magic number. I lost track of how many days had elapsed since the historical moment crossing the 38th Parallel. According to the company sergeant, our orders were to take Wonsan Port, the largest port city on the east coast, as soon as possible to prevent the North Korean forces from regrouping there.

Dry autumn air quickened the foliage to brown in this highland away from the sea. Ripened soybeans remained in the fields along the roads, as the war had prevented farmers from harvesting them in time. They were so dry that the bean shells cracked open themselves. After the fields, we climbed a steep pass under a canopy of wild grapevines. Purple grape clumps hung heavy on the vines. I picked some and found them mouth-wateringly sweet. This reminded me of a picture of the Diamond Mountains from an old magazine, which I had read earlier. The mountains, considered the most beautiful scenery in the peninsula, must have been close by, but because our advancing route turned west, we did not see them.

While we were marching along a narrow, dirt highway between soybean fields, a loud squeal of brakes frightened me from my sleepwalking. Instinctively, I halted and saw that a supply truck driven by a drafted civilian driver had veered into a soybean field. It had run over a soldier and stopped with its right front wheel over the soldier's neck. His legs kicked the air a couple of times and quivered for a moment, then were still. Everyone was too shocked to speak. We quickly surrounded the truck and lifted it to relieve the soldier from under the tire, but he was already dead. His Platoon Sergeant, Quon, hysterically wailed, "You killed my boy, you killed my boy!" and started beating the driver. The shocked man, shivering wildly, shrieked, "Oh my God. Heaven forgive me. Why couldn't I keep my eyes open?" He crouched on the field and began to cry loudly. Apparently, he too had dozed off.

The company executive officer, the platoon sergeant, and a few soldiers were left behind to take care of the dead man, while the rest of us continued to march north. No one spoke for a long while, and then Corporal Pak murmured, "He survived the three tough months at the beginning of the war, and now we are winning. Why was he killed this way?" Corporal Chun echoed, "You never know!" and he began to hum the Korean folk song *Arirang*. Perhaps, he was singing to calm his homesickness or nervousness about an uncertain future.

I had witnessed so many deaths since the inception of the war, but this freak accident made me think about the 160 recruits who had joined the army with me two years earlier. We had gone through basic training together, becoming good friends and comrades-in-arms. Some had been transferred to other units before the war, but many had been killed or gone missing in action during the last few months. Only a couple dozen remained in the same company. I hoped everyone would make it home safely.

CHAPTER 17

Advancing North

October 1950

LOST

After we had sprung out of the Pusan Perimeter, our last defensive foothold, almost four weeks earlier, we had been marching north without significant enemy resistance along trails and narrow roads that crossed the rugged but stunning Sobaek and Taebaek Mountain Ranges. Despite grueling marches in the middle of the war, sometimes the lack of fighting made us feel as if we were hiking for pleasure along multi-colored scenic routes.

One October evening, we began to climb a gently rising mountain pass. After marching all night, we reached the crest of the pass by mid-morning. The mountains dropped sharply to a vast farmland stretching north as far as our eyes could see. As the morning sun warmed the earth, the thin fog dried up. A black railroad track sliced straight across the plain from southwest to northeast, while a river meandered through the rich farmland. Judging from my smattering of geography, I assumed the track was a part of the line connecting Seoul and Wonsan City until the country was split five years ago. I saw a town in haze on the far side of the plain.

The company sergeant shouted, "Fifteen minutes rest." The company commander consulted his map with the sergeant and said, "The town must be Singosan. Beyond it is Anbyon-up, and then Wonsan City. We should take the city within the next few days." His comments caused my heart to pound— we would be taking the largest city in the entire east coast of the peninsula.

When our company entered Singosan early that evening, the residents came out in droves and welcomed us with rousing *Gukgun Mansei*, as had those of the previous towns. An elderly man in a traditional white Korean costume, accompanied by townspeople, grabbed our commander's hands and said, "Thank you for liberating us from the communist dictator." Tears streamed down his cheeks. "Young men, you must be hungry. After learning that you would be arriving here soon, we hurriedly prepared meals for you." Then they led us to a big house. The elder ushered the officers and the company sergeant into a large room, and the rest of us took seats in the courtyard. We all were treated to a bowl of rice in hot beef soup, a feast. It was the first hot meal we had had since the outbreak of the war. We thanked them for their enthusiasm and generosity.

After the sumptuous supper, when we were about to resume our march, the regiment headquarters ordered our company to bivouac in town overnight. Despite being anxious to take Wonsan City as soon as possible, we welcomed the unexpected overnight rest.

The next morning, we were scheduled to move by truck convoy to Anbyon-up, a town closer to Wonsan City, about nine miles farther north, but the convoy was not large enough to carry the entire company. A couple dozen of us were left behind, including me, to wait for a truck to return within two hours. We waited for several hours, but no truck returned as the convoy leader had promised. We became restless and cursed the leader in rich military language.

Being a North Korean native, I was eager to be a part of the Wonsan campaign. My patience was wearing thin enough to venture on by foot. I asked the townspeople for a shortcut to our destination. An elderly resident showed me a country road which led to a heavily wooded mountain. He said, "It will be about an eight-mile walk. Early this morning a score of South Korean soldiers took the route," implying that there would be no enemy stragglers along the way. Even though I was unfamiliar with the region, I thought I could complete the trip within five hours, before sunset. I asked for volunteers to go with me, but only Sgt. Man-E decided to join. He was a temperamental character but was a brave soldier.

With permission from MSgt. Lee, we set out for our trip like boys on a hike. We talked about nothing in particular. Then out of the blue, he asked, "Tae-hyok, have you ever had sex?" Giving me no chance to answer, he said to himself, "I don't think so. You are a nineteen-year-old virgin. Aren't you? You're stupid. You might die without knowing how delicious sex is!" and he laughed boisterously.

I said, "You are the stupid one, not me. Did you forget you had contracted gonorrhea before, and it took some time before you got rid of it? When the war is over, I shall get my education, marry an educated, beautiful girl, and find out how delicious sex will be with her."

"Oh, yeah? It's a noble idea, but there is no guarantee that you will survive the war. We might be ambushed any moment and killed," and he teasingly recited, "Sex is good."

"Hey Man-E, shut your dirty mouth. If I die, I die clean." We laughed heartily.

Suddenly lightning flashed across the gray sky. Ear-splitting thunder followed, frightening us from our leisurely talk. Because we were walking under a dense oak canopy, we hadn't realized that the blue autumn sky had yielded to thick clouds. A gust twisted the oaks, sending fallen leaves flying in all directions, and a heavy shower began. We hurriedly put our raincoats on. The surrounding environment became so dark that we lost our trail. Fighting the bad weather, we continued to climb the hill, hoping that higher ground might provide a decent view. Fortunately, the gust died down as quickly as it had started, but the heavy rain continued. The wet fallen leaves made our footing slippery. Despite wearing raincoats, we were soaked by the shower. A few hours later, we reached a ridge, but a thick gray fog swallowed the whole world. We couldn't see anything but a few oaks nearby. We sat on a ledge speechless and rested our heads on our rifles.

I broke the silence, "Man-E, we got lost."

"Yeah, we did. What shall we do? Shall we turn back?"

"Turn back? I don't think we can find the back-trail. Even if we made it to the town, our group may not be there anymore. The best way is to climb down the valley."

"I'm scared. Aren't you, Tae-hyok?"

"I'm as scared as you are, if not more. But we must move on." To mitigate our fear, I said, "Don't you know the old Korean saying? 'Even if heaven falls on you, there is a hole for you to climb up through to safety.'"

"That's bullshit, but right now I believe it," and he stood up, slinging his rifle on his shoulder. "Sergeant Kim, lift up your heavy ass. Let's move!" We started climbing down what I presumed to be the north side of the valley.

The heavy rain slowed to a trickle, and a relatively strong wind began to blow. We hoped it would clear the thick fog, and it did, though slowly. Patches of blue sky started to appear, and mountain peaks began to show. The pale October sun shone over the crest of the western mountain ranges for a moment, then sank behind them as quickly as it had appeared. But it showed us that we were heading in the right direction.

As we continued our trek, a sudden fear gripped me. We might have come behind the enemy line. Or were we falling into an ambush at one of their villages?

I called, "Hey, Man-E, we must watch out for an ambush. Let's move as quietly as we can." I was getting uptight.

Man-E responded, "You're thinking exactly what I'm thinking. Follow close behind me so that we won't get separated. If we encounter an ambush, we should duck first, and then return fire."

"If we return fire, we will expose our exact location. Then they might attack us with grenades. Why don't we keep silent for a few moments, find their location, and then hurl our grenades at them. Then we begin our rifle attacks, instead of panicking. It's too dark for them to see us."

"That's a good idea, virgin boy. You are smarter than I thought. Panic is our enemy. Before throwing, you move forward to my left, a few feet apart, and then we throw the grenades together to make the firepower as spectacular as possible. I have three grenades; how many do you have?"

I answered, "Two."

"Five will do it. Immediately after the grenades, we'll start to fire our rifles until we kill them all or they retreat. Let's move." A few steps later, he turned around and murmured into my ears, "Tae-hyok, sex is delicious. Remember that," and giggled.

"Shut up. You're crazy. This is no time for joking." But surprisingly his joke loosened my anxiety. I was glad he was with me, a good friend in arms who knew how to break tension in a dangerous situation. But a weird feeling arose in my mind: Am I going to be killed before knowing a woman? Is it a tragedy for a man to die before finding out how delicious sex is?

Suddenly an animal ran in front of us. I was frightened and instinctively ready to shoot.

"Relax. It's only an animal," Man-E said. "If it was an enemy, he would have shot at us. Follow me."

"That damn animal scared me to death." I was fretting. I regretted that I had dared to take this trek. I wished MSgt. Lee had not given us permission to take this shortcut.

We continued to move cautiously down the valley. We were cold, hungry, and wet. After many hours' trekking, we arrived at the outskirts of a quiet farm village. A few dogs began to bark in unison. The town was dark except for a couple of houses. We stealthily approached the log fence of the brightly lit house. Peering between poles, we saw a festive crowd gathered around a bonfire in the courtyard. We heard one man excitedly announcing that the South Korean Army had entered Wonsan City that morning, and the crowd shouting, "Hurray!"

Realizing they were friendly people, we went to the front gate and greeted them, "Good evening, sirs. We are *Gukgun* soldiers."

Despite our announcement, the unexpected presence of fully armed soldiers frightened them, so much so that they abruptly stopped all their activities and watched us silently. Perhaps they suspected us of being disguised North Korean soldiers.

We assured them that we were South Korean soldiers by telling them our names and ranks and explaining that we had gotten lost while heading to Anbyon-up.

The whole crowd exploded, "Welcome, *Gukgun* soldiers. Please come in." A few men approached and led us to a big room lit by a few castor oil lamps, where elderly townspeople were sitting cross-legged on the heated floor. We greeted the elders respectfully, "*Harabeoji, Halmeoni, an-yung hasipnika?* (Sirs and ladies, how do you do? Glad to meet you.)" and bowed politely.

Traditionally, Korean elders do not stand up to greet their younger guests, but the elders in this room spontaneously stood up and welcomed us heartily. "Welcome, young soldiers." Some frail elders struggled to get up.

Overwhelmed and humbled, we pleaded, "Sirs and ladies, please don't bother to stand up. We are young men," and helped them sit.

The elders invited us to sit with them by tapping the floor. "Young soldiers, you must be cold. Sit down here, the warmest spot on the heated floor."

We thanked them and sat down. It was soothingly warm! An old hand-wound clock on the wall showed almost ten o'clock. We had been lost for more than twelve hours.

Then the elders asked the young men who had led us inside to bring some food. The old man next to me said that the North Korean soldiers, including the internal security forces and local Communist Party members, had fled farther north a couple of days earlier. After learning that Anbyon-up had been taken by the South Korean Army early that morning, the townspeople had opened the grain storage, where the communist authorities had confiscated more than 30 percent of their harvest without compensation. They prepared this feast with that grain. The old man said, "Thanks to *Gukgun*, now we have our grain back," and fondly tapped us on the shoulders, smiling. Shortly a sumptuous amount of food in china bowls was brought in on a low-legged, lacquered rectangular table. The elders urged, "Young men, help yourselves."

"Thank you, sirs," we said. The heated floor warmed my butt, and the hot, spicy food made me sweat. My wet clothes began to dry. My stomach was full; I felt warm and content. I wanted to talk with the gentlemen, but fatigue caught up with me and I fell asleep.

Loud snoring woke me. Man-E was the culprit. Someone had put a quilt over us, and the old man who had urged us to eat our supper was sleeping next to us under a different quilt.

I stealthily got up and went outside. The brilliant sun in the spotless blue sky shone on the marvelous autumn foliage. Billions of dew drops sparkled like a wonderland. What a gorgeous morning it was, so peaceful and quiet. Where is the war?

Suddenly someone called out, "Good morning, young man. Did you have a good rest?" It was the homeowner.

"Good morning, sir. Yes, I did. It's a beautiful morning, isn't it?"

"Indeed. The way it's going, the war may be over very soon."

"I hope so, sir. By the way, how far is it to Anbyon-up?"

"Oh, about three miles."

"Pa, Pa. Breakfast is ready," hollered his wife.

We entered the room and found Man-E still sleeping. I kicked him lightly, "Hey, Maneong, get up."

He grudgingly awoke. Upon seeing the old man standing beside me, he jumped up and greeted him, "Good morning, sir. Forgive me for my laziness."

The grandfatherly gentleman patted him on the shoulder lovingly and said, "I hope you had a good rest." At that moment, a man in his forties, probably his son, brought breakfast, just like the previous supper. Asking us to help ourselves, they left us alone in the guest room and joined their family in their private quarters.

Gathering our equipment after a quick breakfast, we thanked the family for their hospitality and left for Anbyon-up. Refreshed, we walked briskly, sometimes running, to catch up with our company, hoping that it hadn't left for Wonsan City.

Many thoughts occupied my mind, including how stupid and reckless I had been by leaving my group and venturing out on a trail over unfamiliar mountains where we could have been ambushed. Our group leader would be wondering what the hell had happened to us; or perhaps he was so mad that he might punish us. I rationalized that he should be partially responsible for our misfortune, having given us permission to act independently.

Man-E said, "Tae-hyok, are you ready for hell from Master Sergeant Lee?"

"I am ready, and I will say contritely, 'Sergeant, I am very sorry. Forgive me, sir.'"

Arriving in Anbyon-up, we found that the company had already left the town; only the battalion quartermaster group was still there, though ready to depart anytime. Fortunately, the Quartermaster Sgt. Kwon Seo-jin was a good friend of mine. Kwon was in his mid-twenties, a master sergeant, two grades higher than me.

He said, "What the hell are you guys doing here when your company has already marched out to Wonsan City early this morning? You slept late and fucked up?" We explained what had happened to us the previous day. "Hop up onto my truck. I will take you to your company."

We thanked him, climbed up onto the cargo bay, and sat precariously atop a heap of supplies. After an hour's drive on a bumpy, narrow dirt highway, we caught up with our platoon. Sgt. Kwon stopped his truck in the middle of the road and hollered to my sergeant, "Hey, Sergeant Lee, I have a couple of your boys with me. They said they had gotten lost in the woods yesterday." Then he shouted, "Tae-hyok, get the hell out of my truck. Don't get lost again." He laughed. As soon as we jumped off the truck and thanked him, he drove off.

We promptly reported to MSgt. Lee. He looked into our eyes wordlessly, then barked, "Where the hell have you been?" Before we could answer, he yelled again, "Get into the column. Move!" He hurried to the front of the platoon.

We quickly blended in, keeping a respectful distance from him to avoid his wrath. Man-E joined the column a few soldiers behind me. Some of my friends asked, "Where the hell have you been? We thought you were dead or had deserted us. Welcome, you son of a bitch. What happened to you?" When I explained that we had gotten lost, they said, "We're glad you're alive." In wartime, if someone disappeared for some time and then reappeared, that is how we would welcome him back.

After a few more hours' march, the company sergeant hollered, "Thirty-minute break for lunch." We all sat by the roadside. My Company Sgt. Lee approached and stood in front of me.

I jumped up and saluted him, "Good afternoon, Sergeant," expecting a blast of anger from him.

He sat on the grass and ordered me to sit down. To my surprise, he asked me gently, "Tell me what happened to you guys, and why you couldn't make it to Anbyon-up yesterday."

Man-E joined me, and we explained how the previous afternoon's heavy rain and thick fog had caused us to stray off the trail and wander for more than twelve hours until we came across a friendly village where we were treated well and where we stayed overnight.

"I thought something very serious had happened to you and woke up a few times during the night to check if you had arrived. Anyway, I am glad to see you both in one piece," and he tapped me on the head and left. A big sigh of relief.

This unfortunate venture taught me one important lesson: do not leave your group and act individually in an unfamiliar environment unless it is absolutely unavoidable.

Since the outbreak of the war, our battalion had been fighting in mountains in the central and east coast regions of the peninsula. This made me want to participate in taking Wonsan City to contact civilization. However, regretfully, our orders were to advance north to Kowon-up. Kowon-up was the junction of two railroads, the Pyongyang-Wonsan Line (east-west) and the East Coast Line (north-south). Our company sergeant said the regiment wanted to secure this strategically important junction as soon as possible.

Two days later, we entered Kowon-up without any enemy resistance. The town had been heavily bombed, and the railroad depot lay in destruction. Debris had been strewn all over the streets. Unlike other towns we had passed through, no one was present. Repeated heavy air raids must have forced the residents to evacuate to safer places. Not even a dog barked. There was an eerie silence. But the beautiful October weather lifted my spirit. While marching, I found hundreds of books scattered on the street, and one, titled *Chichi to Go* (Father and Son) in Japanese, caught my eye. I picked it up, cleaned the dust from it, and tucked it into my backpack for future reading when I had time.

We continued to move toward Hamhung, about fifty miles north of Kowon-up, the capital of South Hamgyong Province. I found a bundle of North Korean 100 *won* bills by the roadside—a significant amount of money. I picked it up and kept it in my army jacket pocket until I met a refugee family with three young children headed by an old man in dirty clothes. Thinking that they needed the money more than me, I called out to the old man, "Sir, you can use this money for your young grandchildren," and put it in his hand.

Astonished, he looked at the money and then looked up at me with his mouth wide open. Then he said in a fearful voice, "Thank you, sir, but I cannot accept this large amount of money."

"*Harabeoji* (Grandpa), please take it. I found it by the roadside, and you can use it to buy food and clothes for your grandchildren."

"Young soldier, I have never seen this much money in my life," he said, and bowed. As he reluctantly accepted it, his hands shook.

A couple of my friends later told me that I should have kept some of the money. I responded that the family could have been mine, and that I was happier without it than with it. We moved on.

CAPTURING HAMHUNG CITY

After more than thirty miles of marching, on October 17, 1950, my regiment captured Hamhung City from the North Korean forces. Having secured the city by the 20th, our combat units paraded victoriously through the main boulevard. The city residents came out in droves and welcomed us enthusiastically, waving South Korean flags and shouting, "Viva unification, hurray *Gukgun!*" For the last four months since the outbreak of the war, we had lived a primitive life, moving from one mountaintop to another, fighting the enemy. Now, the triumphal parade and meeting the multitude of jubilant city people made me feel that I had returned to civilization.

While we were in an exuberant mood, MSgt. Lee told us that one of our lead platoons had taken the Hamhung Prison and found many political prisoners summarily machine-gunned down. They had also retrieved the bodies of prisoners from a well in the prison courtyard. They had been dumped in the well alive, their hands and feet tied. How savage were those communist internal security forces to commit such atrocious crimes on their own people? The report of this incredible massacre made me feel depressed. I couldn't help thinking about the safety of my family back in my hometown. Despite being poor farmers, my family did not like communism, especially my two elder brothers who were staunch anti-communists. I turned southwest, the direction of my hometown, and prayed to higher powers to keep them safe from the communists' barbarity.

While I was feeling dejected, someone shouted, "Let's move." I silently followed my squadron. Realizing that there was nothing I could do for my family, I tried not to think about their fate. My squadron sergeant led us to a small, handsomely stone-fenced house on a quiet back street, a few blocks from the boisterous boulevard. As we stepped inside the courtyard, a delicious aroma of Korean-charcoal steak wafted from a guest room into my nostrils— the same aroma I had smelled a few years earlier at Namyang Construction, when the company had entertained their important vendors.

Entering the neatly decorated guest room, I saw a few senior NCOs, including our Company Sgt. Lee, eating sizzling steak and drinking *soju* with three beautiful young ladies in their early twenties. Corporal Lee Jong-kook followed right behind me. Quartermaster Sgt. Kwon handed a china cup to the girl next to him and filled it.

Upon seeing us come in, the quartermaster hollered in a good-natured voice, "Come in. What kept you boys so late?"

Jong-kook spoke quietly and said, "Umm, Tae-hyok, those girls are prostitutes." We deliberately sat in a corner to eat.

Lee laughed heartily and said, "Look at those young boys. They are so shy that they can't sit next to this gorgeous girl." He put his arm around her waist, offering her another drink.

I quietly picked up a large piece of charcoal steak with a pair of chopsticks and put it into my mouth to hide my embarrassment. It was a mouth-watering delicacy. I gulped it down and took second and third pieces, forgetting MSgt. Lee's teasing.

Soon, the liaison corporal delivered our orders to the company sergeant, who then shouted, "The party is over. Now move on!" We gathered our equipment and departed northward.

I couldn't help but think of my nieces and cousins back in my hometown, hoping they were okay.

INTELLIGENT HIGH SCHOOL GIRL

We marched for a few hours under a golden late October sun, arriving in an orchard village just before sunset. The village was well kept and appeared to be bountiful compared to those towns we had passed through. While our combat units continued to advance farther north, the company commander ordered a dozen of us support personnel to bivouac in the village overnight. Our squad leader, Sergeant First Class Han Geun-bok (who reported to MSgt. Lee) charged me and Sgt. Man-E to locate a couple of large houses which could accommodate our group.

We entered the village separately to expedite our mission. While passing through an apple orchard, I saw a gentleman in his early fifties standing in the courtyard of a large, neatly kept house. I approached and knocked at the gate, greeting him, "Good evening, sir. I am Sergeant Kim from the 3rd Battalion of the 18th Regiment of the South Korean Army." I politely bowed my head to show my respect.

He rushed over and greeted me. Holding my hands, he hollered toward the inner wing of the house, "A *Gukgun* soldier is here. Come and welcome him." Then he led me into the courtyard.

His whole family hurried outside, shouting, "Where?" The family consisted of him, his wife in her mid-forties, a teenage girl in a high school uniform, and a preteen boy. Upon seeing me, they halted abruptly, saluted me with broad smiles, and said, "Welcome, sir."

I returned their salutation with a bow. The lady's use of the word 'sir' embarrassed me so much that I said, "Ma'am, please don't call me 'sir'. I am only a teenager."

Instead of responding to my request, she said to her husband, "*Yeobo*, lead him in, please." Then she asked her daughter to bring some of the choicest apples for me.

As the gentleman led me inside, I asked if he would allow a half dozen of us to stay in his guest quarters overnight.

"Of course, you may stay as long as you want," he said, gesturing for me to enter the guest room.

After thanking him, I asked him to go inside first because he was many years older than me. I sat on the stairs and removed my boots before entering. Then we sat on the clean ondol floor cross-legged, facing each other. He said, "I am glad you are here, Sergeant. I presume you are far away from your hometown in South Korea. I hope your family is safe and well."

"Actually, my hometown is in Hwanghae-do, North Korea, sir." I explained why I had gone to Seoul, and added, "I have not heard from my parents since I left for Seoul two and a half years ago. I hope the war will be over soon so that I may see them. I miss them so much."

He looked at me with a puzzled expression and said, "Did you go to Seoul alone? You said you are a teenage soldier. How old were you when you originally left home?"

"Yes, sir. I went alone. I was then fifteen."

At that moment, his daughter knocked on the door and said politely, "Excuse me, *Appa*. I brought delicious apples for the soldier." She was a slender, intelligent-looking girl. Her oval face was fair; a warm smile danced in her dark eyes. Her countenance looked even fairer against her deep navy-blue school uniform. What a beauty!

Her father responded, "Come in." As she cautiously stepped inside with a basketful of ruby and gold apples, I unconsciously stood up, fixing my eyes on her. He said, "Young sergeant, sit down please, and feel at home." After she sat down next to him, across from me, he proudly introduced her and said that she was a senior at the Hamhung Girls' High School. But because of the war, the school had been temporarily closed, and she stayed home.

I acknowledged her, bowing my head slightly, and said to her father in a nervous voice, "Sir, you have a beautiful daughter. You must be proud of her." I couldn't take my eyes off her.

"Thank you, sergeant. I am proud of her; she is a beautiful girl," and he lovingly patted her on the back.

"*Appa*," she whispered, lowering her head. She blushed. She possessed an ethereal beauty.

I said spontaneously, "Sir, even an angel might envy her beauty."

She protested politely, "Sergeant, you embarrass me, sir. I am not that pretty." She looked at me with a pure angelic smile. Beautiful dimples appeared on her blushed cheeks, resembling a couple of water drops falling on the placid surface of a pond, making calm, round ripples.

"Miss, indeed, you are pretty. May I ask you a favor? Please do not call me 'sir.' As I mentioned to your mother, I am only a teenage soldier, not an officer." Suddenly I felt embarrassed. How could I possibly have made such a bold poetic expression, especially when I had never spoken in front of a young woman before. I had no idea how I had mustered such courage. But I took a deep breath and asked, "Would you mind telling me what they have taught you at your high school? I am interested in what you have learned because I have never had a secondary education."

Her father interjected, "My dear daughter, tell him what they have taught you. Will you peel the apples and serve him please?" Then he stepped out of the room, leaving the two of us alone. I stood up to show my courtesy, and he said, "Sergeant Kim, relax. Feel at home," then held my shoulder and squeezed it with a fatherly smile. Suddenly I felt I was not a stranger to this family, even though we had never met before.

The young lady picked up an apple, twisted the stem off, and started to peel the skin with a small knife. She began from the top of the apple and turned it around while generating a thin ribbon of the skin, exposing the succulent pinkish-white fruit. Her pale, delicate hands and the apple's flesh were difficult to distinguish. The ribbon fell into the basket like a supple spring willow branch. She peeled it so deftly that the ribbon came out in one long strip. She cut the apple into four pieces on the tiny cutting board she had brought and poked a toothpick into each of the four pieces.

I was amazed by how gracefully she had served a guest in such a short time, fancying that her parents must have given her a wonderful home education. She said, "Excuse me, Sergeant. Please have some apples." Then she picked up one piece with a toothpick and handed it to me.

"Thank you, Miss." I took the apple by the stick, but alas the apple piece fell off. Simultaneously, both of us tried to catch it before it hit the floor. Her quick hand caught the apple, but my rough, slow one inadvertently grabbed the back of her silky, soft hand instead. Even though it was an accident, I felt I was holding an angel's hand, and a euphoric sensation filled my heart. "I'm sorry," I apologized to her, releasing her hand reluctantly.

She responded with an incredibly beautiful smile, "Not at all, it was an accident," and opened her hand, showing the juicy apple in her bare palm. I picked it up and took a bite. How sweet it was! In no time, I was ready for more; she was already holding the second piece out to me. After taking it, I asked her again what they had taught her at her high school.

She said that she had learned many different subjects, such as Korean literature, world history, algebra, geometry, trigonometry, science (including physics and chemistry), Russian, and more. They used to teach English until two years ago, when they switched to Russian. "I love English very much. I think it is an eloquent language and sounds softer than Russian, which is guttural. My teacher said that English was an imperialist language, and soon the world would speak Russian, which I don't believe."

She impressed me so much that I couldn't help but respect and adore her. I had some knowledge of Korean literature, algebra, and world history because I had borrowed a couple of books from a high school student in a neighboring town, but had no knowledge of geometry, trigonometry, physics, or chemistry. To me she was a goddess of knowledge, and I was an ignorant backwoods boy. I felt so small. But I mustered all my courage and asked her if she didn't mind teaching me some of what she had learned, especially those subjects I had never heard of before.

With an innocent smile, she said, "I am only a student, not capable of teaching anyone. But I will gladly show you two of my favorite subjects, plane geometry and trigonometry." Then she took a blank sheet of paper and a fat pencil from a low-legged desk in the corner of the room, sat closer to me, and drew a circle and a right triangle. Then she said, "I am sure you know how to calculate the areas of these figures."

Sitting closer to her made me feel ecstatic, yet I suddenly became conscious of how dirty and smelly I was. I had not washed since we had broken the enemy's final offense and begun our advance northward. My last bath was in a shallow creek in mid-September, without soap, six weeks earlier. I felt so embarrassed that I moved a few feet away from her and apologized, "I am sorry that I smell bad."

"Sergeant don't feel bad. I suppose that in war everybody smells, especially fighting soldiers." She moved closer to me with the paper and the pencil and was eager to show me geometry.

I was deeply moved by her gracious gesture and said, "Thank you, Miss." Even though she was only a high school girl, she possessed the grace and sensibility of a grown-up. She made me feel so comfortable.

Putting the drawings in front of me, she repeated that I knew how to calculate the areas of a circle and a triangle.

Without hesitation, I answered, "The area of a circle is the radius times pi, and that of a triangle is the base times the height, divided by 2." Then I secretly took a deep breath.

"Those are parts of plane geometry." After drawing a rectangle inside the circle with each corner touching the circumference, she asked me, "What is the sum of the four angles of the rectangle?"

I promptly answered, "360 degrees," because I had learned it in fifth grade.

Then she drew a small circle centered at the right-angled point of the triangle and asked me how many degrees were outside the right angle. I didn't know, but after scratching my head for a few moments, I hesitantly said, "Is it 270 degrees? I am not sure."

"You are right, it is 270 degrees. Plane geometry progresses from something like this. I am sure you will do well in this subject." She gave me a beautiful smile.

I wished I could have held her hands and expressed my sincere thanks, but because of the culture, I couldn't. I just said politely, "Thank you so much, Miss."

Then suddenly somebody hollered, "Sergeant Kim, where the hell are you?" It was Sgt. Man-E. But, as if I hadn't heard him, I asked her, "What is trigonometry? Is it like algebra?" I wanted not only to learn about the subject but also to spend more time with her.

"Trigonometry is the relationship between the sides and angle of a triangle, expressed in terms like sine, cosine, and tangent," she said.

All those words sounded very strange because I had never heard them before. I felt overwhelmed, but I took the pencil from her without permission and wrote them down on my palm, phonetically in the Korean alphabet.

She took her pencil back, held my hand, and with a broad smile, wrote foreign letters next to my Korean writing. I felt I was melting like an ice chunk in hot water. I trembled, having never experienced such a wonderful moment before. She continued, "Trigonometry is more mathematical than plane geometry. I think geometry is to train logical thinking."

Man-E shouted, "You son of a bitch, Tae-hyok! Sergeant Han wants you to report to him immediately. God damn you."

"Is someone calling you?" she asked, and released my hand, looking alarmed.

"Yes. He is one of my group, a friend of mine," I said. Then I yelled back, "Man-E, don't shout. I am coming out." I hastily but reluctantly bid her goodbye.

At that moment, her father entered the room and asked in an uneasy voice, "Are you alright, dear?" and took her by the arm.

I bowed to him and said, "Sir, she is a wonderful teacher. She taught me geometry and trigonometry. Once again, thank you for allowing my group to stay at your house overnight." I bowed to them. Then I hurriedly came out to join Sgt. Man-E before he got more excited, because he had a peculiar habit of pouring out rich military language when he became upset. I didn't want the beautiful, intelligent young lady to hear my friend's colorful speech.

As soon as I joined him, he barked, "What the hell did you do in that house? Did you f@#$ with somebody?"

I yelled back, "Watch your mouth. I met a wonderful family, and we had a good time."

"Do they have a young girl?"

I hesitated to answer but told him that their daughter was a senior at the Hamhung Girls' High School and had taught me about geometry and trigonometry, proudly showing him what she had written on my palm.

"What the f@#$ is that? It doesn't mean anything to me. Did you f@#$ her?"

I kicked him hard in the shin. "You are a real son of a bitch. You know only f@#$ing."

He yelped and shouted, "F@#$ you, why did you do that to me?"

"Don't talk like that," I yelled, and walked away swiftly. At that instant, I realized that I had come to adore her, so much so that I had kicked my friend.

Man-E cursed me, "Damn you, this hurts."

I turned around and saw him limping. Suddenly I felt sorry that I had kicked him. Despite his foul mouth, we had been comrades-in-arms for a couple of years. Ten days ago, we had gotten lost all night in unknown terrain. I shook his hand and apologized.

"Forget it. Damn it," he said and pulled up his trouser, exposing a reddish bruise on his shin. But he continued needling me. "You must have had a good time with her to react like this. Did you do *ppo-ppo* (kiss) her?"

"God damn you. We didn't do anything like that. I asked her to show me something she had learned at her high school. She kindly agreed and graciously explained what plane geometry and trigonometry were with a few diagrams." I showed him what she had written on my palm again. Alas, it had already begun to fade. "She is a very beautiful, graceful, and intelligent high school girl, and her father was very kind to me. I think I have fallen in love with her."

"You seem to be very serious. You haven't even f@#$ed her yet."

"Shut up. Don't talk like that anymore. I am very serious. I am going to write to her and her father to see if they would allow me to visit them when the war is over." My heart pounded faster.

"Okay. What is her name? Did you get her address?"

I told my friend dejectedly that, unfortunately, in my hurry and nervousness I had forgotten to ask for her name or address. But I would get it that evening when we returned for our overnight bivouac.

Man-E said, "Stupid, you're not going to see her again tonight. I bet you her father has evacuated his family to protect them, especially his daughter, from any problems. Remember that we are a bunch of hungry young soldiers who could cause trouble."

When I returned to the place with my group early that evening, only her father welcomed us. While the gentleman and MSgt. Lee greeted each other, I looked for the adoring, beautiful girl, but she was nowhere to be seen. Her absence disappointed me deeply. I wanted to ask her father for her name and address, but I didn't have the guts to interrupt his conversation with my sergeant. Hoping to see her again the next morning before our departure, I entered the guest room with other soldiers for the night, where earlier that afternoon she had treated me to apples and written on my palm.

The next morning, I got up before my other comrades-in-arms and went out to the courtyard. The chilly morning air made me shiver. I walked around, hoping to come upon the owner so that I might ask him for his address and his daughter's name, but he was nowhere to be seen. Instead, I found steaming water in the big kettle in the guest quarter kitchen. Since the war had begun four months earlier, I had never had the luxury of warm water to wash. I was tempted to clean my dirty face and hands, but I didn't, because I wanted to keep the girl's writing on my palm as long as possible.

MSgt. Lee hollered, "Get up, boys. We are moving out." We hurriedly picked up our equipment and resumed our march northward to Hagaru. Leaving the place without seeing the girl again made my heart ache, but I was determined to visit her when the war was over, perhaps within a few months. Even though it was still going on, the beautiful girl and the bright sunrise brought me hope that I would survive the war and live a happy life.

THE ROAD TO THE CHOSIN RESERVOIR

Reaching the highway, we continued our advance toward the Chosin Reservoir. My group leader estimated that the lake would be about thirty-five miles farther north, and that the Korea-China border lay around ninety miles away. Looking up at a distant mountain range ahead of me, I imagined the road must have to cross many high, rugged mountains like it. A blanket of ominous gray clouds was creeping over the range and blocking the sparkling morning sun. Snowflakes swirled wildly in the sky. As soon as they fell on the ground, they disappeared under our boots.

When we had covered a mile more, a large convoy of trucks loaded with American soldiers drove slowly between our two columns and passed with intermittent honking. Soon afterwards, squads of fat two-engine American Air Force planes flew in and began to drop supply containers, while circling over the open fields. At first, the containers fell very fast, one after another, and then the parachutes popped open, displaying a magnificent array like multicolored waltzing umbrellas. I had never seen parachutes before. The show was so enchanting that I halted and watched the dancing parachutes and the formidable planes until someone behind me shouted, "Move on!" This awe-inspiring spectacle convinced me that the UN forces would conclude the war before long, which meant that I could visit the beautiful girl sooner than I would have expected. A little farther north, the truck convoy had parked in a field, and the American soldiers disembarked. The soldiers gathered the airborne supplies and piled them up here and there.

As we continued marching, another convoy, much larger than the previous one, including field artillery, moved north, raising dust clouds. The American soldiers waved to us, and we waved back. Some of them clasped their hands like boxers who had just won a championship. They kept rolling northward. Then MSgt. Lee hollered unexpectedly, "Fifteen minutes of rest!" The time passed quickly, but no 'Move on!' followed. Some lay on the grass and took a nap, while others chatted. A half-hour later, the Company Commander, Captain Chung, showed up and explained that our Capital Division had come under the U.S. X Corps Command. The Corps had ordered our regiment to advance northeast and to take the Pujon Reservoir. The U.S. First Marine Division would march to the Chosin Reservoir instead of us.

THE MARCH TO THE PUJON RESERVOIR

The Pujon Reservoir was about thirty-five miles east of the Chosin Reservoir over a rugged mountain range. Because there was no shortcut across the range to the reservoir, we had to circumvent the southern foothills of the mountain, which meant we had to turn around for miles and pass through the orchard village where we had camped the previous night. I hoped we would bivouac in the village so that I could see the beautiful girl once more. However, to my disappointment, we passed the town, veered northeastward, and went on for more than six miles, arriving in a hamlet by a river where we bivouacked that evening. It was cold and damp, and each of us had only one army blanket for cover. We were so cold that we collected deadwood from the riverbank and made bonfires to sleep around, like cowboys in Western movies.

I collected rice straw from the nearby fields, spread them on the ground as a mattress and lay on it, using my backpack as a pillow and covering myself with my blanket and raincoat. I quickly fell asleep until I felt so cold that I couldn't sleep any longer. I got up and found that the bonfire had almost gone out, but all the other fellows, except a few guards, kept sleeping soundly. I asked one of the sentries what time it was.

He answered, "I don't know. Damn, it's cold!"

I asked him if he could help me gather some deadwood, which he gladly did. Each of us collected an armful of dried wood from the riverbank and fed the nearly extinct campfire. As the fire roared and spit sparks into the air, I became warm and returned to sleep until a loud shouting woke me. It was MSgt. Lee, yelling, "Boys, get up and cook your own breakfast!" It was pre-dawn, still somewhat dark.

Since I was a slow eater, I jumped up and began to prepare breakfast so that I might have enough time to eat before the sergeant would yell, "Move out!" I promptly took two handfuls of dried rice from my emergency provision sack (one of my extra socks), put it into my deep oval-shaped mess kit, added water, and cooked it over the campfire. Without even salt, the cooked rice tasted bland, but I finished it anyway for the day's long march. Then, I hurriedly rolled my blanket and raincoat, tied them tightly around my knapsack, fastening my mess kit behind it, and was ready to move.

MSgt. Lee barked, "Company, move out!" However, since more than four hundred combat soldiers of our 3rd Battalion preceded us, we had to wait for our turn. We marched on a dirt highway along a river between two lofty mountain ranges. The brilliant morning sun shone on the southern slope of the range on our left, exposing three huge, black water pipelines which ran down side by side from high up, and disappeared behind a smaller mountain. I presumed they would end at the Pujon Hydroelectric Power Plant (the third largest in the Korean Peninsula) somewhere in the foothills of the range. The mountains on our left and right rose so high and the valley fell so deep that even the high-noon sun struggled to reach the bottom of the narrow valley.

After a daylong march of twenty miles along a crooked road, we arrived in a town tucked in the foothills of a high mountain just before dusk, where an elementary school and a town building stood prominently among a few scores of humble farmhouses along a single dirt street, one of the cantons in Sinhung County. Because of the war, the two public buildings had been closed. We were ordered to camp in the town overnight. The combat soldiers of the battalion took the two buildings, and my squad camped in a small, empty house.

In the beginning, the town was eerily quiet. Only a few elderly men by the street suspiciously watched us entering the village. Then, suddenly they shouted, "The South Korean Army!" A few dozen townspeople swarmed out from their hiding places and enthusiastically welcomed us. According to them, a few hundred North Korean soldiers had passed through northwards early that morning. They had drafted able men from the town and forced them to carry their military supplies. The villagers hoped their loved ones would return home safely soon. We hoped so, too.

MSgt. Lee organized the guard duty and posted the first rotation. The rest went into deep sleep, trusting that the faithful sentries would protect us from any surprise attack.

SNOW BURIALS

October 26, 1950. It was a bleak, cold morning. The quartermaster group prepared a breakfast of rice in hot soybean sprout soup and kimchi. They also distributed two bags of army crackers to each soldier for emergency provisions. Each bag contained about thirty silken cocoon-sized hard crackers which tasted bland. They were so hard that if you didn't chew them properly, you could crack a tooth.

While we were eating, the company first sergeant instructed us to fill our canteens with water, because the day's planned route was expected to be a narrow and steep pass to the Kaema Highland, the roof of the Korean Peninsula that was a mile high. He warned us that we should ration our water, because we might not find any watering holes along the pass.

When we had marched over half a mile, the dirt highway suddenly began to rise along a very steep mountain in countless switchbacks. We halted for a few moments and looked up the pass silently, watching hundreds of our fellow soldiers toiling up it, like an army of ants. I thought that this pass was even higher than the Taebaek Pass where I could have fallen into a deep gorge three weeks earlier had I made just one misstep.

MSgt. Lee broke the silence and exclaimed, "This is the pass leading to the roof of the peninsula! Let's move on."

Scaling the steep slope, despite the raw weather, we sweated profusely. Since the stretches between switchbacks were so long, we took shortcuts and beat the battalion commander Major Cho's jeep. After a few hours' climb, the company first sergeant shouted, "Fifteen minutes rest!" While we were taking a sweet hiatus, the major caught up with us. We jumped up and saluted him.

He returned our salute and said with a broad smile, "Take it easy. You are faster than my jeep, my proud soldiers!" Then he ordered his driver to continue.

All too soon, the first sergeant hollered, "Let's move!" The fifteen minutes seemed so brief. I looked up the steep mountain to search for its peak, but all I could see was the snaky road disappearing into the fog. As we climbed higher, the air became colder, and light snow started to fall. By late afternoon it turned into a blizzard, with about half a foot of snow accumulating. The virtual whiteout and slippery road slowed us to a crawl, and the inclement weather continued until dark. An incredibly strong wind began to blow, and the temperature fell rapidly. Soon the wind swept the snow-carrying clouds away, and the full moon shone on the ghostly landscape, making our slow march easier.

Then suddenly enemy machine guns began to fire at us from the peak of the mountain, pinning us down. There was no place to hide. We instinctively dropped to the snow-covered road and counter-attacked, blindly firing our rifles and machine guns at the enemy. Soon our mortar units began bombarding the enemy position with barrages of mortar-shells, and the bombs exploded like spectacular fireworks. The world rumbled around us. As our firepower intensified, the enemy's punch started to wane. After two hours of battle, the enemy machine guns were silenced, but we continued firing until we received a ceasefire order.

No more shooting. A great relief! I got up from the snowy ground, and suddenly felt a frigid wind biting me. My teeth chattered wildly. None of us had a winter coat or long johns. We were completely unprepared for this harsh weather. While fighting, despite lying on the frozen road, I forgot about the unforgiving weather. Now we trotted in place to warm ourselves, while anxiously waiting for marching orders, hoping to get somewhere warmer. Instead, we were ordered to stay overnight where we were, because we had too little intelligence about the enemy's movements.

Hearing the news, SFC Han shouted, "Let's make a bonfire!" and instructed us to gather firewood to keep ourselves from freezing. He said, "It's going to be a very tough night." The bright moonshine made it easy to collect kindling. Soon we made a mound with a bunch of dried grass for tinder. We surrounded our leader to block the gusts of wind so that his cigarette lighter could stay lit long enough for the flame to catch. After a few tries, he succeeded in lighting the grass. We all circled around the fire.

While we were warming ourselves, two corpsmen brought over a wounded soldier on a makeshift stretcher, covered with a blanket, and lowered him by the fire. They rolled the blanket back and cut his bloody jacket with a pair of scissors, exposing the soldier's wound just below his ribcage. They removed the blood-soaked gauze and dressed the wound with a thicker layer. But blood continued to ooze, saturating the new dressing. He groaned weakly in excruciating pain and shivered. Occasionally he murmured, "Cold. I am dying!"

The corpsmen said, "We have a few more men to take care of up there, but fortunately they are not as badly injured as this soldier." They asked us to watch him until they could return and went back to the front.

The weather was getting colder and colder. Even the roaring bonfire couldn't keep us warm. We wrapped ourselves in our army blankets, huddling around the burning wood. But the furious gusts whipped us from all directions. Sometimes the wildly flying cinders landed on us, burning small holes in our blankets, which we put out for each other.

Later at night, the moon sank behind the ghostly silhouette of the range. I felt like we were sucked into a swirling black pit. Even the bonfire was getting dimmer. As it generated less heat, we crouched closer to it, but no one dared to go out to collect firewood on the slippery slope in the dark. Despite the unforgiving weather, we succumbed to fatigue and hunger, and fell asleep one by one.

At last, the brilliant sun woke us, warming our backs, and the biting wind had died down. The bonfire had gone out. I noticed that we had leaned against each other in a tight circle and moved closer to the extinct fire; survival instinct might have made us do so to keep warm. Then tragically, we found that the wounded soldier had died outside the circle. Judging from his cold, rigid body, he might have passed away many hours earlier, perhaps shortly after the two corpsmen had left us to watch him. Had he received proper treatment in time, he might have survived. We all felt terrible, and a bit guilty even though there was nothing we could have done.

SFC Han ordered us to bury him by the roadside. We tried to dig a grave, but the frozen ground was too hard. Instead, we laid him in a ditch, covered his body with snow, and put his rifle by the grave, hoping the battalion quartermasters would retrieve him later and provide a proper burial. I felt strange burying a comrade-in-arms in snow instead of dirt. We lined up and gave a final salute—the formality we couldn't afford during the first four months of the war when the enemy had beaten us in one battle after another. After the brief goodbye, we moved on.

While advancing toward the peak, I took out a handful of Korean Army crackers from my backpack and crunched them to tame my gurgling stomach. The dry, unsalted crackers left my mouth so parched that I couldn't swallow. Despite being hungry, I spit out the powdery food, scooped up a snowball and munched it to wet my mouth, then ate the crackers.

Once my stomach had stopped complaining, I could not help but think about the unfortunate soldier. The war will be over in a couple of months, and he could have returned home and enjoyed life with his loving family. Why did he have to die after surviving the hardest four months of the war? Might I end up like him?

"Fifteen minutes rest," my squad sergeant shouted. SFC Han's announcement woke me from my unpleasant thoughts. I silently thanked him for that.

KAEMA HIGHLAND

After a couple more hours of marching, we reached the crest of the long and steep pass and found a snow-covered plateau which stretched as far as my eyes could see. The magnificent, vast plain glittered under the spotless blue sky. MSgt. Lee exclaimed, "Boys, this is the roof of the Korean Peninsula! The Korea-China border can't be too far. Maybe ninety miles?"

Then unexpectedly Corporal Chun groaned, "Oh, dead *in mingun* (North Korean soldiers). Gross!" We saw two of them near a bomb crater. They must have been hit by our mortar bombardments the previous night and abandoned by their retreating comrades. Shrapnel had plunged into the forehead of one of them, while the second one's face had been shattered beyond recognition. Blood had splashed all over the snow and frozen. The crimson color on the white snow was so vivid that I felt sick to my stomach. I shivered. I had seen many corpses since the war had begun, but their blood had either dried under the burning summer sun or had quickly been absorbed into the soil. Thus, I had never seen anything so dramatic.

MSgt. Lee shouted, "Bury the dead!"

Despite being weary and hungry, we kicked snow over the bodies. I avoided the frozen blood lest it stick to my boots. After the shallow snow burial, we marched on in silence. I wondered why he had ordered us to bury our dead enemies while marching. Perhaps the frozen blood made him feel as sick as me. I tried not to think about the red blood on the white snow, but the image continued coming back for the next few days. It stirred a strange emotion in me—their death meant our survival, but why did we have to kill each other? Aren't we the same people? I cursed Kim Il Sung who had founded Communist North Korea and started this damn war under the auspices of Stalin.

The day turned incredibly balmy, leaving no trace of the previous night's frigid weather. The bright sunshine lifted our spirits, and we began to talk. Yet this vast white plateau made me feel so lonely and small. I sighed. The endless highland reminded me of a ranch scene in an American Western, which I had watched before the war had broken out. I might come here and run a ranch like the one in the movie after the war.

We moved farther into the highland. I noticed tomb-like domes scattered in the fields. Koreans would bury their dead in sloping grounds facing south so that the graves would receive plenty of sunlight and would not be flooded. So, I wondered why there were graves in such a flat landscape. I asked MSgt. Lee if he knew what those mounds were.

He said that those were potato cellars; the climate and soil in this highland were ideal for potato farming. When farmers harvested big, delicious potatoes, they would take home some of the harvest for the winter and store the rest in the field. They would dig a deep hole in the ground, a dozen feet in diameter and below freezing level. Then they insulated the hole with dry hay, stacked the potatoes in it, put thick layers of hay over the stack, and covered it with dirt so it looked like a traditional Korean tomb.

He added that the highland was sparsely populated, mostly by farmers and loggers; the summer climate was too cool to farm rice there. The major staples were potatoes, oats, and barley in the upland. I listened to him with interest.

By midday we arrived in a village of a half dozen farmhouses scattered along the dirt road. We were told to camp there until we received further orders. According to our company first sergeant, we had advanced too fast, too far ahead of the main force of our regiment. While the combat soldiers of our battalion pitched their tents in the fields, a farmer graciously allowed our administrative staff to quarter in his guestroom. Being weary and hungry, we collected our emergency rice and asked the owner's wife to cook it for us, which she gladly did. We shared our food with her family. The lady served her own kimchi, which made our meal savorier. Her husband said, "In this part of the country, rice is hard to come by. Thank you, soldiers, for sharing this delicious food with us."

SIMPLE GRISTMILL

After our meal, I lay on the heated floor and slept contentedly until a distant booming sound woke me. I thought the enemy was firing artillery at us but heard no explosions nearby. Also, the booms were too regular to be artillery bombardments—perhaps five minutes apart. The noise continued, neither intensifying nor diminishing. I fell back sleep. The next morning, the booms continued. Wondering about the source of the noise, I asked the man of the house where it was coming from.

He said that it was from his gristmill. Since there was no fast-flowing river in that flat highland to run a regular hydro-mill, he had built a small mill powered by a creek which flowed through his oat field. He pointed toward a hut two hundred yards away.

His answer piqued my curiosity. With MSgt. Lee's permission, I slung my Carbine rifle over my shoulder and walked across the snow-covered field to the shack. Upon reaching it, suddenly I became nervous; an enemy straggler might be hiding inside. So, I prepared my rifle to shoot and shouted, "Raise your hands. Get out slowly!" while aiming my gun at the door. Silence!

Entering, I saw the farmer's simple gristmill. He had built a small reservoir to collect enough water to run it. It consisted of a long, sturdy log with a barrel at one end and a pestle at the other. He stabilized the log on a fulcrum. When water filled the barrel, the weight raised the pestle high enough to empty the barrel. When it emptied, the pestle fell hard, pounding the grain in a granite mortar, generating booming noises. I thought this was an ingenious creation, and chuckled. The farmer was an extraordinary engineer.

As ordered, we camped in the highland village for the next several days, which gave us unanticipated downtime. Since the war had begun, we had not had even a single day of rest. Also, we were utterly exhausted after more than four hundred miles of marching in the past six weeks. Thus, this hiatus was a gift. For the first two days, I slept constantly, except when eating meals and doing chores, regenerating my physical and mental energies.

Refreshed, on the third morning, I took out the middle school algebra book from my backpack for the first time since the inception of the war. Upon opening it, I found that it had become discolored and wrinkled, and that some pages were stuck together from rain and sweat but were still readable. I quickly reviewed some formulae and word problems. Amazingly, I had remembered them through the four difficult months.

While I was solving some of the factorization problems and daydreaming about the girl I had recently met, a convoy of army trucks moved in with a great racket and parked along the roadside. Many infantrymen disembarked, perhaps one battalion. The fleet also brought us much needed winter fatigues and boots made of gray quilted cotton. We immediately changed out of our dirty, ragged summer clothes and put on new ones. They looked ugly but kept us warm. The company first sergeant ordered us to pile up our dirty, old underwear. He sprinkled gasoline generously over it, struck a match and threw it onto the pile. Instantly, flames engulfed it. It smelled awful, but we were glad to get rid of the lice-infested underwear.

Meanwhile the newly arrived battalion (from the U.S. X Corps) took our place, marching on the route we expected to take, and we were ordered to board the trucks and journey back to Hamhung City, easily driving in one day the same distance it had taken us two weeks to march. While our truck convoy descended the steep pass where we had buried a fallen fellow soldier in snow a week earlier, I tried to find out whether he had been properly buried or not, but I couldn't tell where we had laid him. All I could hope was that someone had given him a proper burial so that his skeleton would not be washed down the valley and into the East Sea.

After a day's ride, we arrived at a school yard in Hamhung City just before sunset and bivouacked there. We fell fast asleep on the bare floor until the next morning when our company sergeant stomped on the floor and shouted, "Get up, boys!"

We marched to the Hamhung Railroad Station and were loaded into cargo trains like livestock. Even though we were packed in, we were still cold, as the train traveled north along the coastline. After two days on the slow-moving train, we joined our main force in a town by the northeastern coast. Our old friends, Oh Munchan, Jin Chin-mae, and others welcomed us and joked, "Where the hell have you been? Did you guys get lost in the highland?" and they laughed boisterously. It felt so good to join them.

CHAPTER 18

March to the Korea-China Border

November 1950

BRAINWASHED

As we marched farther northeast toward the Korea-China Border, we encountered the enemy more frequently, but we continued to advance. By mid-November we reached a small farming village near Myongchon-up, North Hamgyong Province, North Korea, about halfway between Hamhung City and the Korea-China Border. It was a beautiful, balmy afternoon, and the village was peaceful, yet it felt strange.

Then a sudden shout, "Fifteen minutes rest!" broke the spell. Lying on the grass by the roadside, I tried to understand what had made me feel apprehensive. Then I realized that, unlike previous cities and towns that we had come through, no one in this village had come out to welcome us. I rationalized that, anticipating a fierce fight, the villagers had probably taken refuge somewhere safer.

The fifteen-minute rest had passed with no order to move out. No one complained. Despite there being a few more hours left before sunset, we were ordered to camp in the village—an unexpected respite. After my squadron had settled in an empty farmhouse, with my squad sergeant's permission, I slung my rifle on my shoulder and went out to explore the town.

The first person I saw in the village was a young man perched on a jujube branch and singing loudly. I recognized the songs as communist revolutionary chants praising Kim Il Sung. Since he sang such songs in the presence of South Korean soldiers, he must be an ardent communist. I was prepared to shoot him if necessary. Slowly approaching, I found him to be a teenager like me. Yet I was keenly aware that he might have a handgun hidden under his jacket.

I aimed my gun at him and shouted, "Raise your hands! Get off the tree."

He stopped singing and gazed at me. Then he yelled abruptly, "Long live our Great Leader General Kim Il Sung," and pumped his arms into the air.

I was about to pull the trigger, but somehow, I calmed down and shouted, "Boy, come down!" I kept my gun pointed at him. He slowly descended from the tree and kept his arms up, showing no sign of fear or panic. Strange!

I became more alert, fearing this boy's bizarre behavior under such extraordinary circumstances. Pointing my rifle at him with one hand, I searched him with the other for hidden weapons but found none. I relaxed somewhat and told him to sit down on the grass by the roadside and keep his hands on his lap. Then I sat down opposite him.

He looked so young that I asked, "How old are you?"

"Sixteen."

Assuming he was a local boy, I said, "Go home. Your parents must be waiting for you."

"My father sent me to educate those ignorant South Korean reactionaries and show them how great this socialist nation is. He said not to come home until my revolutionary duty was finished. So, I am not going home."

I was utterly stunned at his incredible response. What kind of human being would send his young son to the front lines and tell him not to come home? Had I heard him right? I shuddered. I couldn't help but ask, "What does he do? What is his name? Where does he live?"

"My father is fighting the evil Americans and their running dogs, the South Korean soldiers, on the western front. He is the greatest general of all, the greatest leader. He is Comrade General Kim Il Sung, my father. He will annihilate them all. You, too." Then he began to sing an anthem, praising Kim Il Sung.

At this point, I realized that this boy was mentally ill, had been brainwashed, or both. I knew that he wasn't the son of Kim Il Sung. I also concluded that if I let him go free, he might steal a gun at night and kill us. I had to find his family and put him under their care for everyone's safety, or shoot him, which I didn't want to do. He continued to sing revolutionary songs, which I couldn't stand any longer. I shot my rifle into the air and shouted, "Shut up!" He stopped singing and remained silent as I had ordered.

"Who taught you those stupid songs?"

"Teachers at the Communist Party School."

He had been completely brainwashed. I asked him, "Do you know who I am?"

"You are one of those evil soldiers. I saw many of them like you whom our brave Korean People's Army had captured in Yeongju, Andong, Cheongsong, and Uiseong."

I was surprised by his accurate geographical knowledge and war chronology. In some of those towns, our regiment had fought the North Koreans during the first three months of the war and had sustained many casualties before we crushed the enemy's offense and began to advance. I believed some of our soldiers had become prisoners of the enemy.

Since I didn't want to kill him, I decided to take him to my company sergeant. On the way, I met two elderly men of the village. I greeted them with respect and asked if they knew the boy.

After a quick glance at him, they said simultaneously, "I have never seen him before. He is not one of our boys," and stepped away from him. One of them exclaimed, "Oh my, he looks very angry. Where did you find him?"

"Sir, I first found him sitting on that jujube tree and singing revolutionary songs. He said that his father is General Kim Il Sung. At first, I thought he was one of the town's boys. Obviously, he is not."

One of the old men chuckled and said, "Young soldier, watch him. He seems to be troublesome."

I thanked the elderly gentlemen. Then I ordered the boy to walk toward the farmhouse where my company headquarters bivouacked. Even though he was verbally belligerent, oddly, he did not show any sign of physical resistance. When I reached the headquarters, I led the boy to my Company First Sergeant and told him about the boy's bizarre behavior.

The sergeant told me to leave the boy with him and assigned a guard to watch him. The boy abruptly began to sing an anthem praising Kim Il Sung. At that, the guard hit the boy in the back and yelled, "Shut up!"

I felt greatly relieved to unload the burden of the bizarre boy onto the sergeant. I returned to my squad camp and had a good rest until the next morning. For some reason the image of the mad boy came back to me, which annoyed me. I walked over to the headquarters and asked the guard how the boy had behaved.

He said, "He is gone."

"What do you mean 'he is gone'?"

"We restrained him with telephone cables because he cursed us, shouting 'Long live, General Kim Il Sung,' and kicked the walls, acting wildly all night. He made Captain Chung and others so mad that the commander ordered us to shoot him. So, the guard sergeant and I took him out to a field and executed him."

Strangely, I did not have any feelings about the death of that boy, but I was glad that someone else had killed him. I hated the communists who had drafted and brainwashed him.

BAD NEWS

Since we had crippled the enemy's offensive in mid-September and burst through the Pusan Perimeter, our final defense line, we had won every battle we had fought. By late November, we advanced all the way to the northeasternmost region of North Korea, about sixty miles from the Korea-China Border. We expected to reach the border within a couple of weeks, and the war might be over before the end of the year. Our morale was skyrocketing. I dreamed of visiting my parents and the beautiful, intelligent girl whom I had met earlier in Hamhung City.

Early one morning, while we were waiting for orders to move out, MSgt. Lee, and a few other fellow soldiers huddled around a bonfire. The sergeant said in a somber voice, "The Company Commander told me that the Eighth U.S. Army encountered a massive army from Communist China and is battling along the Ch'ongch'on River in the northwestern region of the peninsula. The U.S. forces are losing the fight." The sergeant paused, took a deep breath, and continued, "Even worse, the old man said that Russian MiG jet fighter planes with swing-back wings challenged the American planes and were faster." He silently stoked the bonfire, then shouted, "I thought only Americans had jet planes. Damn, I don't like it."

The information disappointed me deeply. Suddenly I felt my sweet dream of visiting the pretty girl and my parents disappearing. But I questioned myself, "How could the poorly armed Chinese Communist soldiers possibly be defeating the mighty Americans, who are equipped with the most advanced weaponry?" I didn't believe that the Americans were losing! Even if it was true, I firmly believed that they would regroup quickly and destroy the Chinese, finishing the war soon. I shouted, "We shall win!"

"Move out!" As we marched on the snow-covered highway along the East Sea coast, a couple of miles south of Kyongsong, I saw a gray American Navy ship and a few sailors on the bow with the machine guns ready to fire. I was surprised that such a big gunboat approached the shoreline so closely that it almost touched the land. We waved, and they waved back, acknowledging that we were friends. Seeing the magnificent ship assured me that the Americans' loss on the western front was temporary, and we would surely win the war. The presence of the formidable ship this far north reenergized me, and my morale rose again.

We marched briskly for a few more hours. By mid-morning, we had reached Kyongsong. Thatch-roofed houses were scattered along the dirt road. White smoke rose from the chimneys of several low-lying homes only to be whipped by the strong wintry wind. A few dozen men and children braved the cold morning weather and silently watched us marching north. They were poorly dressed; only a few wore dirty heavy coats. We waved to them, but they didn't respond. I didn't understand then why they were so apathetic. In retrospect, I know that though the South Korean Army was winning in this region and continued to advance toward the Korea-China Border, the local people might have heard that on the western front the U.S. forces had been badly defeated and had begun to retreat. Thus, the locals must have been in a quandary.

CLOSE CALL

By November 28, 1950, our unit had advanced to within forty miles of the Tumen River, which lies on the northeastern border with China. We expected to reach the river by mid-December at the latest. After snowing all night, the weather turned sunny and balmy, and the snow began to melt. We marched in two columns along the slushy Chongjin-Hoeryong Highway. Our battalion commander, Major Cho, drove his Russian-made jeep between the columns. When we had begun our massive counterattack in mid-September, the North Koreans had abandoned their heavy equipment in a hasty retreat. The commander's jeep was one of those vehicles left behind. Ever since, he had proudly ridden in it.

By mid-day we marched, in high spirits, about seven miles north of Chongjin City. Suddenly booming and hissing noises came from the bushes on the right side of the highway. The hissing stopped, which meant the artillery shells would fall nearby. We threw ourselves flat along the frozen roadside and fired our rifles blindly in the direction of the noise. Ear-splitting explosions followed one after another, showering cold dirt over us. The jeep sped forward around a bend to avoid the bombardments. Just after the jeep moved, one shell fell on the very spot where the vehicle had been and exploded thunderously. A few more shells fell here and there, then stopped as quickly as they had begun, but we kept firing for ten or fifteen more minutes before we got up and checked to see if anyone had been hit. No one was hurt. We had been lucky.

Even though the shelling had ceased, I was still shaken. Since the war had begun, I had experienced many artillery attacks much worse than this one. Yet I had not been as badly affected as I was this time. I wondered why. Perhaps because we had been winning every battle we had fought for the last two and half months, I was psychologically unprepared for an unexpected bombardment.

Captain Chung sent a combat platoon to the area to search and kill the enemy still hiding there. About half an hour later, the troops returned. The platoon leader reported that all was clear, and that the North Koreans had abandoned three anti-tank artillery pieces, and no shells were left behind. He said that his soldiers had disabled the big guns by rolling grenades into the barrels.

I thought of the battalion commander. Had the shell fallen a few seconds sooner, he might have been blown to pieces. Major Cho was extremely lucky that day; God saved him, even though not many soldiers under his command liked him. He did not possess the qualities of a good commander; he was known to be selfish and not too intelligent. He couldn't even read military maps because they were written in English.

BURNED ENEMY TRUCK
AND DEAD ENEMY SOLDIER

As we advanced farther north inland, the snow became deeper, almost knee-high in some places, slowing our march. To make matters worse, a wind began to blow from Siberia, over one hundred miles north of us. A couple of burned-out North Korean Army trucks blocked the narrow road. The snow exposed the front of the wreck, piling up a few feet behind it. An extensively burned North Korean soldier dangled upside down from the driver's side, exposing charred jaws so grotesque that I averted my eyes. But curiosity made me look again. Amazingly, the teeth were vibrantly colored antique ivory. Once he had been a living person, but now he was nothing but charcoal. I thought, if I am killed, let me die while we are winning so that our quartermasters can give me a proper burial. Someone behind me urged, "Move!" Not bothering to see who had shouted, I resumed my march, circumventing the wrecked truck and the dead soldier.

FAKE ENEMY

On November 29, 1950, our company reached a mountain range about twenty-five miles south of the China-Korea border. A foot-deep snow had already blanketed this northeasternmost region of the Korean peninsula. Earlier that afternoon, our combat platoons had cleared the area and established a defense perimeter on the ridges. We then marched a couple of miles north, without further enemy contact. Just before sunset, the company commander ordered the administrative and ordnance personnel, including me, to camp in a village for the night, about half a mile behind the line where our combat troops were deployed.

We occupied a couple of humble farmhouses which were very cold. They must have been vacant for a long time. MSgt. Lee directed us to gather firewood for the clay under-floor heating system. According to him, the temperature might tumble below zero degrees Fahrenheit. Because of the extreme weather, he organized a one-hour sentry duty rotation instead of the normal two hours and posted the first sentry. My turn would start at 3 a.m. I quickly prepared to sleep because there wasn't any light available except for the sergeant's flashlight.

In the middle of the night, an urge to pee woke me from a deep sleep. I got up reluctantly and stepped out into the snow-covered courtyard with my rifle slung over my shoulder. The frigid air stung sharply through my thick winter coat, and I shivered. It was hauntingly quiet. The half-moon, frozen in the purple-blue sky, slightly illuminated the landscape. The looming silhouettes of the mountains on both sides of the narrow valley made me feel even colder. In such a freezing environment I could hardly make my fingers unbutton my padded trousers, cotton long johns, and underwear.

While I was urinating in a corner of the yard, someone put a gun to my back and ordered in a deep voice, "Don't move! Raise your hands, slowly."

An incredible jolt of fear ran down my spine. As ordered, I slowly raised my arms. My trousers slipped down to the ground, leaving me exposed and petrified.

He poked my back with his rifle barrel a couple of times and directed, "Keep your arms up higher. Listen to me." He kept silent for a moment which seemed an eternity. Then he continued, "What is your name?"

"Sergeant Kim Tae-hyok," I answered in an almost inaudible voice.

"This is Corporal Lee Jong-kook," he said, then giggled. He was one of my best friends.

I crumbled onto the frozen snow like a dead man. I was so shocked that my bare skin didn't even register the cold. I had no strength to either speak or move.

Jong-kook pulled me up by the hand, put his arm around my neck, and asked, "Did I frighten you, Tae-hyok?" I didn't respond. He continued, "I am sorry, Tae-hyok, but what the hell were you doing out here in the middle of the f@#$&*@ frigid night?"

Instead of answering, I punched him hard in the stomach.

He groaned, "Ow!"

I yelled, "You son of a bitch. You frightened me to death." I slugged him again, saying, "Don't ever do that again. I was peeing." As I pulled up my trousers to cover my freezing privates, I found the front of my pants wet. Despite the extraordinary circumstances, I had not been able to hold it. In a few seconds, the stain was frozen.

Squeezing my shoulder again, he said, "You must have a soybean-sized bladder to make you get up in the middle of this cold night. When is your guard duty?"

"Three."

"You have a couple more hours before your turn. You had better go back to sleep." He pulled his arm from my shoulder and began to trot in place. He gently pushed me toward the house.

I went back inside and lay on the heated floor, warming my frigid body. Fatigue caught up with me, and I dozed off eventually, fancying the war would end soon, and I could reunite with my parents.

ENEMY SCOUTS

Suddenly MSgt. Lee shouted, "Get up, everybody. Enemy scouts have infiltrated the village. Search and kill them!"

We quickly gathered our equipment and ran out to the courtyard. The half-moon slightly illuminated our surroundings. The sergeant split us into three groups and ordered, "You, you search every house on the left; the rest of you search on the right. I will lead the central part. Let's go! Kill them. No prisoners!"

I was teamed up with a private first class. We stopped outside the first house. Seeing no enemies, I directed the soldier to watch the kitchen entrance, while I opened the flimsy door to the living quarters, with my gun ready to shoot, yelling, "Don't move!" But the room was empty.

We cautiously moved on to the next house, which consisted of two quarters, one for guests and the other for family. The guest quarters had a main entrance and a small door at the far end of the building. It was dimly lit on this early morning, which was rather unusual. I gestured to my partner to watch the small door, while I burst into the guest room with my gun ready, and shouted, "Don't move!"

An old man in traditional white Korean attire sat cross-legged in the middle of the small guest room, smoking his pipe. He calmly said, "Please come in, young *Gukgun*" as if he were waiting for me. He appeared to be in his sixties; a Korean's life expectancy was just over fifty at the time.

I hastily responded, "Good morning, sir," and surveyed the room. There was a mid-sized futon on the floor with a thick cotton quilt over it. I saw a man sleeping. My hair stood on end. Aiming my rifle at him, I kicked him lightly and ordered, "Get up, slowly. Hold your hands behind your head." As ordered, he did. I stepped back from the old man and the other man. My eyes darted between the two. I yelled, "Lean against the wall! Keep your hands up!" He was tall, lanky, and undernourished. He had a crew-cut, his face was dirty, and his lips were badly cracked and bleeding. He was trembling. His appearance indicated that he was a North Korean soldier, but he wore padded white cotton civilian clothes instead of a North Korean Army uniform and showed no belligerence. I wondered if he was a deserter.

I surveyed the sparsely furnished room, searching for hidden arms. Finding no weapons, I politely asked the old man to slowly turn the quilt and futon upside down to see if there was any military hardware underneath. Again, nothing was found. I relaxed a little.

I asked the suspected enemy, "You are a North Korean soldier, one of the scouts, aren't you?"

He responded in an almost inaudible, pleading, quivering voice, "No, sir. I am not a North Korean soldier," and dropped his head.

With my rifle aimed at him, I ordered, "Face the wall. Keep your arms up!" Then, I asked the old man, "Sir, do you know this person?"

He mumbled, which convinced me that the other man was an enemy soldier.

Then I heard the soldier murmuring, "Oh, my children. Take care of your mom."

I ordered him to face me, and he did. He looked to be in his late thirties. I asked him how many children he had.

"Four, sir," and he began to sob, audibly. He mumbled, "I was drafted by the North Korean Army a few months ago, but I escaped because I do not believe in their cause. I have not heard from my family ever since."

Suddenly he reminded me of my eldest brother, who still lived in my hometown in North Korea with his wife and three children. He too might have been drafted by the North Korean Army and could have fallen into the same situation.

Although "Kill them. Take no prisoners!" were my orders, I couldn't shoot this unarmed, crying father of four in cold blood. That would be senseless, because we expected the war to end within a few weeks, as General MacArthur had claimed. So, I told him, "Go home, and take care of your family."

As I quickly left the room, the man bowed and said, "Thank you, sir," for his unexpected freedom. I rejoined my partner, hoping he had no inkling that I had disobeyed orders. Since he asked no questions, I didn't say anything. We just moved on. We continued searching, hoping to discover nothing. By the time we investigated the last house, dawn had broken, and we had encountered no one.

My partner said, "Sergeant Kim, I am glad we didn't find any enemy scouts, aren't you?"

"I certainly am." But I wondered what had made our group leader (a gentleman sergeant) issue such harsh orders for us to take no prisoners. Did he know some serious intelligence that we were not aware of?

AN UNEXPECTED HALF DAY RESPITE

When the search operation was over, all the squads huddled around our sergeant in an open, snow-covered field by the house where we had camped overnight and reported that no enemy had been found. I kept silent about my actions.

MSgt. Lee said, "I'm not surprised, because our neighboring platoon found the infiltrators first and attacked them." Then he ordered us to make a bonfire to warm our freezing bodies. We promptly scattered to collect firewood and found a big pile of seasoned pine, which a farmer might have harvested for fuel. We took some and started a fire which quickly grew large with loud cracks, spewing sparks into the sky. The heat was so intense that we had to step back. The brilliant sun shone on the snowy valley, and a group of American fighter bombers flew over us and began to bomb the enemy position only a couple of miles north. Our morale rose, and we talked and laughed, but the sergeant kept very quiet.

Shortly we received orders to stay where we had camped until further notice. MSgt. Lee posted a guard, then directed us to get back to the house. Entering the heated room, I took off my snow-covered boots, put my blanket over my feet, and rubbed my toes to alleviate the numbness, hoping to prevent frostbite. The rest of my comrades-in-arms quickly fell asleep and began snoring. As fatigue caught up with me, I too fell into oblivion.

GENERAL RETREAT ORDER

Suddenly MSgt. Lee yelled, "Get up, boys. Hurry to the courtyard!" We promptly jumped up, gathered our equipment, and went outside. It was around mid-afternoon and cloudy. While we slept, the weather had turned much calmer and milder. The sergeant performed a quick headcount, then ordered us to report to the Company Commander, Captain Chung, within an hour at the headquarters in a village a mile south. He led us to a shortcut across uneven, snowy farm fields. Usually, we chatted while marching until we got tired. But today, we were quiet. Only the monotonous crunching of our heavy boots broke the silence.

Upon arriving at our destination, we found that many soldiers and vehicles crowded the hamlet and the adjacent open fields, perhaps a battalion or more, including a field artillery unit. The howitzers and the trucks were parked along the main highway in a column ready to move south instead of north. I thought there would be more battles to fight before we would reach the China-Korea border for mopping-up operations, thus ending the war. The border lay about twenty-five miles farther north. Then why were the big guns ready to move south? Strange! Not a single civilian was around. I kept moving with my squad, lest I get left behind. Shortly we arrived at our company headquarters, finding that all the other units of the company had already assembled there. Snow began to fall.

As soon as we reported our arrival, the commander stepped onto a boulder and announced that the high command had ordered the entire 1st ROK Army Corps to withdraw immediately from the northeastern region of the peninsula. The entire crowd fell silent.

What, withdraw? My energy drained from every part of my body. I was unable to remain standing. I crumbled onto the freezing snow-covered ground. What do you mean, sir? The China-Korea border is less than twenty-five miles away, sir. For a few moments, my mind went blank.

Then I vaguely heard the commander's voice saying, "We must march back to Sŏngjin Port in three days. We shall depart in an hour. Quartermaster Sergeant, distribute canned rice. Eat supper quickly."

The sergeant and his assistants handed each of us a cold can the size of a beer can and urged us to eat. He murmured, "We have a long journey ahead of us."

MSgt. Lee led us to one of the bonfires. Hardly anyone talked. We sat on our backpacks around the roaring fire and opened the rice cans with our bayonets. It was cooked rice mixed with chopped kelp pieces. The food was dry and unappetizing. I took my baby brass spoon, which I had collected from a bombed-out house a few weeks earlier, from my winter jacket pocket and scooped the food into my mouth. I chewed and tried to swallow, but my emotion-choked throat did not allow the food to pass. I spit it out and threw the can into the bonfire. Soon the can began to sizzle, and I watched it absentmindedly for a few moments. I noticed MSgt. Lee, sitting next to me. I asked, "Sergeant, why are we pulling out of North Korea when we are winning? The Korea-China Border is less than twenty-five miles away."

"Tae-hyok, a massive Communist Chinese army group has trapped the First U.S. Marine Corps Division in the Chosin Reservoir area on our left flank. On the Western Front, the Eighth U.S. Army lost major battles to another huge Chinese army group. They say more than a half a million Chinese are fighting the UN forces. Even though we are winning on the northeastern front, we are in danger of being cut off, because we are too far out in front. That's why the high command has ordered us to retreat."

Then I realized why he had ordered us to take no prisoners. Apparently, he had prior intelligence that we would pull back sooner or later, of which I had not the slightest inkling. I had believed that the mighty UN forces on the central and western fronts had been winning the war, as we were, until that evening. I wondered if having let the sobbing North Korean scout go free was justified or not. He might have rejoined his unit and could now be chasing after us. I should have killed him, but how could I? Disobeying the sergeant's order bothered me, but I chose not to think about it.

My heart ached over the imminent retreat. I buried my head between my knees and thought about my family. I would never see them again, and my sweet dream of marrying the high school girl, who had smiled and scribbled the words 'sine and cosine' on my palm a few weeks earlier, faded.

COMMUNIST CHINA ENTERS THE WAR AND THE BATTLE OF CHOSIN RESERVOIR (CHANGJIN)

October 1950. The United Nations and Republic of Korea troops kept marching north toward the Yalu and Tumen Rivers, the two rivers on the border between North Korea and China. The Eighth Army in command by Lieutenant General Walton Walker was on the west side of the peninsula, and the Tenth Corps (aka X Corps) led by Major General Ned Almond was on the east side. General MacArthur had his sights on the entire peninsula. However, President Truman was so concerned about the possibility of China intervening in the war that he flew to Wake Island in the Pacific to meet with MacArthur on October 15.

It would be the only time they met in person. His main question for the General was about China and the Soviet Union. "What are the chances for Chinese or Soviet interference?" the President asked.[60] Truman feared World War III could occur if they suddenly came into the picture.

MacArthur responded, "Very little. Had they interfered in the first or second months it would have been decisive. We are no longer fearful of their intervention … The Chinese have 300,000 men in Manchuria. Of these probably not more than 100/125,000 are distributed along the Yalu River. Only 50/60,000 could be gotten across the Yalu River … With the Russians it is a little different. They have an Air Force in Siberia and a fairly good one, with excellent pilots equipped with some jets and B–25 and B–29 planes … Our own Air and Ground Forces are not as good as the Marines but they are effective. Between untrained Air and Ground Forces an air umbrella is impossible without a lot of joint training. I believe it just wouldn't work with Chinese Communist ground and Russian air. We are the best."[61]

MacArthur told him that he'd like to "withdraw the Eighth Army to Japan by Christmas."[62] Before leaving, the President awarded MacArthur a Distinguished Service Medal.

Despite MacArthur's reassurances, a twist to the war unfolded. While the North Koreans were retreating, Mao then committed (as promised to Kim Il Sung if the U.S. or Japan entered the war) to sending in his Chinese Communist troops. China was entering the war. The Chinese Army, initially set for Taiwan, were suddenly going to fight for North Korea. There were around 260,000 Communist Chinese who were already in North Korea.[63]

The Battle of Chosin was one of the worst battles fought due to the huge number of enemy forces combined with the cold. It is forever remembered in U.S. Marine Corps history. Its nickname was Frozen Chosin. When the Marines and soldiers got to their positions, they could hardly dig foxholes because the ground was frozen. They were soon surrounded by an unexpected army of thousands of Communist Chinese soldiers.

MacArthur's plan to take the entire peninsula quickly vanished due to the massive number of Chinese entering the war. He met with Almond and Walker on November 28 and decided to move the troops south. The battle lasted from November 27 to December 13.*

During the day, the Chinese would hide under white sheets, blending in with the environment so as not to be seen by the aviators flying in their Corsairs who were planning to perform air strikes on the enemy by using rockets, bombs, and napalm (jellied gasoline which burned the enemy to death). UN planes would also come in to drop ammunition, gasoline, and food.

In the dark, bugles blared, cymbals clashed, and the whistling and yelling of the Chinese forces rang in the ears of the UN forces who were outnumbered in some places 10:1 by the Chinese.[64] They would come, wave after wave. There were upwards of 120,000 Chinese troops in total.

---

* It's important to note that The Battle of Ch'ongch'on River took place on the western side of the Korean peninsula from November 25 to December 2, 1950. UN forces (the Eighth U.S. Army led by Lt. Gen. Walton Walker, ROK II Corps, Turkish Brigade, and the 27th British Commonwealth Brigade) battled the Communist Chinese. Like in Chosin, they faced brutally cold conditions and the Chinese attacked in waves.

Compare this to 30,000 UN troops (including ROK soldiers).[65] But the Chinese were not equipped for the cold, and they held vintage arms. Often, after one wave of Chinese were shot down, the next would pick up their dead comrades' weapons and run forward to attack. What they had was sheer numbers and will.

It was at times minus thirty degrees Fahrenheit.[66] Weapons didn't always work, resulting in hand-to-hand combat. The troops suffered from frostbite and hypothermia. Many, on both sides, froze to death, lying in the snow with their hands raised frozen in the air or without boots. Barricades were created by piling up the dead.[67] There was one benefit from the cold: those who lost their limbs survived due to their blood freezing instead of bleeding out. Clothing would be taken off the dead to keep the wounded warm.[68]

There were a few sparks of hope. Ammunition was low, so a request was made for 60mm mortar shells under the code name "Tootsie Rolls." The individual who got the order didn't know that "Tootsie Rolls" was the code name for ammunition so actual Tootsie Rolls were parachuted down to the troops. The Marines felt like it was Christmas! Not only did the candies taste good, but they also found they could be used to plug bullet holes in their machines so their vehicles, hoses, gas tanks, and other equipment would then be fixed.[69]

The costs, however, in the battle were beyond high. Task Force MacLean/Faith was decimated: out of 3,200 men (700 of whom were ROK soldiers), there were about 1,000 survivors, and of those, 385 were "able-bodied."[70] And still the challenges went beyond the fight between men.

Major General Oliver P. Smith had commissioned Lieutenant Colonel John Partridge to construct an airfield at Hagaru, which was not a small feat given the frozen ground. He accomplished this with his engineering team. And yet, another engineering feat took place. He needed to build a bridge over Funchilin Pass on the main supply route. Thousands of troops depended on that bridge. If they didn't cross it, their lives would be in peril. They airdropped steel pieces from Japan, with one section weighing 2,900 pounds. But this new construction needed support underneath it.

The only thing available? Dead Chinese bodies.[71] With the completion of the bridge repairs, Marines, Army personnel and the British Royal Marines were able to get to Hagaru. Those who were seriously wounded were air-lifted. Once the troops got to Hungnam, they boarded Navy ships. The Navy evacuated thousands, including civilians.

Casualties among the UN and ROK troops totaled 17,883. 7,338 of those were due to the cold. Estimates for the Chinese were 48,156 casualties, including Mao's eldest son.[72]

> *"Fires were built alongside the road. Fires which gave no heat, for the hours near dawn were so cold that nothing could break their grip. Nor did the fires cause concern among the men ... they had long since ceased to worry that they might be next to fall from enemy bullets. Too much exhaustion and pain and death had been their companions. They no longer thought ... or cared.*
>
> *The cold had cut into [a Marine's] face and eyes until even the look of animal survival was gone. When asked what he would have wanted if he could have had any wish, he continued to stand motionless, with empty eyes. Then his lips began to open slightly, and close, as though the effort of a word was too great. He tried again, and failed. He stood just looking into his glove holding the can [of frost-coated beans]. He tried once more ... as he tried his eyes went up into the graying sky, and he said, 'Give me tomorrow.'"[73]*

—David Douglas Duncan,
This is War! A Photo-Narrative of the Korean War

Those who survived are known as The Chosin Few. They had been to a frozen hell and back.

CHAPTER 19

The Long March

November - December 1950

November 30, 1950. The company first sergeant conveyed the division orders that each soldier should carry three or four ammo bandoleers, two grenades, and emergency provisions to expedite our retreat. Any extras were to be piled up at a designated place so that the division corps of engineers could destroy them as soon as we cleared the area. Each bandoleer held six clips of eight rounds. He directed the combat platoons to proceed to the dumping place in alphabetical order, with the administration squad first.

Our sergeant performed a headcount, then ordered in a somber voice, "Soldiers, we have a long march ahead. Let's do our utmost to stay together and help each other. Now let's move out." He led us to an empty field a short distance away, ahead of other units. I knew we had to move, but I wished I hadn't heard him.

Reaching the field, I found a mound of ammunition, including dangerous explosives such as grenades and a few boxes of very powerful 80mm mortar shells. Each box contained two shells. If someone carelessly threw a burning cigarette into it, the mound could catch fire, and a massive explosion would follow. I shivered.

I did not have anything to discard, because I had only three 30-round magazines for my carbine, two grenades, and a bundle of papers, including my company roster and related personnel documents. Being a company clerk, I had to carry those papers with me wherever I went and keep them from falling into enemy hands. Only a couple of my friends unloaded their extra ammo bandoleers onto the mound. Then we quickly proceeded toward the highway leading to Sŏngjin Port where we expected to board an American troop transport ship.

The snow fell heavier by the hour, and dusk had already set in. The moon highlighted the silhouette of the tall poplars along the highway. Poplars were planted along the sides of all major roads, about fifty feet apart, all the way across the country. As we approached the road, many soldiers came into view, marching southward in two orderly columns; between them, a convoy of army trucks moved slowly. When we reached the highway, a few traffic control MPs halted us until the rear of the columns passed by, then directed us to move onto the road before the next unit approached.

As our unit stepped onto the highway, MSgt. Lee performed a headcount one more time to make sure no one had been left behind, which made me respect him more as my leader. We silently followed the columns. The heavy snow continued to fall, turning us into walking snowmen. As we moved on, it became darker, but the poplars lining the roadside kept us from stepping into the drainage ditches. The headlights of intermittently passing trucks helped us as well.

The snow showed no sign of abating; with each step, we sank deeper and felt heavier. Also, I felt hungry, so I took out a small amount of unsalted crackers from my winter jacket pocket and munched them. But I couldn't swallow. My mouth had become so dry that I scooped up a handful of snow, put it into my mouth, and moistened the crackers enough to chew them. My stomach growled. Even though I had a full bag of crackers in my backpack, I didn't take them out because it would take at least five minutes.

I did my best to keep up with my squad. Despite the food which I had eaten, I lagged farther behind my friends. I wished I had eaten the lousy canned rice instead of tossing it into the bonfire earlier that evening. I regretted that I had let my emotions control me.

Then an unfamiliar voice behind me urged, "Move faster!" I did and found myself among strangers, apparently belonging to some other unit of the 3rd Battalion. My squad was nowhere to be seen. Panic! But I took a deep breath and resolved to reach my destination, the Sŏngjin Port.

The snow continued to fall so heavily that only a few soldiers in front of me could be seen. But sheer will kept me in line with the other soldiers. The snow-covered equipment hung heavily on our shoulders. Even the rifles looked like white sticks. No one talked; we just kept moving.

As night progressed, my determination seemed to wane. Soldiers passed by me one after another; I was slowly falling behind.

Then someone pushed me from behind and urged, "Don't sleep! Keep walking." Apparently, I had dozed off and halted. I didn't even have the energy to say thank you. I struggled to keep pace with the others. Then a couple of trucks approached from behind. I stepped aside and raised my hand to flag them down, but neither of them stopped.

I thought the drivers were cold-hearted. Then I noticed that the trucks were already overloaded with supplies and a dozen soldiers and understood why they did not stop. Disappointed, I did my utmost to keep up with the others, walking on the tracks made by the truck wheels.

Sometime later, I found myself trailing the columns again. They seemed to have disappeared into the heavy snow. I didn't see anyone behind me. Cold penetrated my padded fatigues and winter coat. I was no longer sweating but began to shiver. I was so tired that I was tempted to sit down on the roadside to rest, but I resisted because I knew that I would never be able to get up. I forced myself to continue moving. Despite my determination to reach the Sŏngjin Port, I began to doubt if I could really make it.

Then a vehicle approached slowly with headlights blazing, illuminating the snowy highway. I turned around, stood in the middle of the road, and raised my arm high, gesturing for a ride. The vehicle honked, but I kept standing where I was.

To my surprise, it halted a few yards from me. Then somebody climbed down from the vehicle, and shouted, "What the hell are you doing here in the middle of nowhere, you skinny Tae-hyok? Where is the rest of your squad?" It was Battalion Quartermaster Sgt. Kwon. "Climb up onto the cargo bay! I don't have room for you in the cabin." He took a small package from his U.S. Army parka, putting it into my overcoat pocket, and said, "It's some cookies." Then he helped me climb on top of the heaped supplies and tossed me a blanket. "Watch yourself lest you fall off the truck!"

I thanked him for the ride and the cookies. To fend off the wind and snow,

I burrowed between two piles of straw bags filled with rice. I cleared the snow off the place and took my backpack off my shoulders. Then I wrapped myself in Sgt. Kwon's dry blanket, retrieved my own from my backpack, and put it over the other, covering myself from head to toe. They made me feel comfortable and warm.

Once settled, I took the package that Sgt. Kwon had given me from my pocket. I carefully opened it, put a piece in my mouth, and chewed gingerly. The mouth-watering caramel melted and softened my dry mouth. I had never experienced this sweetness before and savored it as long as I could. Then a sudden jolt of the truck almost forced me to spit out the precious cookie, but I quickly swallowed it. I emptied the bag, pacifying my hungry stomach. Despite the jolts, fatigue caught up with me, and I soon fell asleep until the sergeant shouted, "Tae-hyok, get down."

I raised my head from the blanket. It was still snowing and dark. I was buried under a thick snow quilt. The truck was parked in front of a lone farmhouse in the middle of nowhere. The engine of the vehicle continued rumbling, and the headlights illuminated the farmhouse. I didn't know how long and how far we had traveled, but I felt much more rested than when I had struggled alone in the heavy snow. I shook the snow off my blankets, retrieved my backpack and rifle, and climbed down from the truck.

While I was standing, bewildered and cold, in the middle of the courtyard, another supply truck pulled in, and a half dozen soldiers got off the vehicle and joined Sgt. Kwon. They were his staff. He directed them to cook as much rice as they could. He assigned some of them to unload the rice bags from the truck, and others to fetch water from the well in the corner of the courtyard and start a fire in the kitchen oven.

Despite being exhausted, I approached the sergeant, expressed my sincere appreciation again, and asked if I could be of help in any way. He responded, "Skinny kid, get in the house and rest until breakfast is ready. A long march is ahead."

Dragging myself into a room, I found a dozen comrades-in-arms packed in and snoring loudly under a flickering lamp. I peeked into the next room; it was also full of soldiers. The landlord and his family were nowhere to be seen. Perhaps they had followed the retreating soldiers to Sŏngjin Port? I squeezed in between two soldiers, checked if the safety-pin of my carbine was locked, and lay on the heated floor, using my backpack as a pillow. As usual, I held the weapon against my chest like a baby, closing my eyes.

Someone shouted, "Get up!" It was one of the quartermaster staff, holding the door wide open. Cold air swept into the room, shaking us awake. I gathered my equipment and went outside along with the others. Deep white snow blanketed the whole world, and the brilliant morning sun needled my sleepy eyes. A couple of white cloud patches traveled across the powder blue sky. Everything looked so beautiful and peaceful that I almost forgot the war. Then suddenly, with earth-shaking thunder, two groups of American jet fighter planes, three in each group, flying low, came from the East Sea, heading north across the blue sky. Long columns of soldiers marched south along the highway.

I noticed that many refugees mixed with the soldiers, mostly young men, but some were whole families. The men were burdened with heavy stuff on their backs, while the women carried their babies. I wondered how far they could possibly travel in such cold, snowy weather. I hoped they would reach their destination, wherever it might be.

All the other soldiers who had spent the night in the house joined me, but none of them were from my squad. A Sergeant First Class came in front of us and said, "It appears that I am the highest ranking among us. I shall be the temporary leader until each of you rejoins your own company. Any objections?" Unanimously, we said, "No, Sergeant!" I was glad someone with firm leadership qualities had volunteered to lead us.

Then I noticed a soldier approaching us from the highway. It was Corporal Chae from my squad. He was in his mid-twenties, and a warmhearted man with a solid physique. I hollered to him with excitement and asked where the rest of our squad was. He said because of the heavy snow he had lost the group, and continued, "I think they have gone farther ahead of me."

Our temporary group leader, SFC Rim, led us toward the highway where we joined the endless columns of orderly retreating combat soldiers. A convoy of a couple dozen supply trucks and a field artillery battery slowly moved south between the columns of foot soldiers. As they passed, their tires left hard-packed furrows in the snow. We followed in the furrows, where it was easier to walk. The brilliant morning sun reflected on the fresh white snow, intermittently blinding us. Despite the large number of marching soldiers, hardly anyone talked, perhaps because they were too tired and deeply depressed about retreating.

As we marched through a small town farther south, a dozen frightened militia men armed with Russian rifles joined us, some with their wives and children. The women piggybacked their babies, covering them with thick cotton quilts to keep them warm, and the men carried A-frames loaded with emergency provisions and beddings on their backs. They were desperate to move as fast as they could, but not well prepared to cope with the harsh winter climate of this farthest northeastern part of the peninsula.

They said they were anti-communist guerrillas and had fought the North Korean Internal Security Forces detachment to defend their town. Their leader, a man in his thirties, said, "Late afternoon yesterday, a *Gukgun* officer, a native of our town, accompanied by two soldiers, dropped by our militia station and informed us that the South Korean Army would pull out of North Korea and advised us to go to Sŏngjin Port as soon as possible. He took his parents and siblings with him last evening. Surely the communist soldiers and internal security forces will retake our town, hunt us down, and execute us. So, we have to go with you, wherever you are going."

One young militiaman in his late teens next to me murmured, "My hometown is farther north. The *Gukgun* never had a chance to reach that far. I might never see my parents again!" He wiped his eyes.

His muttering was heart-wrenching and took me back to the previous evening; I felt deep empathy with him. Approaching him, I put my hand on his shoulder and said, "My friend, my parents live in Hwanghae-do, North Korea. I have neither seen nor heard from them since I left for Seoul and joined the *Gukgun* over two and a half years ago. When my company commander told us that we would withdraw from North Korea, I cried, too, fearing I might never see them again. Now, you must take care of yourself. Why don't you join the *Gukgun?*"

He looked at me and responded, "That's a good idea. I think I will," and smiled. He quickened his pace and joined his friends. Seeing him cheer up, I felt good.

SFC Rim, signaled the militia to halt. Then he called all of us and said, "It will take at least three days for the militia to reach Sŏngjin Port. As you can see, they do not have much. How about pooling our emergency rice and giving it to them so that they won't starve? This is voluntary. We shall get our resupply when we rejoin our own units."

We all agreed and took out the rice from our backpacks. The sergeant and I removed our helmets and collected it. The rice almost filled them. Then we went over to the nervous militia, and my sergeant said to their leader, "Sir, we pooled our emergency rice for you. It's not much, but you can make a couple of meals out of it."

They were dumbfounded, gazing down at the rice, then looking up at the sergeant for a few moments before saying, "Thank you, Sergeant." The leader accepted our offering and bowed to the sergeant a few times. Then he asked his men if anyone had a sack. One man lowered his A-frame, and retrieved a homemade cotton sack which contained a small amount of millet. The leader carefully poured the rice into the sack and returned our helmets. The whole group expressed their gratitude to us with "*Gamsah-hamnida!*" (Thank you) and bowed. We replied, "*Chun-maneyo* (You are welcome)."

As we marched, my sergeant urged the refugee families to speed up their journey to Sŏngjin Port so that they might find some means of transportation. Then we continued our march, and they set out on their arduous trip. We never saw them again. I hope they arrived safely.

By early afternoon we arrived at a school yard, our 3rd Battalion assembly place. Upon our arrival, our temporary squad split, saying goodbye to each other. Then we rejoined our respective units. Even though it was only for a few hours, I was honored to have had the sergeant with his humanity and excellent leadership guide us. Regretfully, I never met him again.

I soon found my squad and reunited with my old comrades-in-arms. Patting my helmet, they welcomed me with heartwarming words. "You skinny Tae-hyok, good to see you in one piece. We feared you might have frozen to death. Now you are with us." It was so comforting to be with my old friends again.

Our company first sergeant conveyed the battalion orders to resume our march to the next destination about twelve miles southwest along the coast-line, which I assumed would be an all-night endeavor. He ordered us to move out by platoon number, putting the administration squad, including me, in the front.

MSgt. Lee led our squad, and I followed right behind him. I was much more energized and confident that afternoon than the previous day and knew I would not drop behind again. The unseasonably balmy weather made our march much easier than the preceding day. Despite the beautiful weather, hardly anybody talked. We continued our uneventful retreat.

Intermittent convoys of trucks slowly moved between two columns of soldiers and refugees—loaded vehicles southward, empty ones in the opposite direction. Choi complained, "Why are those crazy empty trucks going back instead of giving us a ride?"

Lee answered, "I think they will pick up those combat units who are guarding the rear of our division so that we can safely reach the Sŏngjin Port. They deserve the truck convoy." Choi didn't even acknowledge the sergeant. We all silently continued our march.

The short winter day soon turned to evening, but the gleam of the white snow kept us from stumbling into the drain ditches. Chang in front of me said, "Message, no mess truck tonight. Eat crackers whenever you are hungry." I recited the message to Kim Jae-kook behind me. Despite the disheartening message, no one complained; we just kept moving. Unlike the previous night, the weather was clear.

After a long night's weary trekking, we reached a school yard early the following morning. The school building lay in ruins. A squad of South Korean Army Military Police directed us to the far side of the yard where a fleet of Army trucks were parked with their engines running. I hoped they would take us to the Sŏngjin Port. As our entire battalion of soldiers moved in, a rumor spread that we would ride in the trucks. The weather in this northeasternmost region of the peninsula was freezing. Standing still on the snowy playground made us even colder. I, a chopstick-thin boy, began to shiver. I trotted vigorously in place to generate body heat. I wished I had something hot to drink.

Suddenly the Battalion Sergeant Major's booming voice blared throughout the playground, "We are indeed riding the trucks. Line up by company numbers! Each Company First Sergeant will direct you aboard."

Even though we had subsisted on rock hard, tasteless ROKA crackers for almost twenty hours, we weary foot-soldiers spontaneously shouted, "Hurray!"

As directed, MSgt. Lee led us to a designated truck and let us climb up on the cargo bed. As we did so, he performed a headcount. Although the truck was already almost full, we continued to squeeze in. When Lee boarded, the driver closed the cargo bay door.

Soon the convoy slowly drove out to the highway and traveled southward. We leaned against each other like a bundle of standing logs. Whenever the truck hit a pothole, we were tossed up and down. Despite the rough ride, I fell asleep standing, until someone shook me wildly and shouted, "Goddamnit, wake up. Don't lean against me!"

The brilliant sun shone on my sleepy eyes, and I instinctively covered them with my sleeve for a few moments. It appeared to be mid-afternoon, which suggested that we had driven thirty miles so far. Somehow my helmet had fallen off my head and onto my backpack. I asked the soldier who had shouted at me, "Where are we?" He spat out, "How the hell do I know?"

The convoy later drove into the frozen fields by the highway. Our driver shouted, "Boys, get off my truck! We have to fetch the rest of the regiment." When he opened the cargo bay door, we jumped out and huddled around our respective group leaders. I guessed the vehicle had carried at least two platoons—more than sixty soldiers. Amazing!

After a headcount, MSgt. Lee reported to the Company First Sergeant. When all the company assembled, the First Sergeant delivered our orders that we should reach Sŏngjin Port by the next morning, about fifteen miles, which meant another all-night march. But I was very grateful for the convoy that had saved us from a foot journey of perhaps two days and two nights.

"Move out," the sergeant shouted. The entire company began to march in two columns along the relatively flat, snow-covered highway. The mild weather expedited our journey, and we arrived at Sŏngjin Port the following morning.

Despite the cold early hour, thousands of confused, anxious refugees huddled along the sidewalks, not knowing where to go. The retreating South Korean soldiers ingloriously marched in columns toward the port. Scores of military vehicles slowly drove between the columns with intermittent honks, some with artillery in tandem. Only a few weeks earlier, the citizens of the city had welcomed us, the victorious army, enthusiastically waving home-made South Korean flags. Now we are pulling out of North Korea, where I was born and spent the first fifteen years of my life, and my parents may still be living, I thought. Tears streamed down my cold cheeks. I was dragging my weary feet along with my comrades-in-arms when suddenly MSgt. Lee shouted, "We shall be bivouacking here." He pointed in the direction of a small house near a big well-kept house, which I later found out had been occupied by the battalion commander and his staff.

After entering the small house, I crashed until someone shouted, "Supper!" I wished to sleep more, but after surviving for a few days on only army crackers, I couldn't afford to miss regular food. As soon as I finished the meal, I returned to sleep again until the next morning. I slept about eighteen hours.

TWO NURSE POWS

MSgt. Lee sent me to query the battalion sergeant major about our next move. But when I arrived at the command post, I found no one there except Corporal Pak on guard duty. I asked him, "Where did everyone go? Where can I find the Sergeant Major?"

"They all went over to the regiment headquarters except me. I don't even know where it is. Damn, it's cold. Let's get inside." Then he led me into the building. It was a large clean room, divided into two sections by four sliding doors. They were half open.

I noticed two women in traditional Korean dresses huddled together, their heads almost touching. They were in their early twenties. One appeared slightly younger. I asked the corporal in a low voice, "Who are these women? Are they the commander's relatives?"

The corporal cautiously said, "They are North Korean Army nurse officers, now our POWs."

"Then why are they being kept here instead of being sent to the regiment headquarters?"

He whispered into my ear, "The battalion commander and his staff had sex with them."

"Oh my God, how could they do that?" Feeling sick to my stomach, I turned around and made my way back.

Returning to my camp, I reported to MSgt. Lee that everyone but Corporal Pak had gone over to the regiment headquarters, and he did not even know where the headquarters was located. I did not mention the two female POWs.

The following day MSgt. Lee sent me again to find out if our ship had arrived. But once more I found only Corporal Pak on guard duty. I asked him, "Where the hell has everyone gone?"

"They went over to the regiment headquarters again, leaving me alone. I guess I am low on the totem pole. I do not know what the hell they are doing there." He seemed very unhappy.

I also noticed that the two female POWs were nowhere to be seen. "Where are the two women? Have they been sent to the regiment headquarters?"

Pak somberly, hesitantly responded, "No, they have been executed."

I was horrified. "Oh my God, what do you mean by 'They have been executed'? They were nurses, not combatants." Suddenly the crying enemy scout came to my mind. Only a few days earlier I had let him go home against my leader's order 'Take no prisoners!', because I had believed the war would be over within a few weeks. Thinking about him, I asked Pak, "Who executed them?"

He hesitated for a few moments, then mumbled, "The battalion commander ordered me to do so."

I was speechless. That damn commander, Captain Chung, had had sex with the girls, then ordered the poor corporal to execute the hapless, unarmed nurse POWs? What a brute! Suddenly I thought about my only cousin Bochae and my niece Yun-ok in their late teens, back in my hometown. They could have been drafted by the North Korean Army and fallen into the same situation. I shuddered.

For a while neither of us talked. After a deep breath, I asked, "Did you really shoot them to death? Where did you bury them?"

He silently looked down at the snow-covered ground for some time, then said, "I took them out to a nearby railroad track and shot them." A pause. Then he murmured, "I don't know if I aimed right. Why did he order me to do it?"

Without responding, I made my way back. The commander and his staff had raped the two women prisoners, then executed them. How could they do that? Weren't they just nurses? Weren't they Koreans, too? Damn war, damn commander!

Then someone hollered from behind, "Hey, skinny Tae-hyok!"

I turned around and saw Battalion Quartermaster Sergeant Kwon with his assistants who had given me a lift five nights earlier. I greeted him, "Good morning, Sergeant. Thank you so much for the ride. Without you, I could have frozen to death."

Disregarding my thanks, he shouted, "What the hell are you doing on the street all by yourself? Lost again?" He laughed boisterously, then tapped me on the helmet. He continued, "I am glad you made it. By the way, tell your group leader that our ship will arrive soon. Sergeant Major wants all the platoon sergeants and administration squad leaders to come to headquarters by noon for boarding instructions." He then made his way back to his camp.

I hurried back and conveyed the sergeant major's directive to our leader, MSgt. Lee. He promptly headed for the headquarters.

Meanwhile I joined my friends and chatted with them. But images of the two nurses and Corporal Pak's murmuring 'I don't know if I aimed right' repeatedly returned to my mind. Did he really execute the two helpless female POWs? I doubted he had done so because he was too warmhearted. I knew that he was in his mid-twenties and had a younger sister. Perhaps she was about the same age as the two nurses. I also learned that they had lost their parents when he was in fourth grade; his mom first, then his dad. After their deaths, relatives had fostered them separately. He had to quit school to help on his foster parents' farm, because they were too poor to support his education. Likewise, his sister also quit school and did chores for her new family. He was always concerned about her well-being. When he aimed his rifle at the two nurses, he might have thought about his sister, shot his gun into the air, and let the nurses go.

WAITING FOR THE SHIP

While waiting for MSgt. Lee's return, some of us took a nap, while others played *Hwatu* (a Korean card game). I joined the game to calm my anxiety.

By mid-afternoon MSgt. Lee returned and gathered all of us, then gave us boarding instructions.

He said, "Everyone, bring all of your equipment with you, including your backpacks and canteens." When we all huddled in front of him, he continued, "Listen carefully to what I say and follow it!

Lock the safety of your rifle. Do not unlock it until further notice. Take out the ammo clip from the magazine and secure it in your ammo belt. Check if a round is loaded in the chamber. If it is, take it out immediately. Check if the safety pins of your grenades are securely in place.

Once we board the ship, keep your weapon in a safe place. Do not play with it until we disembark. I emphasize, DO NOT PLAY WITH YOUR WEAPONS UNTIL WE LEAVE THE SHIP!"

Even though we always kept the safety buttons of our weapons locked except when fighting, we checked them and took out the ammunition from the magazines.

When we finished, the sergeant barked, "KEEP THE SAFETY BUTTONS LOCKED! Do you hear me?"

We shouted back, "Yes, Sergeant."

He continued, "According to the sergeant major, if the Sŏngjin Port is not deep enough for an American troop transport ship, it will anchor offshore, and small boats will ferry us to her. Then we will climb up onto the ship using rope ladders."

Corporal Chun interrupted, "Sergeant, what do you mean by rope ladder? I have never seen one before."

He responded, "You dummy, a rope ladder is a rope ladder. I haven't seen one either." We all laughed, which somewhat broke the tension.

The sergeant moved on, "The ship is very big; she can carry more than three thousand men and all their equipment. Once you get on the ferryboat, do the following. Secure your rifle on top of your backpack so that it may not fall into the sea while you are climbing; reach up to a rung and hold it firmly, then carefully put your foot on a rung and start to climb up slowly; do not look down at the sea, which might make you seasick. Instead, just look up and continue climbing. The ladders are hung along the sides of the ship from the deck to the boats. The ropes are as thick as a man's wrist and very strong; they will not break. Any questions?"

There was silence. Everyone seemed overwhelmed.

"Have any of you ever been aboard an oceangoing ship?"

Once again, silence; no one had. I wasn't surprised because our battalion had been organized three years earlier in the most rural region of the South Korean peninsula and recruited locally. Most of us had been farmers before joining the army.

The sergeant stated, "The ship will arrive anytime today or tomorrow. We will stay together and wait for its arrival. Meanwhile, take some rest." Then he sat on the bare floor, leaning his back against the wall with his eyes closed. I sat next to him. He said, "Tae-hyok, I know you came from North Korea. Where is your hometown? How far is it from here?"

"Hwanghae-do Province. Maybe three hundred miles southwest of here."

"How old were you when you left your parents?"

"Fifteen."

"Fifteen—a little boy! You mean they let you leave home alone and cross the 38th Parallel to South Korea? You were a brave boy!" He paused for a few moments, then said, "It appears that we are pulling back to the south of the 38th Parallel. I am sorry that you didn't have a chance to reunite with your parents. Damn war!"

I had neither seen nor heard from my parents for two and a half years. I sighed and looked uncertain.

Tapping my shoulder, the sergeant said, "Tae-hyok, cheer up. Who knows, the UN forces might soon counterattack the goddamn Chinese and push them back to China." He kept quiet for a few moments, then continued, "I hope the port is deep enough for the ship so that we can board her using gangways instead of rope-ladders."

I echoed, "Master Sergeant Lee, I hope so, too. I have never been to the sea before. I saw the ocean from a distance for the first time only two months ago near Gangneung City, while we were victoriously marching northward."

He murmured, "We made an arduous march of about one hundred miles," trailing off with an almost inaudible phrase 'in the deep snow'. He fell silent and began to snore, and his head drooped. During the extraordinary march, he did his utmost to keep our group together under an extreme snowstorm all the way to Sŏngjin Port. I appreciated his leadership. Soon I, too, dozed off until someone shouted, "Supper!"

The company quartermaster and his assistant unloaded two big buckets from their truck, then filled each of our mess kits with chilled rice and kimchi. The kimchi added a delicious kick to the bland rice. I wished for a bowl of hot soup in addition to the spicy vegetables to warm me up.

Then someone shouted from the kitchen, "Anyone want hot water?" It was Corporal Chae. He voluntarily did various chores which other soldiers were reluctant to do. Even though he was one of the lowest ranking soldiers in our group, everyone liked and valued him.

We all gathered around him in the kitchen. Filling our mess kits with hot water, he said, "I thought we needed something hot for the chilled rice. So, I boiled water." We thanked him. Adding hot water to the kimchi and rice produced a pungent acidic odor which made me cough a few times. But I enjoyed it and licked the mess kit.

After supper, we gathered in small groups and chatted to pass the time. Then somebody asked in a somber voice, "Sergeant Lee, it has been two days since our arrival here. I am afraid the enemy might be very close to the city. If the ship does not come soon, we might get into real trouble." Suddenly, the room became quiet, as we anxiously waited for MSgt. Lee's response.

He said calmly, "Don't fret. According to the sergeant major, regimental forces have deployed around the city, and American Air Force fighter bombers and Navy warships are ready to bombard any approaching enemy. We'll be okay. Have a good night." I lay down on the warm floor and fell asleep.

• • •

After two long days of anxiety and boredom, MSgt. Lee shouted, "Hey boys, our ship has finally arrived! We shall be leaving soon."

We all echoed, "The ship has arrived!"

As my initial excitement waned, sadness replaced it. I was leaving the land where I had been born and brought up, and the thought of not reuniting with my parents and siblings subdued me. I quietly sat down in a corner of the room. But the almighty UN forces will regroup and resume to advance all the way to the Korea-China border soon, I thought. There was some hope. A good day will come soon.

On the following morning, we were ordered to assemble at the Sŏngjin dock. When we got there, we found thousands of South Korean soldiers from various units gathered. Some units had already begun boarding their designated ships.

There were many big ships in the port, some big and tall, others low and flat, but all were long. I was awed by those magnificent ships. Heavy military equipment was being lifted on them as we approached. Far off the docks, a few sleek, gray warships were slowly sailing around, perhaps guarding us. A couple of groups of thundering American fighter jets flew from beyond the horizon of the blue sea over us to the north.

We boarded the ship by gangway instead of rope ladders. Then we were led to our designated quarters, about two to three decks below. The beds were hung in many levels one over the other like shelves. I took a middle one.

After settling down, I climbed up to the main deck to watch the loading operations. According to my sergeant, the entire capital division of troops of around nine thousand soldiers and various equipment were boarding.

The ship took us to Hungnam. Near there, the U.S. Marine Corps were trapped in the Chosin Reservoir. We were originally going there to help the Marines, but they were already evacuating by the time we arrived, and we were ordered to stay on the boat. I eventually heard about the suffering they endured at Chosin. Many of these individuals had never even known about Korea before sacrificing their lives for our freedom. I was and still am forever grateful to all those Marines and soldiers.

They and thousands of refugees evacuated from Chosin to Hungnam Port. We stayed on our boat and then took it to Pusan. Our ship brought the refugees to Geoje, where there were twenty thousand refugees. We soldiers took a combination of trains and trucks to Wonju and then to Hongcheon. From there, we marched by foot to Inje.

Note: During our withdrawal, my 18th Regiment, which had belonged to the Capital Division, became attached to the ROK 3rd Division.

NAVAL AND AIR SUPPORT DURING THE KOREAN WAR

The naval and air forces had a significant impact on the outcome of the Korean War. This included, but is not limited to:

- Enabling the UN and ROK Armies to make headway in battles as well as advance north while aviators protected them from the sky.

- The transportation of not only ammunition and supplies, but also soldiers and civilian refugees.

- Bombing key targets to prevent the NKPA from advancing their war efforts.

The following relies significantly on Edward J. Marolda's article "The Cold War's First Conflict" in the June 2010 issue of Naval History Magazine, and the U.S. Department of Defense's document "Korean War Campaigns," last modified May 26, 2010.

Naval Forces

U.S. Naval Forces Far East (specifically the U.S. Seventh Fleet, and under them, the UN Naval Forces and the ROK Navy) took command of the seas surrounding Korea early in the war and maintained it throughout. Military Sea Transportation Service (MSTS) ships, surface warships, submarines, and aircraft carriers all played a critical role in bringing in troops and supplies, protecting ground forces, and attacking the enemy.

In addition to the U.S. Seventh Fleet and ROK Navy, there were also naval forces from Great Britain, Australia, Canada, Colombia, France, the Netherlands, New Zealand, and Thailand who participated. Over 1.1 million Navy personnel served. Per the U.S. Naval Institute, "MSTS transported 5 million passengers, more than 52 million tons of cargo, and 22 million long tons of fuel." Cargo consisted of weapons, tanks, ammunition, trucks, and more.[74]

The amphibious landing at Inchon would not have been possible without the Navy and Marines. 230 ships were involved, as well as air support from the 1st Marine Air Wing.[75] The successful landing changed the tide of the war, enabling friendly troops within the Pusan Perimeter to move north of the 38th Parallel.

Naval aviation played a major role throughout the war, having flown over 275,000 sorties. Corsairs, Panthers, and Skyraiders were among the naval aircraft flown. Navy and Marine aircraft would attack communist troops from above, bomb supply lines to prevent weapons and supplies from getting into enemy hands, drop off supplies to friendly forces, and attack enemy aircraft. Of the latter, the only Korean War Navy ace is Lieutenant Guy P. Bordelon, who took down five enemy aircraft. But being a naval aviator was not without risk. 559 Navy and Marine planes were shot down by antiaircrafts. MiGs shot down five.[76]

Surface warships killed 28,000 enemy troops, and hit buildings, railways, and roads. When troops were evacuating from the Chosin Reservoir to Hungnam, more than 23,000 rockets were fired at communist troops. 105,000 troops and 91,000 refugees boarded the ships along with 350,000 tons of cargo. Fortunately, no UN warship sunk during the war.[77]

Air Forces

While the U.S. Naval Forces Far East took command of the sea, the Far East Air Forces (FEAF) took command of the air. Under the FEAF command were the U.S. Fifth Air Force and Strategic Air Command. Under the Fifth Air Force were the ROK Air Forces and UN Air Forces.

FEAF had an early start to the war by providing cover and transport for Americans as they evacuated from the Republic of Korea from June 26 to 27, 1950. While this was taking place, the Fifth Air Force struck down three North Korean fighters on June 27. On June 29, Americans bombed the Pyongyang airfield, and would destroy any other enemy airfields to keep North Korea from using their planes. While at first, they conducted photo reconnaissance, airlift missions, and air support missions for troops, they moved on to bomb railroads, bridges, and supply dumps to prevent the enemy from resupplying and moving their troops forward. The Fifth Air Force as well as Navy and Marine Air Forces soon gained air superiority.[78]

After the Inchon Landing in September 1950, the Eighth Army was able to move north from the Pusan Perimeter to Osan. During that trip, air controllers would communicate to the ground forces on aerial reconnaissance and bring in air support. Any airfields that had been destroyed would be rebuilt by aviation engineers such as in Pohang, Kimpo, and Suwon.[79]

The Communist Chinese forces entered the war in the fall of 1950. On November 8, the FEAF bombed Sinuiju in northwest Korea.[80] FEAF F-80s battled against MiG-15s—and an American pilot, First Lieutenant Russell J. Brown, took down a MiG.[81] The MiG, however, was a superior aircraft, so to combat these, FEAF brought in their best jet fighters a month later: the F-84 Thunderjets along with F-86 Sabres. By March 1951, the area in northwestern Korea had such a strong number of communist air forces that the Fifth Air Force pilots gave it a name: MiG Alley. At the same time, the Air Force played a major role in the Battle of Chosin Reservoir. 1,500 tons of supplies were airlifted to the Marines in Chosin, as well as parts to assemble the bridge across Funchilin Pass so the Marines could escape.[82]

Throughout the war, FEAF had an immense impact on the course of the war. FEAF:

- Provided air support for the moving ground forces. For example, for a couple of weeks in December 1950, FEAF killed or wounded 33,000 enemy troops, and during the summer and fall of 1952, alongside the Navy and Marines, 2,000 to 4,000 close air support missions were conducted each month.[83]

- Transported personnel via the Air Force's troop carriers such as C-124s and C-47s and provided air medical evacuation.[84]

- Transported cargo in planes such as the C-124s and C-119s.[85]

- Air dropped supplies to ground forces. For instance, 301 tons of equipment and supplies were dropped on October 20, 1950; 1,358 tons from February 23 to 28, 1951; 15,900 tons in April 1951; 21,300 tons in May 1951; 22,472 tons in June 1951; and 1,200 tons from June 28 to July 2, 1953.[86]

- Bombed railroads, bridges, supply centers, marshaling yards, tunnels, airfields, highways, factories, steel plants, power plants, antiaircraft sites, and more.

- Provided cover to protect bombers from MiGs and engaged in aerial combat. On May 20, 1951, 50 MiGs fought 36 Sabres. During this fight, Captain James Jabara struck down 2 MiGs (totaling 6 victories) and thus became the first American jet ace in aviation history. In September 1951, the Air Force engaged with 911 enemy aircraft and shot down 14 MiGs, losing 6 of their own; in December 1951, the 51st and 4th Fighter–Interceptor Wings shot down 26 MiGs, and lost 6 F–86s; from January to April 1952, FEAF shot down 127 enemy aircraft and lost 9 of their own; and from May to July 1953, they had 165 wins while losing 3.[87]

The combined efforts of the Army, Navy, and Air forces resulted in significant progress throughout the war.

CHAPTER 20

My First Christmas Experience

December 1950

It was December 24, 1950 in a mountainous region of Gangwon-do Province in east-central Korea. The unusually cold winter firmly gripped the landscape, blanketing the valleys, fields, and rugged mountain ranges with glittering snow and coating the dark pine trees with ice. The ashen sky hung low, and snowflakes danced wildly as a freezing northerly wind blew over the mountains and down the valleys.

We, the weary troops of the 3rd Battalion from the 18th Regiment, were silently marching in two files on a narrow snow-covered dirt road. We were to be deployed along a mountain range near Inje-up (인제읍), north of the 38th Parallel. Army field backpacks hung heavy on our backs. Some of us carried our rifles on top of those backpacks, while the rest of us carried them on our shoulders. Only the monotonous noise of crunching snow came from under our heavy boots. We had retreated more than 625 miles by land and sea, from the farthest salient point in the northeast Korean Peninsula to this valley, in just four weeks, and were too tired to talk.

Suddenly, Man-E broke the silence with a frustrated, angry holler. "What the hell are we doing here? We are supposed to be patrolling along the bank of the Tumen River!" This river divides the northeastern Korean Peninsula and Eastern Manchuria.

Chun from the rear responded in an equally angry voice, "Because of that son of a bitch Mao Zedong, and son of a bitch *ddong-dae-nom-del.*" *Ddong-dae-nom-del* was a derogatory term for Communist Chinese soldiers.

Kim Jae-kook echoed, "Kill them! Kill them all, damn *ddong-dae-nom-del.*" Almost everybody recited in unison, "Kill them all, kill them all," and then we all burst into loud, frustrated laughter.

The main infantry units of the battalion were deployed on the frontline. The battalion deputy commander, Major Jeong, ordered a dozen of us administrative personnel, myself included, to camp about half a mile behind the line until further notice. The end of the short winter day was approaching rapidly, but unlike American soldiers, we had neither sleeping bags nor tents to protect us from the freezing winter nights. So, SFC Han instructed us to search for a couple of vacated farmhouses to stay in, not too far from the highway, where the regiment headquarters would be camping. We found two empty humble farmhouses with rice straw thatched roofs in a narrow, short, steep valley, just off the road across the river. Apparently, the owners had abandoned them for safer places farther south for fear of imminent fighting. These houses were situated at the uppermost edge of the valley, one hundred feet apart.

The valley was surrounded by thick pine groves. Numerous small rice paddies cascaded down the valley like freshly painted white staircases, laced with a frozen creek on one side. At the far end of the pine groves, rugged but stately mountains rose high into the gray sky—the scenery added an eerie feeling to our low morale. It was even harder for me because my hopes of reuniting with my parents, brothers, and sisters in North Korea had been dashed.

Now we had shelter for the night. Because the quartermaster unit had not yet caught up with us, we did not have any food except a few packs of unleavened Korean Army crackers. SFC Han assigned six to each house and organized sentry duty teams, two per team, each with a two-hour rotation. As usual, he gave us guard duty instructions—three warning shots for anything suspicious, continuous shooting for anyone who gave a wrong nightly password or could not give us one at all. The division headquarters issued a different password every day. He immediately posted Sentry Team 1 on duty to watch the perimeter. The sky started to clear and the cold northerly wind calmed down.

SFC Han split the rest into two groups and then ordered one group to search for food and the other to collect firewood to warm up the *ondol* floors of the farmhouses. We found an urn of buckwheat flour and a jar of kimchi buried under the kitchen floor.

Staff Sgt. Man-E, who had uncanny cooking skills, immediately started making *gooksoo*, the Korean traditional buckwheat noodle. All of us helped him by drawing water from a nearby well, pouring a few buckets into the largest kettle on the earthen oven, and starting a fire to boil the water.

Like a pack of ravenous wolves, we anxiously watched him cooking, which seemed to take forever. A couple of hours later, Man-E hollered, "Come and get it!" We took out our dirty aluminum field mess kits from our backpacks. He filled our containers with hot *gooksoo* in the order of our rank. We thanked him abundantly and devoured the food, licking the bottom of the mess kits clean in no time. What a great feast! It was one of our rare hot meals since the outbreak of the war. We were tired of our daily fare—a fist-size ball of boiled rice sprinkled with salt, sometimes with a chunk of beef boiled in soy sauce. Afterwards, SFC Han replaced Sentry Team 1 on duty with Sentry Team 2 and fed the relieved guards, who joined the rest of us. We huddled in the heated farmhouses and chatted for some time.

As the pale-yellow winter sun was setting behind the western ridges, dusk started rolling into the valley. Lying down on a heated *ondol* floor helped us make up for our sleep deprivation. But I could not dispel a nagging feeling that we were too far from the highway and too close to the thick pine groves—an easy target for North Korean guerilla soldiers.

Somebody hollered in a familiar voice, "Hey, you guys!" We ran out to the courtyard. It was Yu, the battalion headquarters company supply sergeant, with a civilian utility man. They brought some supplies for us using an A-frame.* He said, "I personally brought special gifts for you sons of bitches because you are important." He laughed heartily, and continued, "Since tomorrow is Christmas, the American troops brought a truckload of gifts for our regiment. I brought some for you."

Certainly, he had brought unusual gifts—two big cardboard boxes of exotic candies, chocolate bars, cigarettes, and instant coffee—all American goodies.

---

* American soldiers dubbed the farmer's backpacks A-frames because of their shape. They played an important role in transporting supplies to American soldiers in the rugged mountainous regions.

He distributed different items to each of us. Everybody received two chocolate bars and two packs of cigarettes. The cigarette packs were decorated with
green willows. Years later, I learned that they were Chesterfields. I got a small
bag of cookies and a can of liquid, in addition to cigarettes and chocolate
bars. I did not know what the can contained because I could not read English. I said, "Hey, Sergeant Sim, what is in this can? It looks like something
watery." He answered, "That is cow's milk."

These unexpected and exotic treats were a great surprise to us all. As soon
as Sgt. Yu tossed two packs of cigarettes to each of us, everyone except me
took out a cigarette, put it between his lips, and lit it. They smoked with gusto,
inhaling deeply lest any smoke escape. Then they exhaled smoke through
their noses contentedly. Meanwhile, I tore a chocolate bar open and took a
bite. It melted smoothly and filled my mouth with sweet juice. I had never
had chocolate before. I nibbled the rest slowly so that I could enjoy the sensation as long as possible.

After finishing his first cigarette, Sgt. Man-E collected all the instant coffee
and sugar bags, tore them open, dumped the contents in a big clay jar, and
added hot water. He stirred the mix vigorously with a large wooden scoop
for a few moments. Then, he filled our quarter-moon shaped field canteen
cups with hot steaming coffee for each of us. The strange aroma of the coffee excited my nostrils so much that I could not help but sniff it for some
time before I took a sip. It tasted somewhat bittersweet, a taste I liked immediately even though it was my first cup ever. It added a unique flavor to the
chocolate in my mouth and generated an inexplicably tender taste. But the
cans of condensed milk were the least popular goodies. Nobody knew that
they were for the coffee.

I knew nothing about Christmas. For that matter, I did not even know
who Jesus Christ was and what contribution he had made to the world, except
that he was one of the four ancient holy men. Nonetheless, I thanked him
for these delicious American gifts.

My intellectual curiosity and these generous gifts stirred a desire in me
to learn about Christ and Christmas. I asked, "Sergeant Sim, who was Jesus
Christ? What did he do for Americans? Christmas must be a big deal for them
because they gave us these wonderful gifts."

He explained, "Jesus Christ was born in Palestine two thousand years ago and established a religion called Christianity. Christmas is Christ's birthday. The Western countries observe Christmas as the most important holiday, like Korean Buddhists celebrate Buddha's birthday." Sgt. Sim was considered a very knowledgeable man because not only had he received a secondary education, but also, he had read widely and knew some English. He asked, "Hey, will you swap your American cigarettes for my candy bars?"

I did not smoke and had read somewhere that milk was good for your health, so I swapped with him. Now, I had two cans of condensed milk, three chocolate bars, and a bag of cookies. I punched holes in the lids of the cans with my bayonet point and guzzled both. It tasted somewhat heavy but made me full and content. I put the rest of my food away. Everybody was satisfied with the Christmas gifts.

The front line was eerily quiet except for intermittent trucks driving in the distance. The winter night got deeper. In a relaxed mood, some of us sat cross-legged on the heated *ondol* floor. Some lay on their backs. Everyone except me was smoking contentedly.

Someone said, "My home is only about ten miles due west. I wonder how my family is doing; my one-year-old son, my wife, and my parents." Then he sighed deeply.

I added, "The war would have been over by now if those Chinese had not intervened. By now we should be patrolling on the Korean-Chinese border instead of here, five hundred miles south of it. My home is about 125 miles due northwest. I haven't seen my parents in two and a half years. I hope we advance northward again, kick those sons of bitches out of our country, and reunify the Koreas."

SFC Han said, "Don't bet on it. According to the regiment intelligence chief, about one million Chinese soldiers were sent to help North Korea. I think it's going to take some time before we kick them out of the country." He continued, "My home is about twenty-fives miles east of here. I heard that the South Korean soldiers and the North Korean invaders had a fierce fight near my hometown during the first three days of the war. I hope my folks are all well. My mother is a fragile old lady. Damn it, I have no news about them."

We continued chatting for some time under the flickering light of a kerosene lantern on the wall. The chatting diminished as the fatigue from that day's long march caught up with us. We fell asleep one by one, trusting that the two sentries on duty would give us an early warning in the event of an attack.

Although I enjoyed the buckwheat noodles, the American chocolate bar, and the condensed milk, queasiness kept me from falling asleep. My stomach gurgled noisily. After some time, I managed to fall into a light sleep. Later, stomach cramps woke me up and sent me rushing to the outhouse several times.

A series of distant explosions woke us up. Since the booms sounded far away, we were not too anxious. But SFC Han said, "Let's investigate what the hell is going on out there." We grabbed our rifles and cautiously stepped out of the warm room into the courtyard. Instantly, I felt the wintry air penetrating my bones, already chilled by those trips to the outhouse. We looked around the vicinity and the nearby dark pine groves and found nothing extraordinary. The silvery full moon hung in the pale blue sky. Billions of brilliant moon rays were falling on the blanket of snow and bouncing right back up, making the sky even brighter. The scene was hauntingly beautiful. Strangely, this surreal light and quiet intensified my anxiety to the point that I was ready to shoot at the slightest movement. But stillness and silence prevailed.

Then we heard a distant drone coming from the west. Suddenly, a dark airplane appeared against the bright sky over the western ridge. It continued eastward. All of us watched it with amazement and apprehension. The plane threw a half dozen smoky fireballs behind it, followed by a series of booms. Did someone shoot at it? The plane disappeared into the eastern sky as mysteriously as it had come. "Was that plane ours or the enemy's?" Chae asked.

SFC Han responded, "I don't know. I will call the battalion headquarters. Get back to the room!" All except the two sentries returned to the warm house. He called the battalion headquarters and asked what the plane was. The battalion intelligence officer had no idea but promised to ask the regiment headquarters and let us know. We all anxiously waited for a return call. Sometime later, the battalion intelligence officer informed us that, according to the American Air Force communication liaison officers who were attached to the regiment, the plane was an American reconnaissance plane.

It had been a long day. Everyone but me quickly fell asleep after we had heard the information from battalion intelligence. My stomach started gurgling again from the condensed milk. I tried to sleep, but the discomfort kept me awake. Everybody was fast asleep, some snoring noisily. Finally, I fell asleep. I did not know how long I had slept, but stomach pain and my throbbing feet woke me up. I took off my boots and lay down again, rubbing my abdomen. Somehow, I managed to return to sleep.

The ear-splitting crackling noises of fierce machine gun and rifle fire roused us. "Enemy attack!" someone shouted. "Sounds like there's a lot of them!"

SFC Han yelled, "Everybody, get out! We can't let them encircle us. Run down to the highway before they get closer! Watch out for enemy grenades!" He knew we could not match an enemy armed with machine guns.

I picked up my Carbine rifle and backpack. We all dashed out to the snow-covered courtyard. Suddenly, my feet felt cold. I realized I had not put on my boots. So, I raced back to the room, put them on, and ran back out to the yard. I was alone. Extreme fear gripped me. I bolted out to the open valley to avoid being trapped by the enemy. I jumped into a nearby rice paddy because its banks would provide me with some protection from the enemy fire. The moonlit night was almost as bright as daytime. I saw my friends running toward the lower valley. Then, suddenly, I heard screaming from behind, "Stop there! If you don't, we will shoot you!" while they were shooting at me. Instinctively, I took a quick look back in the direction of the scream. There, a number of North Koreans were charging toward me and firing their submachine guns. Tracing bullets from the enemy machine guns flew over my head. I ran as fast as my legs allowed me to get away from the enemy and catch up with my group. Every four or five steps, I jumped down a few feet to the next lower rice paddy, as if I were running down a gigantic staircase. Every jump put me below the chasing enemy so that their submachine guns were shooting over my head. Halfway down the rice paddy staircase, I finally caught up with my group. We were all running for our lives.

Finally, we reached the river at the foothills of the steep valley. Since there was no bridge, we plunged in. The ice crushed under our feet, and we sank knee-deep in the frigid water. We waded toward the snow-covered opposite bank. The water seeped into my boots and my quilted fatigues; my feet and legs stung. The opposite bank was slippery, but we managed to climb it quickly.

Once we all crossed the river, SFC Han hurriedly regrouped and deployed us along the riverbank. He ordered, "Guys, don't run. Shoot the goddamn sons of bitches," and started to fire his rifle across the river. Everyone followed him. We knew that our counterattack would either kill them or discourage them from crossing the river. We continued to shoot for some time. I emptied my 15-round cartridge before I stopped.

At last, SFC Han shouted, "Cease fire!" He called out each of our names, and said, "Nobody is missing! I don't think the fucking enemy would dare to cross the river. Let's move to the highway."

We hurried across snow-covered fields to the highway. We knew the regiment headquarters had camped somewhere nearby. Approaching the road, we saw a group of figures milling around. Since we did not know who they were, friends or enemies, we halted in the middle of the field and prepared to shoot if they failed to give us the correct *amho* (nightly password).

We called out, "*Amho?*"

They responded, "*Hwarang*," and countered, "What is yours?"

We answered, "*Hwacheon!*"

We had exchanged the proper passwords and identified each other. Feeling relieved, we walked over and joined them. We introduced ourselves and shook hands. The group leader, a staff sergeant, told us that they were a part of the regiment headquarters' security unit. He said, "Since we heard severe machine gun fire across the river, my commander issued a general alert to reinforce the sentries around the regiment camp and dispatched a reconnaissance group. I oversee the group."

After wading across the frigid river, our cotton-padded fatigue trousers were dripping wet and heavy. SFC Han reorganized us into two groups. He put me in charge of one and Sgt. Chang Hyokoen in charge of the other. He said, "Since we have little intelligence about the enemies around this area, we should watch the west and the north. He deployed my group along the highway to guard against a possible attack from the pine groves across the river and put the other behind a farmhouse by the road, about one hundred feet farther north. Lying motionless against the frozen highway bank in wet trousers, I was quickly losing body heat. My feet got very cold, and my wet trousers started to freeze. I feared hypothermia and frostbite.

The moon was sliding down behind the western mountain range, and a faint dawn light started to show in the eastern sky. Before long, brilliant morning sun rays fanned out over the eastern mountaintop across the pale blue sky. There was no sign of the enemy in the vicinity. What a relief! But my teeth were clacking, and my body was shaking violently. My toes felt numb, and my trousers were stiff. We were all shivering.

SFC Han said, "Sergeant Kim, do you see that lonely house between the highway and the river?" He pointed at a snow-covered farmhouse a couple of hundred yards from us. "I think I saw some movement there just before sunrise. I don't like it. Check if there is anything unusual in that house. Take Corporal Lee Jong-kook and a couple of the new soldiers with you. Be careful."

A handful of soldiers fresh out of a training center had joined us the day before. I picked two privates, assigned one to Corporal Lee Jong-kook, and took the other. Before we set out toward the house, I said, "Corporal Lee, you two approach the house from the left; my boy and I will converge from the right. Once you reach the house, you take the back door, and I will take the front. If you find an enemy first, shoot him. If you are shot at, duck and return fire." Since the two new soldiers had not had any battle experience yet, I said, "You two, don't panic. Just follow our orders. Let's go."

We slowly approached the house but saw no sign of movement. Yet we could not be too careful. I saw a few footprints in the snow around the house; some from the highway and some from the river and back. It was quiet. But the footprints alarmed me. I ran from behind the fence to the front door and kicked it open, ready to shoot. My boy followed me. Corporal Lee and his companion came in through the door and joined us. We found only a lone soldier sleeping soundly on a crude table in the kitchen. I yelled, "Get up!" and kicked the table, but he did not respond. I pressed his neck and found him dead. He was a second lieutenant of the South Korean Army Engineering Corps. The back of his army parka was blood-soaked. He appeared to have been bayoneted in the chest. His feet were bare. The enemy must have infiltrated this far, killed him, and taken his shoes and socks. I felt terribly sorry for him. He must have been a loving son to his parents, but now he was dead in this remote part of the rugged mountainous front line. After searching the house thoroughly, we returned to SFC Han and reported what we had found.

After thanking us, he ordered us to make a fire. We ran to a nearby farmhouse, grabbed a few bundles of corn stalks piled against the wall of a shed, and started a fire. Then, we brought big bundles of dried pine branches and logs and dumped them on the burning corn stalks. The pine burned fiercely, generating crackling flames and heat. We gathered around the fire, warming ourselves.

I took off my backpack, sat on it, and removed my boots and socks to warm my freezing feet, rubbing my toes gently. My frozen padded trousers started to drip. I took them off and squeezed the water out of them. Others followed my example. The bonfire was so warm that even my cold naked legs felt too hot despite the freezing winter morning. I felt content watching rising steam from my socks and trousers. The snow around the bonfire melted, exposing dark soil.

When my clothes and boots were dry enough to wear, I put them on, while reflecting on the night's events. Left alone in the courtyard of the humble farmhouse, I could have been killed at the onset of the attack. I thanked the gods of heaven that I was sitting by this fire, and that nobody in my group was injured, killed, or missing.

Then, unexpectedly, two American jeeps pulled up, and four soldiers climbed down and joined us by the bonfire. Two of them were officers. One had sustained a light injury to his arm. Pointing to his wound, he said something which I did not understand. So, I asked Sgt. Sim to translate.

He told me that the good-natured officer had said, "This is my Christmas present." He continued, "These Americans are Air Force communication personnel, dispatched to our regiment to guide U.S. fighter-bombers to enemy targets."

I felt very sorry for the injured officer, and silently expressed my sincere thanks. These soldiers were far away from their loving families and had crossed the Pacific Ocean to help us fight the communist invaders.

My trousers were now steaming hot, so I rolled them up to cool my legs. Then I dozed off. When I woke up, the bonfire was still glowing, and the dazzling morning sun had risen high above the eastern mountain range, casting brilliant rays over the glittering snowy landscape. Millions of snowflakes sparkled. The air was so dry that I felt I could crack it apart like an old twig.

No wind, no gunfire! I stood up, stretched, and turned my cold back to the bonfire. A faint drone from the distant sky broke the silence. I looked up at the powder-blue wintry sky and saw a lone B-29 flying northward, leaving gentle rippling contrails, like silk ribbons, behind it.

SFC Han shouted, "We are moving out. We're heading back to regiment headquarters."

Putting our heavy army knapsacks on our backs and our rifles on our shoulders, we reluctantly bid goodbye to the warm bonfire that had saved my feet from frostbite. We followed the sergeant, wondering what was ahead.

GREEN SOLDIERS

No front line commander wants undertrained soldiers. In wartime, a commander simply does not have the luxury of time to train them. They are more likely to cause problems in battles than to help.

On December 25, in the late afternoon, MSgt. Lee called me to report to him immediately. He told me that our battalion had received a squadron of ten soldiers from regiment headquarters to fill our seriously undermanned front line. Since they were fresh out of basic training, our deputy commander decided to keep them with the headquarters company for a couple of days to minimize their battlefield shock. The sergeant said, "I am putting you in charge of these new men for guard duty at the headquarters until further notice," and handed me the roster.

I had never been a commander at any level before, except for briefly leading a group of five rear-guard sentries a few months earlier. I had fought battles as a rifleman, but never as a squadron leader. I didn't want to lead those green soldiers, especially right after having experienced a surprise attack by the North Koreans earlier that morning. I protested, "Sergeant, there are more qualified and more senior sergeants than me. I am an administrative guy."

"Just shut up! That's an order. Take this roster and go!"

"Yes, sir." In the military, you do as you are ordered. Reluctantly, I took the roster, but asked him to assign Corporal Lee Jong-kook as my helper. Jong-kook and I joined the soldiers, who quietly huddled around a small bonfire. I collected them, and we introduced ourselves. Then I made a roll call, cross-checking each of them by name, dog tag number, and rank. All were privates. They were visibly nervous, being thrown into a war zone for the first time. Even the distant firing of friendly artillery caused them to jump. I asked them how long they had been in the army. They answered that they had just finished six weeks of basic training.

I was surprised that the training center had shipped them out with so little training to fight the enemy. After joining the South Korean Army two years before the North Korean invasion, I had received three months of basic training and a couple of mock battle exercises before being deployed for border guard duty. I had survived numerous battles during that period and after the invasion. Despite those experiences, I still felt nervous whenever a battle loomed. I fully understood why these new soldiers were so nervous.

The winter afternoon faded fast. I needed shelter to keep my soldiers from the bitter cold night. I led them into a nearby partially bombed out small farmhouse, a straw-thatched building with clay walls. The living quarters and the kitchen remained in good condition. I ordered the soldiers to heat the *ondol* floor for the night.

After settling in, I gave them as much verbal training as I could to alleviate their anxiety before they would be taken to battle. I told them what they should do to fight the enemy:

- "Listen to your squadron commander's instructions carefully.

- Memorize the daily passwords and use them properly to distinguish friends from enemies. If anyone gives you the wrong password, shoot him. He is an enemy.

- Dig a foxhole deep and wide so that you can easily maneuver in it. Camouflage yourself as much as possible.

- Don't panic and abandon your foxhole in the face of an enemy attack. You should firmly keep your station and return fire.

- Never fall asleep while on watch and watch fellow soldiers in neighboring foxholes so the enemy doesn't come up on them by surprise.

- Don't think you are the only one scared. Everybody is scared, yet they fight bravely.

- If you see or hear something suspicious, give a three-shot warning.

- If someone calls, 'New recruits, come here!' Do not follow this order. Most likely he is an enemy. Remember that the enemy is Korean and speaks Korean.

- If you keep these points in mind, you will make a good soldier. Tonight, you will be guarding the battalion headquarters."

Then, I inspected their M1 rifles and cautioned them to keep the safety pins of the rifles locked until they were ready to fire to prevent accidental injuries or death. I organized them into five sentry shifts of two men each and deployed the first shift at the two different places chosen by the company sergeant, wondering how well the two inexperienced soldiers would perform their guard duties.

As the winter sun retreated behind the western mountains, and dusk rolled in over the snow-covered farmland, an uneasy feeling about the two guards began to creep into my mind. When dusk turned to darkness, the uneasiness intensified to the point that I picked up my rifle and went out to check on them. As I approached the first guard, he promptly shouted from the back of a big tree, "Stop there! Password."

I gave my password and countered, "What is yours?" to make sure that he was not an enemy. When he gave me the proper response, I said, "I am Sergeant Kim, your squadron leader."

As he came out from behind the tree, he held his rifle ready to fire. His alertness made me happy and established my confidence in him. I gave him unqualified praise and told him that his replacement would be coming within an hour.

The second sentinel was a completely different story. Arriving at the second guard post, I found the guard walking casually on a wide-open, snow-covered field under the bright moonlight, with his rifle slung over his shoulder. As I came closer, he asked in a friendly civilian manner, "Who is there?" instead of shouting, "Stop there! Password?" Incredible!

I answered, "This is your squadron leader, Sergeant Kim."

"Oh, Sergeant Kim. How are you, sir?"

"Fine. Soldier, show me your rifle."

He took his rifle from his shoulder and handed it to me without question.

Stunned, I returned his rifle and ordered him, "Go back to the head-quarters, and send Corporal Lee to me immediately!" I replaced him until Jong-kook took over. When I explained to Jong-kook what the green private had done, he said that we could all have been killed in our sleep had I not replaced that idiot.

Upon returning to the squadron, I immediately gathered the fresh soldiers and repeated my instructions, emphasizing calling for the password and readiness. I underscored that failure to do so could result in serious consequences. I told them about what had happened earlier that evening without mentioning the soldier's name.

That evening, when I led Shift 3 to replace Shift 2, I found that the guards on duty performed exactly as they should. I also recognized that my simple verbal training had improved those soldiers' guard duty effectiveness. Every two hours, I had to lead a shift change, which deprived me of sleep.

At last, the sun rose in the eastern sky, fanning out billions of brilliant rays over the frozen land. I was glad we got through the night without a serious incident. That afternoon, the battalion commander ordered that those green soldiers be sent to him at his forward command post (FCP), relieving me as their squadron sergeant.

When I handed them over to a senior sergeant from the FCP, I felt a heavy yoke lifted from my shoulders. I wished these soldiers had received more training before being deployed in their foxholes, and silently prayed for their safety.

CHAPTER 21

Learning English

February 1951

February 1951 was one of the coldest winters on record. The Korean War entered its eighth month. The Chinese and North Korean armies' massive winter offense pushed the UN and South Korean armies back deep into southern Korea. My company was in a hamlet in the Taebaek Mountain Range region in the southeastern Gangwon-do Province. We nearly froze to death on multiple occasions the past couple of months.

Since we did not have a tent, the six of us company administrative personnel occupied an abandoned straw-thatched farmhouse to keep warm overnight. Surprisingly, this remote poor farmer had a dozen books, including Karl Marx's *Capitalism* and a self-study English communication book from Waseda University, a well-known private college in Tokyo. All of them were written in Japanese. Having received my elementary education in Japanese during the Japanese occupation, I could read those books. However, I didn't even touch Karl Marx's book because two years earlier I had been falsely accused of being a communist, tortured, and jailed for almost two months. Even though I had little knowledge of English except for a few letters, the English book attracted my interest, so I took it with me. Thus, my book inventory grew to two. Unlike today's thick American textbooks, these were thin trade paperbacks.

The few letters I knew came from my algebra book: they were a, b, c, x, y, and z. I didn't even know how to read them. I just memorized them as symbols, such as a, b, and c as coefficients, and x, y, and z as variables in each algebraic equation. I began to read the book. It showed phonetic expressions in the Japanese alphabet for each letter of English. Most Asian languages do not have the sounds of f, v, ph, th, and r. Thus, those phonetic expressions were not close to the real sound.

For the next few months, when there was a lull in the front line, I taught myself English from the self-study book, usually while in my foxhole, to distract me from the cold. However, I didn't understand all the vocabulary. When I read the words or simple sentences with their funny pronunciations, some of my friends made fun of me, while others said, "I don't know what you're saying, but I admire your tenacity. Keep going!" I wished I had an English-Korean dictionary to provide me with the meanings of the words and accurate sounds. One day, a friend of mine at the battalion quartermasters went to Pusan, to get supplies. I asked him to buy me an English-Korean dictionary. Alas, he bought an English grammar book instead.

This grammar book was even more frustrating because the various parts of speech, voices, and rules were totally new to me. The weirdest thing of all was that the order of English sentences is the reverse of that of Korean. English usually has the subject, the verb, the object, or the predicate in that order, while a Korean sentence often omits the subject, and the object comes before the verb. For instance, 'Did you eat dinner?' would be expressed in Korean '*Dinner ate?*'

Even worse is that English requires articles in front of most nouns, while Korean hardly uses articles. I was so confused that I wanted to give up on learning English altogether.

However, two important factors kept me from quitting: the dream and the necessity. The dream was to get a good education. Once the war was over, if I survived it, I was determined to enter high school and eventually advance to college. High schools required entrance examinations which included English, math, and Korean literature. I had taught myself Korean literature and middle school level algebra. However, I had never been exposed to English before, and needed to study it to realize my dream. This necessity inspired me to continue to study.

GENERAL MACARTHUR RELIEVED OF HIS DUTY

After the massive Chinese offensive during the winter, which surprised UN and ROK forces, General MacArthur, who was known to be aggressive and to forge ahead, wanted to use nuclear weapons against the Chinese Communist forces. Bombing China would have gone against keeping the conflict a limited war, and President Truman did not want a World War III.

MacArthur believed in eradicating communism from all of Korea. He ignored the Commander in Chief's orders and continued to order his troops north. On April 11, 1951, Truman relieved General MacArthur of his duty for insubordination. The public did not agree with the President's actions.

Truman addressed the American people on April 11:

> *"What we are doing in Korea is this: We are trying to prevent a third world war…[most people in this country] warmly supported the decision of the Government to help the Republic of Korea against the Communist aggressors…*
>
> *By fighting a limited war in Korea, we have prevented aggression from succeeding and bringing on a general war. And the ability of the whole free world to resist Communist aggression has been greatly improved…*
>
> *We must try to limit war to Korea for these vital reasons: to make sure that the precious lives of our fighting men are not wasted; to see that the security of our country and the free world is not needlessly jeopardized; and to prevent a third world war.*
>
> *A number of events have made it evident that General MacArthur did not agree with that policy. I have therefore considered it essential to relieve General MacArthur so that there would be no doubt or confusion as to the real purpose and aim of our policy…*
>
> *Our military objective [is] to repel attack and to restore peace…*
>
> *The struggle of the United Nations in Korea is a struggle for peace.*

The free nations have united their strength in an effort to pre-vent a third world war.

That war can come if the Communist rulers want it to come. But this Nation and its allies will not be responsible for its coming.

We do not want to widen the conflict. We will use every effort to prevent that disaster. And in so doing we know that we are follow-ing the great principles of peace, freedom, and justice."[88]

Lieutenant General Matthew Ridgway replaced MacArthur. However, MacArthur was welcomed home to a parade and spoke to Congress on April 19, ending his speech with an army ballad, "Old soldiers never die; they just fade away." He said, "Like the old soldier of that ballad, I now close my military career and just fade away, an old soldier who tried to do his duty as God gave him the light to see that duty. Goodbye."[89]

One must wonder about the outcome of the war had MacArthur remained in his position. Would World War III have taken place? Or would the United Nations have eliminated communism from the entire Korean pen-insula? Would North Korea be a free democratic nation today, united with South Korea?

CHAPTER 22

Is This My Last Day?

May 1951

It was May 18, 1951, a calm spring morning. The fierce fighting throughout the night came to an unexpected lull. This respite was welcome. We, the 18th Infantry Regiment of the 3rd ROKA Division, had been fighting the North Korean and Chinese armies for the last three weeks in the mountains a couple of miles north of Hyeon-ri, a small town in the east-central region of Gangwon-do Province, where I had experienced my first Christmas five months earlier. Since February, we had been fighting battles in Jeongseon, Pyeongchang, Gangneung, Odaesan, and Seoraksan.

The 7th Division was positioned at our left. Since the region was so wide, and its terrain so rugged, all available combat units were thinly deployed along the long, rough mountain ranges, leaving no reserve. Normally, each regiment kept a battalion on reserve to render help along the line or replace battle-worn units. The headquarters personnel of our battalion camped by a river a little over a mile south of the front line. The river flowed through the Hyeon-ri Basin. The forward headquarters of the two divisions crowded the basin, while the main headquarters were stationed in the Sangnam-ri Valley, about three miles south of Hyeon-ri, over a mountain trail so narrow that two vehicles could not pass each other. This trail caused a huge logistical nightmare.

After stretching and inhaling fresh air, I washed my face in the crystal clear, cold water from the river, without soap. Refreshed, I looked around the unspoiled mountains and fields, forgetting the war, as if I was cherishing a peaceful spring day for the first time since I had joined the army. A few of my friends came out of the tents and joined me. Chestnuts, oaks, pines, and many other deciduous trees dressed the surrounding mountains in a young spring green color. As a gentle zephyr blew, pine pollen flew into the blue sky as if a magician sprayed yellow dust. Many colorful wildflowers adorned the narrow strips of land along the river. Oblivious to this terrible war, bees buzzed from one flower to another, collecting nectar. Exquisite butterflies flew any which way like drunkards. Some perched precariously on flowers, flipping their wings and sucking honey; others continued to fly or were blown away by the breeze. Everything appeared so peaceful.

Suddenly, loud explosions yanked me out of my absorption in nature. A pillar of smoke rose from the top of the bottleneck trail behind us. We thought it was a bad traffic accident. More followed. They sounded like mortar shell explosions. Machine guns began firing. Were these war games? The firing intensified. We cursed, "Who the hell are these idiots?" Then a powerful, rumbling blast came from Sangnam Valley, on the south side of the trail, where the two divisions' main headquarters and all the supply depots, including ammunition, were located. Secondary explosions followed. Moments later, gigantic towers of smoke eerily rose against the spotless blue sky. We became alert. Our battalion deputy commander, Major Jeong, called the battalion intelligence officer to inquire about the blasts. He knew nothing. So, Major Jeong contacted the regiment intelligence chief. He also had no information. No one suspected that those explosions were enemy bombardments because the trail was far from the front line, at least five miles from the enemy, just south of the division's forward headquarters.

A few minutes later, the battalion executive officer informed the major that a small enemy group had infiltrated the gap between the 3rd and 7th divisions and tried to cut off the supply line. He conveyed the battalion commander's order to be combat ready. We all checked and loaded our rifles. Then each of us put two ammo belts across our shoulders and secured two grenades on the utility belts around our waists. After that, I packed the records of our battalion personnel in my army backpack. Despite being nervous, we were naively confident that the division headquarters' guard unit would easily repel the enemy because the division's forward headquarters was within a stone's throw. The guards were well-trained and experienced fighters.

According to Major Jeong, the guard commander sent a platoon to repel the enemy. Less than an hour after the initial explosion, we heard the enemy and our fighters exchanging fierce rifle and machine gunfire. The enemy mortars pounded on the platoon's position. For some reason, our guard platoon did not respond with mortars; perhaps they did not have any because their primary responsibility was guard duty, not combat. From the beginning, the enemy had the upper hand because of their mortars. Nevertheless, our soldiers continued to attack.

By midday, we learned that the guard platoon had failed to repel the enemy. The enemy force was much larger than we had thought and had completely cut off our supply route. The division's commanding general decided to pull one battalion from the front to reopen our vital supply line. This tactical move deeply concerned Major Jeong. He feared that it would make the front line even thinner, and that it might cause a catastrophe. He also knew that redeploying six hundred soldiers would take many hours, no matter how quickly they might move. By the time the redeployment was completed, the enemy might have brought in reinforcements. Even I, a simple soldier, saw this order as risky and dangerous. I wished that someone higher in the chain of command would organize a large-scale counterattack, using the headquarters personnel of all levels, and stall the enemy's advance until the arrival of the battalion. Meanwhile, the enemy mortar attack was intensifying and getting closer.

By late afternoon, a few American Air Force transportation planes arrived and dropped supplies for us, while circling over us. The cargo shot out of the plane's side door and the attached parachutes opened like a row of colorful beach umbrellas. They were descending gracefully, like a flock of cranes. It was a fantastic display, and it boosted our morale. I was impressed by this speedy airborne operation, only five hours after the situation had deteriorated badly. They landed mostly in the vicinity of the division's forward headquarters, yet I saw no one collect them.

Just before sunset, a fierce fight broke out along the trail, exchanging mortar and machine gunfire. Our field artillery guns pounded the enemy. Major Jeong informed us that finally one battalion had arrived from the front line and begun a counterattack. He was now confident that the battalion force would surely defeat the enemy and reopen the supply line. Despite his confidence, he ordered us to be on the highest alert. He also instructed us to cook supper using our emergency ration. Because all the vehicles were mobilized to transport the battalion from the front line to the trail area, no regular supper would be coming that evening. We collected deadwood, made a fire, and cooked plain, bland rice using our field mess kits. I wished I had some salt but forced myself to eat as much as possible. We might not eat for many days if the situation became worse. Those without field mess kits boiled rice in their helmets. The fire melted the helmet paint and mixed it with the rice. They ate it anyway.

The intense battle continued into the night. I tried to get some sleep, but the artillery explosions kept me awake. Late in the evening, Major Jeong gathered us and said gravely, "Soldiers, the situation has become serious. The battalion is not able to reopen the trail. A large enemy force has infiltrated deep behind our position. We are ordered to retreat individually on foot. Destroy anything you cannot carry. Unload extra ammunition in one place as Lieutenant Park (the battalion's ordnance officer) directs you. Our fighter bombers will bomb them in the morning." He paused for a few moments. He cleared his throat and continued, "Then, climb up the range on the south leading to Odaesan Mountain. Meet in the southern foothills. You should make it. Good luck! Now, move!"

Anxiety gripped me. Now another life-or-death situation was brewing. Nobody talked, but I knew that the same agony tormented all the others, too. I put my backpack on and slung my rifle over my shoulder. I reduced my ammo to two hand grenades and two cartridges of bullets (thirty rounds each), making myself as light as possible. I wanted to dispose of my extra ammunition properly, but it was too dark to find the ordnance officer. Someone nearby said in a distressed tone, "I don't even know where the ammo disposal place is. I don't care," and hurled his ammo into the river. Then he left for the mountain. His hurried departure reminded me that a few short moments might determine my fate, so I dumped my extra ammo into a nearby thicket and followed him, as did others. We crossed the shallow river by which we had camped for the last couple of weeks. We met a group of soldiers who did not know which way they should go. I didn't see any of my close friends among them. Perhaps they had already left for the mountain. We told the group to follow. Many more joined us. As we reached the foot-hills, hundreds of soldiers gathered. It was utter chaos. A familiar voice was directing. I recognized that it was Major Jeong's and was elated. I elbowed through the crowd, reached him, and hollered, "Major Jeong!"

Even though it was dark, he instantly recognized me and responded, "Sergeant Kim, is anyone else from our battalion with you?"

"No, sir. I am afraid we have lost each other."

"I hope they all make it to the mountain. Sergeant Kim, you take this ridge and follow these guys all the way to the top. Once you reach it, bear with the top ridge leading southeast. If you meet anyone you know, tell him what I told you. Stick together. Now, go! I will join you soon."

There must have been many officers, including the division commanding general, ranked higher than Major Jeong, but the major was the only officer directing the confused, scared, and tired soldiers. I was fortunate to be under his command.

With no moon, twinkling starlight from the deep, black sky was the only light we had. When we entered a thick forest along the ridge, the tall trees hid the stars from us. This made the already dark night even darker. As Major Jeong had directed, I followed the groups climbing the ridge. Many hundred more trailed behind. I didn't know who they were, or to what unit they belonged. The higher I climbed, the more I panted, and the thirstier I became. Sweat drenched me. I stumbled over rocks often or bumped into big tree trunks. It hurt, but I had no time for self-pity. Hardly anybody talked. It was a long, quiet march of a huge body of defeated soldiers. Occasionally, the sound of deadwood cracking under our heavy boots broke the eerie silence.

After five hours of inglorious marching along an uncharted, rugged trail, the pale morning sunlight filtered through the green leaves. By then, my canteen was empty. I was exhausted and severely dehydrated, sweating no more. My lips started to crack, my tongue stuck to my palate, and my vision became blurry. My feet weighed tons. All I wanted was water. I asked the soldiers around me if they had any with them, but they did not. I desperately searched for a heavy canteen. Then, a lowly private passed by me. His canteen hung heavy on his utility belt. I grabbed it and said desperately, "Water, please!" Without his permission, I took it out of its holder. I hastily opened the cap and gulped the water. My barbaric behavior stunned him. He stood still and silently watched me swallowing his precious water. Perhaps my higher rank kept him from protesting. I took a deep, satisfying breath and licked my lips lest I waste any. Within a few moments, my strength came back. With profound satisfaction and sincerity, I said, "Thank you! You have saved me!" and returned the canteen even though I needed more.

As he put it back into its holder, he murmured, "The water belongs to my platoon commander. He is going to be mad at me."

"No commander should make another soldier carry his water. If it is his water, he should carry it himself. I am a platoon sergeant, but I've never burdened my soldiers with my personal stuff." I saw a second lieutenant watching us nearby. I presumed him to be this poor private's platoon commander. I purposely yelled, "Give him my thanks for the water and tell him that he should carry his own." On battlefields, fresh platoon commanders (second lieutenants) often rely on their experienced platoon sergeants. Apparently, he knew this, and did not challenge me.

Reenergized, I looked down to see what was going on in the valley that we had abandoned in chaos the previous evening. A thick blanket of morning fog filled the valley, and I saw nothing. I turned around and searched for the crest of the mountain. I saw many lines of weary soldiers snaking upward through the big trees, but nowhere was the crest in view. Then, I looked over another ridge, not too far from my right, and saw a long line of people slowly climbing. I couldn't tell whether they were our soldiers or the enemy's. I approached the platoon commander and said, "Lieutenant, do you see people on the ridgeline to our right?"

"Yes, I do," he responded.

"Are they the enemy's soldiers, or ours?"

"I can't tell."

"Obviously, they can see us, too. But they do not fire at us. Most likely, they are ours. Don't you agree, sir?"

"I do."

"Lieutenant, thank you very much for the water. And I apologize for my harsh language."

He graciously accepted my apology, and we encouraged each other, climbing along the steep, heavily wooded slope. A couple of hours later, we reached the crest, where we merged with those from the other ridges. Then the lieutenant and I got separated in the multitude of retreating soldiers. I never saw him again.

Someone ahead hollered, "Waterhole!" The word '*Waterhole!*' electrified me. I wanted to run there but could only walk. Then I met a soldier coming toward me. A few canteens hung heavily on each of his hands, hitting each other and generating sweet tinkling sounds. Apparently, he had fetched water for himself and his friends. I asked, "Soldier, where did you get the water?"

He stopped and answered, "Sergeant, continue on the ridge for about twenty yards, then climb down the northern slope for a short distance. You will find a cold spring where a bunch of soldiers are filling their canteens." Then he said, "Sergeant, drink some water. You must be thirsty," and offered me one of his canteens.

I grabbed it and took many gulps of water. I thanked him profusely. I followed his directions, and he went on to join his friends. Soon I saw a few clusters of weary soldiers climbing down the northern slope. I followed them. More soldiers followed me. While climbing down, I met a couple of groups returning from the spring. Unlike the soldiers going my way, these returning soldiers were chatting and laughing. Some of them wiped dripping water off their foreheads. Apparently, the cold spring water had restored their vigor.

I knew that the mountains around this region were at least three thousand feet high. So, I imagined that the spring would be a trickle and worried if it would produce enough for all of us. I also thought that I would have to wait a long time for my turn. After a short, slippery trail, I arrived at the fountain. I found it at the base of a small rock wall. Six soldiers circled around it; some impatiently scooped up handfuls of water and slurped them, while others filled their canteens. Suddenly, a soldier jumped up and exclaimed, "Now I am alive again!" while pouring water on his head.

Unconsciously, I responded to him with a loud hoorah, ran to the waterhole, and lay on my stomach by the edge of the spring, between two soldiers. I plunged my head into the ice-cold water and gulped without a pause until my stomach told me, "Enough!" I raised my head and took a deep, satisfying breath. I sat down, wiped the dripping water from my face with my filthy fatigue sleeves, and said, "Spirit of this great mountain, thank you for this cold spring. You have saved me." After filling my canteen, I stood up and gratefully looked at this life-saving waterhole. It was an oval-shaped natural well, about five feet long and three feet wide, overflowing with clear water. I was utterly amazed at this abundant flow. What a miracle! No doubt, this spring water saved many dehydrated men that day.

After getting my strength back, I returned to the crest, rejoined the long, slow-moving line, and continued on the southeast bound ridge. Normally, soldiers put their right arms through the straps of their rifles and let their weapons hang from their right shoulders while holding the straps with their right hands. But now, they carried their weapons in other ways. Few talked.

After an hour's climb, the trail leveled out. Some took their rest in clusters. Others, including me, kept going. Soon hunger slowed me, but I pressed on for thirty more minutes. I wished I had something to eat but had nothing. Then, I saw a soldier eating rice out of his field mess kit with his bare hand. This reminded me of a small amount of rice left over from my previous evening's supper. I had completely forgotten that I carried it with me. Immediately, I unloaded my mess kit from my backpack. I cut a thin, smooth branch of a highland bush with my bayonet, made a pair of improvised chopsticks, and ate my rice with them while walking. It was so delicious, even without a side dish. Then, I met a group resting. There was a one-star general and a beautiful young woman among them. She watched me eating my rice enviously and said, "Oh, he is eating rice! I wish I had some."

Her words pained me. My heart said, "Share the rice with her!" But the greedy side of me jumped in and whispered, "Don't! You do not have enough for yourself. Besides, she enjoys a comfortable living with the general while you spend every day, hot or cold, rain or snow, in a dirty foxhole." This internal conflict robbed me of my rational thinking. I chose to pretend that I hadn't heard her.

I finished the rice as quickly as I could lest someone snatch it from me. This small amount of rice gave me some energy. About a quarter mile of trail later, my conscience returned and I wanted to go back to her and apologize for my shameful act. She needed food, not my apology. But I had no food left.

While I was feeling guilty, I heard a familiar voice from behind. It was one of my closest friends, Sgt. Chang Hyokoen. I turned around and called, "Hyokoen!"

He looked in my direction, ran toward me, put his arm around my neck, shook me, and excitedly responded, "Hey, Tae-hyok. You are alive! Are you okay?"

"Yeah, I am okay. Have you seen anyone from our company on the way?"

"None since we split last night. We lost each other. I hope everybody makes it to the rendezvous."

"I hope so, too. I met Major Jeong at the foothill last night, directing soldiers. Did you see him there, too?"

"No, I didn't."

"He is a good commander. I wish he was with us now. Want some cold water?" I asked, giving him my canteen.

He took it and said, "I have some in mine, but yours is cold. Where did you get it?"

"About half a mile back, there is a big waterhole. Obviously, you missed it."

After a few gulps, he said, "It's good water. Thanks." Returning the canteen, he continued, "Two years ago, I was assigned to this region to collect intelligence about the North Korean Army activities. I was stationed here for a few months and became familiar with the geography around the Hyeon-ri - Sangnam-ri Valley. Whoever chose this trail knows the region very well. We are on the right track. After about a mile, the trail will descend to a narrow valley with a small river. We should follow the river upstream for about three miles to the northern foothill of the Odaesan Mountain that we need to cross to reach our rendezvous."

I listened to him, but my heart was heavy because of the girl. Finally, I asked, "Did you see a young woman and a one-star general on the way?"

"Yes, I did. They are not too far behind us. The general is accompanied by an entourage."

"How was the woman doing? Was she alright?"

"She seemed okay. Why, do you know her?"

"No, I don't." I told him what had happened and added that I felt ashamed. He silently listened to my story. Then he said, "You are too sensitive. To begin with, you didn't have enough rice to share. More importantly, she did not starve to death. I saw her walking as rigorously as any of her group. So, cheer up!" He slapped me on the helmet.

"Thank you. That makes me feel better," I responded. But soon, we ceased to talk.

The trail became rockier and started ascending. The highland bushes here were just starting to yield yellowish-green young leaves while the vegetation down in the valleys was lush. The May sun poured warmth bountifully on this high mountain and the valleys below. The clumps of white clouds lazily moved across the blue sky, indifferent to our dire plight. A cool breeze gently shook the young leaves and softly rubbed my cheeks before it drifted down the slope. I had already emptied my canteen halfway. Only a few hours earlier, when I had been suffering from dehydration, I did not sweat, but now my army fatigue jacket was drenched.

Suddenly, with a thundering noise, eight American Air Force jet fighter bombers in two separate groups flew over us to the north. From this high ridge, at more than a five-thousand-foot elevation, the planes looked larger, faster, more furious, and more magnificent than they would have looked from the lowland. I could easily see the vivid white stars on the avocado green wings. They disappeared as fast as they had appeared.

Hyokoen said, "I am sure those planes are going to bomb the weapons, vehicles and other supplies which we abandoned last night so that the North Koreans cannot use them." A few moments later, he turned in the direction of the Hyeon-ri Valley and shouted excitedly, "Tae-hyok, look at those planes! They are bombing!"

We weary soldiers stopped, turned, and watched the attack. In the distance, the planes flew in a big circle. Then, one of them swooped down like a bullet, fired its rockets at its target, rose as fast as it had descended, and joined the others. As soon as the first one started to rise, the second one darted toward the target and executed the same attack as the first had done. Then, the rest followed one after another. They kept repeating the attack. Ominous towers of black smoke rose behind the mountain range that we had trekked through all night. Some shouted, "Destroy them all!" But others silently watched until the planes flew south after finishing their mission. The bombing did not last long, perhaps ten minutes. We resumed our trail in long, disarrayed lines, wishing for the destruction of everything we had abandoned.

Someone behind me hollered, "We were winning the battle and were ready to advance farther until yesterday morning. I don't understand why the whole division collapsed so quickly. Now, we are retreating. Why?" But no one responded, maybe because we were too tired or did not know exactly what had gone wrong. Right now, the enemy had the upper hand and could cut off our retreat unless we moved fast.

After a long rise, the mountain began to descend. Sgt. Hyokoen stopped abruptly and said, "Tae-hyok, can you see a river down there? That's the one I told you about. We will follow it upstream."

I halted and looked down the valley. A long line of soldiers snaked along the river southeastward. More emerged from the foothills and joined the line. The dazzling early afternoon sun shone on the dancing river. Expecting to reach an abundance of cool water soon, I drank my water to the last drop before starting to descend. It was easier to go down than to climb up even though the trail was as rugged as before. As soon as we arrived at the riverbank, we jumped into the river, slurped water, scooped it, and dumped it on our heads, exclaiming, "Oh, it's good! I've wanted this for a long time." After wiping off the dripping water, we refilled our canteens and hurriedly joined the line.

Shortly after our rest, Hyokoen started to lag behind and became quiet. Normally, he was a pleasant, optimistic person. Only a few hours ago, he had encouraged me and other soldiers. Now, without a word, he stepped to the roadside and sat down, using his rifle as a support. His head drooped between his knees. I sat next to him and said, "You look very tired. This water will give you some strength," and gave him my canteen.

He pushed it away and said weakly, "I want to sleep," and lay on his side. "You go ahead. I will join you after my sleep." Apparently, he was suffering from exhaustion and hunger. He wasn't coherent.

I worried that if he fell asleep, he might never wake up, or the enemy might capture him. I shouted, "You are not going to sleep here. Get up!" I kicked his butt and pulled him up by the arm. He didn't move. In desperation, I took out my canteen, poured some water on his face, and yelled, "You son of a bitch, get up! Move!"

He opened his eyes, and said, "Why did you do that?" and closed them again. I slapped him hard in the face a few times and helped him get up. He struggled to stand. I took his rifle, slung it on my shoulder with mine, held him with my free hand, and pushed him forward. When we covered a couple of hundred feet, he murmured, "I'm hungry."

Alas, I didn't have any food. I asked the passing soldiers if they had any food with them, but they did not. When we had walked another thirty feet, we met two soldiers sitting on the roadside eating their Korean Army crackers. After I let Hyokoen sit down, I approached them and said, "Hello, I think you are miracle workers. My friend is in a dangerous situation from extreme hunger. Unless he eats now, he may not make the rendezvous. Would you share some of your crackers?"

Without hesitation, they said, "Sure, no problem! Take this and feed him, Sergeant!" and gave me half a bag of crackers. "We wish we could give you more."

I was overwhelmed by their generosity. "Thank you very much. You have saved my friend," I said, extending my hands and grasping each of theirs firmly. "Good luck! I hope I see you again at the rendezvous." They were ranked lower than me but had big hearts.

I came back with the crackers and found Hyokoen lying with his eyes closed. Since the water in my canteen had become warm from my body heat, I replaced it with cooler water from the river. Then, I shook him and said, "Hyokoen, wake up! I have some food for you," and lifted his head against my chest. I poured cold water on his head. He opened his eyes halfway and groaned, "I am tired. Let me sleep." He closed his eyes again. I shouted, "Wake up! I have some food!" I crushed a piece of cracker in my dirty palm, put it into his mouth, and gave him some water. He slowly swallowed it and licked his lips. He did not open his eyes. I continued feeding him in the same manner for fifteen minutes. Many soldiers passed us. Some of them inquired if he was okay. But no one stopped to help. Since I knew that we couldn't spend too much time here, I pulled him up by the arm and supported him by placing his arm over my shoulders. He hung heavy on me. It was not easy to carry him and his rifle. However, the more crackers I fed him, the stronger he became. Since I was hungry, too, the temptation to have some of them was intense, but I suppressed it because my friend needed them more. By the time he had finished the last piece, he was able to walk without my support, but it took a while before he became fully coherent.

"Tae-hyok, you have saved my life. I owe you so much," he said wanly. "I think I am getting my strength back." Suddenly, he halted and said, "I have lost my rifle."

"No, you didn't. I have it with me. Do you want it back?" I returned it.

"Thank you, Tae-hyok." He took it and slung it on his shoulder. He was overwhelmed; he continued to move quietly, and then abruptly asked, "Where are we?"

"We are in the valley with a river that you told me about this morning. You said that we should follow the river upstream to the Odaesan Mountain. Maybe two more miles will bring us there."

"Oh?" he said. He kept walking silently for a long time. Then, he put his hand on my shoulder and said in a serious tone, "Tae-hyok, once again, thank you. When this goddamn, lousy war is over, and the country is reunified, you will come with me to my parents' home to meet them and my sister. She is a beautiful girl. They will be happy to meet you. As I told you before, my parents own the largest department store in the city of Sinuiju. They will gladly give you a job, and you can attend Sinuiju Middle School. I have yet to meet a soldier like you, studying mathematics and English on the front line, when we do not even know whether we will still be alive or not in the next moment. I told you before that, because of your spirit and sincerity, I wanted to match you up with my only sister when this war was over. But you took it as a joke. Now, I am telling you this again; take it seriously. My parents have only two children, my sister and me. They will eventually turn their business over to me. I want you to become a member of my family. I will treat you as if you were my younger brother." Then, he paused. He seemed to be reflecting on his life and thinking about his future.

As I quietly listened to him, my heart swelled. I pictured his sister as a sophisticated city girl, and wondered if she would like a farm boy. I imagined myself in a middle school uniform, carrying a book bag. I did not know how to answer my friend. So, I said, "Thank you very much, Hyokoen. Obviously, you come from a wealthy family. You must have enjoyed a good living. Why did you come to the South and join the army?"

He kept silent for a few moments, took a deep breath, and answered, "I was a senior at Sinuiju Middle School in November 1945. The leaders of the student body organized the first anti-communist rally in North Korea and mobilized almost the entire student body. Then, we marched through the streets with banners reading *DOWN WITH COMMUNISM; GO HOME, RUSSIANS! WE DON'T NEED YOU.* Of course, the Russian occupiers didn't like it. They ruthlessly crushed the rally, rounded up the organizers, and put them in jail. I was one of them. My father, one of the wealthiest men in the city, bribed the authorities and freed me. But I was expelled from the school just a couple of months before my graduation. After the expulsion, I helped with my parents' business. As the Communists solidified their power and their grip on people's daily lives, I felt pressure from the authorities. After I discussed the situation with my parents, I fled to the South in 1947 and joined the South Korean Army early the following year. It's already been more than four years since I left my family. Oh, I miss them," he sighed. After a few minutes of silence, he said, "I guess you, too, miss your parents."

I said, "Yes, I do! But, right now, we must make the rendezvous. Are you strong enough to walk?"

"Yes, thanks to you," he said, and started to walk faster.

He was gaining strength, but I was becoming weaker. Exhaustion overtook me, and I began to lag behind. He slowed down to keep pace with me and tried to encourage me, but I kept silent. Eventually, he, too, stopped talking. As the afternoon wore on, I got tired and stopped more frequently to rest. Suddenly, cool water drops fell on my neck. It was raining. I hadn't even noticed the brilliant sunshine yielding to gray, sullen clouds. I took my raincoat from my backpack and put it on. Today it was much heavier than before. Raindrops fell from the edge of my helmet. Weary soldiers with drooping heads dragged past us in clusters of five or six.

At last, we reached the northern foothills of the Odaesan Mountain Range. I looked at the steep and rugged trail shrouded in gray fog. A long line of tired soldiers slowly snaked upward and disappeared into the thick mist. I thought that, except for wild ginseng collectors, few people had ever dared to venture up this scabrous mountain. *Do I have to climb up this hellish ridge? I am already utterly exhausted, hungry, and cold. How can I?* I decided to take another rest before starting to climb. I sat on a boulder and rested my head on my rifle. Hyokoen quietly settled next to me. I immediately fell asleep until he shook my shoulder and said, "Tae-hyok, we have to go," and pulled me up by the arm, as I had done to him a few hours earlier. I reluctantly got up and started climbing up the trail. I managed about fifty steps with Hyokoen's support, but I could go no farther. I stopped again and sat on the wet grass. My exhaustion was so intense that I didn't feel anything; all I wanted was some sleep. I said, "Hyokoen, you move on. I am going to take a good rest and then follow you. Please move!"

He responded, "No, I am not going anywhere without you," and sat down. "You must meet my sister. Let's move!" he pleaded. He tried to lift me up, but I couldn't move.

"Hyokoen, this mountain is over five thousand feet high. There is no way I can climb over it to the rendezvous without a good rest. So, please leave me alone!" Then, I lay on a rock and closed my eyes.

Hyokoen pulled me by the arm and shouted, "Get up!" He pushed me from behind. After a few more steps, I crumbled. He tried to lift me up a few more times and pleaded.

"Hyokoen, please take my diary from my backpack for me!" He took it out. I asked, "If I do not make the rendezvous within the next couple of days, would you please keep it with you and mail it to my father when the war is over? It has my parents' names and address. Write to him about my last day, please. I know that you cannot carry me to the crest of this mountain because you are tired, too! Neither of us has any food. Right now, there is nothing you can do for me. If you think I am your best friend, then you take this diary with you and move on. There is absolutely no reason for you to stay with me. Go!"

He hung his head and listened quietly to me. After a few minutes of silence, he said, "I will keep your diary with me, and I will visit your parents and deliver it to them personally." He held me tightly in his arms and said in a broken voice, "I shall leave, but I want to see you at the rendezvous." He let me lie down. He dragged his feet and disappeared into the fog.

I lay flat on my back. Cold rain fell on my face, but I didn't care. Soon, I fell into deep oblivion. Then, someone sat on my chest, ringed my neck with his hands, and choked me. I tried to get rid of his hands, but he was too strong; I kicked the air in vain. I screamed for help, but no sound came out. Somehow, I managed to poke my fingers into his eyes. He screamed in pain, fell off me, and ran away. I instinctively sat up and rubbed my neck. I coughed violently and spit out watery mucous. Water streamed from my nostrils. I did not see my assailant; there was no one except weary stragglers trudging the steep trail with their heads bowed. I realized I had been dreaming or hallucinating, and the rain had made me choke. As the water trickled from my nose, my cough slowly abated. Finally, the cough ceased.

This nightmare consumed whatever strength I had. I just sat distractedly and watched those dog-tired soldiers struggling to climb up. No one paid any attention to me. As time progressed, the traffic became thinner, and finally there was no more. It was so quiet, except for the sound of the rain. Suddenly, I was scared and cold. I managed to get up using my rifle as a support and climbed up a few steps, but my legs did not move farther. I sat on the wet grass and slid more than I had climbed. Tears welled in my eyes and overflowed, warming my cheeks. I reflected on my life and murmured, "Dad and Mom, I became a twenty-year-old man just three weeks ago. I am not the sixteen-year-old boy anymore whom you last saw. But today might be my last day in this world. We are not going to see each other again. Mom, forgive me for all the heartbreak I caused you because I fought with Yun-ok. I wish I had been a gentler uncle to her instead of a jealous one. Mom and Dad, I miss you so much. Be healthy until we meet again in the next world. Goodbye!" I also called my brothers, sisters, sisters-in-law, and all their children by name, and bid farewell to each of them. I saw the opportunity to meet a girl and gain an education slipping through my fingers. I was overwhelmed. I dropped my head between my knees and sobbed shamelessly for a few minutes. The tears stopped. I raised my head and took a deep breath. Mysteriously, tranquility filled my heart; my fear and sadness were gone. I looked northwest, in the direction of my hometown, thinking about my boyhood days, and saw the big, orange sun peeking through the broken black clouds. I had seen the orange sun many times before, but today it was more beautiful and precious. It disappeared behind the dark clouds as quickly as it had appeared. I wished it had stayed longer. I looked back down the trail that

I had traveled that afternoon and felt good about having saved my friend. This assuaged my guilt at not having shared my rice with the hungry young woman earlier that morning. I prayed to some supreme power, "Please lead that young woman to the rendezvous."

The rain changed to drizzle, and dusk stealthily rolled over the land. I heard the noises of vehicles in the distance. I presumed the enemy had begun their transportation activities under the cover of darkness. By day, they did not dare to move, because our air force mercilessly hunted them down. Then, I realized that they were approaching me. Yet this did not scare me at all. You will not capture me. You will not put me in a coalmine. My resolution not to be caught and imprisoned again inspired me to act before they could reach me. I removed nonessentials from my backpack to lighten my load, starting with my field mess kit. But I kept my algebra and English books and an extra pair of socks; I don't know why. I discarded my heavy metal helmet, keeping its plastic liner. I used to carry two grenades and two magazines of ammunition. I decided to retain one of each, discarding the extras, but I took one cartridge from the second magazine and put it in my jacket pocket to use to terminate my life if I had to. When I stood up, my legs wobbled. I started to climb the trail and vainly searched for footprints. It was too dark to find any. I thought that if I managed to reach the crest of the range, I would turn right and continue on the ridge until the sun rose. Then, I could find the footprints of the soldiers who had preceded me and follow them to the rendezvous.

As I slowly ascended the trail, my strength trickled back. Until a couple of hours ago, I couldn't even move ten steps, and had given up all hope. Now, joy and hope filled my heart and pushed me to quicken my pace. But to avoid further exhaustion, I took it slowly. I continued to climb for two or three more hours. The rain gradually changed to wet snow. The mix of the snow and the wet dead leaves made the trail very slippery. As the elevation increased, the snow intensified, and it turned into whiteout. *Oh my gosh, snow in the middle of May? Am I going to die frozen instead of by the enemy's hands?* But it was a brief blizzard, and the snow ended. Soon, the clouds broke apart, and the silvery moon appeared over the ridge, illuminating the trail dimly. As the moon rose higher, I could see the fallen leaves and some footprints. I was elated to find them. My morale improved, and I realized I would make it to the rendezvous.

The higher the trail climbed, the deeper the snow became. My fingers were freezing. I took out the pair of socks that I had saved and used them as gloves. The bright moon and the white snow made it easier to follow the track. It was a mystery that only six hours ago starvation had driven me to give up the hope of survival. Now my strength was returning without any food intake. When I gave up my hope of making the rendezvous, my mind was so peaceful. I feared nothing. But, as my strength and hope rose, anxiety crept back into my heart. *Could I really catch up with my fellow soldiers? If the enemy had taken the rendezvous place before I could reach it, what would I do?* But I encouraged myself by saying, "Sure, I can. I will make it to the rendezvous! No enemy will beat me there. Relax! Keep going!"

At last, I reached the peak of the mountain. My confidence improved. The moon smiled and showed me the trail. I saw many clear footprints on the ridge and followed them for about half a mile. Unexpectedly, slight noises came from the front. Instinctively, I stopped, held my breath, and listened. They were human voices. I wondered whether they were friends or foes. The last group of South Korean soldiers that had passed me was six hours ago. I figured they would be two miles ahead. Thus, these guys must be the enemy, not my fellow soldiers. *Trapped! This is it, my last day!* A chill ran down my spine. My heart sank. My legs weakened. I wondered how my enemies had come this fast and this far? I sat on the snow to determine my next steps. I knew that I could not go back or move forward. So, I took my rifle from my shoulder, released the safety pin, and stealthily approached them. When I could hear them more clearly, I stopped and listened to their conversation to identify them. I heard someone calling, "Sergeant Lee." and "Yeah, what do you want?" I recognized the responder's voice. It was my Company Sergeant! I kneeled and murmured, "Thank God, I have made it!" I was so excited that I could not get up for a few moments. After calming down, I hollered, "Master Sergeant Lee! This is Kim Tae-hyok. Don't shoot!" I picked up my pace.

As I approached them, I repeated, "Master Sergeant Lee, this is Sergeant Kim Tae-hyok," to let him know that I was one of his soldiers, not a foe. They were taking their rest. Even though the moon was bright, I did not recognize them because of their helmets.

MSgt. Lee answered, "Kim Tae-hyok, come over here!" and stood up. When I reached him, he grabbed my shoulder firmly and said, "You made it! Glad to see you." Before I could express my thanks, he asked, "Did you see anyone from our company?"

"Only Sergeant Chang Hyokoen was with me, but we were separated. It was early evening." I did not tell him how we had split. "He should have been ahead of me because I saw no one behind me for a long time. Was anyone from our company with you, Sergeant?"

"Yeah, Sergeant Maneong and Corporal Pak," he answered. Then he hollered, "Sergeant Maneong and Corporal Pak, come over here! Kim Tae-hyok is here."

The two joined us and welcomed me warmly. Man-E said, "You skinny son of a bitch, I'm glad to see you again."

Corporal Pak added, "So glad you've made it, Sergeant Kim."

Before I could respond, MSgt. Lee said, "We should stick together. I know this mountain area fairly well. Follow me." As we departed, a dozen stragglers whom we did not know followed us.

Only six hours ago, I had given up all hope of survival. But mysteriously, my strength had slowly returned along the trail, enough to catch up with those friends.

We trekked along the rugged, snow-covered ridge. Soon the four of us began to intermingle with the other soldiers. MSgt. Lee worked hard to keep us together, calling each of us by name frequently, and the bright moon helped us to stay close. But soon the fickle weather brought a thick shield of dark clouds over us. The moon disappeared completely, leaving the path invisible. To make matters worse, sleet started to fall, making the trail slippery. MSgt. Lee gathered us and said, "These conditions make it difficult for us to act as a group, but we must. You guys follow me closely, first Tae-hyok, then Maneong, and then Pak. Don't drop behind too far! If you can't see the person in front of you, holler. This is the best way to make it through the night. Remember to act as if we are one body! Now, let's move!"

Despite our best efforts, we were separated and reunited a few times during the night. Each time, we halted and waited until we got together again. This slowed our progress. The bad weather did not make me cold, perhaps because I continued to move. After a few hours of arduous trekking, MSgt.

Lee led us down the mountain along a steep southern canyon. Climbing down in the darkness turned out to be dangerous and difficult. I frequently tripped over rocks and fell. Sometimes, the slope was so steep that I slid down on my rear end. On one occasion, to our horror, we all tumbled off a large ledge. But amazingly, none of us sustained a severe injury.

After stumbling and sliding, we finally reached the foothill of the mountain where a small creek flowed, and a narrow country road snaked beside it. Perhaps people gathering firewood might have used the road. MSgt. Lee said, "Let's take a few minutes of rest here before proceeding. The rendezvous place may not be too far." We huddled on the wet grass. It was not as dark as before, as dawn must have begun to break. We all felt relieved. I noticed that none of the soldiers from other units, who had joined us, were with us anymore. I asked MSgt. Lee what had happened to them. He said that while we had regrouped on the mountain, they had gone ahead instead of waiting for us. He did not know which way they had gone. He hoped they were not stranded.

Man-E took out a cigarette and said, "This is my last cigarette." He lit it and gave it to MSgt. Lee. "Sergeant, you smoke it first because you are the Company Sergeant."

MSgt. Lee accepted it and puffed. "Oh, it is delicious! I've been craving a cigarette for a long time. Thank you, Maneong." After a few puffs, he returned it.

"You're welcome!" Man-E said. He, too, puffed it with gusto. "Certainly, it is delicious. I have never had a cigarette as delicious as this before." Although I had seen cigarettes burning red many times before, today, his looked so mesmerizing. The smoke wafted to my nostrils, and I sneezed. I didn't like the smell.

Corporal Pak said impatiently, "Man-E, I am waiting," while sniffing the smoke.

"I am sorry, Pak," Man-E said. He puffed one more time before passing it over.

After inhaling deeply, Pak added, "Oh, how sweet this cigarette is." After another satisfying long smoke, he asked, "Tae-hyok, will you try just one puff?"

Before I could respond, Man-E interjected, "Tae-hyok, do you know what you are missing in life by not smoking? Especially in this goddamn war? Well, you do not even know a woman yet."

"I just don't like stinking cigarettes. If it is so delicious, keep it with you, Pak. I don't need it!" I sneezed again.

Pak said, "Tae-hyok, you are like an innocent middle school kid. Whenever you have time, you read that crazy number book. You are still a virgin, aren't you?" and chuckled.

What he said reminded me that my twentieth birthday had come and gone a few weeks earlier, and that I was no longer a teenager. I felt sad at the thought that I could die without ever knowing a woman.

Then MSgt. Lee interrupted, "Hey guys, leave him alone! He is a good schoolboy." He laughed, too. After circulating the cigarette for the last puff, he said, "Soon daylight will break. Then we will know how far we are to the rendezvous. Right now, it is too dark to tell exactly how much farther we have. Let's move!" We resumed marching.

Strangely, those good-natured jibes relieved me from the tension that had built up during the retreat. I thought I was fortunate to be with my friends, who could joke even in dire circumstances. The wet snow had changed to rain, indicating that the temperature was rising.

After we had covered about one mile, suddenly, MSgt. Lee halted and hushed us. "Quiet! I hear people talking ahead of us. I don't know if they are friends or foes."

Man-E whispered, "They must be our soldiers. No enemy soldiers could have penetrated this far. I have not seen any enemies for the last two days."

I added, "Do you remember that the enemy infiltrated behind our line and cut off our supply line two days ago? Because of that, our entire front collapsed, and we are now retreating miserably. We shouldn't assume they are our friends."

MSgt. Lee said, "We must identify them before we act. Since we do not have a nightly password, the only way to identify them is by listening to their conversations. If they call each other *comrade*, then they are the enemy. I will reconnoiter. You stay behind."

My heart beat fast, but I was determined to live, and believed that we would make it to the rendezvous. I suggested, "Master Sergeant Lee, let us all go together."

He said, "Okay. We will, but very quietly. If they are the enemy, we will fire at them simultaneously; charge loudly, and kill as many as we can. Then, under the cover of darkness and in their confusion, we will run through any survivors as fast as we can. Now, follow me!"

The rain fell steadily, which made the approach easier. The closer we got, the more clearly we could hear them. Suddenly, we saw a flashlight. We halted, ducked, and held our breaths. The flashlight was pointed away from us. Apparently, they were trying to read something. We sneaked closer and listened, hearing them call each other Sergeant or Corporal, not Comrade. We sighed with relief.

MSgt. Lee cautiously stood up and hollered, "This is Sergeant Lee from the 18th Regiment of the 3rd Division. Three others are with me. What unit are you from?"

"We are from the 1st Battalion of the same regiment as yours. What is your battalion?" they responded.

MSgt. Lee answered, "The 3rd Battalion! Phew! You are our friends." We all rushed and joined them. We grabbed their hands as if we were old friends, exchanging greetings. MSgt. Lee asked, "How many more soldiers are there besides you three?"

"None," the leader of the group answered. "I am the squadron sergeant. After receiving the retreat order, our whole company of about 130 left the front and took a mountain trail. I led the nine men from my squadron. During the retreat, we became separated despite our best effort to stick together. Now, only the three of us are left. I hope they make it to the rendezvous." He sighed. "The creek splits into two branches here. We are in a quandary about which one we should take. Sergeant Lee, do you have any idea?"

"No, I don't. But my instinct tells me that the larger one will lead us southeastward. Our rendezvous is in that direction. Soon, daylight will break. Then, we will find a way to the gathering place. What do you think?"

The squadron sergeant said, "Let's get going!" He led us, wasting no time. I could read the qualities of a battlefield leader in him, and my confidence grew stronger. We filed behind him. MSgt. Lee was first, and I followed him. In the beginning, we conversed briefly, but soon became silent. We were too tired to talk. Then, someone in the back broke the silence and said, "It is a hundred times easier to walk on this smooth road than on the rugged mountain trail." I agreed with him wholeheartedly.

Another chimed in, "Anyone have a cigarette? I am dying for one."

I could hardly understand why those guys preferred cigarettes over food. I wanted something to eat.

"We smoked our last cigarette a while back," MSgt. Lee answered.

The squadron sergeant responded, "Did you forget that we had smoked our last one back on the trail? Don't think about cigarettes. Just keep moving!"

We all fell silent again and moved on. The rain changed to drizzle. Shortly, the dawn broke over the misty valley, giving us better visibility. As we continued on, a group of seven soldiers climbed down from a ridge and joined us. We did not know them, but we welcomed them anyway.

They were tremendously relieved to see us. They said, "All night, we walked on uncharted rugged mountain trails without knowing where we were heading. We're so glad to meet you."

Soon another small group came from a small canyon and happily joined us. Of course, we were happy, too. They had endured the same arduous trek. They came from a different regiment which had been deployed farther east. They were as concerned about their missing friends as we were about ours. They looked as haggard and dirty as we were. But I felt much safer with those men.

After another quarter of a mile, the canyon abruptly ended, and the creek flowed into a river. When we reached the riverbank, a long line of weary soldiers came into view, moving slowly along the opposite bank. We instantly recognized them as our fellow South Korean soldiers. We were overjoyed to see them.

MSgt. Lee and the squadron leader called out, "Hello, we are from the 18th Regiment of the 3rd Division. What's yours?" while we waved. Those soldiers who had just joined us shouted, "Anyone from the 17th Regiment?"

They halted and responded loudly. Some said, "Hey, the 18th Regiment. Come over here!" Others shouted back, "The 17th Regiment. Welcome you guys. Come over!" They all waved back wildly.

Once again, I thought about how some higher power had restored my strength and brought me this far. I knew that I would survive this ordeal. I was overwhelmed with gratitude for this divine entity, whoever he might have been, for saving me from the brink of death. Despite going hungry for the last two days, my strength and morale soared. I waved and yelled, "The 3rd Battalion of the 18th Regiment?" hoping to hear familiar voices.

We all rushed into the river and waded through the fast moving, knee-deep water. When we reached the other side, they helped us climb up to the bank. "Come on, hurry up, guys!" I knew none of them, but they welcomed us with earnest battlefield camaraderie. We learned that they belonged to the 3rd Division. After thanking them, we joined our corresponding units. The seven of us from the 18th Regiment met fifteen more of our men. Despite the leaden sky and the drizzle, we all rejoiced. A sergeant from the group told us that because they had no idea which trail they should have taken, they had followed his compass until they had met the larger group.

Exhaustion and hunger quickly subdued our excitement, and we all lapsed into silence. Besides, we knew that this bad weather would keep our fighter-bombers grounded, and that the enemy could make a bold move without fearing our air attacks. They could catch up with us anytime. We could not afford much time for our joyful reunion. Thus, we immediately resumed our trek.

Shortly, I found the landscape along the river and hills familiar. A little farther upstream, I saw a small farmhouse with a wood-shingled roof by the roadside. This reminded me of an earlier trip. A fellow soldier and I had traveled through this area to visit the Battalion OP in mid-March. A day earlier, the 3rd Battalion had been engaged in a battle resulting in many casualties. My trip was to update the battalion roll. I recognized the mountain in front of me and the trail over it. This trail would lead to the rendezvous, perhaps a couple more miles beyond the mountain. Then, I knew exactly where we were. This lifted my spirits so much that I wanted to run, but extreme fatigue kept my legs dragging.

Many people trudged along this narrow, almost pristine, wet trail that had turned into mire, like a muddy rice paddy. The drizzle changed back to a steady rain. This slowed us to a crawl. Sometime later, I noticed a man lying on the slimy roadside without his shirt. His eyes were closed; he was rubbing his dirty belly and writhing. His shaved head indicated that he was an enemy because all the North Korean foot soldiers had their heads shaved while the South Korean soldiers grew out their hair. I don't know how he had managed to infiltrate so far and so fast. Now, he was dying of sickness or starvation. But nobody came to help him. Perhaps that was because we were fighting for our own lives, or because he had come to kill us, or both. I felt sad for him, but I wouldn't help him under that circumstance. I just passed him, as all the others had, and continued on my way.

Shortly after that, I found a small piece of cracker on the slushy roadside. My eyes opened wide. It was swollen and mixed with mud. I halted, stooped, and scooped it up with the utmost care lest it escape between my fingers. It was as if I had found a precious gemstone. Then I cautiously slurped it and licked my palms.

Meanwhile, I had lost sight of my friends. But I didn't worry because the rendezvous was only a couple more miles beyond the mountain ahead of me. I knew the way. A long line of hundreds of weary soldiers trekked slowly up the trail and along the river. The line extended beyond my view; the head of it disappeared into the clouds that shrouded the mountain, and the tail faded into the lower rainy valley. This large crowd made little noise, except that of their heavy boots sloshing through the slime.

When I reached the foothill of the mountain and looked up the pass, I was overwhelmed and wondered if I could make it. But I assured myself, "You know this road. Unlike those rugged, uncharted trails which you have trekked during the past two days, this is a short mountain pass. Remember the rendezvous is just beyond this hill! Move on!" I trudged along with the others, although I was hungry and exhausted.

After a long haul across the pass, we finally reached the southern foothill of the mountain. A few narrow patches of farm fields were scattered along the valley. The road became a little bit wider and ran between those fields. I fell asleep while walking. I stumbled, and my helmet and rifle flew away. A soldier behind me helped me get up, and another retrieved my equipment. Even after this fall, my eyes continued to close. So, I took off my helmet liner and lightly hit my head with it. The pain kept me awake.

A few hundred feet farther down the valley, we saw four American Army jeeps parked by the roadside, and American soldiers huddled around them. Some of us excitedly shouted, "Look, down there, American soldiers! We are now safe!" We became reenergized and walked faster. When we came closer, we recognized one two-star general, one one-star general, and a couple of colonels escorted by a squadron of soldiers. We saluted the generals, who returned our salutes. My curiosity made me step to the roadside and watch them with appreciation for a few minutes. The generals and the officers spread a big map on the hood of one of the vehicles and studied it. They raised their heads and surveyed the mountains that we had just come through. The two-star general pointed in the direction of the mountains and conversed with the other officers. I presumed that they were planning a counterattack. I guessed that they were in the U.S. I Corp. I understood that our 3rd Division of the South Korean Army was then operationally under the I Corp Command. Now, the general and officers made me feel so safe that I saluted them again and rejoined the long line of weary fellow soldiers.

After another half mile, we finally reached the rendezvous. Numerous cardboard signs were posted along the road, directing stragglers to their corresponding units. I found one reading "The 3rd Battalion of the 18th Regiment," and there the Battalion Quartermaster Sergeants Kwon and Jeon stood by a truck and called loudly, "The 3rd Battalion of the 18th Regiment, come over here!" I hollered back, "Hey, Sergeant Kwon, Sergeant Jeon!" and hastened toward them. They put their arms over my shoulders and said, "Glad you made it, you skinny Tae-hyok. Take your rest." They led me to the truck. "You must be starving. We prepared rice and brought it up here."

There, I saw heaps of cooked rice in two big wooden pails! My eyes opened wide. I watched them for a few moments, wondering if it was real, then lunged, scooped up the rice with my dirty hands and put it into my mouth.

"Tae-hyok, slow down!" said Jeon. He took out his canteen and offered me his water. "Drink some water lest you choke."

I drank the water, ate the rice without much chewing, and licked my palms. Then I thanked him for the water. He asked for my mess kit so that he could fill it with rice. I told him I had discarded it on the way to reduce my load. He took a mess kit from the truck, filled it, and gave it to me. I thought I could consume the whole heap, but I could only finish half of it. Then I fell asleep until Sgt. Kwon woke me.

The late afternoon sun peeked through the broken clouds. I leaned against one of the truck's wheels and stretched my legs. Despite painful previous experiences, I took off my shoes and socks to nurse my aching feet. They smelled like rotten meat. My soles' outer skin had peeled off and rotted, becoming as thin as an onion skin. As the skin dried, my feet hurt like hell, and I groaned.

I rubbed them as gently as I could in order to alleviate the pain and massaged my toes to tame the muscle cramps. I took out my canteen and poured water slowly on my feet, which allayed the pain somewhat.

I noticed that there were only a few of us soldiers besides the two sergeants. This was supposed to be the battalion's assembly place, and there should be more men here. So, I asked, "Sergeant Kwon, isn't this our rendezvous? Are we the only ones who've made it here? Where are all the others?"

"Tae-hyok, we set up a rendezvous at a local elementary school, two miles farther down the valley, just south of the Gangneung Highway. We brought food up here to feed hungry soldiers like you as soon as possible. So far, we have fed a couple hundred."

I asked, "How did you and your friends avoid the enemy's trap and come here so fast that you could prepare a rendezvous and food for us?"

"We were damn lucky that disastrous day. We picked up some supplies from the division's supply depot in the Sangnam Village. After receiving our supplies, on the way back, we reached the checkpoint at the southern foothill of the bottleneck one-way pass. While waiting for our turn to crawl up the snakelike dirt road, suddenly, machine guns began to crackle at the summit of the trail. Mortar shell bombardments followed. Immediately, the traffic MPs instructed us to move off the road to an open field and await further notice. Not knowing who was firing, we turned around toward the field. On the way, numerous mortar shells hit an ammunition pile, and explosions shook the whole valley. All hell broke loose. The MPs shouted that all the personnel and vehicles should evacuate from the depot area to the outskirts of the village, and we hurriedly moved farther south. Fear and confusion overwhelmed us. A rumor spread that the enemy had broken through part of the front line. In the confusion, the supply depot director ordered us to retreat to Pyeongchang and to set up a rendezvous. We drove all night and arrived in the town yesterday morning. Then we set up a gathering place and an impromptu kitchen at a local schoolyard. Again, we were awfully fortunate."

I inquired about my friends Hyokoen, Lee, Man-E, and Pak. He said that Sgt. Chang Hyokoen had made it a few hours ago, and the other three were just ahead of me. "Now, you had better get going."

I was relieved to learn that they had made it. When I put on my boots, my feet hurt badly. Walking made them even worse, but I knew that I had to move on. After a couple of hours of hobbling, I finally arrived at our destination with some other soldiers. I saw a few hundred exhausted soldiers lying on the ground. Only a few remained standing. One of them was Major Jeong, our deputy battalion commander. He was conversing with one other officer whom I did not know. I reported to the major. He welcomed me and said, "I am glad you made it. Is anyone else with you?"

"No, sir!"

"Why don't you get some rest and then help Master Sergeant Lee take a headcount."

"Yes, sir!" Instead of resting, I began to search for my friend Hyokoen. But before I found him, exhaustion overtook me, and I crashed.

MSgt. Lee woke me. He had gathered all the company sergeants and said, "Major Jeong ordered me to do a battalion-wide headcount. Each of you, quickly get your company's count and report to me. Normally this is the Battalion Sergeant Major's responsibility, but he has not shown up yet. I hope he joins us soon. Now, get going!" MSgt. Lee picked me to represent him for the headquarters company.

I took out my company roll and did the headcount. About only half of the total personnel had made it to the rendezvous, including the Battalion Commander and Major Jeong. The rest were missing. While doing the headcount, I looked for my friend Hyokoen, but I did not see him. I wondered where he was. Among the missing were Company Commander Captain Chung, Sergeant Kim Jae-kook, and Sergeant Ha, Senior Sergeant of the Battalion Intelligence Section. I reported my results to MSgt. Lee. The total count was a little over two hundred, less than a third of the battalion in full force; two thirds were still missing. I wondered about the fate of those missing soldiers, and my heart ached. Many of them had joined the army with me, and we had received basic training together.

Someone shouted, "Tae-hyok!" I looked up to see Hyokoen standing in front of me. I jumped up. We embraced tightly. Emotion choked us both. Speechless, we held each other for a few moments. He murmured, "You made it! I knew you would."

I released him from my arms and said, "Of course. I didn't want to die. Let's sit down." We sank onto our backpacks. "A miracle happened to me."

He quietly listened to my story, then held me by the shoulders and said, "I am so happy that you have made it." He reached into his backpack, took out my diary, and returned it to me. "I am glad that I don't have to give this to your parents. Tae-hyok, when this horrible war is over, and the country is reunited, come and see my family."

I held my journal silently for a few moments before putting it in my backpack. My hands were shaking. I wanted to say 'Thank you!' until I calmed down.

In subsequent days, many of the missing soldiers fought through the enemy's siege and joined us; some had been captured but managed to escape in the confusion when our air force attacked. Eventually, the total grew to more than four hundred. About one third of the battalion force remained missing in action. Our battalion sergeant major, as well as Captain Chung and Sergeants Kim Jae-kook and Ha were among them. I still had hope that my friend Kim Jae-kook was alive.

A week later, I heard that Sergeant Lee Jong-kook, one of my best friends, had been killed while trying to break through the enemy siege, and his fellow soldiers had been unable to bring his body with them. I choked and bent over, trying to breathe, when hearing this news. He was one year older and much stronger and more solidly built than me—an excellent soldier with a warm heart. He had carried my raincoat during a long march as I struggled with my rifle and backpack. The gear was too heavy for me. I remembered our wonderful friendship. His loss pained me for a long time. I had lost a brother.

CHAPTER 23

Leaving the Army

October 1951 - July 1953

HOSPITAL ADMITTANCE

We fought a lot on the front lines around Inje and Odaesan. For months, I had a severe cough. In October 1951, when it continued to get worse, I decided to talk to my group leader about it. I didn't want it to slow me down or make me weak while fighting the enemy.

"Master Sergeant Lee, I'm constantly coughing up blood. I thought this would go away, but it's not. I think I just need the right medicine to get better." Lee consulted our company commander, who decided to send me to an army hospital.

My friends said goodbye to me. We all thought it would be a super quick trip where I needed just a few weeks of medical attention before returning to my squad. Corporal Pak came to me to say goodbye and I asked him if he had really killed the two nurse POWs. He said, "Skinny Sergeant Kim, I'll let you figure it out for yourself. Take care." He squeezed my hand with a warm smile and left. His lighthearted gesture suggested that he had let them go free, which made me feel better. I imagined the women making their way home to reunite with their families, no longer separated by war.

We were in Inje, and I took a boat to Pusan. An ambulance brought me from the boat to the hospital, where I was admitted for a lung condition. The hospital had been a high school. It had a big auditorium where all the beds were and six classrooms. There were about sixty patients. My futon was as dirty as everyone else's.

With friends at the Army Hospital on October 27, 1951. Tae-hyok is on the far right.

Mrs. Kim was the army hospital chaplain. I was unable to eat anything, so she made homemade applesauce and fed me for more than a week because I was so sick. The months I was there, she told me about Christ. I became a Christian when I was in that hospital.

The war kept going on, but in the hospital, I met different people. I made friends with the preacher who had been in a seminary school in North Korea before the authorities closed it down. Right after that, he became an anti-communist guerilla, and later, when the South Korean Army was retreating, he and his group joined them, but eventually, he became wounded and was sent here. I met another soldier from the ROK Army who had served at Chosin Reservoir with the U.S. Marines. He had lost both arms and both legs up to his knees due to frostbite. ROKA wintertime gear wasn't as warm as that of others who served in the war, but at the same time, it was known that many died at the Battle of Chosin due to cold or frostbite. Despite this, he was in good spirits, but sometimes he had days where he was depressed and wished he had died at Chosin. I was shocked by the stories he told and saddened by all the lives lost.

Once I felt better, I sneaked out of the hospital and attended an evening academy for English and math. The school was nearby, and the hospital guard would let me sneak out. I would then go back to the hospital and study in my bed. It was boring in the hospital compared to the battlefield. I missed my friends. I dreamed of being a tanker sergeant once I was redeployed, mainly because I wouldn't have to march as much as before. I kept coughing up blood, so I couldn't go back to my company yet.

In July 1952, after nine months in the hospital, I received a medical discharge from the army for a respiratory disease after four years and two months in the service. My redeployment never came. I felt homeless because I couldn't return to North Korea to see my family. I worked for the Army Hospital, helping with the Sunday and Wednesday services as well as with the patients. Many patients had lost their limbs, so I'd help feed them. I also entered a high school in Pusan for refugees in the second semester where I was a twenty-one-year-old 10th grader—the oldest student. The temporary building of the school was constructed on a hilltop overlooking the Pusan Harbor, with flimsy frames covered with thin pine boards and neither insulation nor

Army Hospital on Christmas Day 1951. Tae-hyok is the third row from the bottom on the left.

Tae-hyok and Tae-wook. July 12, 1952.　　Tae-jun

Tae-wook working as a policeman

sheetrock inside. The floor was muddy. I was thankful to the school's principal for not only admitting me despite my lack of junior high education but also for waiving the tuition.

That same summer, I went to visit Mr. Kim Tae-yun and his family in Seoul.

"Tae-hyok! It is great to see you!" I was warmly welcomed by them, and he gave me wonderful news. "Your brothers and Won-sik are here in South Korea!"

I was shocked and couldn't believe my ears! I learned from Mr. Tae-yun that he had received a U.S. Army contract for a construction project and had hired my oldest brother, Tae-jun. Tae-wook, meanwhile, had become a policeman. We all soon saw each other, and we hugged and were emotionally overwhelmed. It was bittersweet. I was happy to finally see them and Won-sik, but they weren't with the rest of our family.

They had crossed the 38th Parallel in late December 1950 and arrived in South Korea in January 1951. Twenty-five to thirty men from our valley crossed together to avoid being drafted by the North Korean Army. My brothers were die-hard anti-communists, and one of our hometown friends had already been executed by the North Koreans. It was such a cold winter, and too dangerous for their wives and younger children to cross. They thought that the withdrawal of the UN forces and South Korean Army from North Korea was tactical and temporary. They believed that these forces would return to North Korea within a couple of months, and they would come back and be reunited with them soon enough. So, the women and young children remained at home. Alas, the forces never returned.

JULY 1951 – JULY 1953 AND THE ARMISTICE

Truce talks between the United Nations and the communists began on July 10, 1951. These talks would last for over two years. This was due to the communists' first demanding that foreign troops leave Korea, and then where the border would lie, and lastly the prisoner exchange, which became the main issue.

During this time, the battles continued. However, there was less action during the winter of 1951. Neither side wanted to have to fight the freezing cold which had caused so many deaths the previous year. Spring and summer came, and the war's largest air raid, the bombing of Pyongyang, took place on August 29, 1952. By mid–1953, cities like Pyongyang had been devastated by American bombings. The North Koreans, to this day, remember this.

> *"Over a period of three years or so, we killed*
> *off—what—20 percent of the population."*[90]
> **—U.S. Air Force General Curtis LeMay, head of the**
> **Strategic Air Command during the Korean War**

> *"[The United States bombed] everything that moved*
> *in North Korea, every brick standing on top of another."*[91]
> **—Dean Rusk, Assistant Secretary of State for Far**
> **Eastern Affairs (later U.S. Secretary of State)**

Dwight Eisenhower became President of the United States in January 1953, promising that he would end the war. Another significant event took place two months later regarding a world leader: Stalin died in March 1953. The communists knew the hostilities were coming to an end, so they continued their fight to gain as much land as possible.

On July 27, 1953, an armistice was agreed upon by the UN, North Korea, and Communist China. South Korea verbally accepted the agreement but refused to sign anything. It served as a ceasefire to stop the hostilities so that a peace agreement could be signed. The Demilitarized Zone (DMZ) was set up, a border that is 155 miles long and 2.5 miles wide and still heavily guarded today. South Korea got 1,500 square miles more than they had when the 38th Parallel was the border, but the old border and the DMZ are close to each other. The sides agreed that the POWs could choose to go where they liked. Many North Koreans and Chinese prisoners chose not to go back to their homes. A Neutral Nations Commission for Repatriation was set up and Operation Big Switch began on August 5, 1953. One by one, prisoners were interviewed and chose to go to North Korea, China, South Korea, Taiwan, or a neutral country. The operation exchanged 75,823 prisoners to the communists and 12,773 to the UN.[92]*

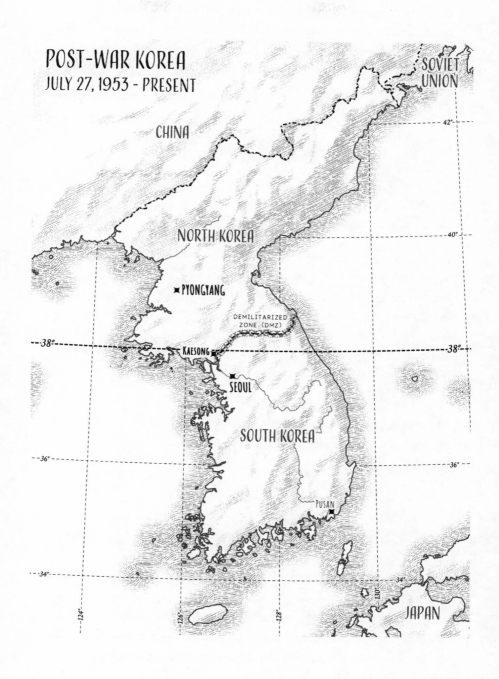

POST-WAR KOREA
JULY 27, 1953 - PRESENT

SOVIET
UNION

CHINA

NORTH KOREA

— 42°

— 40°

✶ PYONGYANG

DEMILITARIZED
ZONE (DMZ)

--38°-- Kaesong ✶

--38°--

✶ SEOUL

SOUTH KOREA

-- 36° --

-- 36° --

PUSAN ✶

-- 34° --

34°

JAPAN

-124-

-126-

-128-

-130-

Casualty numbers vary, but it's estimated that 4 million people died in the Korean War.[93] Over 50 percent were civilians[94] or 10 percent[95] to 20 percent[96] of Korea's pre-war population. This percentage is higher than World War II and the Vietnam War's percentage of civilian deaths within the total war death rate.

As for the United States military, 5,720 Army personnel, 908 Air Force personnel, 276 Navy personnel, and 641 Marines are unaccounted for.[97]

Over 1,000,000 Koreans moved from the North to the South during the war to escape communism, many of which used the UN's military operations to do so.[98] Some, sadly, did not make it due to disease and starvation as well as battling against the cold winter.

The Korean War, while known as "The Forgotten War" has another nickname: "The Never-Ending War." While there was an armistice agreement, technically the war did not ever end. No peace treaty was ever signed. The two nations still stand in stark contrast to one another: communism rules the North whereas a democratic society is in the South. Tensions still exist today between North Korea and South Korea, as well as between North Korea and the western world.

*Operation Little Switch took place from April 20 to May 3, 1953, and returned 6,670 Chinese and North Korean prisoners and 669 UN prisoners, all of whom were sick or wounded.[99]

THE CEASEFIRE

I was taking summer classes in July 1953 during my junior year when most students were on summer vacation. There were about forty students during the summer, whereas usually the high school had over three hundred students at a time. Classes stopped and the school announced that the ceasefire took place. It was somber throughout the school. My heart dropped.

I had no news of my parents or of my sisters. Some people sat on the school floor, unable to hold themselves up after hearing the news, while others cried. Tears ran down my cheeks uncontrollably. I could hardly breathe.

About half the students had been born and raised in South Korea and the other half in North Korea, and we North Korean refugees lost all hope of returning home and seeing our families.

The 1953 Ceasefire divided Korea in two and created the infamous Demilitarized Zone. Both Koreas built heavily fortified lines along the zone. No one was allowed to cross the line or communicate with each other. We never saw our families again; I do not even know if any of my relatives who stayed in North Korea survived the war. Tae-jun and Tae-wook eventually remarried years later. Tae-jun remarried a South Korean woman, and they had six children, seven when including Won-sik. Tae-wook remarried a South Korean widow with two children from her previous marriage, and they had six more children.

We found out in late 1955 from a hometown friend that our parents had died during the war in January 1951. That friend was forced to join the Korean People's Army but then surrendered to the ROK Army during the war. He came to South Korea and told us that our parents had passed and said it could have been from sickness. I believe it was from heartbreak. All their sons and grandson had left, separating their family. Tae-jun, Tae-wook, Won-sik and I cried over their loss. We found ourselves yet again experiencing profound grief.

In May of 1948, 160 men and I enlisted into the 5th Company of the 8th Regiment of the South Korean Army. I was then seventeen, the youngest in the group. More than two thirds of them were either killed or missing in action during the three long years of the war. I lost some of my best friends, including Lee Jong-kook, Bong Jong-tae, Kim Jae-kook (we never saw him again after he went MIA during the North Korean offensive in spring 1951), as well as many comrades-in-arms. Their loss saddens me, and it scares me that some were taken as prisoners of war and must have been tortured. Others survived. We mainly reconnected by word of mouth, learning that a fellow comrade had survived.

After the war, one of my best friends, Oh Munchan, and I met again in Seoul through a network of the Korean War Veterans Association. We embraced each other tightly for a few minutes without a word. Finally, we let go and simultaneously exclaimed, "You are alive!" He said that his father and his younger brother had taken refuge in South Korea to avoid being drafted by the North Korean Army when the American and South Korean Armies retreated from North Korea in December 1950, like my brothers. Since like most North Korean refugees, they naively believed that the mighty American and South Korean forces would come back within a couple of months, and the winter was so brutal, his mother and younger siblings had decided to stay home, expecting that the war would soon end, and the family would reunite. He choked. Like his father, Oh Munchan went into the movie business and got a job as a film operator.

Captain Lee had been promoted to major and then battalion commander and had seven to eight hundred men under him. I later heard he had been killed. I visited his wife and son after the war to pay my respects. His wife was so delighted to see me. I heard later that his son had gone to the Korea Military Academy, the South Korean equivalent of West Point. I credit my survival of the war to Company Commander Captain Lee. He had transferred me to the personnel department as a company clerk. I was still on the front lines but not as often as my friends. If it hadn't been for him, I'd likely have been killed or taken as a POW.

Major Jeong, a leader everyone respected, eventually rose to the rank of general and served as Chief of Staff of the Korean Army in the late 1970s. He was arrested and imprisoned with the accusation that he was involved in the assassination of President Park Chung-hee. I was shocked when I found this out and didn't believe it. After seventeen years, his name was completely cleared.

I'm not sure what happened to some of the others or what they did after the war if they did survive. Kim Hakdong was transferred to the 8th Battalion and kept getting promoted; he survived the war. Master Sergeant Chang Hee-chul was cleared of being a communist suspect and released a few months after I was released from prison; he survived the war and returned home. Jin Chin-mae survived and we kept in touch for years but eventually lost contact; he ran a public bathhouse after the war. Sergeant Lee Chunwoo survived, and after the war he worked in the Army Personnel department. Master Sergeant Lee (my company leader for the personnel department) was a Sergeant Major by the time I was discharged, and eventually commissioned to a Second Lieutenant officer still in the ROK Army Headquarters and personnel department, and later promoted to Captain. He stayed in the Army after the war. I'm thankful that he was my leader. Sergeant Chang Hyokoen survived and became a farmer. Like so many others, he never saw his parents or sister again, as they lived in North Korea. Sergeant Choi survived and joined his family afterward. I saw Lee Yeong-sik after the war. He completely lost his arm but had a fake one. He was in good spirits even though he could not return home because he was from north of the DMZ. He ended up going to college and then working in a university. Corporal Pak survived and later returned home. Quartermaster Sergeant Kwon survived, and I visited him at his home; after the war, he led an army supply business. If he hadn't picked me up in his truck, I would have frozen during the long march. Sergeant Man-E became a platoon sergeant, and after the war he married a girl from his hometown. Master Sergeant Choo was promoted to an officer—a Second Lieutenant—during the war. I visited him in the early 1960s and he was still an easygoing guy. Corporal Chun survived and I met him in Seoul while I was attending the Veterans High School. It was always great catching up with him, as he would continue to crack jokes and bring up funny stories, which brought back good memories of our friends. Sergeant First Class Han was promoted, and after the war, he returned home.

I only saw a couple dozen members of my company. We kept in touch over the years, but unlike today's modern technology, it was mainly through letters. But one by one, they died, as I was the youngest of them all. I was the only one who had moved to America, and as far as I know, the only one among the survivors of my company who learned English, at least enough to share my story and express my feelings in this language. We used to send each other Christmas or holiday cards, but as time went on, some cards would be returned, unable to reach the intended recipient. They may have moved, but after a returned mail, I wouldn't hear from them again. I knew then that they had passed away. We continued to send holiday cards back and forth until 2011.

PART FIVE:

A New Life

1953 - 1970

CHAPTER 24

An Education

September 1953 - December 1958

THAT CAN'T BE ME

In September 1953, when the South Korean Government moved back to the capital city, Seoul, the refugees from Seoul, along with my high school, also returned. I, too, followed the government institution because I stayed with the veterans' accommodation facilities run by the Department of Social Affairs.

During my junior year, in April 1954, I applied for a special entrance examination for standby senior students at Daegwang High School, one of the top high schools in Seoul. On the qualification exam day, I competed with dozens of applicants for only two positions. All the others looked younger than me by at least five years. The exam consisted of English, math, and Korean literature, one hour for each subject. The following afternoon, the names were posted. I was one of the two who made the cut—a twenty-three-year-old senior—and I then transferred to this high school.

• • •

One hot, steamy August day in 1954, the Administrator of Chung-yang Won wanted to see me in his office. Chung-yang Won was a special dormitory in downtown Seoul funded and run by the Social Welfare Ministry of the South Korean Government that accommodated more than one hundred of us Korean War veterans who attended various high schools and colleges. Most of the residents did not have families because the Korean War had

Attending high school with friends. Tae-hyok is the third from the left, standing.

With veterans from the Republic of Korea Army after the war. Tae-hyok is the third from the left on the top row.

divided the country and split their families apart. I was then a high school senior, studying hard to make up for the educational opportunities which I had lost because of the war.

The Administrator told me that the dorm planned to celebrate Liberation Day on August 15 at Oksu Elementary School playground. This holiday observes Korea's liberation from the four decades of Japanese occupation on August 15, 1945, at the end of World War II. It is of paramount political and emotional importance among Koreans. A few dignitaries would attend, including the Deputy Minister of the Social Welfare Ministry and the Commissioner of the Veterans' Affairs Bureau.

The Administrator emphasized that the coming event should be even more meaningful because it would be the first Liberation Day celebration in the capital city since Seoul had been recaptured from the North Koreans and our government had returned to the city. He said that all the dorm residents should attend the ceremony, and stressed, "I want you there!"

I wondered why he had said that. His remark made me feel embarrassed and somewhat displeased because I felt singled out. But I responded, "I will, sir," and left his office. On August 15, just as I finished breakfast, the student president of the dormitory came to my room and said, "Hey, Tae-hyok. The Administrator asked me to make sure that you come to the ceremony. Now, let's go!" With the help of my four roommates, he practically dragged me a couple of miles to the elementary school. Most of the other students were already there, chatting and laughing.

The student president left us and had a brief conference with the Administrator. Then he stood in front of the crowd and shouted into a megaphone, "My fellow war veterans, please form columns of twenty." We ex-soldiers adroitly filed in parade formation, except those who had lost their legs, who remained seated on chairs in front.

Soon, the Social Welfare Deputy Minister and the Chief of the Veterans Affairs arrived and settled on the VIP seats. The dorm Administrator presided over the ceremony. He began the event with a short speech, thanking the dignitaries and the student body for attending. Then he led the national anthem, which we sang proudly at the top of our lungs with our right hands on our chests. A few who had lost their right arms used their left hands.

After the anthem, we prayed silently for those Korean and United Nations forces' soldiers who had lost their lives for our country. Then the deputy minister delivered a speech, thanking us for our contribution to the defense of our nation. He said, "Our government is very proud of you Korean War veteran students. You put nightmarish war experiences behind you and dedicated your energy to higher education." He concluded with the charge that we should get as much education as we could and prepare ourselves to become leaders of the country.

After the deputy minister's speech, the Administrator came to the podium and announced that he had requested that the student council nominate three candidates who met certain criteria for the Model Student Award of 1954.

He boasted that more than 90 percent of the student body had participated in electing the winner, which surprised me because I didn't even know such a vote had been conducted. Apparently, they had executed the whole process during the week when I was visiting my older brother, who was working for the First U.S. Marine Corps Division as an auxiliary policeman near the DMZ. So, I was one of the few who had missed the vote. He then made his announcement.

The audience applauded loudly, but I didn't hear who the winner was because I was deep in thought, trying to solve a solid geometry problem which I had struggled with for several days. I was completely oblivious to the Administrator's announcement.

He urged, "Mr. Kim, please come to the podium!"

I vaguely heard him calling, "Mr. Kim," but I thought it was someone else. After all, about one third of Korean people have the surname Kim. Assuming the winner would be a college student, I returned to my solid geometry problem.

Then, someone from behind tapped me on the shoulder and said, "What the hell are you doing? Go to the podium. You are the winner. Hurry up!"

"No way, that can't be me."

The Administrator hollered again, "Kim Tae-hyok, please come forward!"

I still didn't believe it and hesitated.

My friend pushed me forward. "Hurry up!"

I went up to the podium. The Administrator unrolled a parchment and read:

"Mr. Kim Tae-hyok, a resident student of this institution, has abided by the rules of the institution, has taken initiatives to enhance the cleanliness of not only his own dwelling place but also the common facilities of the institution, has attained academic excellence, and has been an outstanding example to the other students. Thus, I hereby commend Mr. Kim Tae-hyok for the 1954 Model Student Award.

August 15, 1954

Kim Jong-sul, Administrator of Chung-yang Won"

He rolled up the parchment, handed it to me, and said, "Congratulations, Tae-hyok!" while shaking my hand. He also gave me a bulky gift wrapped in white paper. All the participants of the ceremony clapped enthusiastically. The Deputy Minister and the Commissioner shook my hand and congratulated me.

I was profoundly humbled and dumbfounded. I wondered if I deserved the award because I was only a high school senior among more than two hundred college students. It is true that I did my best to follow the rules because I was a member of the community. I kept my place and common facilities clean because I hated uncleanliness. I studied hard to advance myself. Even though I had yet to go to college, I had attained a good understanding of calculus, trigonometry, and physics—so much so that some of the college students majoring in engineering came to me for help. However, all my hard work was for me, not for them. But they chose me as the model student.

While I was standing there speechless in front of the crowd, the Administrator led, *"Dae-han-min-guk Mansei!"* The crowd chanted *"Dae-han-min-guk Mansei!"* three times, and the ceremony ended.

Afterward, a dozen of my friends swarmed around me and expressed their sincere congratulations. That's when I finally realized that I really was the winner. I was sorry that I hadn't asked the Administrator for a few minutes to express my appreciation to the student body for choosing me for this award.

My friends asked me what the gift was. I carefully opened it and found high quality cotton fabric with a tag saying it was three feet wide and forty feet long. I wished it were clothes instead of fabric. We admired its high quality, but being a single man, I had no idea what to do with it. Later, I donated it to a lady with two young children, whose husband had been captured by the North Koreans and carried to the North. She made clothes out of the fabric for herself and her children. My brother, Tae-wook, married her a year later.

I SHALL FIGHT, AND I WILL WIN
December 1954 - August 1955

My dormitory was a worn two-story wooden structure with tar-painted walls. The Japanese had used it as a Shinto priest training facility during their occupation. It had survived the three years of the Korean War when many of the surrounding buildings were ruined.

On Christmas Eve, 1954, I had just come back to my dorm from the service at a nearby church. Most of my friends were out celebrating the holiday, leaving the building almost empty. Taking advantage of the silence, I studied solid geometry, my weakest subject. I knew most top college entrance examinations would contain one solid geometry question in the mathematics section.

The dorm was unheated, and the absence of my four roommates made my room even colder. Despite wrapping myself up in my thick cotton quilt, I still shivered. While I was struggling to solve a few problems, my chest felt tight, and I coughed hard and spat out phlegm. Noticing blood spots, I thought my gums were bleeding. Although I was initially unconcerned, after it happened a few more times, I became alarmed and collected the saliva in a small glass bottle. I remembered that I had been given a medical discharge from the army because of an unspecified lung problem.

The next morning, I took my sample to the Seoul City Clinic lab, but it was closed for the Christmas holiday. I returned the following day. The technician who received the bottle asked me to return for the lab test results in three days. After three long days of waiting, I returned to the lab. Avoiding my eyes, the technician advised me to see a pulmonary doctor immediately, making me feel worried.

I took the lab report to my pulmonary specialist, Dr. Choi, who, four months earlier, had X-rayed my lungs, examined the picture, and declared me okay. His office occupied the second floor of the undamaged half of a townhouse-like building. The rickety stairs grunted as if I weighed too much. The office had two bare light bulbs dangling from the ceiling. A couple of broken glass panes were patched with pieces of plywood to shield off snow and rain. But the mid-day light pleasantly brightened the office.

I knew Dr. Choi well. He was one of the five elders serving in a Presbyterian church which I attended. He was in his mid-fifties, a kind gentleman with a perpetual smile on his face. He had escaped North Korea to Seoul with his family a few years before the war broke out. His parents remained in their hometown in North Korea.

As soon as I entered his office, he gave me a surgical mask to wear. I gave him my lab report. He read it carefully, took out my file and my old X-ray from an old wooden filing cabinet, put it against a glass pane of the south side window, and scrutinized it without a word. Then, he murmured, "There was a tiny dot in the upper left lung, but I didn't think it was a scar because it was so small." Then he weighed me on a big, outdated scale and exclaimed, "Only eighty pounds!" He read my file and said, "You have lost thirteen pounds since your last visit." Then he examined my chest with his stethoscope.

I asked nervously, "Doctor, how am I doing? What does the lab report say?"

He answered hesitantly, "I am sorry, but your lungs do not sound normal. And the test report shows that tuberculosis was detected in your spit sample, but I am not sure if the germs caused the bleeding. To be sure, I will take another X-ray."

Even though I had expected unpleasant news, the word *tuberculosis* devastated me, and I collapsed into a chair and remained speechless for a few minutes. In Korea, tuberculosis was the leading cause of death. Widespread malnutrition and a lack of proper treatment turned it into a terminal disease.

The doctor said something to soothe my anguish, but I didn't understand him. He led me to the X-ray machine. This time, he took two chest X-rays, one from the front and the other from the side and asked me to return for the results the next day. He also advised me to keep wearing the mask. Before I left his office, he gave me an injection of streptomycin in my buttocks. It was the most painful shot I had ever received. The pain lasted almost two days.

I left the doctor's office, wishing the report had been wrong. I felt anxious at the idea that I might have a terminal disease. I walked through the streets of Seoul, trying to distract myself from the thought that death had put a noose around my neck. "Terminal" continued to ring in my brain. I returned to my dorm but hesitated to enter the room that I shared with four close friends. I stood by a hall window outside the room, watching people briskly pass by. The pale afternoon sunlight filtered through the window and thawed my frigid body, but my heart remained cold.

One of my roommates saw me and asked, "What are you looking at?"

"Nothing in particular," I answered, and fell silent again. My thoughts drifted back to the past. Now that I finally had educational opportunities, and college entrance examinations and my high school graduation coming up, I also had tuberculosis. Why now? I felt homesick and overwhelmed, and I prayed for better health and a chance to finish my education.

Then, I promised myself I would fight the disease and win. This filled my heart with immense strength. I asked my roommates to come out to the hallway, where I calmly announced that I had contracted tuberculosis, but I was determined to defeat it. I reassured them that my doctor had told me that wearing a mask would prevent the germs from spreading, and that from now on, I would wear it and maintain my distance from them when communicating. I stressed that Dr. Choi had told me that the TB organisms would dissipate and die within a few minutes in the air. I needed their help and understanding to win my war against this horrible disease. I asked their permission to put a wall between the room and a part of the hall with the window to isolate myself and provide fresh air.

At first, they were shocked. Then they expressed their sincere sympathy. They offered me any help I needed. What moved me most was that they voluntarily chipped in to buy several pieces of pine boards and studs, and built a wall, creating a new four feet by six feet room with a window allowing good airflow and light. They sacrificed their southern exposure and bright sunlight for me, leaving themselves only the north side window. Their room became darker. I thanked them but told them that my room was off limits. I asked them to keep a good distance when we communicated, which they did. I wallpapered the wall with newspaper to prevent the infectious organisms from filtering through the cracks into my friends' room.

The following morning, I visited Dr. Choi again, wearing my surgical mask. He wore one, too. He led me to a chair in front of his desk where my file waited for me. He had two X-rays displayed side by side on the sill of the southern window.

He said calmly, "Mr. Kim, your case seems acute." He pointed his pen at an empty-looking space in the upper part of the first film. "This X-ray I took yesterday shows a whitish area which tuberculosis bacteria have damaged." Then he tapped his pen at a miniscule speck in the next picture, almost invisible to my untrained eyes, and continued, "This picture is the one taken four months ago. Can you see this speck? It has grown almost five centimeters in only four months." His pen switched back to the new film. "Only four months! I never suspected that speck was a tuberculosis-induced scar."

Silently thanking him for his honesty, I decided to trust him. Unlike the previous day, I listened to him calmly. His candid explanation made my resolution to fight the disease stronger.

"I am going to give you intensive treatment for the next six months. I will give you one streptomycin shot at my office every three days along with this oral medicine."

I shuddered at the thought; the pain from the previous day's shot was still lingering. But I had to endure it.

He continued, "You will take one pill of this medicine once a day with food," and gave me a bottle of red-coated oval pills. "It might cause diarrhea, but do not skip it. When you have finished it, I will give you more."

I desperately needed this treatment, but how could I pay? Without it, I might soon be a goner. I said, "Dr. Choi, this procedure will cost more than I can afford. Is there a less costly way?"

"Indeed, this program is expensive. But fortunately, an American Christian charity group is providing me with free tuberculosis medicine, including antibiotics and X-ray supplies. Since I know that you are a war veteran student without family, I will put you in this special program. I will not charge you for my service. Just come in twice every week until I say that you have been cured.

Astonished, I kept silent for a moment, then asked, "Dr. Choi, do you mean that you will treat me for free?"

"Yes, I will."

Overwhelmed, I said, "Thank you, Dr. Choi!" and I bowed to him.

"You are welcome. You should thank the good Samaritans from America who have made this possible. I thank them as well as those missionaries who have arranged this aid for me. I thank God for everything. I strongly believe God will heal you. Do not despair! See you again in three days."

I thanked him and left his office, feeling incredibly encouraged. I praised God and resolved not to let tuberculosis prevent me from getting my education. I continued preparing for the college entrance examinations, but I decided to sleep six hours a night instead of four, as I had been doing for the last two years to make up for the nine years I had lost.

Isolated from my roommates, my small room with the large window was very cold. The draft coming through the cracks made the room even colder. The glass panes became ice sheets. It was so cold that I slept in my clothes and wore my hat. Yet, I felt safe and happy because my small room had a good flow of fresh air to keep germs from spreading to my friends. I had complete confidence that God, the good Samaritans, and Dr. Choi would heal me.

Meanwhile, I applied for the pre-med program at Yonhi University (which later changed its name to Yonsei University), a Korean Ivy League. I decided to pursue pre-med because I was motivated to help others. Having come from a poor farming community where we couldn't afford access to doctors and medicine, I saw a lot of individuals fall ill in my hometown, along with the unfortunate suffering and loss of soldiers in the war. Those experiences solidified my decision to become a doctor. The college entrance exam day arrived in early March. The exam consisted of Korean literature, English, math, Korean history, and world geography. I took the exam along with thousands of other applicants, including three of my best classmates.

All four of us passed. We congratulated each other and enjoyed the moment. Then, I found out that we needed to pass a physical examination. I knew I'd be dropped as physically unfit, cutting short my excitement.

The physical was scheduled three days later. I agonized over whether to go because I knew that any doctor could easily detect my tuberculosis. But I went to the exam at the university auditorium anyway. Lined up in our underwear, we snaked through a half dozen examiners. When I entered the room, I recognized one of the doctors who had been my doctor at the army hospital. I was embarrassed and tried to avoid her, but she saw me and said,

"Sergeant Kim, come over here!" She put her stethoscope on my chest for a few seconds. "Go out to the lobby and wait for me. I want to talk with you. I shall be with you in a few minutes."

My exam had been cut short. I went into the lobby with a pounding heart.

Soon, she walked in with her stethoscope dangling from her neck and asked, "Have you had a chest X-ray?"

I lowered my head and said, "Yes."

"Studying is important, but your health is more important. Have you had any treatment?"

I told her that I was under an intensive six-month treatment with Dr. Choi.

She continued, "You have already made the cut in the written exam with this prestigious college. I passed you because I had seen you studying hard at the army hospital, and I didn't have the heart to fail you in the physical. You should take care of your health first, then study. If you need help, don't hesitate to ask me." She left the room.

I thanked her and sighed deeply. Soon I would be a college freshman. The burden of anguish was lifted from me, and suddenly, I felt so tired that I fell asleep on a bench despite the noise from other applicants conversing.

During my six months of intensive treatment, Dr. Choi checked my chest frequently, jotting things down in my file. He took an X-ray of my chest every month and compared it with the previous ones, but he said nothing about my progress. I didn't ask him about it either because I was afraid that he might say, "No progress," or "It is getting worse." Finally, at the end of the fourth month, he held the latest X-ray up to the bright sunlight and exclaimed, "At last, it has started to shrink!" and showed it to me.

Instead of looking at the X-ray, I jumped up from my chair and shouted, "Has it?" Excitement choked my throat. I stood there motionless and speechless until the doctor patted me on the shoulder. Then, I said, "Thank you, Dr. Choi!"

"Let's praise God for this progress and give thanks to those Christian brothers and sisters who provided us with the medicines. If the next X-ray shows significant progress, I might reduce the shots to once a week instead of two, starting next month. Let's pray for this!" He squeezed my shoulders, humming contently. "Let me give you today's shot!"

The streptomycin had not changed, but it did not hurt me as much as before. I left his office feeling more hopeful about my future. The forsythia by the ruined building next to the office looked so much more beautiful now than it had an hour earlier. I sat in front of the blossoms and closed my eyes, thanking God, the doctor, and the good Samaritans in America.

The next month moved too slowly for me as I waited for my new X-ray. The colorful spring flowers around my university campus and my busy classes tempered my impatience. But after a weekly shot, I asked my doctor if he could take an X-ray sooner. He said, "Be patient!"

After a long two weeks, he took a new X-ray before giving me the shot and said the result would be available the next day. Unlike today, the X-ray films were developed in watery chemicals in a darkroom and dried before doctors could examine them. My anxiety about the results kept me awake at night.

The following afternoon, I went straight to the doctor's office from my last class on a public bus. As usual, I wore my surgical mask on the bus. One passenger looked askance at me a few times and asked why I was wearing a mask on a warm spring day. I told him that I didn't want to inhale germs in the thick air on the bus, instead of telling him the truth. He murmured that I was a pretentious young SOB, but I pretended not to hear him.

As soon as I got off the bus, I ran up the squeaky stairs to the doctor's office. Fortunately, he was free. I greeted him in short breaths and asked him for my results.

He welcomed me with a smile and said, "Be seated and take a deep breath." I sat down on the edge of the chair in front of his desk. "Mr. Kim, your recovery progress is remarkable. Your lung is rapidly healing."

I sprang up from my chair, grabbed his hand, bowed, and said, "Thank you, Dr. Choi!" over and over until he pulled his hand from mine and squeezed my shoulders.

"Congratulations, Mr. Kim! I am going to reduce the shot to once a week. Today, there is no shot! Come in next Friday for your next shot. I think the tuberculosis bacteria have begun going dormant. You don't have to wear the mask anymore. Let's praise God for this. See you next Friday."

I hurriedly bid him goodbye, flew down the stairs, took the bus, and ran to my dorm. I swung open my roommates' door and shouted, jumping up and down, "Hey, you guys, I am healed! I don't have to wear a mask any-more," even though I had not been completely cured.

My friends swarmed out to me and said, "Congratulations!" holding my arms and hands, and affectionately rubbing my head. "Let's celebrate. Let's go to a *makgeolli* (cheap rice wine) house." Then one of them teasingly said, "This son of a bitch doesn't drink *makgeolli*!" and they laughed. "Let's go to a teahouse instead." They toasted my remarkable progress over a cup of tea.

My extraordinary progress should have made me sleep better, but a severe ear ringing kept me awake. This ringing had begun almost unnoticeably a couple of weeks after my treatment had begun. It grew louder and louder, as if a few jet fighter planes were constantly flying around in my ears. When I tried to concentrate on my books, this tinnitus drove me crazy.

Knowing the ringing would be with me day and night, I resolved to learn how to live with it just as I was determined to recover from tuberculosis. When I went to bed, I would count numerals or read science books until I fell asleep. This method worked well in training me to live with my tinnitus. I did not know what caused this problem until many years later, an ear, nose, and throat specialist in New York City told me that the high dosage of streptomycin must have been the culprit, and that there was no treatment for it.

Despite this new discomfort, my healing continued to progress well, enough to reduce my streptomycin shot from once a week to once every two weeks. Slowly, my stamina returned. Feeling upbeat, I studied diligently, especially chemistry and biology. Then, one August day, after examining my chest with his stethoscope, Dr. Choi took a monthly X-ray of my chest and asked me to come back for the result the following day. He also skipped my biweekly shot. All those things made me anticipate something good.

I wanted to go to the doctor's office early but appeared on time. When I entered his office, the doctor asked me to sit down, and smiled from ear to ear. He said, "You are completely healed. Congratulations!"

Even though I had expected good news, I was stunned. I was so over-whelmed that I buried my head between my knees for a few moments, mur-muring "Now, I have a new life!" Then I rose and bowed, "Thank you, Dr. Choi. I will never forget your care and generosity." I had won this battle against tuberculosis with the help of the American church charity group, Dr. Choi's care, and my willpower.

"Now go home. See you again, not in my office, but at church." He led me to the door.

FULL SCHOLARSHIP
March - October 1955

As my high school graduation approached, I applied for the 1955 college entrance exam at Yonhi University. The examination consisted of mathematics, English, Korean, and Korean history, and I passed them all. I was proud. Unfortunately, I couldn't register for my premedical freshman year because I did not have money for tuition.

I went to the dean of students, explained my dire situation, and asked him to arrange financial aid. He flatly denied my request. Undaunted, I went to the dean of the academy and pleaded my case. I told him that I had come from North Korea and served in the South Korean Army for four years, but I did not have the financial means to pay the tuition. I was confident that I had scored well in the college entrance exam in all four subjects; and I earnestly requested some financial aid. Unlike the dean of students, he listened to me patiently and said, "Let me see what I can do for you." He asked me to see him again a week later.

After a long week, in the early morning, I went to the college and waited for him, wondering what he would tell me. His comments had given me a ray of hope, but uncertainty occupied my mind because all colleges in war-ravaged Korea operated on a shoestring budget. Scholarships were practically non-existent. If he couldn't help me, I wondered what my next step would be. While I was lost in thought, somebody said, "Good morning!" It was the dean. Embarrassed, I bowed and responded, "Good morning, sir."

He asked me to follow him into his office. Then he said with a smile, "Dr. Chang, the dean of the Science and Engineering (SAE) College, and I reviewed your college entrance scores and your high school grades. We also studied your application file. We confirmed that you are a Korean War veteran. But we found that your application file only had the record of your senior year. Why?"

I explained that I had completed only two and a half years of high school education and transferred high schools at the start of my senior year, which was what they had a record of. Additionally, I never attended middle school because I didn't have the opportunity. As a result, I had no other grades on file. I also told him that during the war I had obtained Waseda University's (a Japanese university) communication books at a bombed house and taught myself algebra and basic English on the front line.

He quietly listened to me and then said, "Well, President Dr. Baek along with Dr. Chang and I have agreed to grant you a tuition scholarship for the first semester because your combined score for the entrance examination was in the top 5 percent; your high school grades were excellent; and you are a war veteran. Congratulations! Study hard!"

"Thank you, sir!" I stood up and bowed.

"Go to Dr. Chang and thank him. Then enroll for the semester!"

I bowed to him again and left. I walked briskly over to Dr. Chang in the Engineering Building. He was alone in his office. I knocked, and he called me in. I bowed to him and introduced myself, expressing my sincere thanks for the tuition grant.

He shook my hand and said, "Congratulations! We made a special grant for you despite the university's scholarship fund being virtually empty because of the war. I believe that you will make an excellent student." He handed me an envelope to take to the registration office for my enrollment.

I thanked him again and went directly to the registration office across from the engineering building. The gentleman behind the counter took my envelope and processed my enrollment without a word. He issued my student ID card and a blue shield-shaped lapel pin showing the *Yonhi University* logo. He said, "You are a special case. Good luck!" and closed the window.

Overwhelmed, I held my ID card and the pin in my hands, looked at them, and read the *Yonhi University* logo over and over. Then I went to a quiet place in the wooded university amphitheater, turned in the direction of my hometown in North Korea, holding the ID and pin in my open hands, and shouted, "Mom and Dad, can you see my student ID card and lapel pin from Yonhi University, one of the most prestigious colleges in Korea? I am a student at this university. Do you remember that nine years ago, I left you both for Seoul with the dream of getting a college education? Now, I am a college student. I am going to be a medical doctor. I want to share this exciting occasion with you." But the only response was the brush of a zephyr that gently touched my face and was gone. I missed them so much, wondering if I would ever see them again. My head drooped and my legs sagged to the ground.

• • •

On April 1, 1955, I was in my first college class—calculus. The professor took the roll call, "Kim Tae-hyok!" "Here, sir," I answered loudly. My college life began with this "Here, sir." I resolved to make the most of my tuition grant. I studied diligently and excelled in physics, algebra, calculus, and English. In the beginning, I struggled in chemistry and biology because I had studied those two subjects for less than a year at high school. However, as

Attending college

the semester progressed, I improved and came out with an A- in chemistry and a B in biology. I enjoyed college life tremendously and was happy with what I had achieved for the semester.

I would sit apart from other students to avoid close contact, wearing a surgical mask, because I had been undergoing tuberculosis treatment. Throughout the semester, the only isolated seat happened to be in the middle of the first row in almost every one of my classes.

The semester came to an end quickly. Then, financial reality hit me again because the college had exempted me from tuition only for the first semester. There was simply no summer job available in the war-wasted land. The summer vacation was only four weeks—not enough time to earn tuition even if I had a job. I had no money for the second semester!

The second semester began, and without registering, I continued the same classes plus analytical geometry, which Dr. Chang taught, while seeking financial aid, to no avail. One month into the semester, the dean called me into his office and regretfully told me that the university policy did not allow anyone to attend classes without paying tuition. I had no choice but to drop out. I was devastated.

I looked for colleges which might offer me some financial aid, while concurrently searching for a job. The Eighth U.S. Army stationed in Korea was the largest employer in the country. I considered applying for a houseboy job with the army, but my tuberculosis treatment precluded that even though I was making a remarkable recovery. I also thought about construction work. I then weighed only eighty pounds, so I could not lift heavy things such as a ninety-pound cement bag. Furthermore, I feared that physical strain might jeopardize my tuberculosis treatment, so I discarded that idea, too.

Five weeks after I had dropped out, one of my classmates brought me a message that the dean of the Science and Engineering (SAE) College wanted to see me as soon as possible. Hoping for good news, I visited him early the next morning.

He welcomed me and explained that the Ministry of the Education had established a national scholarship fund for eighty college students. The amount would be 50,000 *won* per year for each recipient. He said that it would be enough to cover my tuition, books, and various fees. The ministry sent out a directive nationwide, asking each university and college to choose two students for the national scholarship examination, and Dr. Baek, the university president, allocated one to be chosen from the SAE College and the other from all other colleges of the university. He said that the faculty members had chosen me as a candidate to take the scholarship examination.

At first, I was dumbfounded. Then I rose from my seat and bowed to him, expressing profound thanks.

He said, "Not so fast. You must pass the examination first. Then you can thank me and the other faculty members. Attend any classes you want until you take the exam. If you pass, then you may register for the semester. Now, return to your classes!"

I bowed to him again and left for my class. I knew that among the six hundred students at the SAE College, there were many kids who were smarter than me. But I had been chosen because the dean had taken my difficult situation into consideration. The second candidate was an education major who had scored the highest in the entrance examination and was considered brainy. He deserved to represent the university more than I did.

Two weeks later, the assistant dean of the academy escorted us both to the Ministry of Education, where we registered for the exam. About three hundred bright and confident students from all over the country assembled to compete for the eighty scholarships.

An official from the ministry greeted us and gave the instructions for the examination. He said that it consisted of two subjects, essay writing and science (physics and chemistry). Then those who passed the written exams would have oral interviews. After the orientation, we were divided into smaller groups and led into various classrooms at a nearby elementary school.

The first exam was essay writing. An official from the ministry handed out two blank sheets, and wrote the essay topic on the blackboard, "Civilian Diplomacy." We had two hours to complete the assignment. Agonized groans rose from some who complained that the subject was too ambiguous and broad. But the official said, "Don't blame me. I didn't choose it."

I was not a political science major, and I knew very little about diplomacy. But I had to write something. Since the ceasefire had been signed less than two years earlier, the South Korean government had worked hard to bring as many neutral nations as it could to join our side against North Korea. I narrowed the subject to "What We Civilians Should Do with the People of Neutral Nations." I chose India to develop my thesis because it claimed to be neutral but was really leaning toward North Korea. I wrote that we civilians should open up pen pal diplomacy with Indians, introduce our culture, treat Indian diplomats stationed in Korea with respect, and make friends; we should learn their culture; and we should not alienate them just because their government was friendlier to North Korea.

The science exam heavily stressed atoms. Since I had diligently studied atomic structure and the role of electrons in chemical reactions, I did well. A few days later, the director of Science Education at the ministry interviewed those candidates who had passed the written exams. He was a well-known astrophysicist who had found a new star that was named after him to honor his contribution to science. I became very nervous standing in front of him. To calm myself, I broke the ice by saying, "Sir, standing in front of such a giant like you makes me nervous. Would you please ask me easy questions?"

He laughed and said, "Don't worry. I am not going to be hard on you." Then he began his interview. He asked me to describe the uranium atom structure and properties and the periodic table of elements and their properties. I answered calmly step by step. He was satisfied and let me go. Certainly, he did not ask difficult questions.

On the day the results were announced, the assistant dean, the other candidate and I went to the ministry building where hundreds of anxious students gathered, waiting for the finalists' list. An official brought a roll and posted it on the ministry's bulletin board. As the names unfolded, excited shouts rose here and there. I watched the unfolding intently, and my mouth went dry. Then I, too, shouted, "There is my name. I am receiving 50,000 *won!*"

The assistant dean tapped my shoulder and said, "Congratulations, Tae-hyok! I am proud of you," shaking my hand firmly with his other hand.

I thanked him. After my initial excitement, I thought about my fellow student. I assumed that he, too, had made the final cut because he was so intelligent. I wanted to congratulate him and to share our happiness but found him nowhere. I asked the assistant dean about him. The dean said that he had not passed the exam and had gone home. It was hard for me to understand that such a smart kid had failed.

At the bottom of the roll, there was a written note, "The exam scores are available in the office of Science Education. If you are interested, ask the office manager for your scores." To satisfy my curiosity, I went to the office manager. He opened a thick folder and exclaimed, "Oh my God, you scored the highest in the essay writing. Congratulations!" He then turned the file toward me so that I could see. The names were ranked according to the scores, high to low. My name was at the top, with 95 points. I couldn't believe my eyes, so I looked again. Yes, my name was at the top. I was so elated that I left the office without finding out my science scores.

• • •

The South Korea Defense Department eventually interfered with the Department of Education and changed the terms so that veterans who had been medically discharged would not qualify (the wounded would, however, which I understood) for a full scholarship. Unfortunately, I didn't have the money to pay the tuition, so I had to withdraw from my pre-med program after my freshman year.

Tae-hyok working for KMAG

I started searching for jobs and found an ad in the newspaper for a clerk position with the U.S. Army. They were the largest employer in South Korea; thousands of people worked for them. I applied and interviewed. During the interview, they tested my English. The U.S. Army had a library of military publications that people could check out, and they made me an army publications stock-room clerk, like a librarian. This helped improve my English even more as I was constantly reading. The army had lots of regulations, from defense regulations to weapons system manuals. I learned the Army weapon system as well as the Air Force weapon system. I ended up working in the U.S. Military Advisory Group to Korea (KMAG) for seven years.

CHAPTER 25

Miss Lee

December 1958 - December 1959

In the 1950s, Western style dating culture had not yet been popularized in Korea. Therefore, most Koreans had arranged marriages. Relatives, friends of a prospective bride or bridegroom, or even a professional matchmaker would approach a prospect's parents to describe the personality and family background of a possible match. If the parents of both sides showed interest, then the matchmaker would gather vital statistics about the two prospects, such as the date and time of birth and family history. Then the matchmaker would present the information to the opposite side's parents.

In turn, the prospects' parents would consult their trusted astrologer for *gunghap* (marital harmony). The astrologer would analyze the vital statistics and predict *gunghap*. If the *gunghap* research resulted in a good prediction, then the two sets of parents would arrange a *sun*, a preliminary visit by the prospective groom to present himself to the prospective bride and her parents. This visit was brief. Most of the time, the young man didn't have a chance to meet his future bride face to face because the girl usually sat behind her parents.

If the *sun* went well, then the two sides would announce a formal engagement to their relatives and friends. The wedding date would be determined based on astrological analysis. In this process, the prospective couple had very little say.

Since my parents has passed away in North Korea, few people approached me about marriage. I was twenty-seven, but I didn't think about it myself either. Then one day, unexpectedly, one of my good friends, a minister of a

country church, visited me. He hinted that it was about time for me to start
a family. He said that his wife wanted to introduce me to one of her former
classmates, Miss Lee, a twenty-six-year-old elementary school teacher, the
eldest of seven children. His wife offered to arrange a meeting at his church
on Christmas Eve. He emphasized that Miss Lee had a job. At that time, very
few jobs were available to women.

Even though I was interested in meeting her, just thinking of starting
my own family scared me to death. I had a job but had not yet finished college. How could I support a wife? Nevertheless, out of curiosity, I agreed to
the meeting.

As Christmas approached, I felt anxious, and wondered if I had been too
hasty. I hadn't even seen her, and if I wasn't interested, her feelings might be hurt.

Before I knew it, Christmas Eve arrived. My office closed mid-day. I took a
city bus to Kyoung-gi Bus Terminal by Dongdaemun (East Gate) where most
long-distance buses for the southeast routes departed. But that's as far as I got.

My minister friend was the pastor of a church in Daessangnyeong (or
Daessang), a small farm community about twenty miles southeast of Seoul.
With today's modern highway system, it takes less than an hour to get there.
But a long-distance commercial bus would take three to four hours along
unpaved roads.

I was supposed to meet Miss Lee in Daessang but worry so gripped me that
I couldn't force myself to buy a bus ticket. Instead, I returned to my apartment, wondering whether I should go. If I didn't, I would not only betray
my friend's trust but also insult Miss Lee. After hours of agony, I returned
to the depot. Its lobby was dimly lit, cold, and small, without even a bench.
I asked the ticket clerk about the schedule to Daessang.

He told me that the last bus to the town had left one hour earlier; the last
bus in that direction would be leaving at 6 p.m., but it would only go as far as
Kyoungan-up (now called Gwangju), about three miles short of Daessang. He
glanced at the wall clock behind him and said, "You only have a few minutes."

"Three miles!" Disheartened, I stood silently in front of the ticket window,
cursing myself for having wasted those precious few hours. I had never traveled through that region and thought about whether to go.

"Do you want a ticket?" the clerk asked.

Without thinking further, I said, "Yes. One please." Outside the hall, a woman conductor hollered, "Bus to Kyoungan-up, bus to Kyoungan-up!" The bus was packed with boisterous country folk. Even though it had no heating system, the passengers' body heat made it warm. I managed to find a place to sit on a grain bag in the back.

Buses in war-torn Korea were made from converted American military trucks. Technicians banged discarded military gas drums and welded them together into bus-shells. Thus, unlike today's luxurious carriers, those make-shift buses were rickety and uncomfortable, but they took passengers where they wanted to go.

The departure time came and went, but the conductor continued to holler, "Last bus to Kyoungan-up, last bus to Kyoungan-up!" A few more passengers climbed in and elbowed through the standing passengers, vainly searching for a place to sit. Despite the winter weather, the body odor from the packed passengers was nauseating.

Half an hour after we should have departed, the driver showed up and said, "Let's go," while taking his seat. He made no apology, but nobody complained because that's the way these buses operated. But I was disappointed because now I would have to walk in the dark.

As the bus moved, the passengers calmed down. Some of them snored. But I wondered about the extra three miles along strange country roads by night. I consoled myself by remembering how I had crossed the border between the two Koreas at night when I was only fifteen. "Now I am twenty-seven. No one will be shooting at me. I will be alright."

Once the bus left the paved city streets for unpaved country roads, it bounced wildly, knocking my breath out and painfully twisting my internal organs. However, the pain temporarily relieved me from my nervousness. The bus seemed to stop at every single village along the route.

After three long hours, the conductor announced, "This is Kyoungan-up, the last stop." The bus pulled up in front of a barrack. I approached the conductor and asked for the directions to Daessang. Kindly, she asked the passengers if anyone was heading in that direction.

Fortunately, three young men volunteered to show me the way. I followed them up a winding dirt road. The bright moonlight and the unusually mild weather for Christmas Eve made our journey easier. As we walked, they talked of trivial things and laughed. One man remarked that as a city gentleman, I must have been having difficulty walking on that path.

I responded that I had once been a farmer, too, and had served in the army for four years during the Korean War, so it was nothing. When I mentioned that I was visiting a friend at Daessang Presbyterian Church, he told me that he thought that they were going to have a midnight service to celebrate Christmas.

After about an hour, we reached a fork at the top of the path. They said, "You should bear with the main road for about five ris (approximately 1.3 miles). You will enter the town and find the church on the right. It is easy to find. Have a good trip." Then, they took the branch road.

Now alone, my fears returned. How would I introduce myself to her? What would I say? I quickened my pace and headed down the road, stumbling over the rocks a few times.

After more than five hours of journeying by bus and on foot, I entered the town. It was almost 11 p.m. Thanks to the bright moon, I found the church quite easily. I looked in through the windows. A few kerosene lamps hanging from the ceiling lit the sanctuary, and people sat in groups on the bare wooden floor. There were no pews. I spotted Rev. Choi chatting with a few men in the middle of the hall. I quietly entered the church and tiptoed up to my friend without attracting the congregation's attention. I tapped him lightly on the shoulder and said, "Reverend Choi, it's me."

He turned around and exclaimed, "Tae-hyok, you made it. I was worried about you." He embraced me. "I was talking about you with these people." After introducing me to them, he led me to his residence. "Miss Lee arrived around seven this evening, and she is with my wife now. I thought you weren't going to make it."

I said, "I'm sorry I'm so late. I missed the buses to Daessang, so I took the last carrier to Kyoungan-up and walked the rest of the way." As we approached his house, my heart began to pound, and my mouth went dry. Soon we arrived at his humble, rice-thatched farmhouse.

Outside the entrance, my friend called his wife loudly, "*Yeobo*, Mr. Kim is here," and waited.

Instantly, Mrs. Choi opened the door and said excitedly, "Mr. Kim, welcome. Come in please! We have been waiting for you."

When we stepped inside, I saw another young lady standing behind Mrs. Choi. Heat flashed through my body. I presumed that she was Miss Lee, but I couldn't see her clearly because the flickering kerosene lamp behind her kept her in the shade. Mrs. Choi said, "Mr. Kim, this is my friend Miss Lee."

I bowed slightly, and said in a nervous voice, "I am Kim Tae-hyok. It's a pleasure to meet you, Miss Lee." I felt my heart pounding wildly.

She responded in a calm, clear voice, "My name is Lee Soonnyum. Nice to meet you, too." She bowed politely.

After we sat down on the heated floor, Rev. Choi returned to the church. Meanwhile, Mrs. Choi prepared dinner on a low-legged traditional Korean table for Miss Lee and me. Then, she excused herself to join her husband for the midnight Christmas Eve service, leaving us alone. She told us to join her after dinner.

Miss Lee and I sat across the table and bowed our heads for grace. After a long journey, I should have been hungry, but I couldn't eat much. Miss Lee kept quiet, pretending to eat, but her dinner remained almost intact. To break the ice, I said awkwardly, "Miss Lee, I am sorry that I kept you waiting. How was your trip?"

Keeping her head down, she said, "It was not bad at all. How about yours, Mr. Kim?"

"I missed the last bus to Daessang, so I took the bus to Kyoungan-up and walked three miles from there to here. The bright moon made my trip easier. It was rather romantic."

She looked up, meeting my eyes for the first time. She exclaimed, "Oh my goodness. You walked three miles in the dark for me? I am sorry, Mr. Kim, but I am glad you came." Then she lowered her gaze and stopped eating her dinner. She put her spoon on the table cautiously and said in a gentle, caring voice, "After a long trip, you must be hungry. Please help yourself."

Her tone cleared me of all anxiety and fatigue, leaving my heart joyful and exalted. It also convinced me that she possessed a warm, loving personality. I said, "Thank you, Miss Lee," and began to devour my dinner, but then I became self-conscious of my table manners and stopped eating.

"Shall we go to church, Miss Lee?" I helped her put on her winter coat and opened the door for her, which Korean men rarely did, but I had seen my American colleagues do so for their wives. At first, she seemed somewhat puzzled, but she turned around and graciously thanked me.

While we silently walked the short distance to the church under the bright moonlight, I wanted to hold her hand, but I didn't dare; Koreans considered such things improper. I broke the silence by asking about her family and teaching job.

She said that her father was in his early sixties and her mother in her late fifties. He was a retired school principal. She had three sisters and three brothers, and she really enjoyed teaching children.

I cherished walking with her. We arrived at the church too soon. I wished the walk had been longer. I opened the church door and let her enter first, which again confused her, because men usually led the way. She cautiously walked in and sat in the women's section, and I deliberately sat in the back of the men's section so that I could see Miss Lee without attracting people's attention. I stealthily looked at her. I didn't hear one word my minister friend preached.

Soon the service was over, and the minister, his wife, Miss Lee, and I returned to his residence. It was way past midnight. The residence had only two bedrooms, so his wife prepared bedding for her husband and me in the adjacent room, and for Miss Lee and herself in the main room, which was warmer than the other. Feeling content with having met Miss Lee, I soon fell asleep.

My friend woke me up on Christmas morning. The brilliant sunshine and balmy weather coaxed me out for a walk on a narrow dirt road along a small creek. I thought about my short date with Miss Lee. I hadn't been able to see her clearly the previous evening because of the poor lighting. I wondered what she really looked like. She was tiny, but was she as beautiful as I had thought the previous night? Did she possess a warm, loving personality? Did she like me or not? I hadn't come to Daessang for a frivolous date, but for a serious meeting. This trip might result in the most important event in my life.

Suddenly, the road ended, and I found myself standing at the edge of a steaming spring. Well-nourished oak and chestnut trees surrounded the pool like heavenly angels guarding a sacred well of living water. The creek originated here. I couldn't help but go down to the spring and scoop up a handful of the clean water to drink. It tasted good and warm, so warm that I rolled up my jacket sleeves and washed my face. That fresh water brought me out of many unwarranted fancies and worries.

Entering the courtyard, I found Miss Lee enjoying the brilliant Christmas morning. She did not notice me entering. I said, "Good morning, Miss Lee."

She turned around and responded, "Good morning, Mr. Kim. Did you have a good rest?" Her wavy deep brown hair dazzled in the morning sun. An ethereal smile danced softly on her mouth. Her sparkling eyes made her face even fairer and her light pink lips brighter. The narrow, snow-white collar of her burgundy Korean jacket formed a neat V just below her neck. As she moved, her long pleated black skirt gently waved, like weeping willow branches in a sweet spring zephyr. She was petite, a living doll. What a beautiful girl!

Captivated, I watched her speechlessly, unable to respond, until she coughed lightly. I mumbled, "Yes, I did." Then I said awkwardly, "It's getting chilly. Shall we go inside?"

While we walked side by side across the yard, I accidentally touched her hand. A tingling sensation swept through me. I apologized. She looked at me and said with a sweet smile, "That's okay." I felt so good.

After our breakfast, we all went to the church early to help Rev. Choi prepare for Christmas morning service. He rang the church bell, heralding worship in one hour. He and I brought in firewood and started a fire in a small cast-iron stove. The ladies swept the plain pine plank floor.

About thirty worshipers filtered in from the surrounding villages and sat on the bare floor. Some brought their own cushions. Rev. Choi began the service with an invocation and led a few Christmas carols. The church was too poor to own an organ. Just before his sermon, Rev. Choi announced that Miss Lee would sing a special song. She walked to the front of the podium and sang *Silent Night* in an extraordinarily beautiful voice without any instrumental accompaniment. She interpreted the music so well that I felt as if I were seeing the holy infant peacefully sleeping in a humble manger. I was so deeply absorbed that I didn't notice that the last verse had already been sung until the congregation exclaimed, "Amen." What a wonderful talent she had! She looked even prettier.

After the service, the whole congregation enjoyed Christmas luncheon at the church. I wanted to eat with Miss Lee, but she sat with the other ladies, and I with the men. Shortly after the luncheon, Miss Lee had to leave. Rev. Choi, his wife, and I accompanied her to the roadside to catch the bus to Seolseong, where she taught, about a three-hour journey.

While waiting for the bus, Miss Lee looked at me and hesitantly asked, "Mr. Kim, would you mind giving me a picture of yourself if you have one? I would like to show it to my parents." She smiled.

I felt my heart pounding and wondered if it was a good omen. I didn't know if I had a picture, but I searched in my wallet anyway. I found one which had been taken a few years earlier when I applied for my citizen's ID. I handed it to her.

She thanked me, looked at the photograph for a moment, and carefully put it into her handbag with a barely visible smile. I asked her if she had one of herself for me. She apologized that she didn't but gave me her address.

Shortly, her bus arrived in a huge cloud of dust. She was the only passenger from Daessang. We bid farewell to each other, and she climbed up into the packed bus. It departed, and she was gone.

Our visit had been too short, not enough time to get acquainted, yet I felt as if I had known her for a long time. Her departure left an empty feeling in my heart even though I didn't know what she thought of me. I watched the disappearing bus, feeling lonesome.

Mrs. Choi asked, "Mr. Kim, what do you think about Miss Lee? Do you like her?"

Her unexpected question put me at a loss for a moment. But I answered that I liked her very much, and I wished that we had had more time to get to know each other.

Then a Seoul-bound bus came from the opposite direction and stopped, raising more dust clouds. After bidding goodbye to my friends, I hopped onto the bus, which had standing room only. As the bus rolled on, the physical distance between Miss Lee and me increased, but I dreamed that her heart and mine were coming closer together.

As soon as I arrived home, I picked up a pen and a sheet of paper and began to write a letter to her, but my mind went blank. After some struggle,

I wrote that it had been a pleasure meeting her; I wished we had had more time; and I wanted to see her again if she pleased.

I began to check my mailbox the day after I had mailed my letter even though I knew that the Korean postal service moved at a snail's pace. After more than a week's wait, I finally received a letter from her. I ran up three flights of stairs to my apartment, but didn't dare open the letter for a few moments, fearing that she might reject me. I took a couple of deep breaths to calm myself, then opened it.

She answered that she, too, had enjoyed meeting me, and would like to see me in early January when she visited her sister in Seoul. Her bus would be arriving between 5 and 6 p.m. on January 4, and she wanted to meet me at the Kyoung-gi Bus Station. Her sister's residence was a few blocks away from there. I was so elated to receive her reply that I shouted, "All right! She is coming." I read the letter one more time. Then I realized it would be the next day—less than twenty-four hours away.

I pondered what I would talk about with her. Judging from our short date, I believed that she was an honest, beautiful, intelligent, and unpretentious girl. I would present myself honestly, too, and if she accepted me for who I was, I would propose to her, telling her we would build a happy life together.

The next twenty-four hours crawled by. The last few hours took an eternity. Finally, her bus arrived, and she stepped down. I wanted to run to her and hug her, but our culture made me hold back. I said, "Hello, Miss Lee," and bowed slightly, beaming with joy. "How was the trip?"

She responded with a radiant smile. "How are you, Mr. Kim? I am glad you came," and she, too, bowed. "On the bus, my feet were freezing."

Taking her small travel bag from her, I said, "It must have been a five-hour trip. You must be tired and hungry. I will treat you to dinner. What would you like, Chinese food or Korean food?"

She chose Chinese food. I led her to a nearby Chinese restaurant. The hostess guided us to a cozy private room. We sat across the table from one another while the hostess brought two cups and a kettle of hot green tea. It was delicious, warm, and perfect for such a cold day.

We felt much more comfortable and relaxed than the first time we had met. While waiting for our food, we talked about the weather. Then I gradually moved on to my personal history. I told her about my parents, that I was the youngest of five children; that I had left my home for Seoul to search for educational opportunities when I was fifteen. I went on to tell her about joining the South Korean Army and fighting in the Korean War. After the war, I told her, I had attended Yonhi University Medical School on a full scholarship from the Education Ministry of the South Korean Government, but then a year later, I had had to drop out because of the tuition. I finished by telling her that I worked for KMAG in Yongsan as a clerk.

She listened to me intently and said, "I am sorry that the tuition forced you to leave the college." She paused, lowering her head for a while. "Can you return to medical school eventually?"

Tae-hyok and Soonnyum's wedding in December 1959

"No, I must retake an entrance exam. Even if I made the cut, I still could not afford the tuition and other expenses."

"Even though my salary is not big, I would like to help you."

Instead of responding to her offer, I stretched my arms across the table, took her hand, and said, "I love you. Will you marry me?"

She put her other hand over mine, squeezed hard, and said, "Yes, I will." Tears welled in her eyes. "Yes, I will."

Holding her hand, I walked over, kissed her, and said, "Thank you!" Eleven months later, she changed her name from Miss Lee to Mrs. Kim.

• • •

My wife and I bought a house that looked like a shack on the outskirts of Seoul. We had a daughter, Mi-jung, and a son, Hong-sik—just two children, because we wanted to be able to afford a good education for both. There were no free or public schools. For five years, we had to live separately because my wife's job was transferred to the countryside, so we moved our family there, and I stayed with my parents-in-law, whose home was closer to my job. I would come visit my wife and children every weekend. We had little, but our love was incredibly strong.

CHAPTER 26

America

September 1965 - September 1970

"*Yeobo*, go to *Miguk* (America), get your education and a good job, and then send for us." Those were my wife's last words before I set out for America on September 18, 1965. America was the dream because it had more opportunities for us as a family. We had 67,200 *won* (about $420 U.S. dollars) in debt; a significant amount, as the South Korean GDP per capita at the time was less than $80 U.S. dollars. We had to borrow the money from a few different friends to cover my trip to the United States, but we would repay them in twelve monthly installments with interest. My wife said that she could manage to pay the installments from her monthly salary as a schoolteacher and still take care of our children. I estimated that she would have only 2,400 *won* (about $15) remaining after she had paid the monthly obligation of 5,600 *won* ($35) out of her paycheck. That was way below a shoestring budget for her and our two children, but she pointed out that many Koreans lived with less.

After thirty-five days of traveling by sea, I entered America in Portland, Oregon on October 24, 1965. My destination was New York City, where one of my premed classmates was doing an internship at Bellevue Medical Center, hoping that he might help me find a job. A one-way Greyhound bus ticket from Portland to New York City was $67.50. But I had only $9.50. While I was pondering what to do, help came serendipitously. A reporter from the *Seoul Daily News* who had traveled on the same ship offered me a loan of $67.50 to buy a ticket to New York City. She, too, was headed for New York and said that I could pay her back when I got a job, which I did. I thanked her profoundly for her gracious offer and accepted it. After four days and five nights on the bus, I arrived at the New York City Port Authority Bus Terminal with only $3.50 in my pocket. I stayed with my former premed classmate while starting my search for work and a place to live. Two weeks later, I found a laminated paper cutting position for $1.20 an hour.

Even though my wife encouraged me by saying, "Honey, don't worry about us. I will manage everything," I knew she would face difficulties taking care of our children with only $15 a month as winter approached. I had to send her some money. To save money, I set up a monthly budget and was determined to stick to it no matter what.

The budget consisted of $32 for rent; $30 for food; $6 for subway tolls; and $10 for miscellaneous expenses. This enabled me to save $118 out of my $192 monthly income. These savings could pay off our $420 debt in four months. The prospect of becoming debt-free lifted my spirits sky high, and my heart pounded with excitement. I promptly wrote to my wife, informing

The Kim family before Tae-hyok leaves for America, 1965

her that I had found a job and would make almost $200 a month. I enclosed a ten-dollar bill with my letter.

Two weeks later, I received her reply telling me that everything was under control, and our beautiful children were growing and healthy. They often asked why *Appa* did not come home, especially at dinner time. With a lump in my throat and tears in my eyes, I couldn't continue to read until my emotions were under control. She said that the $10 had helped her buy fuel and one hundred grams of beef. She pounded the beef and made two small hamburgers for our children. They really loved them. She ended the letter with, "I love you. Do not worry about us back here. Just study hard for your children and me!" She kissed the bottom of the page, leaving a bright pink print of her lips. This letter made me the happiest man in the world.

At work, everyone but the owner spoke Spanish. Some of them could speak English, but theirs was as bad as mine, making it impossible to improve my English on the job. After working for two weeks, I visited the New York State Employment Division in Brooklyn and applied for a clerical job in an English-speaking environment. After testing me for my math and English

Mi-jung and Hong-sik in South Korea

proficiency, they sent me to Staff Builder's Temporary Placement Agency, which placed me at Cartier Jewelry Retail Store in Manhattan as an errand boy for $1.35 an hour—a 15¢ pay raise. Furthermore, this job provided me with plenty of opportunities to converse in English.

This 15¢ increase enabled me to send $24 more to my wife every four weeks. I opened a savings account with a nearby branch of Chase Manhattan Bank and deposited my weekly paychecks. The customer representative gave me a black savings account book, printing the amount in it. It was my first experience with a bank, and I looked at the balance several times before putting it carefully in my jacket pocket. My fourth paycheck increased my bank total to more than $130 after my weekly expenses, and my morale soared, thinking of paying off at least one quarter of our debt.

The South Korean government practiced a fixed exchange rate between the Korean and American currencies, way below the real value. If I sent $100 to my wife through the Korean Central Bank, it would pay her about 17,000 *won* and auction the dollars off for three to four times that amount, profiting more than 300 percent. I didn't want the government to exploit my hard-earned dollars. So, I decided to send the money to my wife through a secret method so that she could sell it on the black market for its real value.

I converted $120 into two bills, a $100 and a $20, and discreetly kept them in the inner pocket of my jacket. Even though my office was so warm that my coworkers took off their coats, I kept mine on until I came home. On the way home, I stopped at a Woolworth's and bought a small bottle of Elmer's glue and four children's books, the kind with thick cardboard pages, two for my five-year-old daughter and two for my two-year-old son. The books contained many colorful animals and large letters.

Arriving at my apartment, I closed the door to my room and picked the thickest book from the four which I had bought. Then I chose one page and carefully peeled it into two pieces using a razor to slice apart the upper corner of the page. Next, I inserted the $100 bill and glued the page together with extreme care so as not to damage the bill and to restore the page to its original form. After doing the same for the $20 bill with a second book, I mailed them to my wife with an encrypted letter, requesting that she confirm receipt of the package as soon as possible. To make this method successful, she and

I devised a set of secret codes such as "your birthday was 7/24" which meant "check pages 7 and 24 for some U.S. dollars."

As I waited to hear from her, I found that one dollar a day for food did not go very far. My diet consisted of two small cans of chili, one for breakfast and the other for lunch, and plain spaghetti sprinkled with a little bit of salt and tomato ketchup for supper. After a couple of weeks, I got tired of my diet, especially the spaghetti. Every day, I had to pass a steakhouse and the aroma of sizzling beef drove me crazy. Unable to resist any longer, I bought the cheapest can of beef I could find at a nearby grocery store. It cost 70¢, 70 percent of my daily food budget. Upon opening the can, a very strong, disagreeable smell came from it, but I heated it anyway and mixed it with a lot of ketchup to eliminate the odor. Despite my craving for meat, I barely finished one half of the beef and discarded the rest. 70 percent of my daily food budget went into the wastebasket, and the stench led me to the empty can. I read the label carefully. It was dog food! Feeling embarrassed, I never shared this episode with anybody.

Four weeks after I had mailed the package, I still had no news from my wife, and feared that she was sick or that the package had gotten lost. Meanwhile, after one and a half months of temporary employment, Cartier offered me a full-time job as an assistant bookkeeper for $60 a week with health insurance and two weeks of paid vacation. I took it without hesitation.

After a couple of weeks of training, my boss, Gene Tiejun, let me perform my responsibilities alone. A few days later, he offered me overtime. I jumped on it. Knowing that I needed money, he gave me so much overtime that I worked from 9 a.m. to midnight every day except Wednesday, when I went to take computer classes. I also worked on Saturdays. This grueling schedule kept me too busy to be lonely. This employment paid almost $150 a week, allowing me to raise my food budget to $3 a day. No more dog food!

Despite my request, my wife did not write back for more than six weeks. Only affluent Koreans could afford telephones. She did not have one. Thus, air mail was our only means of communication. My anxiety grew daily. Despite having no news, I decided to send $300 more in $100 bills. This time I used many postcard-size pictures of me taken around New York City. I picked three pictures and peeled each of them into two pieces. I folded each of the three bills in half and ironed them flat. Then I inserted each bill between the pieces of the photo, glued them back carefully to their original form, and pressed them under a thick book. When they dried, I doctored the pictures by cutting off any excessive glue with a razorblade. I mixed them randomly with the other pictures and spread them face down on the floor, trying to identify the doctored ones. It took a long time before I could pick them out. I packed all the pictures in a padded envelope and mailed them to my wife with an encrypted letter.

Two weeks later, I finally heard from her. She said that she had received both packages; she had sold the dollars for a significant amount of Korean money at its real value in the black market and paid off our debt, leaving her with a good amount. Being debt free enabled her to keep her paychecks in full. The children were so delighted to see my pictures and kissed them. She apologized for not writing letters for many weeks due to an injury. She said that after paying the monthly obligations from her paychecks, she had no money left to buy coal for heating. So, one cold January day, she went into the nearby hills to collect firewood and accidently cut her right shin with the sickle. She treated the injury with home remedies, and it took more than one month to heal. She didn't write because she did not want to cause unnecessary anxiety for me in a distant land. She sacrificed herself for our children and me.

In less than six months, her devotion, our belt-tightening budget, and my new job bailed our family out of considerable debt. I continued to send her $100 every month to help with my family's living costs while saving for my college. I worked for Cartier for nineteen months until I had saved enough money for one year of college expenses and a lump sum of $1,000 for my family. That freedom from debt lifted my spirits, my happiness, and my hopes in this land of opportunity.

In September 1967, I enrolled at Brigham Young University (BYU) as a thirty-six-year-old sophomore, majoring in statistics. I chose the school because the tuition was so much cheaper than other universities. BYU cost $95 per semester whereas other universities cost $1,000 to $1,600 per semester. After my enrollment, my wife and I discussed by mail how to reunite our family as soon as possible. Because of our financial situation, we made a very difficult decision that she should come to America first, leaving our seven- and four-year-old children behind with their maternal grandmother. It was extremely painful for my wife. After three long years of separation, she joined me in Las Vegas in June 1968, while I had a summer job. Because she couldn't bring our children with her, ours was a bittersweet reunion. She got a job as a seamstress at a local ladies' garment factory. We saved every penny for our children to join us. Two years later, we brought them (then nine and six years old) from Korea. It took five long years before we were all reunited.

Hong-sik and Mi-jung arriving in America, 1970

Epilogue

by Nicole Rogers

My grandfather received a B.S. in 1970 and an M.S. in 1972, both in statistics from Brigham Young University. He had finally accomplished his dream of getting an education, as well as living the American dream, albeit with challenges and sacrifices.

My grandparents had to adjust to living in a completely different culture. The language barrier was just one of those, mainly for my grandmother, who didn't speak English prior to coming to America. But she taught herself. She gave up her teaching job to come to the United States and worked as a hotel

Graduated from Brigham Young University

The Kim and Rogers family, 1990s. From left to right: Soonnyum Kim, Michelle (Mi-jung) Rogers, Bill Rogers, Nicole Rogers, Tae-hyok Kim, and Harold (Hong-sik) Kim.

Tae-hyok and Soonnyum in California, 2018

maid and in a sewing factory. She had her story as well. She was born in Seoul, the oldest of seven children. Her family lost everything during the Korean War. Her home and her parents' business (a retail store) were destroyed; they were bombed by the Americans at the beginning of the war when the North Koreans were concentrated in Icheon, South Korea. She was farming when she saw her home being bombed; thankfully, her parents and siblings survived. Despite this, she became a survivor and helped raise her younger siblings. She didn't marry before she was twenty-six because she wanted to focus on her job and provide money for her family.

I will always remember her as the best Korean cook I've ever known. She had an organic garden in her backyard, where she grew Korean herbs and vegetables. She also sewed beautiful clothes and sang in her church choir for years. My grandfather once wrote, "Our love has ripened from green to golden-brown, inseparable. We hope to cross the bridge of no return together, hand in hand, in the bliss of our unchangeable love." She passed away in 2022.

After getting a master's degree at the age of forty-one, my grandfather went on to work for American Hoechst Pharmaceuticals, *Reader's Digest*, AIM, AT&T

The Kim and Rogers family, 2019. From left to right: Bill Rogers, Griffin Kim, Tae-hyok Kim, Connor Kim, Soonnyum Kim, Nicole Rogers, and Michelle Rogers.

Universal Card Services, and Crestar Bank. He came to my high school field hockey games and track meets to cheer me on. He would always whistle, too! He ran half marathons, and took classes at a community college as well as at my old town's library. He always had a dictionary at home and would learn the 'word of the day' every single day; now that's turned into the word of the day on dictionary.com on his iPad. He is a lifelong learner, and always stays positive.

WASHINGTON D.C., MAY 2009

FREEDOM IS NOT FREE. My grandfather's worn hand slid down the silver engraved letters. We were outside at the Korean War Memorial in Washington, D.C. It was my graduation week; I had just gotten my undergraduate degree at The George Washington University. I knew I had to bring my grandparents to this memorial. My parents and uncle came, too.

"It's not," he looked at me, his mouth slightly open like he was about to say something more. He stood there in his chinos and blue and white button-down shirt, his glasses hiding some of the wrinkles on his face. He looked into the distance, as if his memories were resurfacing. I had never seen him this frozen before.

"Dad?" my mom called out. My grandmother had left his side to take in the entire memorial. She started walking along the United Nations Curb, which showcased the names of twenty-two countries from the United Nations (including the Republic of Korea) that had served in the war.

He shook himself out of his reverie. He looked at the men approaching him. Statues on high alert, their heads were tilted as if they had heard something, while marching through a rice paddy, the cold, bitter wind hitting their parkas. "It's not free," he said silently.

"So many people came to help us. I would not be here today if they had not come to fight our enemy. They didn't know about our land, but they still came. They could not speak our language, yet they still fought alongside us. I had never seen such bravery before. They were the heroes. I will forever be grateful to all those who fought for our freedom."

My mom clenched his hand, and my uncle put his arm around my grandfather's back. My grandfather turned and said, "Mi-jung, Hong-sik," addressing my mom and uncle by their Korean names. "Nicole," he continued, looking at me. "Don't ever forget."

We wouldn't. The cost of the war included human losses (including many civilians); refugees stranded from their homes; cities and towns that were bombed, and individuals trying to relocate south by walking miles in the frozen winter. Brothers and sisters, children and parents were torn apart, divided by a permanent border.

And yet, there were hundreds of thousands of heroes who came from around the world to this small, mountainous land. They made such a sacrifice for families like ours, leaving their own behind. I was reminded of the two American soldiers who found a way to keep the Korean family together by improvising seats on their truck and giving them a ride. This was just one small act of the spirit of American humanitarianism. There were heroes within Korea, too—military personnel and civilians alike—who fought for freedom. Many lost their lives. Others were separated from their families. Those heroes, who have often been forgotten, saved so many Korean people. We would not be standing here today if it weren't for them.

We need to remember all of Korea; all its people—those who were hoping to be in South Korea when the DMZ was created but were (and still are) forever in the North; those who fought for their own country against communism. Many North Koreans went south to join the Republic of Korea Armed Forces when the war broke out, hoping to reunify their country under a banner of freedom. We need to remember all the countries and men and women who came to Korea's aid at a time of need, and the courage and love they showed for people they did not know.

"We won't, grandpa," I answered him.

We joined my grandmother and my dad, who were now looking at the hundreds of photographs of service members stenciled into the mural wall.

So, let's remember.

Let's remember the Korean people throughout the peninsula who speak one language and share the same history and culture.

Let's remember that Korea was one nation, and that with the creation of the border on the 38th Parallel, its people were suddenly forcibly split.

Let's remember that terrible wars can break out due to a few men's desires for more power.

Let's remember that the call for democracy was heard and answered by twenty-one other nations.

Let's remember the cost of war, and the importance of political and military decisions on a war's outcome and a nation's civilians. Could the United States have listened more to the Republic of Korea's warnings? Should they have armed them with more weapons? Should the UN forces have kept moving north past the 38th Parallel? If they hadn't, would the Communist Chinese not have intervened? Would World War III have taken place if Truman hadn't relieved MacArthur of his duties? Could there have been a way to save more North Korean civilians?

But we cannot forget that if the U.S. and UN countries had not come to the Republic of Korea's aid, South Korea would not be a country today—a buzzing economy (currently ranked the tenth country in the world by GDP[100]) and people who happily live in a democratic state. We cannot forget that if these nations had not gotten involved, and the North had communized the South, communism would likely have continued to spread in Asia.

Let's remember all the military personnel who sacrificed their lives to bring freedom to a nation they had never heard of and a people whom they did not know. Let's remember that the Republic of Korea—soldiers, civilians, and even student volunteers—rose to fight for democracy. Let's continue to rise and stand up for freedom. To all those who served in the Korean War, thank you. We owe a debt of gratitude to you. Thank you for your service and sacrifice, and for your outstanding bravery.

Let's remember that the Korean people have endured so much hardship and still march forward. That their homes were bombed. That they lost their children. That families were forever split. But also, many Koreans and their families got the freedom that they so desired and for which they fought so valiantly.

And for the people who didn't, I'm sure that they still say to themselves, "a good day will come soon."

Let's always remember.

ACKNOWLEDGMENTS

by Nicole Rogers

In 2018, after my grandfather had a stroke, my family and I were helping him organize his papers and came across his writings. I had grown up hearing his stories, and he had e-mailed me a few of them on occasion, but I would usually skim them.

Fast forward to the pandemic, when we were all sheltering in place in California. I watched *Band of Brothers* and *The Pacific*. I sat on my couch thinking I wanted to continue watching. "What's next?" I thought. "What about my own story?" My mind shifted back to the conversations where my grandfather used to tell me about serving in the Korean War. So, I dug up those stories. I printed out hundreds of pages and pieced them together.

There are many people to thank for their help in completing this book. But first, I'd like to thank my grandfather. He has had so many setbacks in life, some of which you've read about in these pages. Nonetheless, he continues moving forward with pure determination and with the most positive energy of anyone I know, always smiling and looking at the bright side of things. So, thank you, Grandpa, for taking those calls every day for the past three years to answer my questions and help me fill in the gaps. Thank you for being patient with me as I went over character after character with you and had you relive those moments. Thank you for letting me share your story. My grandfather always said, "I hope others read it! But I think you're the only one who'd be interested in my story, Nicole." That may be so, but in my opinion, more people need to know about Korea's history, how far South Korea has come, how far North Korea has not, and what the Korean people experienced and continue to experience today.

To my grandmother, Soonnyum Kim, who passed away in 2022. You were there by his side in every dream and aspiration he's had and pursued. Not enough thanks have been given to you for the sacrifices you've made—giving up your teaching job to come to America, working as a hotel maid and in a sewing factory while Grandpa got his master's degree, and later owning a dry-cleaning business. You always worked hard and put your family above yourself. I wish I had asked you more about your own story.

To all the countries who came to Korea's aid at its time of need, and to the leaders of those countries, who had to make timely and difficult decisions, thank you for stepping up.

To the veterans of the Republic of Korea and the United Nations, thank you for your service and sacrifice. While you served in "The Forgotten War," you have not been forgotten. Without your actions, a whole nation would be under the rule of communism today. There are individuals and families who wake up every day thankful for all of you who fought for the freedom of so many.

To my grandfather's friends with whom he served and those above him in command, thank you for looking after "Skinny Sergeant." You each have your own stories, which were not captured in this book, and which I wish I knew. My uncle (Tae-hyok's son), who served in the U.S. Navy, once told me that in addition to serving your country, it's all about the "people and the experiences" in the military and how some of the people you serve with become closer than your blood relatives. That "band of brothers" creates a bond that we see throughout war stories to this day. I'm grateful for your having been a brother to my grandfather. To the families of those who passed, know that they served their country well and that we're so grateful for all they've done.

To my grandfather's family. Your memory will live on for those of you who never made it to South Korea. My heart goes out to all of you as well as families like your own who were forever separated. To his family in South Korea, thank you for hosting my mom and me during our last visit. Your closeness with each other shows the love that has grown out of hardship. Won-sik, it was so nice to see you again. Your smile and that twinkle in your eyes are just like my grandfather's. Kyeong-ja, thank you for being our tour guide for days and for always keeping in touch.

To my mom, Michelle (Mi-jung) Rogers. I have seen so much outpouring of your love for your parents. It goes above and beyond. You continue to have that will and determination that your parents passed on and showed you at a young age, which can be seen every day. You have an endless spark of joy and energy that you bring into each person's life.

To my dad, Bill Rogers. For all your coffee chats, technology discussions, and news recaps that you've provided to Grandpa. Thank you and mom for always believing in me, and for showing me what hard work looks like. And thank you for watching Korean history and Korean War documentaries with me.

To my uncle, Harold (Hong-sik) Kim. And his family Heather, Connor, and Griffin. Harold, this story was originally dedicated to you and Michelle, when you first asked in the car years ago as a kid who your grandparents were. It was then that Tae decided to write his story down. Thank you for asking, for being there for your dad, and for your service. Heather, Connor, and Griffin, I hope you enjoy the story, which was originally meant for you, too.

To Sora Chung. You were the first reader of the entire manuscript. You provided feedback and asked me questions throughout the process. Thank you for being interested in this story, but mainly for always being one of the best friends I have ever had. To more adventures ahead.

To Conway Chen. You're always a phone call away. I should really put you on speed dial. Thank you for always answering my endless questions about this project. As I write this, I can't wait for our next catch-up call.

To Chris Rogers, Gail Rogers, Robin Daniels, Adam Massey, Mark Urton, and Andrew Chapello. Thank you for pre-reading this prior to its publication. Chris, you once said, "I would pay big money to live five minutes of your grandfather's life." I hope this story gave you all more than a five-minute glimpse. I'm very appreciative of this group of close friends taking the time to read it.

To Lukas Atwood. For all the military questions you answered. Thank you for taking the time to explain military terminology, rank, and weaponry to me. You're still like a younger brother to me, and I will always remember our pizza and movie nights with your family. And thank you for your service.

To my grandfather's assisted living community. Thank you to those who took the time to hear these stories. I hope you enjoyed them. And thank you for being a family to my grandfather (and to my grandmother when she was alive). To Rivier University, where my grandfather took writing classes, and to Hollis Social Library, where he was a part of the writers' club. Thank you to all those individuals who taught him about writing.

To Jaya Chatterjee. I'm very fortunate to have worked with you as an editor who is extremely knowledgeable about world history, geopolitics, and international relations. I remember getting the manuscript back and smiling because of all your edits. Thank you for meticulously editing the manuscript line by line, and polishing and honing it to where it is today. It wouldn't be the same if it wasn't for your professional eye.

To Nat Case. Nat, I never knew that I'd ever collaborate with a cartographer in my lifetime, and I'm so glad I did. Your knowledge of history is incredible, as is your skill at creating maps for the accompanying era. I thought I'd pass on what I needed but the creation of these maps became a partnership to draw the "right" ones for the story. Thank you for making it such a cool experience.

To Owen Gent. I was immediately impressed when you told me you watched the documentaries I sent you and read the historical links. Thank you for your interest in Korean history and my grandfather's story, and the collaboration on the creative concepts, sketches, and details of the beautiful design. "Reflection" does speak of his memories of home and how they are always with him, but also of the divide between the two countries. Whenever I look at it, I feel like it captures his looking ahead and moving forward.

To Andy Bridge. Thank you for the artistic sketches and designs, capturing the essence of Korea's scenic beauty from the serene rice paddies to the farming scenes and majestic mountains. It's been an absolute pleasure working with you on all the visual elements and the details those entailed and putting this all together as one beautiful design.

To Steve Kuhn. Talk about speed. Thank you for answering all my questions—there were a lot! And for all the time you took to make the interior beautifully formatted, transforming the manuscript into visually stunning pages of an actual book.

To Jack, Linyan, JD, and Liz. Thank you for being a part of this journey, and for all the calls and emails that have helped prepare this book for launch.

To the Korea Institute of Military History. I pored over your books on the history of the Korean War. I often came across the American account, but your books gave me the Korean perspective I needed.

To so many authors who have already written on Korea's past and the Korean War. Thank you for expanding awareness so that more people know of its history.

To the reader, I hope this makes you a bit more knowledgeable about Korea and some of its history (there is more—thousands of years to catch up on!) and its people. I also hope this story inspires you to ask your elders—family or acquaintances—questions about their lives. Every person has a fascinating story to share. I'm thankful I got to know a bit more of mine.

And last but certainly not least. To the Korean people. Those who live in both North and South Korea, we will always remember that your country was unified at one point, and all the suffering and hardship you experienced. I admire your determination and resilience. There are many more of these stories out there which I hope get written down. I look forward to reading them someday.

Bibliography

ACADEMIC JOURNALS:

Koh, B. C. "The War's Impact on the Korean Peninsula." The Journal of American-East Asian Relations 2, no. 1 (Spring 1993): 57. https://www.jstor.org/stable/23612666.

BOOKS:

Chae, Han Kook, Chung, Suk Kyun, and Yang, Yong Cho. The Korean War Volume One. Seoul, Korea: Korea Institute of Military History, 1997.

Chae, Han Kook, Chung, Suk Kyun, and Son, Moon Sik. The Korean War Volume Two. Seoul, Korea: Korea Institute of Military History, 1998.

Duncan, David Douglas. This is War! A Photo-Narrative of the Korean War. Little, Brown & Company (Canada) Limited, 1951.

Halberstam, David. The Coldest Winter: America and the Korean War. New York: Hyperion, 2007.

Seth, Michael J. Korea: A Very Short Introduction. Oxford: Oxford University Press, 2019.

Sides, Hampton. On Desperate Ground: The Marines at the Reservoir, the Korean War's Greatest Battle. New York: Doubleday, 2018.

DOCUMENTARIES:

Chosin. Directed by Brian Iglesias. September 10, 2010.

Korea: The Never-Ending War. Written and produced by John Maggio. Produced by WETA Washington, D.C., KBS, ZED, ARK Media, and the BBC. Published April 29, 2019. Funding provided by the National Endowment for the Humanities, The Arthur Vining Davis Foundations, and PBS.

The Battle of Chosin. Directed by Randall MacLowry. A Film Posse, Inc. Production for American Experience. WGBH Educational Foundation, 2016.

The Forgotten War. Directed by Daniel Leonard Bernardi. 2020.

MAGAZINES:

Marolda, Edward J. "The Cold War's First Conflict." Naval History Magazine. June 2010, Volume 24, Number 3. https://www.usni.org/magazines/naval-history-magazine/2010/june/cold-wars-first-conflict.

OFFICIAL REPORTS:

The U.S. Air Force in Korea: Campaigns, Units, and Stations, 1950–1953. Compiled by Organizational History Branch, Research Division, Air Force Historical Research Agency. https://media.defense.gov/2010/May/26/2001330297/-1/-1/0/Korea_Campaigns.pdf.

"Resolution 83 (1950)." United Nations Digital Library. https://digitallibrary.un.org/record/112026?ln=en.

"Resolution 84 (1950)." United Nations Digital Library. https://digitallibrary.un.org/record/112027?ln=en

ONLINE GOVERNMENT DOCUMENT:

United States Department of State. "Substance of Statements Made at Wake Island Conference on 15 October 1950." Foreign Relations of the United States, 1950, Volume VII, Korea, Document 680. https://history.state.gov/historicaldocuments/frus1950v07/d680.

WEBSITES:

"Chosin Reservoir." Museum of Honor. https://mohmuseum.org/chosinreservoir/.

Cummings, Bruce. "The U.S. War Crime North Korea Won't Forget." Washington Post. March 24, 2015. https://www.washingtonpost.com/opinions/the-us-war-crime-north-korea-wont-forget/2015/03/20/fb525694-ce80-11e4-8c54-ffb5ba6f2f69_story.html.

Fry, Michael. "National Geographic, Korea, and the 38th Parallel." National Geographic, August 4, 2013. https://www.nationalgeographic.com/science/article/130805-korean-war-dmz-armistice-38-parallel-geography.

"Korean War." The History Channel. https://www.history.com/topics/asian-history/korean-war.

"Korean War Commemoration: Quotes." United States Marine Corps. Marine Corps University, Research, Marine Corps History Division. https://www.usmcu.edu/Research/Marine-Corps-History-Division/Brief-Histories/Korean-War-Commemoration/Quotes/.

Lewis, Larry and Smith, Scott D. "Counting the Dead at Hiroshima and Nagasaki." The Bulletin, August 3, 2020. https://thebulletin.org/2020/08/counting-the-dead-at-hiroshima-and-nagasaki/.

"Military Personnel Unaccounted For." Defense POW/MIA Accounting Agency. Accessed January 6, 2023. https://www.dpaa.mil/Our-Missing/Korean-War/Korean-War-POW-MIA-List/.

"New Evidence on North Korean War Losses." Wilson Center, August 1, 2001. https://www.wilsoncenter.org/article/new-evidence-north-korean-war-losses.

"Old Soldiers Never Die" Address by Gen. Douglas MacArthur, April 19, 1951." Iowa Department of Cultural Affairs. https://iowaculture.gov/history/education/educator-resources/primary-source-sets/cold-war/old-soldiers-never-die-address-gen.

Pickrell, Ryan. "These Are 10 of the Toughest and Most Important Battles US Marines Ever Fought." Business Insider, November 10, 2020. https://www.businessinsider.com/these-are-some-of-the-most-iconic-battles-the-us-marines-ever-fought-2018-11.

"Prewar Context: Western." Memory Bank. Korean War Legacy Foundation. https://koreanwarlegacy.org/chapters/prewar-context-western/.

"Prisoners of War." National Museum of the U.S. Air Force. https://www.nationalmuseum.af.mil/Visit/Museum-Exhibits/Fact-Sheets/Display/Article/195883/prisoners-of-war/.

Ray, Michael. "Korean War Timeline." Britannica. Accessed May 20, 2023. https://www.britannica.com/list/korean-war-timeline.

"Recall of General Douglas MacArthur (1951)." U.S. Embassy & Consulates in Germany. https://usa.usembassy.de/etexts/democrac/58.htm.

"Soviets Boycott United Nations Security Council." This Day in History. History.com. https://www.history.com/this-day-in-history/soviets-boycott-united-nations-security-council.

"Statement by the President, Truman on Korea." Wilson Center, Digital Archive. https://digitalarchive.wilsoncenter.org/document/116192.pdf?v=cd0b66b71d6a0412d275a5088a18db5d.

"Task Force Faith Heroism in Korea 1950." HistoryNet. https://www.historynet.com/task-force-faith-heroism-korea-1950/.

"This Day in Aviation." November 8, 1950. https://www.thisdayinaviation.com/8-november-1950/.

"Top 15 Countries by GDP in 2022." Global PEO Services. https://globalpeoservices.com/top-15-countries-by-gdp-in-2022/.

Zabecki, David T. "Stand or Die - 1950 Defense of Korea's Pusan Perimeter." Historynet.com, May 1, 2009. https://www.historynet.com/stand-or-die-1950-defense-of-koreas-pusan-perimeter/.

Notes

1. 'the 4ᵗʰ to the 7ᵗʰ century, three states existed in Korea', 'fought each other', 'unification of Korea' : Seth, Korea: A Very Short Introduction, 10-12.

2. Roughly 110,000 to 210,000 people were killed : Lewis and Smith, "Counting the Dead."

3. wanting Seoul and Inchon to be in the American sector : Fry, "National Geographic, Korea, and the 38th Parallel" taken from Dean Rusk's memoir, *As I Saw It*

4. 'thirty minutes' (said by Sue Mi Terry (Former CIA Analyst) in this documentary). No one from Korea was consulted about it : Korea: The Never-Ending War, written and produced by John Maggio, 2019.

5. 150,000 troops : US War Department Intelligence Division, *Intelligence Review*, June 20, 1946 as cited in Chae, Han Kook, et al., The Korean War Volume One, 13.

6. '77,600 to the south of the border,' 'withdraw their troops in 1948', and '2,000 military advisors' : Chae, Han Kook, et al., The Korean War Volume One, 17, 43.

7. 'meeting in December 1948 with representatives from North Korea and Communist China', 'strengthen the North Korean People's Army', 'invade South Korea by mid-1950' : Ibid., 43.

8. March 5, 1949 meeting and the 'unification of the Korean peninsula', 'Soviet Union would loan $40 million' : Ministry of Foreign Affairs, *Soviet Documents* (3), pp. 6-12. Korea Institute of Military History, *Soviet Source Materials*, of the conference between Kim Il Sung and Bulganin as cited in Chae, Han Kook, et al., The Korean War Volume One, 44.

9. 'March 1949 … more military assistance' : Ibid., 133.

10. World War II equipment, some of which was deteriorated : Author interview with Ray Mansour, Korean War Veteran (former U.S. Marine) on March 31, 2023.

11. 'howitzers had half the range', 'antitank rocket launchers could not destroy enemy tanks', 'equipment was meant for 50,000 men, but by March 1950, the ROK forces had 104,000' : Chae, Han Kook, et al., The Korean War Volume One, 80-81.

12. Ibid., 80.

13. 'April 28, 1949, Kim Il Sung met with Mao', 'accord he had signed with the Soviet Union on March 17', 'provide the NKPA with Korean veterans,' Ibid., 104-105.

14. 50,000 veterans : WHCC, *History of the Korean War*, vol. 1, pp. 94095; WHCC, *History of the Korean War*, vol. 1 (old edition), pp. 689-690 as cited in Chae, Han Kook, et al., The Korean War Volume One, 45.

15. 'By May 17, 1949…agreed on war,' and 'meetings continued' : Chae, Han Kook, et al., The Korean War Volume One, 106-111.

16. 'August 20, 1949, Syngman Rhee wrote a letter … only had enough ammunition for two', Ibid., 81.

17. 400,000 men : The 400,000 men consisted of "100,000 in the standing army, 50,000 in the reserves, 50,000 in the police, and 200,000 reinforcements." Letter from Ambassador Muccio to US State Secretary Dean Acheson; WHCC, *History of National Defense*, vol. 1 p. 322 as cited in Chae, Han Kook, et al., The Korean War Volume One, 81.

18. '$10.2 million to ROK in 1950,' 'KMAG … said they needed $20 million' : Chae, Han Kook, et al., The Korean War Volume One, 87-88.

19. Jacob Malik … left the Security Council … proposal for a PRC representative : "This Day in History: Soviets Boycott United Nations Security Council," History.com.

20. intelligence report on December 27, 1949 : WHCC, *History of the Korean War*, vol. 1, p. 567 as cited in Chae, Han Kook, et al., The Korean War Volume One, 134-135.

21. shared with the UN Commission : Chae, Han Kook, et al., The Korean War Volume One, 134.

22. press conferences with foreign journalists : WHCC, *History of the Korean* War, vol. 1, p. 567 as cited in Chae, Han Kook, et al., The Korean War Volume One, 134-136.

23. Plan … build up the North Korean military, then to propose to South Korea the idea of unifying the two states …North Korea would then start the war : Chae, Han Kook, et al., The Korean War Volume One, 110.

24. border skirmishes from 1945 to 1950, causing 10,000 casualties : "Korean War," The History Channel.

25. MacArthur wrote an intelligence report to Washington and said he had intelligence that North Korea would invade in June : WHCC, *History of the Korean War*, vol. 1, p. 758 as cited in Chae, Han Kook, et al., The Korean War Volume One, 152.

26. Strength and equipment of North Korean People's Army : WHCC, *History of the Korean* War, vol. 1 (old edition), pp. 697-702; Ministry of Foreign Affairs, *Soviet Documents* (4), p. 28 as cited in Chae, Han Kook, et al., The Korean War Volume One, 50-51. Strength and equipment of ROK Armed Forces : Chae, Han Kook, et al., The Korean War Volume One, 89-90. ROK Estimate of Enemy Situation (December 27, 1949) : WHCC, *History of the Korean War*, vol. 1, p. 567 as cited in Chae, Han Kook, et al., The Korean War Volume One, 135. ROK Estimate of Enemy Situation (May 12, 1950) : Chae, Han Kook, et al., The Korean War Volume One, 137.

27. 'invasion plan was finished on May 29, 1950,' 'plan was in Russian, thus showcasing that it was put together by Soviet military advisors, and then it was translated into Korean', 'end the war in a month… new government being formed by August 15, Liberation Day in Korea,' 'China said that if Japan or the U.S. entered the war, they would send in troops to back up North Korea,' Chae, Han Kook, et al., The Korean War Volume One, 106, 110-112.

28. ratio was 1:4 and 1:7. Ratios provided were actually 1:4.1 and 1:7.1 to be precise. : "The strength comparison is based on the figures from Appleman, *South to the Naktong, North to the Yalu*, p. 11 and 15, but see *History of the Korean War*, vol. 1, p. 245 for the figure on the strength of the Separate Armor Regiment in

the Inje Area. As no precise data were available on the strength of the 549ᵗʰ Detachment, it was estimated as one-third that of a naval combat team. Figures in the blanks represent the strength and the ratio exclusion those ROK troops on leave." as cited in Chae, Han Kook, et al., The Korean War Volume One, 147.

29. '$10,970,000 in military assistance (earlier saying $10.2 million) in March 1950. However, less than $1,000 had been sent to South Korea by June 25' : Schnabel, *Policy and Direction,* p. 36; Sawyer, *KMAG,* pp. 96-104 as cited in Chae, Han Kook, et al., The Korean War Volume One, 88.

30. '105,752 people … 198,380,' 'As for equipment, ROK had zero tanks and 22 airplanes, no antitank weapons for armored attack, and no antiaircraft guns. The NKPA had 242 T-34 tanks and 211 airplanes. ROKA could not use 15% of its weapons and 35% of its vehicles' : Chae, Han Kook, et al., The Korean War Volume One, 146-147.

31. 'strengthened their security and then went under emergency alert,' '45 days,' 'lifted on June 24,' 'One-third of the soldiers went on leave,' 'Some went to help their families during the farming season' : Ibid.,152-154.

32. 100,000 soldiers : Ray, Michael. "Korean War Timeline." Britannica.

33. "Domino Theory", President Harry Truman said, "If we let Korea down, the Soviet[s] will keep right on going and swallow up one piece of Asia after another." : "Prewar Context: Western," Korean War Legacy Foundation.

34. 'June 28 … Army Chief of Staff Chae ordered the Han River bridges to be blown up' (sources vary between 1:45 am to 2:30 am), '500-800 people died,' '40-50 cars were affected by the blast not on the bridge, thus bringing injuries to citizens', 'citizens who hadn't crossed would now be under North Korean rule.' : Chae, Han Kook, et al., The Korean War Volume One, 235-237.

35. "Resolution 83 (1950)." United Nations Digital Library.

36. "The attack upon Korea … peace and security" : "Statement by the President, Truman on Korea," Wilson Center, Digital Archive.

37. '"human bullet" attacks,'; unable to envelop their forces' : Chae, Han Kook, et al., The Korean War Volume One, 239, 243.

38. 'U.S. committed to sending ground forces to Korea on June 30, and General Douglas MacArthur ordered the 24ᵗʰ Division of the Eighth U.S. Army to be sent in from Japan', '…already sent naval and air forces' : Ibid., 283-285.

39. Task Force Smith : Appleman, *South to the Naktong, North to the Yalu,* p. 60; Charles E. Heller and William A. Stoff (eds.), *America's First Battle (1776-1965);* Roy K. Flint, *T.F. Smith and the 24ᵗʰ Division: Delay and Withdrawal, 5-19 July 1959* (Univ. of Kansas Press, 1988), p. 274. as cited in Chae, Han Kook, et al., The Korean War Volume One, 286.

40. "Resolution 84 (1950)." United Nations Digital Library.

41. 'July 14, the command of the ROK forces…' : Chae, Han Kook, et al., The Korean War Volume One, 347.

42. Command Structure of the United Nations Command : WHCC, *Summary of the Korean War,* p. 206 as cited in Chae, Han Kook, et al., The Korean War Volume One, 344.

43. Lt. Gen. Walton Walker's 'Stand or Die' speech : Zebecki, "Stand or Die – 1950 Defense of Korea's Pusan Perimeter."

44. 'Lt. Gen. Walker achieved more than what he's acknowledged for in the battles up till September 1950',

'He knew the importance of Daegu', 'He even would fly right above his men fighting and would scream at his troops, risking his own life while doing so.' : Halberstam, The Coldest Winter, 254-255.

45. "I can almost hear…and I shall crush them," : "Korean War Commemoration: Quotes," United States Marine Corps.

46. 'recruited Major General Oliver Prince Smith at the end of August to come up with the plans,' 'Smith would be reporting to his complete opposite, Major General Edward Almond, also known as "Ned the Dread,"' : Sides, On Desperate Ground, 9, 17-18.

47. Thirteen thousand troops : Halberstam, The Coldest Winter, 306.

48. "The amphibious landing … all naval history." : Brodie, Bernard. A Guide to Naval Strategy. Princeton: Princeton University Press, 1944 as cited in "Korean War Commemoration: Quotes," United States Marine Corps.

49. Forty thousand men : Halberstam, The Coldest Winter, 308.

50. 'barricades, mines, and snipers' : Sides, On Desperate Ground, 39.

51. 'fight in the mountains and hills … performing flanking maneuvers' : Chae, Han Kook, et al., The Korean War Volume One, 432.

52. 'Students volunteered … partake in combat missions', 'fought in the Battle of Pohang', 'female students enlisted', 'The Korean Student Volunteer Army was formed', 'the ROK Army Troop Information and Education Office created a Student Cadre's Unit sending 1,500 students to the front line', 'training schools', and 'The Korean Military Academy merged with the ROKA Infantry School' : Ibid., 448, 514-516.

53. 'Policemen also attached themselves to the army', : "Bradley J. Haldy, *Korean Service Corps-Past and Present,*" Army Logistician (July-August, 1987), pp. 22-23; The War History Compilation Committee, *The History of Korean War,* vol. 3, 1970, p. 590; Early of August, 1950, 5,800 South Korean policemen together with about 10,000 combat police forces had been deployed at Taegu front. Yoo Kwan Chong, *the History of the ROK Police* (Library of Modern Police, 1982), p. 104" this is a note on pg 575 as cited in Chae, Han Kook, et al., The Korean War Volume One, 449.

54. 'carrying weapons and supplies up the hills to the battle ground, performing engineering duties like building airstrips and roads, and evacuating the wounded.' : Chae, Han Kook, et al., The Korean War Volume One, 449, 479, 517.

55. about 50-60 volunteers per ROKA battalion : WHCC, *The Battle of Tabudong* (1981) p. 41, p. 124 as cited in Chae, Han Kook, et al., The Korean War Volume One, 448.

56. "Too little … to the offensive." : Chae, Han Kook, et al., The Korean War Volume One, 711.

57. 'a third of the men in a division were forcibly conscripted', 'forced to carry loads of supplies and food for the NKPA, or build and repair items.' : Chae, Han Kook, et al., The Korean War Volume One, 508-509.

58. 'hands tied behind their backs and shot in front of trench', 'end of September 1950, 5,000-7,000 South Korean civilians were found dead in Taejon city, with just six surviving to tell the story.' : Appleman, *South to the Naktong, North to the Yalu,* p. 887 as cited in Chae, Han Kook, et al., The Korean War Volume One, 702-703.

59. 'October 1950, in Wonsan, North Korea, 600 Koreans had been killed', '12,000 civilians were killed in Hamhung' : Chae, Han Kook, et al., The Korean War Volume One, 778, 859.

60. "What are the chances for Chinese or Soviet interference?" : U.S. Department of State, "Substance of Statements Made at Wake Island Conference on 15 October 1950," FRUS 1950, Vol. VII, Doc. 680.

61. "Very little … We are the best." : Ibid.

62. "withdraw the Eighth Army to Japan by Christmas" : Ibid.

63. 260,000 Communist Chinese : The Korea Research Institute for Strategy, tr., p. 6; The Central Research Office of Chinese Archives, op. cit., p. 561. as cited in Chae, Chung, and Son, The Korean War Volume Two, 102.

64. Outnumbered 10:1 : The Battle of Chosin, dir. Randall MacLowry.

65. 120,000 Chinese troops : Pickrell, "These Are 10 of the Toughest and Most Important Battles US Marines Ever Fought."

66. Temperature varies across multiple sources. Some say -20 and others upwards of -45 degrees Fahrenheit.

67. Barricades : Pickrell, "These Are 10 of the Toughest and Most Important Battles US Marines Ever Fought."

68. 'those who lost their limbs survived due to their blood freezing instead of bleeding out', 'Clothing would be taken off the dead' : The Battle of Chosin, dir. Randall MacLowry.

69. "Tootsie Rolls" story : Sides, On Desperate Ground, 262-263. Hampton Sides also writes in his notes: "See "How Tootsie Rolls Accidentally Saved Marines During War," at the Marine Corps Community Services website (www.usmc-mccs.org)."

70. 3,200 men (seven hundred of whom were ROK soldiers) … one thousand survivors, … 385 were "able-bodied." : "Task Force Faith Heroism in Korea 1950," HistoryNet.

71. 'Major General Oliver P. Smith had commissioned Lieutenant Colonel John Partridge to construct an airfield at Hagaru … He needed to build a bridge over Funchilin Pass on the main supply route … They airdropped steel pieces from Japan, with one section weighing 2,900 pounds. But this new construction needed support underneath it … Dead Chinese bodies' : Read full story in Sides, On Desperate Ground, 120-122, 185, 258-259, 278, 311-312.

72. Casualty numbers : "Chosin Reservoir," Museum of Honor.

73. "Fires were built … 'Give me tomorrow.'" : Duncan, This is War!

74. 'naval forces from Great Britain, Australia, Canada, Colombia, France, the Netherlands, New Zealand, and Thailand who participated. Over 1.1 million Navy personnel served … Cargo consisted of weapons, tanks, ammunition, trucks' : Marolda, Edward J. "The Cold War's First Conflict," Naval History Magazine.

75. 230 ships : Ibid.

76. '275,000 sorties … Corsairs, Panthers, and Skyraiders were among the naval aircraft flown … the only Korean War Navy ace is Lieutenant Guy P. Bordelon, who took down five enemy aircraft … 559 Navy and Marine planes were shot down by antiaircrafts. MiGs shot down five'. : Ibid.

77. 'killed 28,000 enemy troops … 23,000 rockets were fired at communist troops …105,000 troops and 91,000 refugees boarded the ships along with 350,000 tons of cargo … no UN warship sunk during the war,' : Ibid.

78. 'evacuated from the Republic of Korea from June 26 to 27, 1950 … struck down three North Korean fighters

on June 27 … On June 29, Americans bombed the Pyongyang airfield … they conducted photo reconnaissance, airlift missions, and air support missions for troops, they moved on to bomb railroads, bridges, and supply dumps to prevent the enemy from resupplying and moving their troops forward' : "The U.S. Air Force in Korea: Campaigns, Units, and Stations, 1950–1953," 7-8.

79. 'air controllers would communicate to the ground forces on aerial reconnaissance and bring in air support' … 'airfield rebuilt in Pohang, Kimpo, and Suwon' : Ibid., 11-12.

80. FEAF bombed Sinuiju : Ibid., 15.

81. Russell J. Brown, took down a MiG : "This Day in Aviation."

82. 'FEAF brought in their best jet fighters a month later: the F-84 Thunderjets along with F-86 Sabres … 'MiG Alley' … major role in the Battle of Chosin Reservoir … 1,500 tons of supplies were airlifted to the Marines in Chosin, as well as parts to assemble the bridge across Funchilin Pass' : "The U.S. Air Force in Korea: Campaigns, Units, and Stations, 1950–1953," 15-16, 19.

83. 'December 1950, FEAF killed or wounded 33,000 enemy troops … summer and fall of 1952 … 2,000 to 4,000 close air support missions were conducted each month' : Ibid., 16, 36.

84. Transported personnel via the air force's troop carriers such as C-124s and C-47s and provided air medical evacuation : Ibid., 36.

85. Transported cargo in planes such as the C-124s and C-119s : Ibid., 36.

86. 301 tons of equipment and supplies dropped on October 20, 1950; 1,358 tons from February 23 to 28, 1951; 15,900 tons in April 1951; 21,300 tons in May 1951; 22,472 tons in June 1951; and 1,200 tons from June 28 to July 2, 1953 : Ibid., 12, 19, 24, 43.

87. May 20, 1951, 50 MiGs fought 36 Sabres … Captain James Jabara struck down 2 MiGs (totaling 6 victories) and thus became the first American jet ace in aviation history … September 1951, the Air Force engaged with 911 enemy aircraft and shot down 14 MiGs, losing 6 of their own; in December 1951, the 51st and 4th Fighter-Interceptor Wings shot down 26 MiGs, and lost 6 F-86s; from January to April 1952, FEAF shot down 127 enemy aircraft and lost 9 of their own; and from May to July 1953, they had 165 wins while losing 3 : Ibid., 24, 27, 31, 43.

88. Truman addressed the American people on April 11, 1951 : "Recall of General Douglas MacArthur (1951)," U.S. Embassy & Consulates in Germany.

89. ""Old Soldiers Never Die" Address by Gen. Douglas MacArthur, April 19, 1951," Iowa Department of Cultural Affairs.

90. "Over a period …20 percent of the population" : Cummings, "The U.S. War Crime."

91. "[The United States bombed] … on top of another" : Ibid.

92. Operation Big Switch … exchanged 75,823 prisoners to the communists and 12,773 : "Prisoners of War," National Museum of the U.S. Air Force.

93. 4 million people died : B. C. Koh, "The War's Impact on the Korean Peninsula," 57.

94. 50 percent were civilians : "Korean War." The History Channel.

95. 10 percent : "Korean War." The History Channel.

96. 20 percent : "New Evidence on North Korean War Losses." Wilson Center.

97. U.S. Military: 5,720 Army personnel, 908 Air Force personnel, 276 Navy personnel, and 641 Marines are unaccounted for : "Military Personnel Unaccounted For." Defense POW/MIA Accounting Agency.

98. 1,000,000 Koreans moved from the North to the South : Chae, Chung, and Son, The Korean War Volume Two, 333.

99. Operation Little Switch took place from April 20 to May 3, 1953, and returned 6,670 Chinese and North Korean prisoners and 669 UN prisoners, all of whom were sick or wounded : "Prisoners of War," National Museum of the U.S. Air Force.

100. Ranked the tenth country in the world by GDP is according to 2022 data : "Top 15 Countries by GDP in 2022," Global PEO Services.

Tae-hyok and Nicole, 2022

TAE-HYOK KIM

Tae-hyok Kim grew up in North Korea when it was under Japanese rule in the 1930s. Following Japan's surrender in World War II, he experienced the division of Korea into two separate states, North Korea and South Korea, in 1945. Seeking an education, Tae-hyok embarked on a journey to South Korea. He later joined the South Korean Army, fighting for the Republic of Korea Army (ROKA) during the Korean War, not knowing whether he was fighting against his own brothers and friends. After the war, Tae-hyok married Soonnyum Lee, and they had two children. Tae-hyok pursued his dreams and came to America, where he received an education at Brigham Young University. He worked for many companies, spending the most time at Reader's Digest. Despite the challenges and hurdles that have come his way, Tae-hyok always has a smile on his face and keeps pushing forward with a positive attitude, embodying the enduring spirit of resilience. His friends know him as Tae (pronounced 'Tie').

NICOLE KIM ROGERS

Nicole Kim Rogers is the granddaughter of Tae-hyok Kim. She grew up captivated by her grandfather's remarkable tales of adventures in Korea. In 2020, she started reading all her grandfather's stories and piecing them together, interviewing him daily. She has worked in marketing for companies including Ektron (now Optimizely), Box, Google, WeWork, and Matterport. Beyond pursuing a career in tech, Nicole is passionate about the outdoors. Whether running, climbing, biking, or hiking, she has a love for the mountains. Her passion for exploration has taken her to all seven continents, allowing her to embrace the diverse cultures of the world. Nicole is based in the San Francisco Bay Area, the hub of technology and innovation.

Made in the USA
Middletown, DE
19 July 2023

35426458R00312